T0296793

Ubiquitous Computing and Technological Innovation for Universal Healthcare

Arumugam Suresh Kumar
Jain University (Deemed), India

Ramesh Sekaran
Jain University (Deemed), India

Geetha Ganesan
Jain University (Deemed), India

Batri Krishnan
Jain University (Deemed), India

N. V. Kousik
Arden University, UK

A volume in the Advances in Medical Technologies and Clinical Practice (AMTCP) Book Series

Published in the United States of America by
IGI Global
Medical Information Science Reference (an imprint of IGI Global)
701 E. Chocolate Avenue
Hershey PA, USA 17033
Tel: 717-533-8845
Fax: 717-533-8661
E-mail: cust@igi-global.com
Web site: http://www.igi-global.com

Copyright © 2024 by IGI Global. All rights reserved. No part of this publication may be reproduced, stored or distributed in any form or by any means, electronic or mechanical, including photocopying, without written permission from the publisher.
Product or company names used in this set are for identification purposes only. Inclusion of the names of the products or companies does not indicate a claim of ownership by IGI Global of the trademark or registered trademark.

Library of Congress Cataloging-in-Publication Data

Names: Suresh Kumar, Arumugam, 1979- editor. I Ganesan, Geetha, 1970-
   editor. I Sekaran, Ramesh, 1987- editor. I Krishnan, Batri, 1980-
   editor. I Veerappan, Kousik, 1982- editor.
Title: Ubiquitous computing and technological innovation for universal
   healthcare / [edited by] Arumugam Suresh Kumar, Geetha Ganesan, Ramesh
   Sekaran, Batri Krishnan, Kousik Veerappan.
Description: Hershey, PA : Medical Information Science Reference, [2024] I
   Includes bibliographical references and index. I Summary: "This book
   also brings a broad discussion on the essential developments in
   ubiquitous computing considering them from economic, social, and
   technical perspectives. It clearly examines different sectors and
   application areas that benefit most from the potential of pervasive
   computing"-- Provided by publisher.
Identifiers: LCCN 2023057966 (print) I LCCN 2023057967 (ebook) I ISBN
   9798369322680 (hardcover) I ISBN 9798369322697 (ebook)
Subjects: MESH: Universal Health Care I Medical Informatics Computing
Classification: LCC R855.3 (print) I LCC R855.3 (ebook) I NLM W 67.1 I
   DDC 610.285--dc23/eng/20240202
LC record available at https://lccn.loc.gov/2023057966
LC ebook record available at https://lccn.loc.gov/2023057967

British Cataloguing in Publication Data
A Cataloguing in Publication record for this book is available from the British Library.

All work contributed to this book is new, previously-unpublished material.
The views expressed in this book are those of the authors, but not necessarily of the publisher.

For electronic access to this publication, please contact: eresources@igi-global.com.

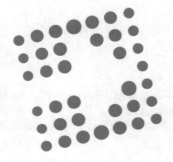

Advances in Medical Technologies and Clinical Practice (AMTCP) Book Series

Srikanta Patnaik
SOA University, India
Priti Das
S.C.B. Medical College, India

ISSN:2327-9354
EISSN:2327-9370

MISSION

Medical technological innovation continues to provide avenues of research for faster and safer diagnosis and treatments for patients. Practitioners must stay up to date with these latest advancements to provide the best care for nursing and clinical practices.

The **Advances in Medical Technologies and Clinical Practice (AMTCP) Book Series** brings together the most recent research on the latest technology used in areas of nursing informatics, clinical technology, biomedicine, diagnostic technologies, and more. Researchers, students, and practitioners in this field will benefit from this fundamental coverage on the use of technology in clinical practices.

Coverage

- Clinical Nutrition
- Clinical Studies
- Diagnostic Technologies
- Medical Imaging
- Nutrition
- Patient-Centered Care

IGI Global is currently accepting manuscripts for publication within this series. To submit a proposal for a volume in this series, please contact our Acquisition Editors at Acquisitions@igi-global.com or visit: http://www.igi-global.com/publish/.

The (ISSN) is published by IGI Global, 701 E. Chocolate Avenue, Hershey, PA 17033-1240, USA, www.igi-global. com. This series is composed of titles available for purchase individually; each title is edited to be contextually exclusive from any other title within the series. For pricing and ordering information please visit http://www.igi-global.com/ book-series/advances-medical-technologies-clinical-practice/73682. Postmaster: Send all address changes to above address. Copyright © IGI Global. All rights, including translation in other languages reserved by the publisher. No part of this series may be reproduced or used in any form or by any means – graphics, electronic, or mechanical, including photocopying, recording, taping, or information and retrieval systems – without written permission from the publisher, except for non commercial, educational use, including classroom teaching purposes. The views expressed in this series are those of the authors, but not necessarily of IGI Global.

Titles in this Series

For a list of additional titles in this series, please visit: www.igi-global.com/book-series

Technologies for Sustainable Healthcare Development
Thangavel Murugan (United Arab Emirates University, Al Ain, UAE) Jaisingh W. (Presidency University, India) and Varalakshmi P. (Anna University, India)
Medical Information Science Reference • copyright 2024 • 427pp • H/C (ISBN: 9798369329016) • US $445.00 (our price)

Modernizing Maternal Care With Digital Technologies
Dattatray Takale (Vishwakarma Institute of Information Technology, India) Parikshit Mahalle (Vishwakarma Institute of Information Technology, India) Meera Narvekar (University of Mumbai, India) and Rupali Mahajan (Vishwakarma Institute of Information Technology, India)
Medical Information Science Reference • copyright 2024 • 535pp • H/C (ISBN: 9798369337110) • US $485.00 (our price)

Revolutionizing the Healthcare Sector with AI
Babita Singla (Chitkara Business School, Chitkara University, Punjab, India) Kumar Shalender (Chitkara Business School, Chitkara University, Punjab, India) and Katja Stamer (DHBW Stuttgart Campus Horb, Germany)
Medical Information Science Reference • copyright 2024 • 471pp • H/C (ISBN: 9798369337318) • US $485.00 (our price)

Artificial Intelligence Transformations for Healthcare Applications Medical Diagnosis, Treatment, and Patient Care
Thangavel Murugan (United Arab Emirates University, UAE) Jaisingh W. (Presidency University, India) and Varalakshmi P. (Anna University, India)
Medical Information Science Reference • copyright 2024 • 423pp • H/C (ISBN: 9798369374627) • US $465.00 (our price)

701 East Chocolate Avenue, Hershey, PA 17033, USA
Tel: 717-533-8845 x100 • Fax: 717-533-8661
E-Mail: cust@igi-global.com • www.igi-global.com

Table of Contents

Detailed Table of Contents

Chapter 1
Venkatesh Raju, PSNA College of Engineering and Technology
(Autonomous), Dindigul, India

The chapter "Origins and Evolution of Pervasive Computing: A Historical Perspective" takes readers on a comprehensive journey through the history of pervasive computing, tracing its impact on the convergence of digital and physical realms. It explores the historical roots of this field, beginning with pioneers like Mark Weiser, who introduced the concept of "ubiquitous computing." The chapter highlights the crucial roles of wireless communication and sensor technologies in enabling pervasive computing, showcasing projects like the internet of things (IoT) and smart cities. It also addresses ethical dilemmas, including privacy and security concerns, underscoring the interdisciplinary nature of this domain. This chapter equips readers with a deep understanding of the forces shaping interconnected and intelligent systems and offers insights into future directions, fostering ongoing research and innovation in this dynamic field.

Chapter 2

    A. Gayathiri, Vivekanandha College of Arts and Sciences for Women
      (Autonomous), India
    S. Sabitha, Vivekanandha College of Arts and Sciences for Women
      (Autonomous), India
    G. Sathiya, Vivekanandha College of Arts and Sciences for Women
      (Autonomous), India
    P. Sumitra, Vivekanandha College of Arts and Sciences for Women
      (Autonomous), India
    M. Sathiya, Vivekanandha College of Arts and Sciences for Women
      (Autonomous), India
    George Ghinea, Brunel University, Brunei

Pervasive is also acknowledged as ubiquitous computing, which incorporates connecting all objects in the surroundings through its functionalities. When it is connected it will integrate as a single system and all together work as a whole single unit. It is used for computer capacity as an embedded device and is used for communication. It communicates well and achieves the dropping of end users' need to communicate with computer. This pervasive computing is used in various areas in the real world. Today, people have a smart watch which connects with smart phones and receives many notifications from the office employees while not at work. As this, there are many examples in the real world of pervasive computing. In this chapter the authors are going to know about the pervasive computing origin, which are the places where pervasive computing is used and how it is working with heterogeneous network and also with the future generation network.

In the rapidly evolving landscape of healthcare, the emergence of the Metaverse presents a promising yet complex frontier. The chapter begins by providing an overview of the Metaverse, exploring its fundamental concepts, and highlighting its potential benefits for the healthcare industry. It then proceeds for challenges that healthcare professionals, researchers, and stakeholders may encounter in this transformative journey. With the Metaverse's immersive and interconnected nature, safeguarding patient data and ensuring secure communication channels are paramount. The chapter examines the vulnerabilities in the Metaverse and explores strategies to protect sensitive medical information. The chapter concludes with a forward-looking perspective on how the healthcare industry can harness the Metaverse's potential while mitigating the associated issues and challenges. It emphasizes the importance of interdisciplinary collaboration between healthcare professionals, technologists, policymakers, and ethicists to navigate this uncharted terrain successfully.

Chapter 4

The Metaverse, often referred to as the immersive internet, is widely considered the next significant technological disruption on the horizon, with the potential to reshape clinician-patient interactions, enhance the patient experience, transform innovation and research and development processes. The Metaverse is currently in its developmental phase, and the establishment of a definitive framework is an ongoing endeavor. In recent years, the concept of the Metaverse has gained substantial traction and has evolved into a multifaceted virtual universe with limitless possibilities. This chapter provides a glimpse into the evolving landscape of healthcare, where the Metaverse's immersive and interconnected experiences have the power to revolutionize how we perceive, access, and deliver healthcare services. From virtual clinics and medical simulations to AI-assisted diagnostics, this chapter explores the multifaceted ways in which the Metaverse is reshaping healthcare and creating new opportunities for improved patient outcomes, education, and research.

Chapter 5

    Annamalai Selvarajan, Jain University (Deemed), India
    Sangeetha Nagamani, City Engineering College, Bangalore, India
    Suresh Kumar A., Jain University (Deemed), India
    Tejavarma Dommaraju, Jain University (Deemed), India
    Harsha Vardhan Gandhodi, Jain University (Deemed), India
    Dimitrios A. Karras, National and Kapodistrian University of Athens,
        Greece

Nowadays, Metaverse continues to be a boon for virtual space. The word Metaverse was coined by Neal Stephenson in his science fiction novel "Snow Crash." It has become the next iteration of the internet. Metaverse is defined as a distinct, ubiquitous, deeply engaged, insistent, 3D virtual space where we can virtually create a life better than the physical world. The real world has evolved tremendously since the COVID-19 pandemic. People have isolated themselves from gatherings and other activities. Organisations began to use new technology for remote work. Metaverse had pushed forward to fix the problem by employing augmented reality (AR), virtual reality (VR), mixed reality (MR) and extended reality (ER). Furthermore, the metaverse is regarded as a web of a virtual environment in which avatars interact to provide an immersive experience. Metaverse features include digital avatars, decentralisation, highly effective remote work, security, and privacy.

> *Raghavendra M. Devadas, Department of Information Technology,*
> > *Manipal Institute of Technology Bengaluru, Manipal Academy of*
> > *Higher Education, Manipal, India*
> *Vani Hiremani, Symbiosis Institute of Technology, Symbiosis*
> > *International University (Deemed), India*
> *Praveen Gujjar J., Faculty of Management Studies, Jain University*
> > *(Deemed), India*

The study addresses the complexity of Fibromyalgia syndrome (FMS) by integrating multi-criteria decision-making (MCDM) TOPSIS with fuzzy logic for accurate prognosis. A comprehensive set of criteria, including clinical, psychological, and physiological factors, is employed. Fuzzy logic models uncertainties and subjective expert opinions. The method systematically evaluates and ranks FMS prognoses, contributing to transparency in decision-making. Incorporating sensitivity analysis with small variations enhances reliability. Considering symptoms, patients, and expert ratings, the study identifies patient 5 as more likely to have FMS (closeness coefficient 0.881), while patient 1 is less prone (closeness coefficient 0.088).

> *S. Radha, Vivekanandha College of Engineering for Women, India*
> *C. Visali, Vivekanandha College of Engineering for Women, India*
> *C. Aparna, Sengunthar Engineering College, India*
> *C. Aarthi, Sengunthar Engineering College, India*
> *R. Logambal, Vivekanandha College of Engineering for Women, India*

The healthcare industry has witnessed significant advancements in recent years, driven by the integration of technology and data analytics. Smarter healthcare systems aim to enhance the quality of patient care, improve efficiency, and reduce costs through the intelligent use of technology. This chapter explores existing models, proposes a new model, discusses the requirements and architectures for smarter healthcare systems, addresses security issues, and highlights the emerging motivations for adopting these solutions. One prominent model is the electronic health record (EHR) system, which enables the digital storage and sharing of patient medical records. Additionally, wearable devices and mobile health applications empower individuals to track their health, collect data, and receive personalized insights. A proposed model for smarter healthcare is the integration of artificial intelligence (AI) and machine learning (ML) algorithms. These technologies can analyze vast amounts of medical data, identify patterns, and provide accurate predictions and diagnoses.

Unmanned aerial vehicles (UAVs) play a vital role in healthcare applications, specifically in rural and isolated regions. The metaverse, a collective virtual shared place, offers a one-of-a-kind platform for immersive and collaborative healthcare data analysis. Improved patient outcomes and healthcare efficiency can be achieved by the widespread adoption of computer vision (CV) tools and techniques in clinical settings. The synergy between CV, metaverse analysis, and UAV communication offers a transformative approach to healthcare delivery. This study investigates the incorporation of computer vision methodologies and strategies into the metaverse framework to augment healthcare services provided by UAV communication. UAVs with extensive communication capabilities act as a link between the physical and metaverse, allowing for seamless data flow and analysis. This multidisciplinary approach offers real-time, immersive insights that improve diagnosis, decision-making, and overall patient care, and it has the potential to completely transform the way healthcare is delivered.

In the not-so-distant future, the confluence of cutting-edge technologies such as artificial intelligence (AI), telemedicine, and blockchain is transforming the way we perceive and interact with the world. A pivotal component of this paradigm shift is the use of unmanned aerial vehicles (UAVs) to enable seamless communication within the Metaverse, where physical and digital realms blend harmoniously. This chapter delves into the intricate web of UAV communication, exploring its applications, challenges, and potential for shaping the metaverse of tomorrow.

    M. Sathiya, Vivekanandha College of Arts and Sciences for Women
        (Autonomous), India
    P. Sumitra, Vivekanandha College of Arts and Sciences for Women
        (Autonomous), India
    G. Sathya, Vivekanandha College of Arts and Sciences for Women
        (Autonomous), India
    A. Gayathiri, Vivekanandha College of Arts and Sciences for Women
        (Autonomous), India
    S. Sabitha, Vivekanandha College of Arts and Sciences for Women
        (Autonomous), India
    George Ghinea, Brunel University, Brunei

Unmanned aerial vehicles (UAV) are appropriate as viable instruments in communication systems. The concept of the unmanned aerial vehicle fits with the internet of things (IoT), which frequently deploys an outsized number of sensors across a large area. To deliver wireless communications, UAVs have been employed as an airborne communication platform. To show the idea's viability, the authors present a UAV-based architecture for communicating with BANs in a dependable and power-efficient manner. The design that has been suggested employs the wakeup-radio-based communication paradigm between a UAV and plenty BANs. The authors examine the proposed protocol's performance in terms of throughput and latency by designating different priority to hubs and gateways. The authors also highlight outstanding research topics and obstacles for building effective procedures for UAV-based data collecting in smart healthcare systems.

Akshay Bhuvaneswari Ramakrishnan, SASTRA University, India
S. Srijanani, Velammal Engineering College, India
Mukunth Madavan, SASTRA University, India
R Manikandan, SASTRA University, India
S. Magesh, Dr. M.G.R Educational and Research Institute, India

The revolutionary integration of unmanned aerial vehicle (UAV) communication, metaverse technology, learning techniques, and cloud computing in the healthcare industry is investigated in this chapter. Unmanned aerial vehicles (UAVs) are capable of collecting a wide variety of data, which can then be viewed in the metaverse. In order to detect illnesses at an earlier stage, machine learning is powered by cloud computing. At the same time that ethical concerns and regulatory problems are being highlighted, the necessity of international collaboration is being emphasized. Applications in the real world illustrate a future in which medical care is not limited by geographic boundaries; it will be possible to receive treatment remotely and receive medical education on a global scale. The chapter is a representation of a collective aspiration to make healthcare a fundamental human right, so rewriting the history of human compassion and the advancement of medical technology.

Mukunth Madavan, SASTRA University, India
Akshay Kumar R., TL Consulting Group, Australia
Akshay Bhuvaneswari Ramakrishnan, SASTRA University, India
Manikandan R., SASTRA University, India
S. Magesh, Dr. M.G.R. Educational and Research Institute, India

The integration of computer vision, unmanned aerial vehicles (UAVs), and metaverse analysis has potential to transform healthcare and offers solutions to geographical challenges. Emphasizing real-world applications, it details how computer vision aids in real-time patient monitoring and disease detection, while the metaverse enables immersive medical simulations and remote patient monitoring. Unmanned aerial vehicles help break the geographical barriers and give people access to healthcare services. The synergy between computer vision and metaverse analysis facilitates revolutionary data analysis and has multiple applications. Augmented reality (AR) and virtual reality (VR) tools enhance user engagement, enabling remote patient monitoring and medical simulations. The integration of metaverse analysis with UAVs introduces applications such as remote operation, telemedicine, propelling healthcare into a new era.

    Daksh Srivastava, VIT-AP University, India
    Nandini Mahanag, VIT-AP University, India

Blockchain technology is revolutionizing healthcare data management by introducing unprecedented levels of security, privacy, and interoperability. It provides a tamper-resistant, decentralized ledger for storing patient records and enables secure, transparent sharing of medical data among healthcare providers and patients. With blockchain, patients have more control over their data, ensuring their privacy while enhancing data accuracy. Moreover, healthcare institutions can streamline administrative processes and reduce fraud. This innovative approach promises to improve patient care, reduce costs, and reshape the healthcare industry's data management landscape. The Department of Health and Human Services keeps track of and posts the data breaches. The battle against the COVID-19 pandemic highlighted the importance of the blockchain technology.

The expansion of the internet and the growing use of technology in the healthcare system have helped doctors monitor their patients remotely through the use of real-time smart health devices. In spite of this sophisticated system, there are many concerns regarding the sensitive data of the patients being exposed to the world by hackers. Thus, the shortcomings of the healthcare framework can be resolved by leveraging blockchain tools. The mechanism of the blockchain health system works in such a way that an id is assigned to a patient health record, and they can give access to view their health records to the specific health provider of their choice. Eventually, by using this mechanism, the patient's health record is secured from the hackers. Thus, this chapter deals with data privacy of the patient's health, research objectives, issues, and challenges that can be easily understandable and helpful for beginners in their research progress.

Graph theory in computer science is an innovative answer to the increasingly complicated modern infrastructure of healthcare, where security and connection are critical and it has a wide range of applications, such as drug development, epidemiological analysis, personalized medicine, and so on. Through the utilization of graph databases and analytics, healthcare practitioners can obtain significant knowledge, improve their decision-making procedures, and optimize their operations. Real-world case studies illustrate successful implementations, such as remote patient monitoring and smart healthcare environments through graph-theoretic solutions The healthcare sector stands to gain from increased patient outcomes, data-driven decision support, and increased efficiency through the incorporation of graph technology. The study describes the field's challenges and future directions. It looks at new trends, untapped applications of graph theory in healthcare optimization, and approaches to ethical and legal issues.

This chapter aims to establish an approach for IVHM requirements elucidation. A meticulous literature study served as the bedrock of this research, offering critical insights into existing methodologies and challenges in IVHM for UAS. Leveraging this knowledge, the study innovatively introduced the IVHM-RD method, a culmination of extensive data analysis. This approach not only grounded the study in established theories but also pushed the boundaries of understanding in IVHM, ushering in transformative possibilities for UAS design. This method consolidates diverse stakeholder demands through extensive data analysis, resulting in a prioritized set of IVHM requirements. The study's innovative approach, bridging the gap between theory and practice, promises transformative implications for UAS design processes.

This chapter is conceptual in character and concentrates on two more recent technology innovations the fashion industry is making use of both virtual reality (VR) and augmented reality (AR).Using examples from contemporary fashion, the technology acceptance model (TAM) will be used to further assess the perceived utility and usability of AR and VR from a consumer perspective. The chapter ends with a discussion of potential future study areas. Academics and business alike are paying an increasing amount of attention to mobile augmented reality, or mobile AR. Application-based and hardware-based are the two leading platforms for mobile augmented reality applications. Even with the deployment through apps requiring additional downloading and installation beforehand making it painstaking for many platforms distribution, mobile augmented reality implementation through hardware is known to be costly and lacking in flexibility. This chapter looks at the newest technological advancements, active mobile augmented reality deployments, auxiliary technologies, and issues that come up with AR.

Preface

In recent years, the integration of Unmanned Aerial Vehicles (UAVs) into healthcare has marked a significant leap forward in the technological landscape, transforming out-of-hospital care models and setting new standards for medical practice. This evolution is pivotal for healthcare enterprises, enabling the efficient collection, analysis, and utilization of data. Smart healthcare systems, designed to detect and transmit individual health status data to clinicians regardless of location, are becoming increasingly critical, particularly in addressing medical personnel shortages. Through cognitive algorithms, innovative intelligent systems are being developed to enhance and automate diagnostic processes, using essential clinical data to ensure timely health prevention and protection during emergencies.

We are witnessing a revolutionary shift in computing paradigms with the rise of Pervasive (Ubiquitous) Computing, which promises to reshape interactions with mobile devices, physical spaces, personal computers, and various stakeholders. This technology envisions a future where sensors, embedded processors, computers, and digital communications are omnipresent and affordable, creating a seamless, comfortable environment for users. Ubiquitous computing will populate our surroundings with countless sensor devices, offering novel functionalities and specialized services that enhance human interaction.

The advent of Metaverse healthcare analysis presents a groundbreaking approach to delivering treatment, reducing costs, and significantly improving patient outcomes. This approach merges Artificial Intelligence (AI), Augmented Reality (AR), and Virtual Reality (VR) to create immersive, interactive experiences. While these technologies hold immense potential, their application in healthcare is still emerging. The next generation of healthcare solutions will be shaped by the integration of these diverse disciplines into everyday life.

This book delves into the transformative impact of behavioral activities on evolving traditional medical systems into intelligent ones. It explores the development and integration of treatment programs leveraging UAV communication, AI, Telemedicine, Blockchain, Digital Twins, AR, and VR for metaverse intelligent systems. These technologies enable instant information sharing among healthcare professionals, facilitating quicker identification of disease causes. Additionally, monitoring patient activity in the metaverse aids in tracking compliance and improving diagnosis and treatment.

We invite contributions that cover theory, applications, and design schemes of UAV communication for metaverse intelligent systems, vision techniques, and biomedical applications. The book emphasizes the necessity of developing stable, efficient, and scalable intelligent algorithms to enhance decision-making in emergency healthcare scenarios using UAV communications.

Furthermore, this book addresses the economic, social, and environmental impacts of metaverse healthcare systems. It aims to provide a comprehensive understanding of metaverse analysis-supported applications, employing advanced smart computing methods and intelligent algorithms. Detailed assessments of AR, VR, IoT sensors, actuators, communication technologies, and standards are included, alongside discussions on the challenges faced by these smart healthcare systems, such as connectivity, sensing, computation, complexity, and security issues.

Designed to offer innovative solutions to these challenges, this book explores the dynamics of metaverse health analysis for future generations. It also examines the essential developments in ubiquitous computing from economic, social, and technical perspectives, highlighting sectors and application areas poised to benefit the most from pervasive computing. Future directions and the need for active, complex solutions and pervasive management are also discussed.

This book is targeted at researchers, academicians, industry professionals, policymakers, and system designers working on the development and application of UAV Communication and Pervasive Computing for Metaverse in Smart Healthcare. Additionally, it serves as a valuable resource for medical professionals, IoT solution developers, and students in biomedical and computer science engineering, providing insights into recent trends, scopes, and technologies in IoT applications in healthcare.

Chapter 1: Origins and Evolution of Pervasive Computing - A Historical Perspective by Venkatesh Raju, PSNA College of Engineering and Technology (Autonomous), Dindigul, India

The opening chapter, "Origins and Evolution of Pervasive Computing: A Historical Perspective," provides a detailed exploration of the field's development, tracing the integration of digital and physical worlds from its inception. Starting with the foundational work of pioneers like Mark Weiser and the introduction of "ubiquitous computing," the chapter highlights the pivotal roles of wireless communication and sensor technologies. It delves into significant projects such as the Internet of Things (IoT) and smart cities, while also addressing ethical concerns related to privacy and security. This comprehensive overview not only underscores the interdisciplinary nature of pervasive computing but also offers valuable insights into future trends and innovations in this dynamic field.

Chapter 2: Real Time Applications of Ubiquitous Computing on Heterogeneous Next Generation Networks by Gayathiri A, Sabitha S, Sathiya G, Sumitra P, Sathiya M, Vivekanandha College of Arts and Sciences for Women (Autonomous), India, and George Ghinea, Brunel University, Brunei Darussalam

Chapter 2, "Real-Time Applications of Ubiquitous Computing on Heterogeneous Next Generation Networks," explores the real-world applications of pervasive computing, also known as ubiquitous computing. The chapter elucidates how interconnected devices form a single system, enhancing communication and reducing the need for direct human-computer interaction. It provides practical examples, such as smartwatches linked to smartphones for office notifications, and examines the use of pervasive computing in various domains. The discussion extends to the integration of these technologies with heterogeneous and next-generation networks, offering a glimpse into future advancements.

Chapter 3: Issues and Challenges of Metaverse in the Healthcare Domain by Guru Prasad M S, Praveen Gujjar J, Raghavendra M Devadas, Bhavya B S, Amith K Jain, A Suresh Kumar

This chapter delves into the emerging Metaverse in healthcare, highlighting its potential benefits and the challenges it presents. Beginning with an overview of the Metaverse and its concepts, it examines how this immersive, interconnected environment can revolutionize healthcare. The authors discuss the paramount importance of safeguarding patient data and secure communication, addressing vulnerabilities within the Metaverse. The chapter concludes with strategies to harness the Metaverse's potential while mitigating associated risks, emphasizing interdisciplinary collaboration to navigate this transformative journey.

Chapter 4: Emerging Implications of Metaverse in the Healthcare Domain by Praveen Gujjar J, Guru Prasad M S, Harold Andrew Patrick, M H Sharieff, Naveen Kumar H N

Chapter 4 provides a forward-looking perspective on the Metaverse as the next technological disruption in healthcare. The chapter explores the transformative potential of the Metaverse, from virtual clinics and medical simulations to AI-assisted diagnostics. It emphasizes the ongoing development of a comprehensive framework for the Metaverse, discussing its evolving nature and the myriad opportunities it offers for improving patient outcomes, education, and research.

Chapter 5: Emerging Implications of Metaverse Healthcare Analysis to the Individual and the Society: Metaverse Healthcare by Annamalai Selvarajan, Sangeetha Nagamani, A Suresh Kumar, Tejavarma Dommaraju, Harsha Vardhan Gandhodi, Dimitrios A.K arras

This chapter explores the profound impact of the Metaverse on healthcare during and after the COVID-19 pandemic. It traces the concept's origin from Neal Stephenson's "Snow Crash" to its current role as a vital virtual space for augmented, virtual, mixed, and extended reality. Highlighting features such as digital avatars, decentralization, and enhanced remote work, the authors discuss how the Metaverse has revolutionized healthcare, addressing challenges brought by the pandemic and offering new solutions for security and privacy.

Chapter 6: Aiding In Prognosis Of Fibromyalgia Syndrome Utilizing Mcdm Topsis Method In Fusion With Fuzzy Logic By Raghavendra Devadas, Vani Hiremani, Praveen Gujjar J.

This chapter addresses the complexities of diagnosing Fibromyalgia Syndrome (FMS) through an innovative integration of Multi-Criteria Decision-Making (MCDM) TOPSIS and fuzzy logic. By combining clinical, psychological, and physiological criteria, the authors create a transparent and reliable prognosis model. The chapter showcases how fuzzy logic handles uncertainties and expert opinions, enhancing the accuracy and reliability of FMS diagnosis.

Chapter 7: Applications, Requirements, Architectures, Security Issues and Emerging Motivation for Smarter Healthcare by Radha S, Visali C, Aparna C, Aarthi C, Thangadurai E, Logambal R

Chapter 7 explores the integration of technology and data analytics in smarter healthcare systems. The authors discuss existing models like Electronic Health Records (EHR) and wearable devices, proposing new models integrating AI and ML algorithms for enhanced patient care. The chapter addresses security issues and highlights emerging motivations for adopting smarter healthcare solutions, aiming to improve efficiency, reduce costs, and elevate the quality of patient care.

Chapter 8: Integration of Computer Vision Techniques, UAV, and Metaverse Analysis to Uplift Healthcare Services by Naveen Kumar H N, Guru Prasad M S, Chandrappa S, Praveen Gujjar J, A Suresh Kumar

This chapter examines the transformative potential of integrating computer vision techniques, UAVs, and Metaverse analysis in healthcare. Focusing on real-world applications, it explores how computer vision aids in patient monitoring and disease detection, while the Metaverse enables immersive medical simulations. UAVs bridge geographical gaps, facilitating remote healthcare services and enhancing overall patient care through seamless data flow and analysis.

Chapter 9: UAV Communication for Metaverse Intelligent Systems with Blockchain Technology by Vasim Babu M, Ramprabhu S, Ramesh Sekaran

This chapter explores the convergence of UAV communication, blockchain technology, and the Metaverse. The authors discuss how UAVs enable seamless communication within the Metaverse, blending physical and digital realms. The chapter delves into applications, challenges, and the transformative potential of this integration, envisioning a future where AI, telemedicine, and blockchain redefine our interactions with the world.

Chapter 10: Impact of UAV Communication in the Healthcare Sector on IoT Framework by Sathiya M, Sumitra P, Sathya G, Gayathiri A, Sabitha S, George Ghinea

This chapter explores the increasing viability of UAVs in IoT-based healthcare systems. The authors present a UAV-based architecture for reliable and power-efficient communication with Body Area Networks (BANs). By examining throughput and latency, the chapter highlights the protocol's performance and addresses research challenges in developing effective UAV-based data collection for smart healthcare systems.

Chapter 11: UAV Communication for Various Learning Approaches in Metaverse Healthcare Analysis using Cloud Computing by Akshay Ramakrishnan, Srijanani S, Mukunth Madavan, R Manikandan, S Magesh

This chapter investigates the revolutionary integration of UAV communication, Metaverse technology, learning techniques, and cloud computing in healthcare. The authors explore how UAVs collect diverse data for Metaverse analysis, powered by machine learning and cloud computing for early disease detection. The chapter emphasizes the need for international collaboration to address ethical and regulatory issues, envisioning a future where healthcare transcends geographical boundaries.

Chapter 12: Incorporation of Computer Vision and Metaverse Analysis using UAV Communications for Healthcare Applications by Mukunth Madavan, Akshay Kumar R, Akshay Ramakrishnan, MANIKANDAN R, S Magesh

This chapter focuses on the integration of computer vision, UAVs, and Metaverse analysis to overcome geographical challenges in healthcare. Highlighting real-world applications, the authors detail how computer vision aids in patient monitoring and disease detection, while the Metaverse facilitates immersive simulations. UAVs bridge geographical gaps, enabling remote healthcare services and revolutionary data analysis.

Chapter 13: Blockchain in Healthcare Department: Blockchain in Healthcare Data Management by Daksh Srivastava, Nandini Mahanag

This chapter explores the transformative impact of blockchain technology on healthcare data management. The authors discuss how blockchain enhances security, privacy, and interoperability, providing a tamper-resistant ledger for patient records. Blockchain enables secure data sharing among healthcare providers, giving patients control over their data and improving accuracy. The chapter highlights blockchain's potential to streamline administrative processes, reduce fraud, and reshape healthcare data management.

Chapter 14: Challenges with the Blockchain-Powered Healthcare Secure System by Sumitra P, Sathiya M, Gayathiri A, Sathya G, Sabitha S, George Ghinea

This chapter addresses the challenges of implementing blockchain in healthcare systems. The authors discuss how blockchain can enhance data privacy and security, protecting patient records from hackers. The chapter explores the mechanism of assigning patient health records an ID, allowing controlled access to healthcare providers. By leveraging blockchain, the authors highlight strategies to overcome data privacy concerns and streamline research progress in healthcare.

Chapter 15: Graph-theoretic Approaches to Optimizing Connectivity and Security in Ubiquitous Healthcare Systems by R. Sowrirajan, Manimekalai S

Chapter 15 delves into the innovative application of graph theory in healthcare. The authors explore how graph databases and analytics enhance decision-making, optimize operations, and improve patient outcomes. Real-world case studies illustrate successful implementations, such as remote patient monitoring and smart healthcare environments. The chapter also addresses challenges and future directions for applying graph theory in healthcare optimization.

Chapter 16: Navigating Complexity: Unraveling the IVHM Requirements Puzzle in Unmanned Aerial Systems Through Innovative IVHM-RD Method by Rita Komalasari

This chapter introduces an innovative approach to elucidating IVHM requirements for Unmanned Aerial Systems (UAS). The IVHM-RD Method aims to overcome the challenges posed by ambiguous and imprecise requirements, streamlining the analysis of system-level requirements and bolstering the decision-making process. The chapter highlights the method's capacity to address the intricacies of IVHM requirements and enhance the design and development of UAS systems.

Chapter 17: A Bright Future For AR And VR On Mobile: Current Status, Obstacles, And Perceptions by Sathya G, Gayathiri A, Sumitra P, Sathiya M, Sabitha S, and George Ghinea

This chapter explores the current status, challenges, and future prospects of mobile augmented reality (AR) and virtual reality (VR) applications in the fashion industry. Using the Technology Acceptance Model (TAM), it assesses consumer perceptions of AR and VR utility and usability while examining application-based and hardware-based platforms. The chapter concludes by discussing technological advancements, deployment issues, and potential future research areas in mobile AR and VR.

As editors of this reference book, we are delighted to present a comprehensive exploration of the transformative impact of Unmanned Aerial Vehicles (UAVs) and Pervasive Computing in healthcare. This collection of chapters provides an in-depth analysis of the latest advancements and future directions in integrating UAV communication, artificial intelligence, telemedicine, blockchain, digital twins, augmented reality, and virtual reality within smart healthcare systems.

Throughout this book, our contributors have meticulously detailed the origins and evolution of pervasive computing, the real-time applications of ubiquitous computing on next-generation networks, and the emerging implications of the Metaverse in the healthcare domain. Each chapter delves into specific technological innovations and their potential to revolutionize patient care, diagnostics, and treatment, offering novel insights into how these technologies can enhance healthcare delivery and patient outcomes.

The chapters explore a variety of critical topics, including the use of computer vision techniques, UAVs, and metaverse analysis to uplift healthcare services, the integration of blockchain technology for secure data management, and the application of graph-theoretic approaches to optimize connectivity and security in ubiquitous healthcare systems. The authors also address the challenges and opportunities presented by these technologies, providing practical solutions and highlighting the importance of interdisciplinary collaboration.

We believe this book serves as a valuable resource for researchers, academicians, industry professionals, policymakers, and system designers working on the development and application of UAV communication and pervasive computing for metaverse in smart healthcare. Additionally, medical professionals, IoT solution developers, and students in biomedical and computer science engineering will find this book insightful and informative, offering a thorough understanding of recent trends, technologies, and the scope of IoT applications in healthcare.

As we move forward into a new era of technological innovation, it is crucial to continue exploring and harnessing the potential of these cutting-edge technologies to improve healthcare systems and patient care. We hope this book inspires further research and development in this exciting field, fostering a future where advanced smart healthcare solutions become an integral part of our everyday lives.

We extend our heartfelt gratitude to all the contributors for their exceptional work and dedication. Their expertise and insights have been instrumental in creating this comprehensive guide. We also thank our readers for their interest in this groundbreaking topic, and we hope this book provides a rich source of knowledge and inspiration for advancing smart healthcare systems.

Editors:

A. Suresh Kumar
Jain Deemed to be University, India

Geetha Ganesan
Jain Deemed to be University, India

Ramesh Sekaran
Jain Deemed to be University, India

Batri Krishnan
Jain Deemed to be University, India

Kousik Veerappan
Arden University, United Kingdom

Chapter 1
Origins and Evolution of Pervasive Computing:
A Historical Perspective

Venkatesh Raju
https://orcid.org/0000-0002-0355-8857
PSNA College of Engineering and Technology (Autonomous), Dindigul, India

ABSTRACT

The chapter "Origins and Evolution of Pervasive Computing: A Historical Perspective" takes readers on a comprehensive journey through the history of pervasive computing, tracing its impact on the convergence of digital and physical realms. It explores the historical roots of this field, beginning with pioneers like Mark Weiser, who introduced the concept of "ubiquitous computing." The chapter highlights the crucial roles of wireless communication and sensor technologies in enabling pervasive computing, showcasing projects like the internet of things (IoT) and smart cities. It also addresses ethical dilemmas, including privacy and security concerns, underscoring the interdisciplinary nature of this domain. This chapter equips readers with a deep understanding of the forces shaping interconnected and intelligent systems and offers insights into future directions, fostering ongoing research and innovation in this dynamic field.

INTRODUCTION: PERVASIVE COMPUTING UNVEILED

Pervasive computing, also known as ubiquitous computing, represents a paradigm shift in the way humans interact with technology. It envisions a world where computing capabilities seamlessly integrate into the environment, becoming an intrinsic part of everyday life (Taylor, 2009). This literature review delves into the

DOI: 10.4018/979-8-3693-2268-0.ch001

Copyright © 2024, IGI Global. Copying or distributing in print or electronic forms without written permission of IGI Global is prohibited.

origins and evolution of pervasive computing, tracing its historical development from its conceptualization to its current state.

Conceptual Foundation: The roots of pervasive computing can be traced back to the late 1980s and early 1990s when researchers at Xerox PARC, including Mark Weiser, introduced the concept of ubiquitous computing. Weiser envisioned a future where computing would fade into the background, becoming invisible yet omnipresent, with interconnected devices facilitating effortless interaction. His seminal paper, "The Computer for the 21st Century," published in Scientific American in 1991, laid the conceptual foundation for pervasive computing.

Early Development and Research: Following Weiser's pioneering work, the 1990s witnessed significant research endeavors aimed at realizing the vision of ubiquitous computing. Projects such as MIT's Project Oxygen and the University of Washington's Gaia explored novel ways of embedding computing capabilities into everyday objects and environments. These initiatives focused on developing context-aware systems capable of adapting to users' needs and preferences seamlessly.

Technological Advancements: The turn of the century marked a crucial period for pervasive computing, driven by rapid advancements in technology. Miniaturization of hardware components, wireless communication protocols, and sensor technologies paved the way for the proliferation of smart devices and sensor networks. Additionally, the emergence of cloud computing and edge computing frameworks provided the infrastructure needed to support pervasive applications across diverse environments.

Commercialization and Mainstream Adoption: The early 2000s witnessed the commercialization of pervasive computing technologies, with the introduction of smartphones, wearable devices, and smart home automation systems. Companies like Apple, Google, and Samsung played a pivotal role in popularizing these technologies, bringing them into the mainstream consumer market. The integration of pervasive computing into various domains, including healthcare, transportation, and entertainment, further fueled its adoption and growth.

Challenges and Future Directions: Despite significant progress, pervasive computing still faces several challenges, including privacy concerns, interoperability issues, and ethical considerations. Addressing these challenges requires interdisciplinary collaboration and innovative solutions. Moreover, as technologies such as artificial intelligence, Internet of Things (IoT), and augmented reality continue to evolve, the future of pervasive computing holds immense promise. Emerging trends such as edge AI, immersive interfaces, and decentralized architectures are poised to shape the next phase of its evolution.

In a world where technology has become an inseparable part of our daily existence, the concept of pervasive computing has emerged as a revolutionary force, challenging the boundaries of thought was possible. It is a journey that transcends the confines of traditional computing, promising a future where technology is not just an accessory but an integral part of our lives, our environments, and our interactions (Want, 2009).

Pervasive computing, also known as ubiquitous or ambient computing, envisions a world where technology is seamlessly integrated into our surroundings, creating a web of interconnected devices and systems that understand our needs and adapt to our preferences (Abdulrab et al., 2011). It is a world where homes, cities, and workplaces become smarter, more responsive, and more efficient. In this world, information is always at our fingertips, services are anticipatory, and our physical surroundings are enhanced by the digital.

Market Size and Growth: The pervasive computing market has experienced significant growth over the years. According to various market research reports, the global pervasive computing market was valued at several billion dollars and was expected to continue growing at a healthy rate due to increasing adoption across various industries.

Smart Devices and IoT Adoption: The proliferation of smart devices and the Internet of Things (IoT) has been a driving force behind the evolution of pervasive computing. Statistical data would likely show a steady increase in the number of connected devices worldwide, with estimates ranging from billions to trillions by certain years.

Mobile and Wearable Technology: The rise of smartphones and wearable devices has played a crucial role in making pervasive computing a reality. Statistical data would reflect the growing penetration of smartphones and wearables among consumers, along with trends in usage patterns and preferences.

Cloud Computing and Edge Computing: The adoption of cloud computing and edge computing frameworks has provided the necessary infrastructure to support pervasive computing applications. Statistical data might show the growth of cloud service providers, data center deployments, and investments in edge computing technologies.

Applications Across Industries: Pervasive computing has found applications across various industries, including healthcare, transportation, manufacturing, and retail. Statistical data would likely highlight the market size, growth rates, and key players within each industry segment.

Research and Development Investments: Governments, academia, and industry players have invested significant resources in research and development related to pervasive computing. Statistical data might include funding allocations, research output, and patent filings in relevant areas.

Challenges and Adoption Rates: Statistical data could provide insights into the challenges faced by pervasive computing, such as privacy concerns, interoperability issues, and adoption rates among different demographics or regions. Surveys, market studies, and industry reports may offer valuable statistics in this regard.

Figure 1. Exploration of pervasive computing

This exploration of pervasive computing (figure1) will journey through its history, from its conceptual origins to the impactful present. It will delve into the technologies that have brought us to this point, from the interconnected world of the Internet of Things to the ever-advancing capabilities of artificial intelligence and edge computing. It will also reflect on the challenges and ethical considerations that have arisen as technology has become more pervasive, and it will glimpse into the future, where the boundaries of pervasive computing are set to expand even further.

Pervasive computing is not just a technological evolution; it is a transformation of our world. It challenges us to rethink our relationships with technology, our environments, and one another. It prompts us to consider how it can leverage the power of interconnected systems for the greater good while safeguarding our privacy and security (Jakob et al., 2006). It is a journey of promise and potential, and its unveiling is an invitation to explore the ever-expanding horizons of technology in our lives.

The Pervasiveness of Pervasive Computing

Pervasive computing, as implied by its name, is distinguished by its all-encompassing presence. It epitomizes technology's capacity to be omnipresent, seamlessly weaving itself into our everyday existence, surroundings, and encounters. The very term "pervasive" underscores the degree to which technology has evolved into an enduring and boundary-defying influence, reshaping our interactions with the world. In this exploration, it will delve into the myriad aspects that demonstrate the ubiquitous nature of pervasive computing.

Ubiquitous Connectivity

One of the foundational aspects of pervasive computing is its ability to connect an extensive array of devices, systems, and sensors. The proliferation of the IoT and wireless communication technologies has made it possible for everyday objects, from household appliances to industrial machinery, to be interconnected. This connectivity extends from our homes and workplaces to smart cities and beyond, creating a network that spans the globe.

Seamless Integration

Pervasive computing excels in seamlessly integrating technology into our physical surroundings. It is a world where technology doesn't stand out but blends in. Smart homes adjust lighting and temperature based on your preferences. Smart cities use sensors to optimize traffic flow and conserve resources. Augmented reality apps overlay digital information onto the physical world, making it an integral part of our experiences.

Context-Awareness

Pervasive computing is inherently context-aware. It understands the context in which it operates, whether it's the time of day, your location, or your personal preferences. This context-awareness enables systems to anticipate your needs and adapt accordingly. For example, your smartphone knows when to mute itself during a meeting or your car adjusts its settings based on your driving habits.

Interconnected Ecosystems

The pervasiveness of pervasive computing extends to the creation of interconnected ecosystems. The devices and systems that make up pervasive computing
don't operate in isolation. Instead, they communicate and collaborate to enhance
our experiences. This interconnectedness means that your wearable fitness tracker
can seamlessly sync with your smartphone, which, in turn, communicates with your
home automation system.

Enhanced Intelligence

Artificial intelligence (AI) and machine learning play a pivotal role in the pervasiveness of pervasive computing. These technologies make systems smarter and
more responsive. They learn from your behaviors and adapt to your preferences.
For instance, AI-driven digital assistants can understand your voice commands and
provide you with personalized recommendations.

Ethical Considerations and Challenges

The pervasiveness of technology also brings about ethical considerations and
challenges. As technology becomes deeply ingrained in our lives, concerns about
privacy, data security, and the ethical use of AI and automation become more significant. Striking the balance between convenience and the protection of individual
rights is an ongoing challenge.

The Future of Pervasive Computing

Pervasive computing, with its commitment to the effortless incorporation of
technology into every dimension of our existence, remains a dynamic field that
continues to evolve and mold the future in captivating ways. As we gaze towards the
expansive domain of pervasive computing, we can foresee numerous groundbreaking
trends and developments that will reimagine our connection with technology and
our physical environment (Hong, 2017).

Ambient Intelligence and Contextual Awareness

The future of pervasive computing is set to be marked by a profound level of
ambient intelligence and contextual awareness. Devices and systems will not only
be interconnected but will also possess a keen understanding of the context in
which they operate. This contextual intelligence will enable predictive features,

as technology adapts to our surroundings and anticipates our needs. For example, your home will sense your arrival and adjust the lighting and temperature to your liking before you even enter.

Decentralization and Edge Computing

With the surge in data generated by pervasive computing, the need for faster and more efficient data processing is pushing the boundaries of decentralization. Edge computing, where data is processed closer to its source, will become more prevalent. This reduces latency and enhances the real-time capabilities of pervasive systems, making them more responsive and reliable.

Human-Machine Collaboration

The future of pervasive computing will involve even more sophisticated human-machine collaboration. Advanced AI and natural language processing will enable us to communicate with our devices more naturally and intuitively. Think of your digital assistant as a true conversational partner, understanding nuances and context as it discusses our needs and preferences.

Wearable Technology and Implants

Wearable technology is just the beginning. In the future, it may witness a shift towards technology implants, where devices are seamlessly integrated into our bodies. These implants could enhance our sensory perception, monitor our health, and provide new ways of interacting with the digital world.

Ethical Considerations and Regulation

As pervasive computing becomes even more ingrained in our lives, ethical considerations regarding privacy, security, and data ownership will become paramount. It has more comprehensive regulations and standards to protect users and ensure their rights are respected. Balancing the convenience of pervasive computing with ethical concerns will be an ongoing challenge.

Sustainability and Green Computing

Sustainability will be a critical theme in the future of pervasive computing. The environmental impact of technology will be carefully scrutinized, and efforts will be made to reduce energy consumption, minimize e-waste, and create eco-friendly computing solutions.

Global Collaboration and Interconnectedness

Pervasive computing will continue to foster global collaboration and interconnectedness. Cross-border projects and initiatives will aim to tackle international challenges such as climate change, healthcare, and disaster response. The global community will harness pervasive computing to address complex problems more effectively.

Transformative Industries

Pervasive computing will reshape industries in unexpected ways. Healthcare will benefit from remote monitoring and personalized treatments. Transportation will see the rise of autonomous vehicles and efficient traffic management. Education will embrace immersive learning experiences. Agriculture will become more data-driven and sustainable. These transformations will have far-reaching implications for society.

The future of pervasive computing promises an exciting, interconnected world where technology blends seamlessly into the fabric of our lives. With the rise of ambient intelligence, increased decentralization, and more sophisticated human-machine collaboration, on the cusp of an era where our interactions with technology are more intuitive and responsive than ever before (Mangaraj & Aparajita, 2010). As it navigates these changes, it is crucial that the evolution of pervasive computing is guided by ethical considerations, environmental responsibility, and a commitment to the well-being of individuals and society as a whole.

The Aim and Structure of the Chapter

This chapter is an exploration of the complex and captivating history of pervasive computing. Our objective is to provide readers with a comprehensive historical account of the key developments that have shaped the field. It will focus on the seminal ideas, pivotal milestones, and the evolution of technologies that have culminated in the present era of pervasive computing.

The narrative begins with the early visions of luminaries such as Mark Weiser, whose pioneering work on "ubiquitous computing" (fig.2) laid the foundation for the field. From there, it traverses through time, examining how the concept of embedding computation into everyday objects and environments gradually gained traction. It will delve into the birth of wireless communication and sensor technologies, recognizing their crucial role in enabling the proliferation of pervasive computing.

Figure 2. Ubiquitous computing systems

The chapter will also spotlight the influential projects and initiatives that have propelled research and innovation in this field. Among these, it explores the IoT revolution and the advent of smart cities as real-world manifestations of pervasive computing's potential.

Privacy concerns, security implications, and societal impacts will be examined in detail. It will also illuminate the convergence of various disciplines, such as computer science, telecommunications, and human-computer interaction, in shaping the trajectory of pervasive computing (Zhu et al., 2012).

It provides readers with a profound understanding of the technological, cultural, and social forces that have brought us to the present era of interconnected and intelligent systems. Furthermore, it will offer insights into the potential future directions and challenges in the field, paving the way for further research and innovation in the realm of pervasive computing. Let us embark on this enlightening journey through the historical tapestry of pervasive computing.

THE VISIONARIES: MARK WEISER AND THE BIRTH OF UBIQUITOUS COMPUTING

The story of pervasive or ubiquitous computing finds its roots in the visionary ideas and pioneering work of computer scientist Mark Weiser. His groundbreaking concepts laid the foundation for what know as a world where technology is seamlessly woven into the fabric of our lives.

Figure 3. Mark Weiser

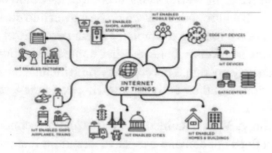

Mark Weiser (fig.3), often referred to as the "father of ubiquitous computing," was the Chief Technologist at Xerox PARC (Palo Alto Research Center Incorporated) during the late 20th century. It was here that he articulated his vision for computing that was integrated into everyday life rather than being confined to specific machines or devices.

Ubiquitous Computing Defined

Weiser's vision of ubiquitous computing, which he introduced in his 1991 essay titled "The Computer for the 21st Century," was revolutionary in its simplicity and insight. He proposed a world where computers would be invisible and integrated into the environment, where technology would be so prevalent that it would fade into the background. Weiser described this concept as "calm technology," where the interaction with computers would be non-disruptive and part of our natural surroundings.

In Weiser's vision, computers would be everywhere, but they would be unobtrusive. Rather than focusing on the computer itself, users would interact with the environment and the tasks at hand. He foresaw a world where technology would be responsive to context and anticipate the needs of users.

Key Concepts of Ubiquitous Computing

Weiser introduced several key concepts that have become foundational to the field of pervasive computing:

1. **Ubiquitous Sensing**: Weiser proposed that the environment would be filled with sensors and devices capable of perceiving the world, from temperature and light sensors to motion detectors. These sensors would feed data to computers that could analyze and respond to the environment.
2. **Invisible Computing**: In Weiser's vision, computers would be unobtrusive and disappear into the background. They would be woven into the fabric of everyday objects and locations, making technology a seamless part of our lives.
3. **Context-Awareness**: Weiser believed that computers should understand the context in which they operate. This context would include information about the user, their location, and their activity, allowing computers to provide relevant and timely assistance.
4. **Calm Technology**: Weiser coined the term "calm technology" to describe technology that does not demand excessive attention. It should be unobtrusive and operate quietly in the background, stepping in only when necessary.

Legacy and Impact

Mark Weiser's visionary ideas laid the groundwork for the development of the IoT and pervasive computing as it knows them today. His concepts have inspired researchers, engineers, and designers to create technologies that blend seamlessly into our lives.

Weiser's influence extended beyond academia and research. His ideas continue to shape the way the think about technology and its role in our daily experiences (O'Neill et al., 2013). The legacy of his work is visible in the smart homes, wearable devices, and context-aware applications that have become integral to contemporary life.

In conclusion, Mark Weiser's vision of ubiquitous computing was a revolutionary concept that has had a profound and lasting impact on the field of technology. His foresight in anticipating a world where computers seamlessly integrate into our daily lives, anticipating our needs and operating in the background, has paved the way for the transformative changes are witnessing today in pervasive computing. He was indeed a true visionary whose ideas continue to shape our technological landscape.

Mark Weiser's Vision

Mark Weiser, a renowned computer scientist, is often regarded as the father of ubiquitous computing. In the early 1990s, he introduced the concept of ubiquitous computing in a series of visionary essays published at Xerox PARC (Palo Alto Research Center). Weiser's vision was simple yet profound: he foresaw a world where computing technology would be seamlessly integrated into our everyday environment, so much so that it would become nearly invisible.

Weiser's vision was rooted in the idea that computing would no longer be confined to personal computers or standalone machines. Instead, computation would be woven into the very fabric of our lives, present in the objects, spaces, and interactions engage with daily. He coined the term "calm technology" to describe technology that was unobtrusive and unintrusive, blending harmoniously with our surroundings.

Central to Weiser's vision was the concept of "ubiquitous computing devices" or "smart devices," which were not traditional computers as it knew them but everyday objects imbued with computing capabilities. These smart devices would sense, process, and respond to the world around them, making our lives more efficient, convenient, and connected.

Seminal Works

Mark Weiser's ideas were articulated in a series of influential essays, the most notable of which is his 1991 essay titled "The Computer for the 21st Century." In this essay, Weiser introduced the world to the idea of ubiquitous computing and painted a compelling picture of the future he envisioned. He wrote, "The most profound technologies are those that disappear. They weave themselves into the fabric of everyday life until they are indistinguishable from it."

Weiser's work didn't stop at conceptualization; he actively worked to turn his vision into reality. At Xerox PARC, he oversaw research projects that laid the groundwork for the development of smart devices, sensor networks, and user interfaces that would become fundamental to pervasive computing.

Weiser's influence extended far beyond his writings and projects. His vision had a profound impact on the field of computer science and inspired countless researchers, engineers, and designers to explore and advance the possibilities of ubiquitous computing.

In this section of our historical exploration, it has unveiled the foundational ideas of Mark Weiser and the birth of ubiquitous computing (Ye et al., 2012). It was Weiser's vision that sparked the evolution of pervasive computing, inspiring researchers and innovators to embark on a journey to make technology truly pervasive and integrated into the fabric of our daily lives. As it continues our journey through the historical landscape of pervasive computing, it will witness how Weiser's vision, and the work of those who followed in his footsteps, shaped the field and brought us to the interconnected world.

THE GRADUAL INTEGRATION OF COMPUTATION INTO EVERYDAY LIFE

The integration of computation into everyday life, often referred to as pervasive or ubiquitous computing, has been a gradual and transformative process. It is a journey that spans several decades and is marked by the relentless evolution of technology. The story of this integration is a testament to the power of innovation and the adaptability of humans to seamlessly incorporate technology into our daily experiences.

Figure 4. Vannevar Bush

Early Foundations

The journey of integrating computation into everyday life can be traced back to the mid-20th century. Early computers were colossal machines, inaccessible to most people. However, visionaries like Vannevar Bush (fig**ure** 4), who introduced the idea of the "memex" in the 1940s, laid the conceptual foundation for a more integrated computing experience. Bush's vision of a personal information device foreshadowed a future where technology would become an extension of our cognitive abilities.

Miniaturization and Personal Computing

The development of microprocessors in the 1970s marked a pivotal moment in the gradual integration of computation into daily life. These miniature chips made it possible to create smaller and more affordable computing devices. The advent of personal computers, such as the Apple II and the IBM PC, brought computing to homes and offices, slowly making it a part of everyday work and leisure.

The Internet Revolution

The widespread adoption of the internet in the 1990s was a significant milestone in the integration of computation into daily life. It transformed how to access information, communicate, and conduct business. The World Wide Web made information accessible from anywhere, and email became a ubiquitous means of communication.

Mobile Computing and Smart Devices

The introduction of mobile devices, particularly smartphones and tablets, in the early 21st century brought computation into our pockets and hands. These devices evolved to become central to our daily routines, serving as communication tools, information sources, and personal assistants.

The IoT

The concept of the IoT emerged as a key driver in the gradual integration of computation into everyday life. IoT devices, from smart thermostats to wearable fitness trackers, began to permeate our homes and personal lives, creating an interconnected ecosystem of objects and systems.

Context-Aware Systems

The development of context-aware systems in pervasive computing allowed technology to respond to our surroundings and anticipate our needs. These systems use sensors, location data, and machine learning to provide context-aware services. For example, smart homes can adjust lighting and heating based on the presence and preferences of occupants.

The Future: Pervasive Computing

Looking ahead, the trajectory of the gradual integration of computation into everyday life points to a future characterized by pervasive computing. This is a world where technology is seamlessly woven into our environments, offering ambient intelligence and context-aware services. It's a future where technology is a natural extension of our lives, providing personalized, efficient, and unobtrusive support.

The gradual integration of computation into everyday life is a testament to the transformative power of technology. As it continues on this journey, it is essential to consider the ethical and societal implications of pervasive computing, ensuring that technology remains a tool for enhancing our lives while respecting individual rights and privacy (Lucke & Steinmetz, 2014). The future promises a world where computation becomes an even more integral and natural part of our daily experiences.

The Shift to Embedded Computing

One of the fundamental shifts that occurred in the journey towards pervasive computing was the transition from traditional, standalone computing devices to embedded computing. In traditional computing, it interacted with computers through distinct devices such as desktops or laptops. In contrast, pervasive computing aimed to make computers nearly invisible by embedding them within the environment and everyday objects.

This shift involved rethinking how to design and use technology. Everyday objects like refrigerators, thermostats, and even clothing became potential hosts for computing power. Through miniaturization and innovation in hardware, these embedded systems could sense, process, and respond to data from their surroundings. This shift allowed for a more natural and integrated interaction with technology, reducing the cognitive load on users.

As computation became embedded in objects and environments, it became more context-aware. Devices could respond to the user's needs and adapt to different situations, making technology feel more responsive and tailored to individual preferences. This shift, often referred to as "context-aware computing," was a key aspect of the gradual integration of computation into everyday life.

The Role of Sensor Technologies

A critical enabler of the gradual integration of computation into everyday life was the advancement of sensor technologies. Sensors, which could detect various physical attributes like temperature, light, motion, and more, played a pivotal role in making everyday objects "smart."

These sensors served as the eyes and ears of pervasive computing systems, providing the data needed to make informed decisions and adapt to changing conditions (Bacon, 2002). For example, smart thermostats could use temperature and occupancy sensors to adjust heating and cooling based on the presence of people in a room, optimizing energy usage and comfort.

Sensor networks, often interconnected wirelessly, allowed for the collection of data from multiple sources and their central processing. This development was instrumental in creating the ecosystem of smart devices that could communicate and collaborate with each other.

By infusing everyday objects with sensor technologies, computation could operate in the background, enhancing our lives without demanding our constant attention. The use of sensors also played a crucial role in addressing some of the practical challenges of pervasive computing, such as power efficiency and scalability.

As the journey through the historical landscape of pervasive computing, it finds that the gradual integration of computation into everyday life was not just a technological transformation but a cultural and societal one. It changed how to interacted with our environment, fostering a world where technology adapted to us rather than the other way around. In the next section, it will explore the pivotal role of wireless communication and connectivity in making pervasive computing a reality.

WIRELESS COMMUNICATION AND CONNECTIVITY: PAVING THE WAY FOR PERVASIVE COMPUTING

In our exploration of the historical evolution of pervasive computing, it now arrives at a pivotal milestone: the role of wireless communication and connectivity. The ability to seamlessly connect and communicate between pervasive devices and networks is a cornerstone of the pervasive computing revolution. This section delves into the transformative impact of wireless technologies and their contribution to making pervasive computing a reality.

Wireless Technologies

Wireless communication technologies, in the context of pervasive computing, refer to the various methods of transmitting data and information without physical, wired connections. These technologies range from short-range wireless protocols, such as Bluetooth and Wi-Fi, to long-range wireless solutions like cellular networks.

The adoption and advancement of wireless technologies brought forth a radical change in how pervasive computing systems operated. Traditional wired connections were often restrictive and limited the mobility and flexibility of devices. Wireless technologies, on the other hand, liberated devices from physical constraints, enabling them to communicate and share data across vast distances. This freedom of movement and communication is fundamental to the vision of ubiquitous computing, where devices work in harmony and adapt to our needs, regardless of our location.

Bluetooth, for instance, allowed devices to connect seamlessly over short distances, enabling wireless headsets, smartwatches, and other personal gadgets to communicate with smartphones and other devices (Kumar & Zambonelli, 2007). Wi-Fi empowered homes and businesses with wireless networking, creating interconnected smart homes and workplaces.

In addition to short-range technologies, long-range wireless communication played a crucial role. Cellular networks, 3G, 4G, and eventually 5G, not only facilitated mobile communication but also enabled the IoT. IoT devices, from smart city infrastructure to industrial sensors, could transmit data over cellular networks, creating a vast ecosystem of interconnected devices.

Networking Protocols and Standards

To ensure the seamless interaction of pervasive devices, various networking protocols and standards emerged. These standards provided a common language for devices to communicate and collaborate effectively. Some of the key standards in this domain include:

- **IPv6:** With the proliferation of devices in pervasive computing, the adoption of Internet Protocol version 6 (IPv6) became essential. IPv6 provides a vastly expanded address space, accommodating the numerous devices that form the IoT.
- **Zigbee and Z-Wave:** These are wireless communication protocols designed for low-power, short-range communication between IoT devices. They are often used in home automation and smart device networks.
- **MQTT and CoAP:** Message Queuing Telemetry Transport (MQTT) and Constrained Application Protocol (CoAP) are lightweight communica-

tion protocols tailored for IoT applications. They facilitate efficient and low-overhead communication between devices.

- **Thread:** Thread is an open standard for wireless networking designed to support the IoT. It focuses on creating reliable and secure networks suitable for home and commercial applications.

These networking standards not only ensured interoperability among devices but also contributed to the security and efficiency of pervasive computing systems. Standardization was instrumental in allowing diverse devices to work together seamlessly.

As it examines the role of wireless communication and connectivity in the historical journey of pervasive computing, it becomes evident that these technologies have been the backbone of the pervasive computing ecosystem (Davies, 2013). They have not only enabled the interconnection of devices but have also revolutionized how to interact with technology in our daily lives. In the subsequent section, it will explore influential projects and initiatives that have further advanced the field of pervasive computing.

INFLUENTIAL PROJECTS AND INITIATIVES

It refers to significant undertakings, programs, or efforts that have a profound impact on various aspects of society, technology, the environment, or other domains. These projects and initiatives often serve as catalysts for change, progress, and innovation. They may be launched by governments, organizations, or individuals and aim to address specific challenges, promote positive developments, or drive advancements in a particular field.

Influential projects and initiatives can encompass a wide range of areas, including:

1. **Technological Advancements:** Projects that push the boundaries of technology, such as the development of groundbreaking inventions or initiatives that drive technological innovation, like space exploration programs.
2. **Social and Humanitarian Causes:** Initiatives designed to address social issues, improve living conditions, promote equality, or enhance access to education and healthcare, like humanitarian aid programs or initiatives to eradicate diseases.
3. **Environmental Conservation:** Projects and initiatives focused on protecting the environment, reducing pollution, conserving natural resources, and combating climate change, such as conservation efforts, sustainability programs, and climate agreements.

4. **Healthcare and Medical Research:** Initiatives aimed at advancing medical knowledge, developing new treatments, and improving global health, like research projects to combat diseases or initiatives to enhance healthcare access.
5. **Educational and Cultural Endeavors:** Programs that promote education, cultural exchange, and preservation of heritage, like educational outreach projects or cultural preservation initiatives.
6. **Infrastructure and Urban Development:** Projects focused on improving infrastructure, urban planning, and transportation systems to enhance the quality of life in cities and regions, such as smart city initiatives and public infrastructure development.
7. **Global Collaboration:** International efforts and agreements that foster cooperation among nations to address global challenges, like international treaties on climate change, peacekeeping missions, and efforts to combat poverty.

Influential projects and initiatives often transcend borders, impact large populations, and have a lasting legacy. They may involve significant financial investments, expertise, and long-term commitments.

The IoT Revolution

The IoT has heralded a revolutionary transformation in the way of interact with our environment and the objects within it (fig**ure** 5). This groundbreaking concept has rapidly gained momentum and reshaped various industries, from healthcare to agriculture, transportation to manufacturing. It essentially involves connecting everyday objects and devices to the internet, enabling them to collect and exchange data, thereby offering unprecedented insights and control.

Figure 5. The revolution of IoT

One of the most influential IoT projects is the "Smart Home" revolution. Smart homes are equipped with interconnected devices that can be controlled remotely through smartphones or voice assistants like Amazon's Alexa or Google Assistant. From smart thermostats that optimize energy consumption to security cameras that provide real-time monitoring, the IoT has made homes more efficient, secure, and convenient (Kun, 2019). The Nest Thermostat, for instance, stands as a pioneering example, learning user preferences to adjust temperatures, saving energy and costs.

In agriculture, IoT sensors monitor soil conditions, crop health, and weather patterns, optimizing farming practices. This leads to increased yields, reduced resource consumption, and greater sustainability. John Deere's Farm Sight system is an exemplary project, integrating IoT technology into agriculture, enabling farmers to remotely monitor and manage their machinery and fields.

The healthcare sector has also embraced IoT to enhance patient care. Wearable devices like Fitbit track health metrics, while remote patient monitoring systems keep healthcare providers informed about patients' conditions, reducing hospitalization and enhancing patient outcomes. Philips Healthcare's Health Suite is an initiative that uses IoT to monitor patients and provide actionable data to healthcare professionals.

Transportation has been revolutionized through IoT as well. Connected vehicles communicate with traffic lights and other cars to improve road safety, reduce congestion, and enhance overall mobility. Tesla's Autopilot system is a prominent example, using IoT to enable semi-autonomous driving and vehicle connectivity.

The Smart City Movement

The Smart City movement (Figure 6) is another transformative initiative that has gained traction worldwide. As urbanization accelerates, the challenges of managing cities become more complex. Smart Cities leverage technology and data to address these challenges and make cities more efficient, sustainable, and livable.

One of the key components of Smart Cities is efficient urban infrastructure. Advanced traffic management systems use IoT sensors and data analytics to alleviate congestion and improve traffic flow. The city of Barcelona, for instance, has deployed a smart parking system that helps drivers find available parking spaces, reducing traffic and emissions.

Energy consumption and environmental sustainability are also major concerns in Smart Cities. Many cities have adopted IoT-powered smart grids that optimize energy distribution and consumption. Singapore's Smart Nation project is a comprehensive initiative that uses technology to manage everything from waste disposal to energy efficiency, making it a leader in the Smart City movement.

Figure 6. Smart city movement

Public safety is a paramount focus of Smart Cities. IoT-driven surveillance systems and predictive analytics help law enforcement agencies respond more effectively to emergencies. In New York City, the Domain Awareness System uses IoT to integrate data from various sources, including cameras and sensors, to enhance public safety and counterterrorism efforts.

Quality of life in Smart Cities is further enriched by initiatives in healthcare, education, and social services. For example, in Amsterdam, the "Amsterdam Smart City" program uses data to improve healthcare delivery and create more inclusive services for citizens.

The Smart City movement is continuously evolving, with cities around the world striving to create more efficient, connected, and sustainable urban environments (Harrington & Cahill, 2011). This initiative not only enhances the lives of city dwellers but also serves as a model for addressing the complex challenges of the 21st century.

The Internet of Things and the Smart City movement are two influential projects and initiatives that have reshaped the way it will live and interact with our environment. They have not only improved efficiency but also contributed to sustainability, safety, and overall quality of life in various sectors and urban areas. These initiatives serve as a testament to the power of technology and data in transforming our world for the better.

CHALLENGES AND ETHICAL CONSIDERATIONS

In the era of rapid technological advancement, a myriad of challenges and ethical considerations have arisen across various domains. These challenges are not only technical but also have significant societal, legal, and ethical implications. Here, it explores some of the key challenges and ethical considerations that have come to the forefront in recent years.

Privacy Concerns

Privacy concerns have become a pressing issue in the digital age. The proliferation of data collection and sharing, often without the clear and informed consent of individuals, has raised serious questions about personal privacy and data security.

- **Data Collection:** Companies and organizations routinely collect vast amounts of personal data, leading to concerns about how this data is used, stored, and shared. The collection of sensitive information, such as biometrics and location data, has intensified these concerns.
- **Data Breaches:** High-profile data breaches and leaks have exposed the vulnerabilities of personal data, highlighting the need for robust cybersecurity measures. The ethical challenge here is the responsibility of entities to protect the data they collect.
- **Legislation and Regulation:** The implementation of privacy regulations like the General Data Protection Regulation (GDPR) reflects the growing recognition of privacy as a fundamental right and underscores the need for ethical data handling practices.

Security Implications

The digital world is increasingly vulnerable to various security threats, from cyberattacks to espionage. These challenges encompass both personal and national security concerns.

- **Cybersecurity:** The rise of cyberattacks poses a significant threat to individuals, organizations, and governments. Ethical concerns revolve around responsible and transparent cybersecurity practices.
- **Cyber Warfare:** The use of cyber capabilities in warfare introduces ethical dilemmas related to the rules of engagement, the use of cyber weapons, and the protection of critical infrastructure.
- **Surveillance and Privacy:** The balance between national security and individual privacy is an ongoing ethical debate. The challenge is to ensure that surveillance practices are both effective and respectful of civil liberties.

Societal Impacts

The societal impacts of technology are far-reaching and require careful consideration, especially regarding issues of employment, inequality, and the consequences of automation and artificial intelligence (Kong et al., 2020).

- **Job Displacement:** Automation, artificial intelligence, and robotics have the potential to displace jobs in various industries. Ethical considerations include retraining the workforce and ensuring a just transition.
- **Economic Inequality:** The benefits of technological advancements are not always distributed equitably. Ethical discussions focus on wealth disparities, access to education, and social safety nets.
- **Digital Divide:** Unequal access to technology and the internet creates a digital divide, impacting education, economic opportunities, and social inclusion. Ethical concerns revolve around bridging this gap.
- **Misinformation and Manipulation:** The spread of false information and the manipulation of public opinion through digital platforms have ethical implications for content moderation, freedom of speech, and the responsibilities of tech companies.

These challenges and ethical considerations underscore the need for a multidisciplinary approach to address the complex and evolving landscape of technology in our lives. Ongoing discussions, policies, and regulations are essential to strike a balance between technological progress, individual rights, and societal well-being.

INTERDISCIPLINARY CONVERGENCE: SHAPING THE TRAJECTORY OF PERVASIVE COMPUTING

Pervasive computing, often referred to as ubiquitous or ambient computing, is a transformative field that envisions a world where computing is seamlessly integrated into everyday life (Huang & Wu, 2020). This integration necessitates a convergence of various disciplines, each contributing its unique expertise to shape the trajectory of pervasive computing. It explores the interdisciplinary nature of this field, focusing on the pivotal roles played by computer science, telecommunications, and human-computer interaction.

Computer Science

Computer science serves as the bedrock of pervasive computing, providing the essential theoretical and technical foundations for the development and evolution of this field.

- **Software and System Architecture:** Computer scientists design the software and system architecture that underpin pervasive computing. They develop operating systems, middleware, and application frameworks that facilitate communication and interaction among a myriad of devices.
- **Data Management:** Given the vast amount of data generated in pervasive computing environments, computer scientists develop sophisticated data management systems, including databases, data analytics tools, and machine learning algorithms to extract valuable insights.
- **Security and Privacy:** Ensuring the security and privacy of pervasive computing systems is paramount. Computer scientists design encryption methods, access controls, and security protocols to safeguard data and protect the integrity of devices and systems.
- **Distributed Systems:** The development of efficient algorithms for distributed and decentralized systems is a critical task. Computer scientists create algorithms that optimize resource allocation, reduce latency, and enhance the overall performance of pervasive computing networks.
- **Artificial Intelligence (AI):** AI and machine learning are increasingly integrated into pervasive computing to enable context-awareness and automation. Computer scientists contribute by developing AI algorithms for tasks such as pattern recognition, predictive analysis, and natural language processing.

Telecommunications

Telecommunications plays a pivotal role in the convergence of pervasive computing, providing the infrastructure and communication frameworks that enable seamless connectivity across a diverse array of devices.

- **Wireless Communication:** Pervasive computing heavily relies on wireless technologies, including Wi-Fi, cellular networks, and emerging standards like 5G. Telecommunications experts work to enhance network coverage, capacity, and reliability, facilitating the constant communication required for pervasive computing.
- **IoT:** The IoT is an essential component of pervasive computing, with telecommunications professionals designing communication protocols and standards that allow IoT devices to connect seamlessly to networks and exchange data.
- **Network Architecture:** Telecommunications experts focus on designing network architectures that can efficiently manage the increased data traffic generated by pervasive computing. This includes innovations like edge computing, which processes data closer to its source to reduce latency.
- **Interoperability:** The ability for devices and systems from different manufacturers to communicate necessitates the development of communication standards and protocols. Telecommunications professionals contribute by defining and implementing standards like MQTT and CoAP for IoT communication.

Human-Computer Interaction (HCI)

Human-Computer Interaction (Figure 7) plays a crucial role in shaping the user experience and ensuring that pervasive computing technologies are user-friendly and accessible to all.

Figure 7. Human-Computer interaction (HCI)

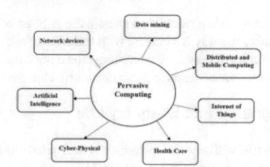

- **User Interface Design:** HCI specialists design user interfaces for pervasive computing systems that are intuitive and user-friendly. They focus on ensuring that users can seamlessly interact with the myriad interconnected devices.
- **Accessibility:** Inclusive design is a core consideration. HCI experts work to create interfaces and interactions that accommodate users with various abilities and needs, ensuring that pervasive computing is accessible to a diverse user base.
- **User Experience (UX) Research:** HCI researchers conduct studies to gain insights into how users interact with pervasive computing systems. This user-centric approach informs iterative improvements in design and functionality.
- **Context-Aware Systems:** HCI experts contribute to the development of context-aware applications. These systems adapt to users' environments and preferences, enhancing the overall user experience and making interactions with pervasive computing more intuitive.
- **Ethical Considerations:** HCI professionals address ethical concerns such as privacy and data security. They advocate for the design of pervasive computing systems that respect user privacy, preferences, and ethical principles.

The trajectory of pervasive computing is significantly influenced by the interdisciplinary convergence of computer science, telecommunications, and human-computer interaction. Computer science provides the technical underpinnings, telecommunications ensure seamless connectivity, and human-computer interaction focuses on usability, accessibility, and ethical considerations (Balint, 1995). Together, these disciplines create a holistic approach that advances pervasive computing and its real-world applications, ultimately realizing the vision of a seamlessly integrated, technology-driven world.

A GLIMPSE INTO THE FUTURE OF PERVASIVE COMPUTING

Pervasive computing, often referred to as ubiquitous or ambient computing, is poised to revolutionize the way it interacts with technology and the world around us. Its peer into the future of pervasive computing, the envision a landscape characterized by remarkable advancements and transformative changes (Kim et al., 2012).

Seamless Integration Into Everyday Life

Pervasive computing will become so seamlessly integrated into our daily lives that even notice it's there. Our surroundings, whether it's our homes, offices, or public spaces, will be embedded with smart devices and sensors that work harmoniously to enhance our experiences. These systems will adapt to our preferences and needs, creating a truly personalized environment.

Context-Aware and Predictive Systems

Future pervasive computing systems will exhibit an unprecedented level of context-awareness. They will understand the context of their users, drawing from data like location, time of day, personal preferences, and even biometrics. This contextual intelligence will enable predictive features, such as anticipating your needs before you explicitly request them. For instance, your home may adjust the lighting and temperature to your liking as you enter the room.

Ambient Intelligence and Automation

Ambient intelligence will take center stage, making our environments intelligent and responsive. Pervasive computing systems will autonomously manage routine tasks, freeing us to focus on more meaningful activities. For example, your home will take care of energy management, security, and even grocery replenishments based on your patterns and preferences.

Interconnected Ecosystems

The various components of pervasive computing, including IoT devices, wearable tech, and intelligent infrastructure, will form interconnected ecosystems. These ecosystems will seamlessly communicate with each other, breaking down the silos between devices and applications. This connectivity will lead to a more holistic and efficient user experience.

Enhanced Augmented Reality

Augmented reality (AR) will play a pivotal role in the way the interact with the digital world. AR glasses or contact lenses will provide a heads-up display, overlaying digital information onto our physical surroundings. Whether for work, entertainment, or education, AR will become an integral part of our lives.

Advanced AI and Machine Learning

Artificial intelligence (AI) and machine learning will continue to advance, powering the intelligent decision-making processes of pervasive computing systems. These technologies will not only understand our preferences but also learn and adapt to our behaviors, creating a more intuitive and responsive digital environment.

Enhanced Healthcare and Well-Being

Pervasive computing will revolutionize healthcare by continuously monitoring our health and well-being. Wearable and implantable devices will provide real-time data, enabling early disease detection and personalized treatment plans. Telemedicine will become the norm, offering efficient and accessible healthcare services.

Ethical Considerations and Regulation

As pervasive computing becomes more ingrained in our lives, ethical considerations surrounding privacy, data security, and digital rights will grow. Governments and regulatory bodies will play an essential role in crafting policies and standards that protect individuals while fostering innovation (Duquenoy & Burmeister, 2009).

Sustainability and Green Computing

Sustainability will be a core theme in the future of pervasive computing. Energy-efficient devices, responsible e-waste management, and eco-friendly computing practices will be essential in reducing the environmental impact of technology.

The future of pervasive computing holds the promise of a world where technology seamlessly blends into the fabric of our lives, making our interactions with digital systems more intuitive and responsive (Tailor, 2012). However, this future also comes with the need to address unresolved challenges, including privacy, security, standards, environmental impact, and social inclusion. As it navigates these changes, it is essential that the growth of pervasive computing is guided by ethical considerations, environmental responsibility, and a commitment to the well-being of individuals and society as a whole.

CONCLUSION: THE PAST, PRESENT, AND FUTURE OF PERVASIVE COMPUTING

The evolution of pervasive computing, spanning from its origins to the present and onward into the future, stands as a tribute to human ingenuity and our unwavering quest for a more interconnected and intelligent digital realm. As it draws our exploration to a close, it can summarize our insights into two essential elements: the path traversed thus far and the perpetual process of evolution.

Reflecting on the Journey

Pervasive computing emerged as a visionary response to the limitations of traditional computing models. Early pioneers and visionaries envisioned a world where technology would not be a separate entity but an integral part of our daily experiences. Over the years, it has witnessed the gradual realization of this vision.

The past of pervasive computing is marked by key milestones. The rise of the internet, the proliferation of mobile devices, and the advent of the IoT have all contributed to the integration of technology into our lives. Our homes, workplaces, and public spaces have become digitally enhanced, creating a world where information and connectivity are ever-present.

However, this journey has been fraught with challenges. Privacy concerns, security vulnerabilities, and ethical considerations have risen to the surface as technology has become more ubiquitous. The balance between convenience and individual rights has been a recurring theme. It has led to the development of legal frameworks and ethical guidelines to ensure that our rights and privacy are respected in this connected world.

The Ever-Present Evolution

The story of pervasive computing is far from over; it is an ongoing narrative that continues to evolve and shape the future. Look ahead, it is clear that pervasive computing is not just a concept but a dynamic force driving innovation and change.

The future promises a world where technology is seamlessly integrated, more intelligent, and responsive to our needs.

Emerging trends, such as ambient intelligence, context-aware systems, augmented reality, advanced AI, and eco-friendly computing, point to a future where technology is deeply intertwined with our daily lives. The digital and physical worlds will blend further, making our experiences more personalized, efficient, and sustainable.

Yet, with this evolution comes new challenges and responsibilities. Ensuring the ethical and responsible development of pervasive computing remains paramount. Privacy concerns, data security, and social inclusivity must be addressed. Technology should be a force for positive change and equality, not division.

The journey of pervasive computing is a story of promise and potential. It is a journey where technology evolves to become an integral part of our lives, a journey where innovation knows no bounds, and a journey where the well-being of individuals and society remains at its core.

As it moves forward, let us do so with a commitment to ethical principles, environmental sustainability, and the betterment of humanity. The past, present, and future of pervasive computing are interconnected chapters in a story that continues to shape the way the live, work, and connect with one another.

This chapter takes readers on a historical journey through the world of pervasive computing, from its inception to its modern-day significance. It covers the visionary ideas of Mark Weiser, the gradual integration of computation into our everyday lives, the pivotal role of wireless communication, influential projects, and the ethical considerations and challenges that have arisen. It also explores the interdisciplinary nature of pervasive computing and provides a glimpse into its future. The chapter aims to offer readers a profound understanding of the forces that have brought us to the interconnected and intelligent systems of today, while also sparking curiosity about the potential directions and challenges that lie ahead in the field of pervasive computing.

REFERENCES

Abdulrab, H., Babkin, E., & Kozyrev, O. (2011). *Semantically Enriched Integration Framework for Ubiquitous Computing Environment*. Ubiquitous Computing. https://doi.org/10.5772/15262

Bacon, J. (2002). Toward pervasive computing. *IEEE Pervasive Computing*, 1(2), 84. https://doi.org/10.1109/mprv.2002.1012341

Bálint, L. (1995). HCI methods and tools in computer-supported interpersonal communication: Towards error-free information exchange in human-to-human interaction. Symbiosis of Human and Artifact - Future Computing and Design for Human-Computer Interaction, Proceedings of the Sixth International Conference on Human-Computer Interaction, (HCI International '95), 819–824. https://doi.org/10.1016/s0921-2647(06)80129-2

Davies, N. (2013). Ethics in Pervasive Computing Research. *IEEE Pervasive Computing*, 12(3), 2–4. https://doi.org/10.1109/mprv.2013.48

Duquenoy, P., & Burmeister, O. K. (2009). *Ethical Issues and Pervasive Computing*. Risk Assessment and Management in Pervasive Computing., https://doi.org/10.4018/9781605662206.ch014

Harrington, A., & Cahill, V. (2011). Model-driven engineering of planning and optimization algorithms for pervasive computing environments. *Pervasive and Mobile Computing*, 7(6), 705–726. https://doi.org/10.1016/j.pmcj.2011.09.005

Hong, J. (2017). The Privacy Landscape of Pervasive Computing. *IEEE Pervasive Computing*, 16(3), 40–48. https://doi.org/10.1109/mprv.2017.2940957

Huang, Y., & Wu, K. (2020). Vibration-based pervasive computing and intelligent sensing. *CCF Transactions on Pervasive Computing and Interaction*, 2(4), 219–239. https://doi.org/10.1007/s42486-020-00049-9

Kim, M. J., Maher, M. L., & Gu, N. (2012). *Mobile and Pervasive Computing: The Future for Design Collaboration. Mobile and Pervasive Computing in Construction*. Portico. https://doi.org/10.1002/9781118422281.ch9

Kong, X., Cao, J., Wu, H., & Hsu, C.-H. (Robert). (2020). Mobile Crowdsourcing and Pervasive Computing for Smart Cities. *Pervasive and Mobile Computing*, 61, 101114. https://doi.org/10.1016/j.pmcj.2020.101114

Kumar, M., & Zambonelli, F. (2007). Middleware for pervasive computing. *Pervasive and Mobile Computing*, 3(4), 329–331. https://doi.org/10.1016/j.pmcj.2007.04.005

Kun, A. L. (2019). Reader and Teacher: Fourteen Books That Can Inspire Teaching in Pervasive Computing (and beyond). *IEEE Pervasive Computing*, 18(2), 85–90. https://doi.org/10.1109/mprv.2019.2912257

Lucke, U., & Steinmetz, R. (2014). Special issue on "Pervasive Education.". *Pervasive and Mobile Computing*, 14, 1–2. https://doi.org/10.1016/j.pmcj.2014.08.001

Mangaraj, B. K., & Aparajita, U. (2010). Cultural Dimension in the Future of Pervasive Computing. Ubiquitous and Pervasive Computing, 974–992. https://doi.org/10.4018/978-1-60566-960-1.ch060

O'Neill, E., Conlan, O., & Lewis, D. (2013). Situation-based testing for pervasive computing environments. *Pervasive and Mobile Computing*, 9(1), 76–97. https://doi.org/10.1016/j.pmcj.2011.12.002

Tailor, J. H. (2012). Green it: Sustainability Plan of Green Computing. *Global Journal for Research Analysis*, 3(4), 38–39. https://doi.org/10.15373/22778160/apr2014/13

Taylor, A. (2009). Ethnography in Ubiquitous Computing. Ubiquitous Computing Fundamentals, 203–236. https://doi.org/10.1201/9781420093612.ch5

Want, R. (2009). An Introduction to Ubiquitous Computing. Ubiquitous Computing Fundamentals, 1–35. https://doi.org/10.1201/9781420093612.ch1

Ye, J., Dobson, S., & McKeever, S. (2012). Situation identification techniques in pervasive computing: A review. *Pervasive and Mobile Computing*, 8(1), 36–66. https://doi.org/10.1016/j.pmcj.2011.01.004

Zhu, F., Carpenter, S., & Kulkarni, A. (2012). Understanding identity exposure in pervasive computing environments. *Pervasive and Mobile Computing*, 8(5), 777–794. https://doi.org/10.1016/j.pmcj.2011.06.007

Chapter 2
Real–Time Applications of Ubiquitous Computing on Heterogeneous Next Generation Networks

A. Gayathiri

Vivekanandha College of Arts and Sciences for Women (Autonomous), India

P. Sumitra

Vivekanandha College of Arts and Sciences for Women (Autonomous), India

S. Sabitha

Vivekanandha College of Arts and Sciences for Women (Autonomous), India

M. Sathiya

Vivekanandha College of Arts and Sciences for Women (Autonomous), India

G. Sathiya

Vivekanandha College of Arts and Sciences for Women (Autonomous), India

George Ghinea

Brunel University, Brunei

ABSTRACT

Pervasive is also acknowledged as ubiquitous computing, which incorporates connecting all objects in the surroundings through its functionalities. When it is connected it will integrate as a single system and all together work as a whole single unit. It is used for computer capacity as an embedded device and is used for communication. It communicates well and achieves the dropping of end users' need to communicate with computer. This pervasive computing is used in various areas in the real world. Today, people have a smart watch which connects with smart phones and receives many notifications from the office employees while not at work. As this, there are

DOI: 10.4018/979-8-3693-2268-0.ch002

Copyright © 2024, IGI Global. Copying or distributing in print or electronic forms without written permission of IGI Global is prohibited.

many examples in the real world of pervasive computing. In this chapter the authors are going to know about the pervasive computing origin, which are the places where pervasive computing is used and how it is working with heterogeneous network and also with the future generation network.

INTRODUCTION

Communication is one of the important and mandatory parts in every minute life. This communication is done through many customs. One such mores is through computer and internet. In this current era even that of using computer is also gone with invent of new technologies. That new technology is already in use but now it is familiarizing. That is embedding the computers, communication technologies, IOT devices with the environment. When we use computers and laptops we will strict to a particular place to work with, but when Pervasive computing or it is known as Ubiquitous computing we can use it anywhere anytime.

Pervasive computing additionally known as ubiquitous computing it can included with any device, anywhere at any time, with any data format, over any network, and with the ability to transfer tasks from one computer to another is all part of ubiquitous computing. These devices have evolved to include Laptops, notebooks, Smartphones, tablets, wearable devices and sensors. Devices like Radio frequency identification (RFID)tags, wearable computers, embedded systems, mobile devices, middleware, and software agents are all commonly associated with ubiquitous computing. Systems supporting ubiquitous computing are able to gather, process and share data; moreover, they are able to adjust to the activity and context of the data. The key components of ubiquitous computing are context awareness, localized scalability, invisibility, and the effective and (Meshram, 2016) efficient utilization of smart places. The study on ubiquitous computing aims to make gadgets more transparent in their use.

What is Ubiquitous Computing?

The growing field of ubiquitous computing emerged as a study area in the middle of 1980s. Professor Mark Weiser of MIT initially coined the phrase in 1988. "Ubiquitous computing #1" and "Ubiquitous computing #2", two brief notes written by Weiser, were published. He imagined a future in which desktop computers would no longer be used for computer power may be used with new quality in various domains, from industrial production to private everyday usage (Friedewald, 2011).

Three technologies merge to form pervasive computing (Geeks for Geeks, 2020):

1. Small, powerful devices and displays with minimal energy usage are made possible by micro electronic technology.
2. Digital communication technology offers global roaming, more bandwidth, and a faster data transmission rate at a reduced cost.
3. The industry and other standardization groups work together to standardize the internet in order to provide the framework for integrating all the parts into a system that is interoperable and has billing, security, and service systems.

Qualities of Pervasive Computing

A range of characteristics that define the scope of its functioning may be used to define ubiquitous computing. Real-world communication has already embraced mobility and ad hoc networking. In the next two to five years, attributes including context awareness, autonomy, and energy autarky are anticipated.

It is believed that contextual awareness and integration with commonplace things are fundamental and formative aspects of ubiquitous computing. On the other hand, energy autarky and system and component autonomy are seen as secondary features. Therefore, it makes sense that as its features increasingly take shape, ubiquitous computing will become more and more established. Autonomy is not projected for another 10 years, even if market-ready ubiquitous computing applications are predicted to be available in the next four to eight years. Additionally, the significance of each feature varies based on the application industry. For instance, the mobility and autarkic power supply of ubiquitous computing components are crucial for communications applications but very insignificant for the smart home.

Therefore, it makes sense that as its features increasingly take shape, ubiquitous computing will become more and more established. Autonomy is not projected for another 10 years, even if market-ready ubiquitous computing applications are predicted to be available in the next four to eight years. Additionally, the significance of each feature varies based on the application industry. For instance, the mobility and autarkic power supply of ubiquitous computing components are crucial for communications applications but very insignificant for the smart home.

Examples of Pervasive Computing

1. **Internet of Things** which is called as IoT entails attaching commonplace items to the internet so they may exchange data. This covers wearable technologies industrial sensors, and smart home appliances.
2. **Wearable computer**, the items that bring computer skills closer to the user include augmented reality glasses, fitness trackers and smart watches.

3. **Smart environments**, where areas include smart houses, smart workplaces, and smart cities that have sensors and actuators that can adapt to the demand of their residents.
4. **Context Aware computing**, this is the capacity of systems to identify and respond to the context in which they are utilized, accounting for elements like user preferences, time, and place.
5. **RFID radio frequency identification technology**, which is widely used in supply chain management, logistics and inventory monitoring tracks and identifies items using radio waves.

Figure 1 .The Pervasive computing and its areas

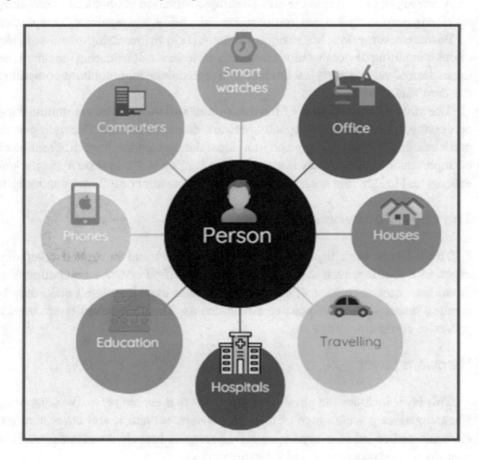

The Technological Basis of Pervasive Computing

In particular, tiny electronics and communications technologies are essential for practically all applications using ubiquitous computing. While energy autarky may not be a crucial aspect of every ubiquitous computing application, energy provisioning is undoubtedly a primary responsibility. Within the next one to four years, ubiquitous computing-relevant technologies should mature and become widely available. In the near future, almost all of the technological prerequisites for ubiquitous computing should be satisfied. unsolved issues with power and technology.

Challenges of Ubiquitous Computing

A few minor obstacles to the effective implementation of ubiquitous computing are resource consumption, environmental sustainability, and regulatory compliance.

Power consumption: Maintaining the batteries in an increasing amount of ubiquitous computing devices wouldn't be feasible. However, considering the functional interaction of various parts is a fundamental prerequisite for ubiquitous computing, standardization is crucial.

The state of equilibrium of hardware and software features: multitasking, processing, memory, storage capacity, network, display, and more. Depending on the particular application, privacy and individual data protection have different levels of importance. While privacy is a significant limiting factor in security, communications, and health, it is not a major problem in industrial or military applications.

The Layers of Pervasive Computing

These layers work together to create a seamless and integrated computing experience that is woven into the fabric of daily life. Pervasive computing aims to enhance user convenience, automate tasks, and improve overall efficiency by creating intelligent and responsive environments. There are seven layers used in pervasive computing. They are,

Hardware Layer

This layer includes the physical components that enable pervasive computing. It encompasses a wide range of devices, sensors, actuators, and other hardware elements embedded in everyday objects. Examples include smart sensors, RFID tags, embedded processors, and wearable devices.

Communication Layer

The communication layer facilitates the exchange of information between different devices and systems in a pervasive computing environment. It involves various communication technologies such as wireless networks like bluetooh wi-fi and zigbee, RFID (radio-frequency identification), NFC (near field communication), and other protocols that enable seamless connectivity.

Middleware Layer

Middleware provides a set of services and protocols that enable communication and interaction between heterogeneous devices and applications. It is quite important in abstracting the underlying complexity in diverse hardware and software components. Middleware ensures interoperability and facilitates the development of applications that can run across different devices.

Software Layer

This layer involves the development of software applications specifically designed for pervasive computing environments. These applications leverage the capabilities of the underlying hardware and communication infrastructure to provide context-aware, adaptive, and intelligent services. Examples include smart home applications, health monitoring software, and location-based services.

Service Layer

Pervasive computing aims to deliver services that are context-aware and can adapt to the user's environment. The service layer involves the development and deployment of various services that enhance the user experience. These services could include location-based services, context-aware applications, intelligent personal assistants, and more.

Security and Privacy Layer

Protection and privacy both be critical concerns in pervasive computing due to the extensive data exchange and connectivity. This layer addresses the implementation of robust security mechanisms to protect data, ensure secure communication, and safeguard user privacy. Techniques such as encryption, authentication, and access control are integral components of this layer.

User Interface Layer

The user interface layer focuses on the design and implementation of interfaces that allow users to interact by means of pervasive computing systems. Because these systems be incorporated addicted to everyday objects and environments, user interfaces need to be intuitive, unobtrusive, and tailored to the context of use. Voice commands, gesture recognition, and augmented reality interfaces are examples of interfaces in pervasive computing.

Embedded System: What Is it?

An embedded system is a type of computer system that performs certain activities related to its job, interacts with physical processes, and functions as a part of a larger system. Additionally, it could feature a unique user interface.

Embedded systems perform a crucial role in providing services for ubiquitous computing. Users of these systems require access to an adaptable user interface in order to display services, therefore using an embedded system with an adaptive interface is a suitable option. Nevertheless, the following objectives are not very successfully achieved by the conventional embedded systems software services (Zhi,-yong, 2011).

The examples of Embedded Systems are,

- Microwave control panel
- Automobile instrument cluster
- Blu-ray player
- Thermostat

Numerous embedded systems are capable of communicating with other embedded systems locally (e.g., hot shoe camera flash), remotely (e.g., GPS units, restaurant notification coasters), and globally (e.g., Nest, Echo, smart TVs). Compared to conventional computer devices, embedded systems frequently have rather distinct issues.

Categories of Ubiquitous Computing

Ubiquitous computing can take different forms. Here is a sample of a few of those forms.

Portable Computing

Computing has been more portable thanks to laptops and handheld computers even if you can take your computer everywhere you go, using it is still essentially the same as using it at your office—you still need to use a more conventional interface.

Pervasive Computing

Smart gadgets have computing technology in unexpected locations. PDAs, pagers, and other information appliances like phones will be the first to use this. In the future, more conventional appliances like toasters, freezers, washing machines, ovens, home security systems, and so forth are anticipated to be included in the scope of ubiquitous computing. Subsequently, the infrastructure will advance to the point where smart gadgets will incorporate devices similar to those found in cars, hotels, airports, and on the road. With your phone-based electronic wallet, you may be able to purchase plane tickets or pay tolls, for instance. Although there are existing prototypes showing these kinds of capabilities, a universal infrastructure with more processing and communication capability will be needed for their general use.

Well-connected, furnished with intelligent appliances and a PC-based system capable of regulating the interior climate are all characteristics of "smart buildings." To save costs and maximise user comfort or security, some appliances require "smarts" to initiate and stop. For instance, a smart home may choose to operate the water heater during periods of low energy cost. It might also decide when to put on the air conditioning or heat depending on which rooms are inhabited at the moment or would likely be filled soon.

Calm Computing

The concept of computing disappearing into the background is realised by this technology. With the help of this technology, we may live with intelligent objects that quietly improve our lives without requiring conscious engagement. The "dangling string" network monitor is one instance of this. To monitor computer network traffic, a typical user interface would gather a lot of data and attempt to display it on a computer screen. On the other hand, the hanging string is powered by a tiny motor and is suspended from the ceiling of a corridor. The motor kicks the string ever so gently when there is network activity. Thus, network activity is shown as the actual hum of the swaying string.

The creation of non-symbolic user interfaces is the fundamental idea underpinning quiet computing. Even though symbols may express a great deal of specific information, in order to understand them, one must pay close attention to them.

Humans, on the other hand, are able to process a great deal of non-symbolic information without explicitly paying attention to it. You can effectively complete your primary activity in a symbolic mode, but you can also be aware of several other activities on the periphery of your attention without focusing on them. This latter group includes the hum of a string, the shadows created by a ceiling fan, and the reflections from a shimmering body of water. Even when your focus is on your word processor or a phone call, you will probably be aware of the flickering shadows and reflections and how quickly they are changing.

Wearable Computing

In this antithesis of quiet computing, you carry the computers on your person as opposed to having them integrated in the surroundings. The user interface is one significant distinction from a standard computer. Hands-free operation is the design of wearable computers. The intended user would frequently be moving about or in a difficult position, as within a small submarine engine room or atop an electric utility pole. One of the first uses of wearable computers was in equipment repair. It lets the user see information using a head-mounted display that projects an image onto their glasses and gives voice instructions.

The user had to practically carry a rucksack with a computer inside of it when it came to the first wearable computers. But thanks to technological advancements, wearable computers might soon be sewed into clothes, worn as pendants, or even included in wristwatches. Typically, these tiny computers are made for certain tasks, such showing text and images and providing web instructions while the user is moving about. In a different application, the wearable computer acts as an interface to a three-dimensional information space, interpreting the user's motions with their head, neck, and eyes as requests to explore certain areas of the environment in greater detail.

Embedded Platforms for Ubiquitous Computing

Embedded smart devices that gather, analyze, and send data in a cooperative and independent manner comprise the network of embedded smart devices that makes up peripatetic computing, also known as ubiquitous computing (Bozorgzadeh, 2017). Web Services have been established to enable distributed applications to be deployed across organizations.

Reducing the complexity of the service interfaces—which simply encode generic semantics—is how loose coupling is achieved. Descriptive messages must have all application-specific semantics contained in them. All parties may understand the open standard format used to write messages, which is often XML. The ubiquitous nature of XML allows any Web Service-enabled device to be accessed and guided by any XML competent programme connected to the network. In order for higher level middleware services like security and transaction management to be deployed across heterogeneous domains and utilized to combine resources and services from various organizations into higher level, added value applications, the Web Service effort is working to standardize these specifications. Nevertheless, the usage of Web services in embedded systems remains hard. It needs web services technologies, which eliminate the need for software to be incorporated into a web server (Cottenier, 2020).

The widespread use of embedded systems running software code for the overall management and monitoring of bigger systems has been made possible by the continually diminishing size of processor chips and memory, as well as the rising speed and processing components. Nearly every piece of contemporary electronic equipment utilised in homes, businesses, vehicles, space exploration, and military combat zones has one or more embedded systems (Sharma, 2013).

Embedded nodes are independent and self contained. They have a clear interface for communication, a single thread of control, and their own state. Nodes interact with one another asynchronously. These gadgets might not operate in a reliable setting. These factors dictate that interactions between various devices must be at arm's length; the malfunction of one gadget shouldn't have an impact on another. Take an intelligent house, for instance, where the coffee machine is activated by an alarm and the clock is networked to it. It shouldn't be possible for the alarm clock to stop working because of a malfunctioning coffee machine. Our described model's autonomy and asynchrony contribute to this kind of fault containment.

Embedded nodes usually have restricted resources, such as a short communication range, very little storage, a short power supply, etc. There are several repercussions from these resource constraints. Due to limited capacity, not all code that could be needed throughout a node's lifespan can be pre-loaded into the device. Some abstractions, such those that need busy waiting to implement, could be too costly to be useful due to limited power supplies.

Ubiquitous Computing Future Trends

According to Gordon Moore, the performance of a microprocessor doubles around every 18 months (Mathur, 2015). Other technological characteristics have also grown, such as the data transfer rate in both directed and unguided media.

According to this tendency, computers will get further smaller in the future and be more widely accessible in simpler shapes and sizes.

Devices such as PDAs, smart phones, laptops, and palmtop computers have begun to partially replace classic computers like workstations, PCs, and servers in the modern day. By using embedded technology, which involves implanting a GPS chip into a common object, computers are connected to commonplace objects, increasing their effectiveness and processing capabilities and transforming them into "smart objects."

One of the most recent technological developments is ubiquitous computing, which is an application of information and communications technology (ICT) permeating daily life. With the widespread use of ICT systems, the objective is to satisfy the statement of everything, always, everywhere for data processing and transmission. Possessing traits like:

1. **Miniaturization:** reducing size of ICT components for their mobility with ease of access.
2. **Embedding:** ICT components are embedded into everyday objects, converting them into smart objects
3. **Networking:** ICT components are linked to each other for communication via radio, Infra or Micro Waves, and are designed to work simultaneously.
4. **Ubiquity:** since embedded ICT components are ubiquitous, they are oblivious or even invisible too, to user.

LITERATURE REVIEW ONE

Luo (2022) implemented the new pervasive computing technology for their medical purposes. The thickening of the arteries caused by the deposits of like cholesterol, fatty substances and any other deposits causes Atherosclerosis which will become stiff and thickened. The authors used pervasive computing for monitoring the above atherosclerosis by using the biological indicators related to atherosclerosis examinations. (iPPG) imaging photoplethysmography also known as remote phtotoplethysmography exploited to measure the blood volume pulsation and calculate approximately physiological parameters using video images. A photoelectric plethysmograph or it is also known as PPG is photoplethysmograph an instrument used to measure the changes in the blood volume tissue. Whereas Imaging photoplethysmography iPPG uses three different cameras like high definition, consumer level and cellphone cameras in their iPPG. High definition cameras are high cost and its expediency. When light is needed in ambient the authors suggested using consumer level cameras which is lesser than high definition cameras respective to cost and convenience. Different cameras can be placed in the human places like head which includes 2 cameras for the pulse arrival time (PAT). Likewise as per the area of interest the embedded devices are used to calculate the human activities.

In the recent years to detect the heart rate cellphone based iPPG applications are used. Here iPad camera is used to detect the images of the human. The phone's flash camera records the colour changes on the finger, which is used to measure heart rate and breathing. Laser Doppler is used to measure the blood flow in the organ. The strong diffuser, the light that is scattered is used to calculate the blood flow rate. The sensors of non invasive are Radio Frequency electromagnetic waves, which are cost effective, used in Doppler shift, used for chest movement. The blood flow in the wrists arteries, such as the ulnar and arteries, is measured using radio frequencies called wrist pulse sensors. Electromagnetic radiation is emitted by the objects which has more than 0 K is is used as basic principle of Thermal Imaging. It makes use of both long wave and medium wave infrared cameras; long wave is typically employed in situations when hot things seem brighter in the medium wavelength. The thermal camera is employed to capture the thermal images, which is used to convert the thermal data to identify the flow of blood. Various thermal images used areas are to notice the respiratory rate, information about breathing in the organ of nostril. The cardiac pulse also can be detected by using thermal imaging. Likewise in various applications thermal imaging is used. Optical Fiber Sensing includes an optical source, a device for transmit and a device for detector. It is now more well-liked. It is used to detect pressure of the blood. Fiber Bragg Grating and Long Period Grating are used to measurable biological reactions that offer information about an individual's health and well-being are called physiological indicators. These indicators might be things like blood pressure, heart rate, temperature, respiration rate, and glucose levels, among other things. The tool used to measure blood pressure, respiration rate, and heart rate is called a piezoelectric sensor. The piezoelectric sensors are used to place beneath the mattress to detect the vibrations. The bedside monitor receives vibration signals from the device automatically, and data is analyzed using sophisticated signal processing techniques. The patient's heart rate and breathing rate are calculated. If there is any emergency the data is sent to the nurse who is in duty.

LITERATURE REVIEW TWO

As per every part of life computers are emerged and the technology related to computer like embedding and working from everywhere becomes the necessary part. Not only Higher education but also schools has been changed from the covid

19 period from traditional type of learning to computer oriented e –learning. This type of learning has ie the through smart phones the school and college education has ran for two years during the covid periods. The students can to learn through laptops and smart phones. Park (2014) use the technology well effectively by using internet. Even in some countries the educational institution allow one day as three screen day to use any electronic gadgets like tabs, laptops, smart phones etc. As per Geeks for Geeks (2020), more than 99 percent college students and more than 95 percent school students use wireless internet. Among them the network they use 3G Mobile communication. Likewise the school and higher education system nowadays use home work, any communication, instant messages all communicated through the whatsapp group. Now as a next generation pervasive computing is used for them. The facilities while using the new pervasive computing are the main thing is flexibility for the learners, independence, location and relation. Park (2014) made a survey where the main use of internet service is for information retrieval as the first place and the second place to watching Television. Thus the students gave main importance for education where information retrieval is done for that. As per the survey also the students prefer to learn in the moderate IT environment is high than all other preferences of usage like, No IT, Limited IT, Extensive IT and Online. The students gave no interest in No IT and entirely online. The student's mentality is to learn in the Moderate IT class room. In this model of classroom it is built with smart boards, traditional boards and with internet facility. When a concept is taught it can shown in the digital board and as well as it can also be taught by black board. Many video classes has been uploaded by the educators in their interested topics. Computing equipment, communications for connection, and user interfaces are the three information and communication technology domains that make up peripatetic computing. The maximum used generations of computers is 4G. The next generation 5G is also implemented in some areas. The highest capacity of 5G is 2 Gbps, with data bandwidth ranging from 1 Gbps to 2. Code division multiple access multiplexing is used, and all packets are switched. The network is IPv6-based and internet-based. In future networks which needs as pervasive computing, it need more dense networks. Multiple picocells with smaller base stations which cover the corresponding target regions within a larger mobile coverage area.

LITERATURE REVIEW THREE

Lin and Shi (2006) used Pervasive computing to automatically filter the spam messages on the portable devices. It was done by using pattern discovery, pattern detection and it also uses the Teiresias. The algorithm used to implement Aho-corasick algorithm. The authors implemented the spam filter in mobile phones. The authors embedded device system is divided as one as an offline trainer and an online filter. The offline trainer is the server which runs on the personal computer and the second online filter runs on the embedded systems. Even though there are many other algorithms used or filtering the spam messages like mathematical and statistical methods. The three distinct algorithms are Bayes, Support Vector Machine, and K-Nearest Neighbour. The authors face many difficulties when they implemented in the embedded systems as floating point hardware is not used in central processing unit. So the authors tried to implement this by using pattern discovery, pattern detection instead of statistical methods and mathematical methods. The patterns are found by the offline trainer from both the HAM message set and the SPAM pattern set. The discovered patterns are made as a message set using the algorithm TEIRESIAS, this is the algorithm which find outs unknown patterns that appears more than ones in a large mass. IBM implemented this in 2004 for anti-spam field and showed the high rate of identification. The different modules used in the implementation are the pattern discovery, negative training, jump table generator, online filter, prefiltering, pattern detection using the algorithm. The discovered pattern is identified as the form of string $\sum(\sum l'.')^* \sum)$. The authors then does the negative training which made the set difference between the SPAM AND HAM set of pattern produced. The messages which is received from the SPAM is set as blacklist and that received from the HAM is set as the whitelist. The message which first enters into the phone is made to pass in the whitelist and then filteration is done in the blacklist. If the identification is yet not ound then the messages are passed to the pattern detection. For this the authors used the Aho Corasick algorithm which is improved in jump table on single, jump table on multi-patterns and pattens tree. Thus, the writers demonstrate text message filtering on embedded devices, demonstrating good filtering performance.

LITERATURE REVIEW FOUR

To understand the patient's health in the timely mode, it is necessary that the patient's information is needed for the intensivist. The past history of the patient's information is mandatory for the intensive care unit treatments for decision making purposes. But it is impossible for the patient's information to be cared along every time in the form of hardcopy. Pereira (2016) suggested the pervasive business intelligence systems for the above situation. The patient's information is first stored in business intelligence and they retrieve in the information any time and any where the decision is needed for the patients. With the information the following process is done like data is available, examinations of the data, the medicine they need, performation of health checkup, as the last step the conclusions are made. This type of approach is very much useful in the healthcare sectors. It is possible with the concept of business intelligence and with the pervasive computing concepts. Bozorgzadeh (2017) explained the integration of the business intelligence with pervasive health-care is explained. The pervasive information systems view the elements in the multi dimensions mode. It includes the human interaction and software engineering. It merges the human data and the computer to the physical world.

LITERATURE REVIEW FIVE

Industry 4.0 and the Internet of Things will use the next generation of networks, known as open platform communications unified architecture time sensitive network-ing (OPC UA TSN). There are different types of Control networks for Industries emerged to reduce wiring, and effective performance like CC Link, DeviceNet, PRO-FIBUS, and Modbus etc. These protocols are still in use because they are reliable, strong, and somewhat simple. There are built in the lower layer communications protocols. The new generation fieldbus standard, which incorporates the industrial internet of things (IIoT), is used by this OPC UA TSN. As the needs of the industry are increased it needs time synchronized and timeliness in needed. For this TSN is used as the next generation computers. The new feature of TSN is part of the OSI tiered model's Second Data Link Layer. In the ISO/OSI layer, it is supported. It also offers a well-defined and transparent interface, effectively handling transmission failures and advancing the mechanism to manage data flow. A (AVB) Audio video bridging standard improves synchronization, which are the applications of the audio and video markets. On the critical traffic, The primary objective of TSN is to reduce end-to-end and worst-case latency. The IEC 62541 is the standard for OPC UA. It links Industry 4.0 with IIOT. It has systems like reliability, security manufacturing, for the information exchange platform independent and the self describing devices for the support of semantic information. It is also scalable.

Pervasive or Ubiquitous Computing in Education

As per new Higher Education policy framed, it allows the education institution to use the hybrid mode of teaching in the education environment. It seems that the education institution can run in the offline and in the online mode of teaching. When online mode of teaching is used it needs new technology which will effectively use for teaching. This type of computing anywhere will make the education system more effective. Anytime anywhere system is opted for Pervasive computing. As already in the Covid type we all have experienced the online teaching method where we use smart boards, white boards, tablets, laptops and desktop computers for teaching. In this mode of teaching it is possible to sit and hear in one place. In contrast, we can learn at anytime and from anyplace thanks to the new technology booming next to online teaching is the ubiquitous computing. The (All India Council for Technical Education, 2022) higher education system also support online certificate courses like SWAYAM (study webs of active learning for young aspiring minds), MOOC (massive open online courses) and NPTEL for the interested learners. The access, equity and quality are the three main education polices that SWAYAM aims to attain. SWAYAM also aims to close the digital gap or the students who have not been able to integrate into the knowledge economy and have not yet been affected by the digital revolution. In SWAYAM a peer group interaction, to clarify doubts a discussion forum. The course ahs well and best teachers in the country and the course is taught from 9th to post graduation. It is like pervasive computing concept o accessed by anyone and from anywhere at any time. The course has no cost or the registration and it is free of cost anywhere in India. It supports high quality learning experience using multimedia on anytime and anywhere basis. Easy to monitor the classes where video are The higher education system makes arrangement for the students to use the online certificate courses as the one that can be included in the curriculum as per the credits. The students can choose any of the courses of interest and get the certificate by viewing the video lectures and assignments. The mark for the online certificate is considered as assignment and the examination marks, both are included. The NPTEL also gives scores as just pass, Elite, Silver, Gold and Platinum. It is as the appreciation or the students. It also has the problem oriented online session and can clarify the doubts. If a student gets the certificate it can also be considered in the semester examination as per the credit courses. The course is not only for the students, the interested educators, teachers, college professors all can write the exam.

The Growth of Pevasive Computing From PC

The Growth of the Pervasive computing starts from the stages of computer growth (Saha, 2005). The personal computer is the first stage of the computer, which was invented by John Blankenbaker in 1970. He invented the PC before microprocessor was invented. The device was aimed for the educational and working on small programmes by the satisfied users, and to demonstrate many programming concepts. The next generation of computer is personal computer with the information technology, where hardware components are well developed with graphical user interface. The next generation computer is the distributed computing with the advent of networks like several forms of networks ie the local area network, wide area network and the personal area network. This type of systems is used to share the data like emails and files in the network. This type of network is referred as distributed networking.

Next comes in the follow up is the World Wide Web, which uses the internet as the platform. It attracted many computer users where such as grid computing is used. The people's aim expected more than sticking to a place and working with computers. As the next stage of change the Web with mobility included came to existence. This mobile computing uses the cellular architecture, user uses SIM subscriber identity module to connect the global system fo mobile communication where the mobile data and voice services are transmitted. The mobile phone applications include calendar, games, text messages, voice messages, voice communications, files / photos transfer, web access and voice recognition are possible.

Figure 2. The generations of PC to pervasive computing

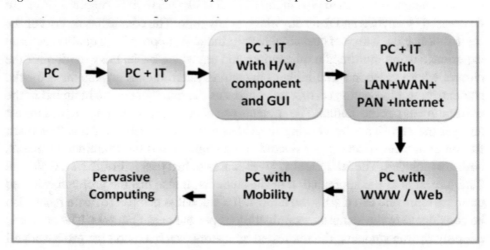

Smart Watch

Now smart watches are the next smart phones where it facilitates not only to connect to your mobile phones, it also able to say more than the time, it provides vibrations on your wrist which indicates the left or right turn while travelling, it also frequently show the direction and it also guides you with the voice guide in the smart phones, fitness and health tracking, notification and communication with the feature of "find phone" the smart phones help to connect to your phone which is missed, it can take calls and reply to the messages instantly, we can connect to the social medias like Face book, Whats App, Snap chat, Instagram and any others, it is completely secure and it is also complete entertainment. Thus the smart phones come as the next generation computer for communication. These all like

PC, PC plus information technology, PC plus improved hardware components and GUI environment, PC with different types of networks like LAN, WAN, PAN and internet, PC with WWW or Web, PC with Mobility components paved the way for the Pervasive computing.

Pervasive Computing in the Area of Business

Through the (RFID) Radio Frequency Identification is a wireless device which uses tags and readers within it. With the help of sensors and RFID supply chains are employed tracking the goods, security monitoring and optimizing. Mainly with the help of sensors the equipments, vehicles and tools are monitored, alters and maintenance and data driven decision making to maximize the asset utilization is also done. Pervasive computing enhances the retail experience by enabling personalized and context aware services. Beacons, RFID, and mobile devices can be leveraged to deliver targeted promotions, streamline checkouts, and provide a seamless omnichannel experience for customers. Business can implement pervasive computing technologies for building automation, energy management, and facilities maintenance. Sensors, actuators and smart devices contribute to energy efficiency, security, and overall operational optimization. It also supports flexible work environment by providing employees with smart devices, wearable's, and IoT enabled tools. It promotes collaboration, improves communication and improves on the whole productivity. It analysis data from sensors, devices and customer interactions can inform strategic decision making, improve processes and identify new business opportunities. In industries the employee's health and safety is monitored through the use of wearables and sensors. In the real time monitoring environmental conditions and worker activities helps prevent accidents and ensures compliance with safety standards. It also facilitates seamless and secure financial transactions like mobile payments, contactless transactions, IoT enabled convenient and efficient payment ecosystem. In the area of transportation, it is used for route optimization, vehicle tracking and predictive maintenance. Chatbots and virtual assistants, enhances customer service by providing customer inquiries and issues by communicating with various integrated devices.

Figure 3. Pervasive computing in the area of business

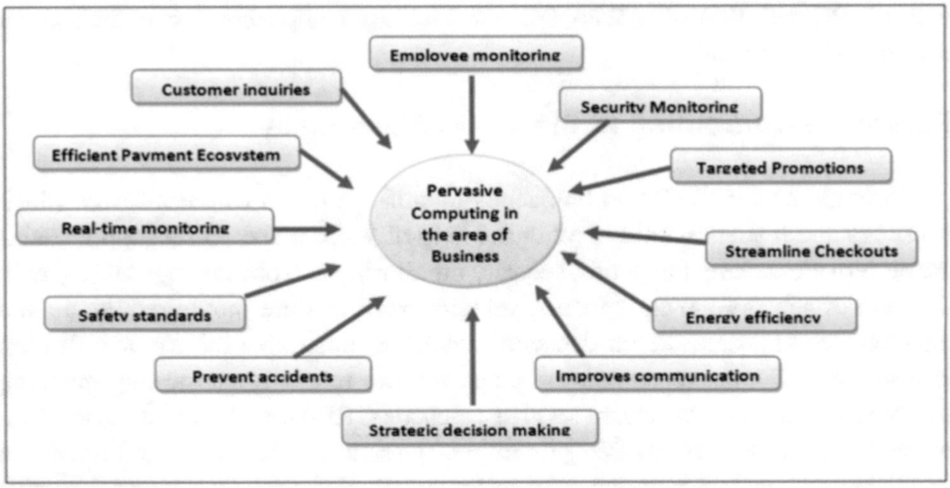

Pervasive Computing in the Area of Education

Pervasive computing converts the traditional classrooms to smart classrooms, interactive spaces by bringing smart boards, interactive displays, IoT devices facilitates collaborative learning and provide multimedia content. It provides to access the educational resources, learning materials and collaborative tools. Apart from learning student's physical activities, health metrics, support language learning are done through wearable devices. To enhance the learning Augmented and Virtual realities are used to make the simulations. It also provides with interactive learning environment. IoT's enable to track and monitor the attendance, usage of resources and it also enhance the security of the campus. Cloud computing enables the collaborative learning. It also dynamically adjusts the speed and content of instruction based on individual student's progress and learning styles. It also enables the real time assessment and feedback mechanisms. Gamification elements like games and simulations can also be integrated experience to make the students more interactive. Remote learning initiatives are provides by the pervasive computing to the students. It also makes the libraries equipped with smart search capabilities, interactive displays and digital resource management systems, enhancing the accessibility and utilization of educational materials.

Figure 4. Pervasive computing in the area of education

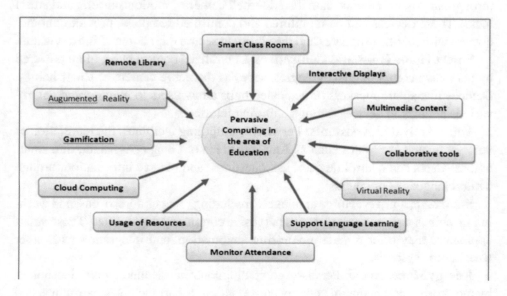

Pervasive Computing in the Area of Smart Homes

Pervasive computing has a profound impact on the concept of smart homes, transforming traditional residences into intelligent, connected environments. The integration of computing technologies into homes enhances automation, security, energy efficiency, and overall convenience. Here are some ways pervasive computing is applied in the area of smart homes:

Home Automation: Pervasive computing enables the automation of various household tasks. Smart devices such as thermostats, lighting systems, door locks, and home appliances can be controlled and automated through a central system or remotely via smartphones and voice commands.

Smart Lighting Systems: Pervasive computing contributes to energy-efficient lighting solutions in smart homes. Smart lighting systems can automatically adjust brightness levels, color temperatures, and turn on/off based on occupancy or natural light conditions.

Smart Thermostats: Intelligent heating, ventilation, and air conditioning (HVAC) systems use pervasive computing to optimize energy usage. Smart thermostats can learn user preferences, adjust temperatures based on occupancy, and be remotely controlled for energy efficiency.

Home Security and Surveillance: Pervasive computing enhances home security through smart surveillance cameras, doorbell cameras, motion sensors, and smart locks. These devices can be monitored and controlled remotely, providing home-owners with real-time updates and the ability to secure their homes from anywhere.

Smart Home Hubs and Controllers: Centralized control hubs, often powered by pervasive computing technologies, serve as the nerve centers of smart homes. Devices like smart speakers or dedicated hubs allow users to manage and control various connected devices through a unified interface.

Voice-Activated Assistants: Pervasive computing facilitates the integration of voice-activated assistants, such as Amazon Alexa or Google Assistant, into smart homes. Users can control devices, ask questions, and receive information through natural language commands.

Smart Appliances: Home appliances, including refrigerators, ovens, and washing machines, can be equipped with pervasive computing capabilities. These smart appliances may offer remote monitoring, automation, and integration with other smart home systems.

Energy Management: Pervasive computing contributes to energy-efficient homes by monitoring and managing energy consumption. Smart meters, smart plugs, and energy management systems provide insights into energy usage patterns, allowing homeowners to optimize consumption and reduce costs.

Health and Wellness Monitoring: Wearable devices and sensors in smart homes can monitor residents' health and well-being. Pervasive computing supports applications such as remote health monitoring, fall detection, and the integration of health data into personalized routines.

Automated Home Entertainment: Pervasive computing enhances home entertainment systems by automating audiovisual components. Smart TVs, streaming devices, and audio systems can be integrated for seamless entertainment experiences.

Environmental Sensors: Pervasive computing facilitates the deployment of environmental sensors to monitor air quality, humidity, and other factors. Automated responses, such as adjusting ventilation or air purifiers, can enhance indoor environmental quality.

Smart Irrigation Systems: Pervasive computing technologies contribute to efficient water management in smart homes. Automated irrigation systems can adjust watering schedules based on weather conditions and soil moisture levels.

Pervasive Computing in the Area of Farmers

Pervasive computing has the potential to bring about transformative changes in agriculture by providing farmers with advanced technologies to enhance productivity, optimize resource use, and improve decision-making. Here are several ways pervasive computing is making an impact in the field of agriculture:

Precision Agriculture: Pervasive computing technologies, such as GPS, sensors, and drones, enable precision agriculture. Farmers can gather real-time data on soil conditions, crop health, and weather patterns. This data is then used to optimize planting, irrigation, and fertilization practices, leading to increased efficiency and reduced resource usage.

IoT in Agriculture: The Internet of Things (IoT) plays a crucial role in smart farming. Connected sensors can be deployed in fields to monitor factors like temperature, humidity, soil moisture, and crop growth. This information allows farmers to make data-driven decisions for crop management.

Smart Irrigation Systems: Pervasive computing facilitates the implementation of smart irrigation systems that automatically adjust watering schedules based on real-time data. This not only conserves water but also ensures that crops receive the optimal amount of moisture for their growth.

Farm Management Software: Pervasive computing technologies support the development of farm management software that integrates data from various sources. Farmers can use these platforms to monitor crop performance, track inventory, manage equipment, and analyze financial data for informed decision-making.

Autonomous Farming Equipment: Pervasive computing enables the use of autonomous machinery in agriculture. Self-driving tractors and harvesters equipped with sensors and GPS can perform tasks such as planting, harvesting, and spraying with precision and efficiency.

Weather Monitoring and Forecasting: Pervasive computing contributes to real-time weather monitoring on farms. Advanced weather stations and sensors provide accurate data, helping farmers anticipate changes in weather conditions and make timely decisions to protect crops.

Livestock Monitoring: IoT devices and sensors can be deployed for monitoring the health and behavior of livestock. Pervasive computing allows farmers to track factors like animal movement, feeding patterns, and health indicators, leading to improved animal welfare and productivity.

Supply Chain Optimization: Pervasive computing technologies aid in optimizing the agricultural supply chain. From monitoring crop storage conditions to tracking transportation logistics, these systems help streamline the movement of agricultural products from farm to market.

Blockchain for Traceability: Pervasive computing, combined with blockchain technology, enhances traceability in agriculture. Farmers can use blockchain to record and verify every step in the supply chain, providing transparency and accountability for consumers and stakeholders.

Mobile Applications for Farmers: Pervasive computing supports the development of mobile applications tailored for farmers. These apps may provide real-time market prices, weather forecasts, pest alerts, and other relevant information, empowering farmers with valuable insights.

Data Analytics for Crop Prediction: Big data analytics, powered by pervasive computing, can analyze historical and real-time data to predict crop yields, disease outbreaks, and market trends. This predictive analytics assists farmers in making strategic decisions for crop planning and marketing.

Remote Monitoring and Control: Farmers can remotely monitor and control various aspects of their operations through pervasive computing. This includes the ability to control irrigation systems, adjust equipment settings, and receive alerts about critical conditions on the farm.

By leveraging pervasive computing technologies, farmers can move towards more sustainable, efficient, and data-driven agricultural practices. These advancements contribute to the ongoing evolution of smart farming and the broader digital transformation of the agriculture sector.

CONCLUSION

Thus the Pervasive computing with the next generation networking, it is going the rule all and every field of the world. In the chapter we have listed out some of the applications of the pervasive computing. Mainly the fields of application of the main areas are the medical field, farmers and the students in the education field. In the world, in the computing era the traditional ways are all changed and the computer its proceedings help the people in all its way.

REFERENCES

All India Council for Technical Education. (2022). *Invitation of Proposals*. All India Council for Technical Education. https://www.aicte-india.org/sites/default/files/40 -35_AICTE_SWAYAM_EOI_2017.pdf

Bozorgzadeh, E. (2017). *Embedded Systems for Pervasive Computing*. Springer. https://www.springeropen.com/collections/espc

Cottenier, T. (2020). *Adaptive Embedded Services for Pervasive Computing*. Illinois Institute of Technology.

Davies, N., Langheinrich, M., Clinch, S., Elhart, I., Friday, A., Kubitza, T., & Surajbali, B. (2014). *Proceedings of the 32nd annual ACM conference on Human factors in computing systems - CHI '14 - Personalisation and privacy in future pervasive display networks*. ACM. 10.1145/2556288.2557287

Friedewald, M. (2011). *Ubiquitous computing: An overview of technology impacts Author links open overlay panel*. Science Direct.

Gajjar, M. (2010). *Ubiquitous Computing Smart Things*. Science Direct. https://www.sciencedirect.com/topics/computer-science/ubiquitous-computing

Geeks for Geeks. (2020). *Introduction to Pervasive Computing*. Geeks for Geeks. https://www.geeksforgeeks.org/introduction-to-pervasive-computing/

Lin, Q., & Shi, X. (2006). A Message Filtering System in Pervasive Computing. *2006 First International Symposium on Pervasive Computing and Applications*. IEEE. 10.1109/SPCA.2006.297446

Luo, J. (2022). Advances in Atherosclerotic Disease Screening Using Pervasive Healthcare. *IEEE Rev Biomed*. doi:10.1109/RBME.2021.3081180.Epub

Mathur, K. (2015). Review and Future Prospects of Ubiquitous Computing. *Indian journal of Research, Palak Chauhan, 4*.

Meshram, V. (2016). *A Survey On Ubiquitous Computing*. Department of Computer Engineering, Vishwakarma Institute of Information Technology, India.10.21917/ijsc.2016.0157

Park, Y. C. (2014). Pervasive Computing and Communication Technologies for U-learning. *Journal of International Education Research (JIER), 10*(4), 265–270. https://www.aicte-india.org/sites/default/files/40-35_AICTE_SWAYAM_EOI_2017 .pdf10.19030/jier.v10i4.8836

Pereira, A. (2016). *Pervasive Business Intelligence: A New Trend in Critical Healthcare*. EUSPN/ICTH.

Saha, D. (2005). *Pervasive computing: A vision to Realize*. Elsevier. .10.1016/S0065-2458(04)64005-8

Sharma, S. (2013). *Embedded Systems -- A Security Paradigm for Pervasive Computing, Surendra Sharma*. Semantic Scholar.

Yang, C., Tampubolon, H., Setyoko, A., Hua, K., Tanveer M., & Wei, W. (2023). Secure and Privacy-Preserving Human Interaction Recognition of Pervasive Healthcare Monitoring. *IEEE Transactions on Network Science and Engineering, 10*(5), 2439-2454. .10.1109/TNSE.2022.3223281

Zhi,-yong, Q. (2011). Pervasive Computing Environment for Embedded System. *Computer Science, 38*(3), 179-181.

Chapter 3
Issues and Challenges of Metaverse in the Healthcare Domain

Guru Prasad M. S.
https://orcid.org/0000-0002-1811-9507
Graphic Era University (Deemed), India

Raghavendra M. Devadas
Department of Information Technology, Manipal Institute of Technology Bengaluru, Manipal Academy of Higher Education, Manipal, India

Praveen Gujjar J.
https://orcid.org/0000-0003-0240-7827
JAIN University (Deemed), India

Bhavya B. S.
Jain University (Deemed), India

Amith K. Jain
SDM Institute of Technology, India

A. Suresh Kumar
Jain University (Deemed), India

ABSTRACT

In the rapidly evolving landscape of healthcare, the emergence of the Metaverse presents a promising yet complex frontier. The chapter begins by providing an overview of the Metaverse, exploring its fundamental concepts, and highlighting its potential benefits for the healthcare industry. It then proceeds for challenges that healthcare professionals, researchers, and stakeholders may encounter in this transformative journey. With the Metaverse's immersive and interconnected nature, safeguarding patient data and ensuring secure communication channels are paramount. The chapter examines the vulnerabilities in the Metaverse and explores strategies to protect sensitive medical information. The chapter concludes with a forward-looking perspective on how the healthcare industry can harness the Metaverse's potential

DOI: 10.4018/979-8-3693-2268-0.ch003

Copyright © 2024, IGI Global. Copying or distributing in print or electronic forms without written permission of IGI Global is prohibited.

while mitigating the associated issues and challenges. It emphasizes the importance of interdisciplinary collaboration between healthcare professionals, technologists, policymakers, and ethicists to navigate this uncharted terrain successfully.

INTRODUCTION

In the digital age, the convergence of technology and healthcare has ushered in a new era of possibilities, paving the way for a profound transformation in the way we deliver and experience medical services. At the heart of this revolution lies the concept of the Metaverse, a multifaceted virtual realm that extends far beyond the boundaries of conventional cyberspace (Prasad,2023). As we navigate the 21st century, the potential of the Metaverse in the healthcare domain is nothing short of revolutionary. The Metaverse, a term originally popularized in science fiction, has transitioned from the realm of imagination into tangible reality, offering an immersive and interconnected digital universe where users can interact, collaborate, and create in ways previously unimaginable (Agarwal, 2023). In the healthcare domain, the promise of the Metaverse is immense, offering innovative solutions for patient care, medical training, and even therapeutic interventions. This amalgamation of digital technology, artificial intelligence, augmented reality, and virtual reality has the potential to redefine the healthcare landscape and enhance the quality of life for individuals around the world. As we navigate this uncharted territory, it is crucial to maintain a delicate balance between embracing the transformative power of the Metaverse and safeguarding the essential human elements of healthcare—compassion, empathy, and human touch. The term "Metaverse" gained widespread recognition when Facebook underwent a corporate rebranding, adopting the name Meta in October 2021, and unveiling intentions to allocate a minimum of $10 billion towards the realization of this concept during that year. Furthermore, not only Meta but also tech industry behemoths such as Google, Microsoft, Nvidia, and Qualcomm have committed substantial financial resources, investing billions of dollars into this emerging concept. The metaverse embodies the collective vision held by many within the computer industry, representing what they anticipate as the forthcoming evolution of the internet. It envisions a unified, immersive, enduring, three-dimensional virtual realm where individuals can encounter life in novel ways that go beyond what the physical world can offer. While certain technologies facilitating access to this virtual domain, like virtual reality (VR) headsets and augmented reality (AR) glasses, are rapidly advancing, other crucial elements required for the metaverse, such as ample bandwidth and standardized interoperability, may still be years away from realization or might never come to fruition (Prabhu,2015). Two pivotal technologies that play a significant role in shaping and expanding the metaverse are virtual reality and augmented reality: Virtual reality immerses users in a simulated 3D environment, facilitating interactions within a virtual space that closely resembles the sensory perceptions of our physical reality (Kumar, 2023). Typically, this simulated reality is accessed through a VR headset that completely occupies the user's field of vision. The integration of haptic feedback mechanisms, such as gloves, vests, and even full-body tracking suits, further enhances the realism of the interaction within the virtual environment. In contrast, augmented reality offers a less immersive experience compared to VR. It overlays digital elements onto the real world, often through some form of wearable lens. Users in augmented reality still retain the ability to interact with their actual surroundings. A prime example of AR in action is the game Pokémon Go, while consumer products like Google Glass and heads-up displays in car windshields are well-recognized instances of AR technology in everyday life.

LITERATURE REVIEW

There is a boom in the innovation of healthcare and new business models that offer an alternative healthcare system through computer-mediated virtual worlds. The scope of digital transformation today is broad. Not limited to virtual communication alone, but it includes digitizing the social network by using metaverse technology in the healthcare sector. The metaverse is a virtual universe that is ubiquitous and immersive (Bansal et al., 2022). The swift advancement of digitalization and automation has caused revolutionary expansion in the healthcare industry by presenting novel approaches for economical treatment provision. Healthcare has a bright future thanks to the burgeoning Metaverse, which is being powered by the convergence of technologies like AI, VR, AR, IoT, robots, and quantum computing (Pai, 2023). This study of the literature offers a thorough investigation of the uses of the Metaverse in healthcare, emphasizing the state of the field today and the technology that makes it possible. It also discusses possible obstacles and suggests future areas of inquiry to optimize the Metaverse's influence on healthcare (Chengoden et al., 2023b). The Metaverse is transforming communication and interpersonal relationships by fusing virtual and augmented reality. Its appearance, especially after Mark Zuckerberg's declaration, has attracted a lot of interest in the medical community. In 2022 and 2023, the Metaverse has the potential to revolutionize the healthcare industry and provide profitable opportunities. It can help with a number of healthcare issues, including social connectedness, mental health, regional health access, and virtual health. This assessment of the literature highlights the possible obstacles to the future deployment of the Metaverse while also summarizing its uses and possibilities in the field of healthcare (Athar et al., 2023b).

Healthcare is investigating how to use the Metaverse to improve patient experiences and accessibility since it has enormous promise for simulating reality. However, there is a dearth of research on practical applications in healthcare. This study focuses on outpatient telemedicine and privacy issues while addressing the state, prospects, and difficulties of the field today (Mejia & Rawat, 2022b). Metaverse applications to improve clinical patient management in the face of mounting demand on healthcare systems. An extensive analysis covers the principles, important technology, and a range of healthcare applications, including emergency response instruction and practical anatomy learning. Through an exploratory approach to qualitative data analysis utilizing scientific databases such as Web of Science and Springer, the potential for Metaverse technology to transform healthcare by enabling remote consultations and providing patients with health information is shown (Ullah et al., 2023). The Internet industry is the Metaverse, which merges the actual and virtual worlds. This research uses the UTAUT2 model with a "switching cost" variable to examine the variables influencing the adoption of the Metaverse in Vietnam. The study, which involved 520 people from Generations Y and Z, shows that factors that favorably promote Metaverse adoption intent include hedonic motivation, value pricing, enabling circumstances, effort expectation, and performance expectancy. Generation Y is heavily affected by social influence. Although there are significant distinctions between Generations Y and Z, switching costs prevent Metaverse adoption, providing insights for sustainable internet sector growth (Turab & Jamil, 2023). Healthcare 5.0, which includes wellness monitoring, telemedicine, patient tracking, and individualized treatment in virtual environments, is the next evolution of smart healthcare. As the Metaverse has the potential to improve healthcare experiences, issues with data privacy and the interactions of digital avatars are brought up. Blockchain technology can help with these problems by giving Metaverse transactions immutability and transparency (Prasad, 2019). This paper presents a case study of telesurgery and discusses possible problems as it investigates the synergistic potential of explainable AI and blockchain in the Metaverse-enabled Healthcare 5.0. (Bhattacharya et al., 2022). digital transformation of the healthcare industry by using blockchain, IoT, AI, and telecommunication networks. The advent of the Metaverse, which combines virtual and augmented reality, allows for immersive communication between people. Avatars and 3D virtual environments have the potential to improve telemedicine, teaching, diagnosis, and therapies in the field of ophthalmology. Innovation in eye care is necessary because implementation calls for careful evaluation of clinical effectiveness, user-friendliness, real-world compatibility, and conformity to healthcare norms (Tan et al., 2022).The Internet of Things, wearable sensors, 3D modeling, and artificial intelligence have all contributed to the rise in interest in The Metaverse, a virtual environment where users adopt avatars. Given its vital relevance, the field of healthcare appears to be a potential one for Metaverse applications. The pandemic's restrictions on access to healthcare have highlighted the need for creative responses. With an emphasis on digital twins in particular, this article provides an overview of Metaverse-based healthcare by highlighting technologies such as augmented reality (AR), virtual reality (VR), and AR. The suggested methodology promotes the use of digital twins for health assessment and maintenance, emphasizing data completeness, update frequency, and accuracy. Personalized risk factors are used to monitor possible illnesses (Song & Qin, 2022b). The COVID-19 epidemic revealed serious flaws in India's healthcare system, including a lack of doctors and necessary supplies. This has led to a group effort to find answers to these problems, making it a crucial matter for experts, public officials, and responsible citizens. In this regard, the metaverse's transformational potential—which is already well recognized in the gaming and social interaction domains—is being investigated as a potent remedy for healthcare. This essay, which focuses on the healthcare industry, describes the ways in which the Metaverse might improve treatment facilities, learning materials, and other aspects of the industry (Pandey et al., 2023b). The 21st century has seen a focus on technology improvement in immersive virtual reality (VR), which has attracted interest from a wide range of fields. There have been little research on immersive VR in major IS publications, indicating that the area of information systems (IS) has fallen behind. Advances in immersive virtual reality technology provide novel prospects for both IS researchers and organizations. The present review emphasizes the benefits of immersive virtual reality (VR), including embodiment and interaction, and examines how these affordances have been used in different fields of study. It also emphasizes how IS academics may contribute to the area by doing metaverse research (Dincelli & Yayla, 2022b). A dynamic digital universe fashioned by state-of-the-art technology, the Metaverse holds the potential to revolutionize many aspects of everyday life. This article explores the use of the Metaverse in healthcare, providing insightful information about the idea and supporting technology. It addresses the obstacles preventing its widespread acceptance in the healthcare industry while examining the vast range of applications, including supply chain management, telemedicine, and medical education. The paper lays the groundwork for future studies that will explore the healthcare industry's potential in using the Metaverse (Musamih et al., 2023b).The Metaverse, which makes use of extended reality technology to facilitate distinctive real-time interactions, is a representation of the Internet's future development. This essay investigates its possible effects on a number of industries, including human resource management, marketing, manufacturing, tourism, education, retail, banking, and healthcare. Every industry is examined, with a focus on prospects, difficulties, and suggested study topics. The thorough analysis of the Metaverse's ramifications highlights its transformational potential across several fields (Koohang et al., 2023c). The possibility for immersive experiences in the metaverse is what drives its use, especially in the medical industry. This project uses big data, the Internet of Things, and 5G networks to investigate the use of the Metaverse in acute care. It explores a number of areas, such as education, prehospital and emergency medicine, applications for diagnosis and treatment, and administrative matters, and it shows how widely augmented reality (AR) and virtual reality (VR) may be used in the healthcare industry. These results demonstrate how the Metaverse in healthcare is changing and offers insightful information for the future of emergency medicine (Wu & Ho, 2023b).The changing face of chronic illnesses demands that healthcare providers adopt novel strategies. The Metaverse theory presents viable approaches to problems like expert load and resource distribution. These problems can be resolved with the use of advanced artificial intelligence (AI) integration in Metaverse healthcare platforms. The promise of Metaverse technology in contemporary digital medicine is examined in this article, which also highlights some of the major obstacles facing the industry (Farahat et al., 2023). The investigation of metaverse services as a business model in the healthcare sector is the main topic of this research. It examines qualitative data from several sources using an exploratory methodology to evaluate the state of the industry and new developments in healthcare metaverse services (Kirubasri, 2023). In order to provide useful insights for strategic decision-making and policy formation in the pursuit of commercial prospects in healthcare and related areas, the paper examines a variety of situations, synthesizes findings, and suggests ways for using metaverse services in the healthcare industry (Lee, 2022c). The Metaverse—which is powered by holograms and avatars—has the potential to completely transform how people interact with the real and virtual worlds. Even while "big tech" touts its revolutionary potential, it can be difficult to distinguish hype from reality. Scholars are gathering more and more evidence about how technology affects industries like as marketing, education, healthcare, and society at large. This includes social interaction, privacy, prejudice, disinformation, and psychological impacts (Prasad, 2023). This thorough analysis provides insights into the metaverse's revolutionary potential and recommends (Dwivedi et al., 2022).

METAVERSE IN HEALTHCARE

The concept of the metaverse holds enormous potential for the healthcare industry, offering a range of innovative opportunities and challenges (Sardar, 2023). The metaverse in healthcare encompasses the use of virtual and augmented reality technologies, artificial intelligence, and immersive digital environments to transform various aspects of the healthcare ecosystem. key areas where the metaverse is making an impact in healthcare are shown in figure1

Figure 1. Key area of metaverse in healthcare

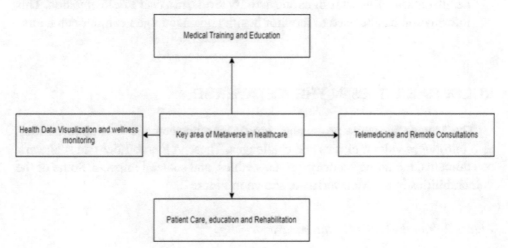

A. Medical Training and Education: Virtual reality (VR) and augmented reality (AR) are being used to train healthcare professionals, such as surgeons, in a safe and realistic environment. These technologies allow for hands-on practice and the simulation of complex medical procedures, enhancing the training and skills development of medical personnel (Shah,2023).

B. Patient Care, education and Rehabilitation: The metaverse provides unique tools for patient care, particularly in rehabilitation and therapy. VR and AR can be used to create immersive, engaging environments for physical therapy and mental health interventions. These technologies can help patients recover from injuries or manage chronic conditions in a more enjoyable and effective manner. Patient Education: Patients can use the metaverse to better understand their medical conditions and treatment options. Interactive 3D models and simulations can be created to educate patients about their health, improving health literacy and decision-making.

C. Telemedicine and Remote Consultations: Virtual medical consultations have become more prevalent, and the metaverse can offer a more immersive and interactive experience. Patients can meet with healthcare providers in 3D virtual environments, improving the quality of remote healthcare services.

D. Health Data Visualization and wellness monitoring: Virtual reality can be employed to visualize complex medical data, such as 3D scans, medical imaging, and patient records. This facilitates better understanding and collaboration among healthcare professionals, ultimately leading to more accurate diagnoses and treatment plans (Singh,2023). Wearable AR devices can provide real-time health data, such as vital signs and activity levels, in a user's field of vision. This information can be used to monitor health and encourage healthier behaviors.

VULNERABILITIES IN THE METAVERSE

The Metaverse, while promising significant advancements and opportunities, also introduces vulnerabilities and challenges. These vulnerabilities can span various domains, including security, privacy, ethics, and societal impacts. Some of the vulnerabilities in the Metaverse are shown in Figure 2.

Figure 2. Vulnerabilities in the metaverse

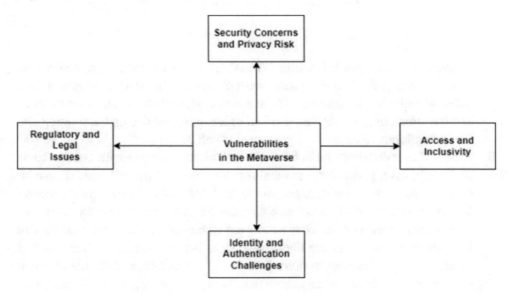

A. **Security Concerns and Privacy Risk:** The vast amount of personal and sensitive data within the Metaverse creates a prime target for hackers and cybercriminals. Data breaches can lead to identity theft, financial fraud, and privacy violations (Raju,2023). Metaverse platforms and ecosystems may be vulnerable to cyberattacks, which can disrupt services, compromise user information, and even lead to real-world consequences if critical infrastructure is interconnected with the Metaverse. Users in the Metaverse generate and share extensive data, including personal information, preferences, and behaviors. Protecting this data from misuse or unauthorized access is a major concern. Constant monitoring and data collection in the Metaverse can lead to unwarranted surveillance, eroding personal privacy. As in other online spaces, the Metaverse is susceptible to harassment, bullying, and abusive behavior. Ensuring appropriate content and behavior is a complex task, particularly in user-generated virtual worlds.

B. **Identity and Authentication Challenges**: The Metaverse may struggle to maintain secure user identities, potentially enabling identity theft and impersonation. Developing robust authentication methods that prevent unauthorized access while maintaining user convenience is an ongoing challenge. The Metaverse may contribute to digital addiction and overconsumption, impacting mental and physical well-being (Santhosh Kumar,2023). Ethical questions arise regarding how AI and algorithms within the Metaverse make decisions, including content recommendations and virtual behavior enforcement.

C. **Access and Inclusivity:** Access to the Metaverse and its benefits may be unequal, leading to a digital divide where not everyone can participate. Ensuring the Metaverse is accessible to individuals with disabilities is a critical consideration.

D. **Regulatory and Legal Issues:** The Metaverse operates in a complex regulatory landscape. The absence of clear laws and regulations can lead to ambiguity and legal challenges. Issues related to copyright, trademarks, and intellectual property protection may arise when users create and exchange content in the Metaverse. Automation and virtual labor can displace traditional jobs, potentially leading to economic and social inequalities (Kukreti, 2023). The Metaverse's impact on face-to-face human interactions and social dynamics is a subject of concern.

ISSUES AND CHALLENGES OF METAVERSE

The integration of the Metaverse into the healthcare domain brings forth a myriad of issues and challenges that involve privacy and data security, with the Metaverse collecting and processing vast amounts of sensitive health data, ensuring privacy and data security is paramount. Unauthorized access, data breaches, and the potential for misuse of personal health information are significant concerns. The Metaverse blurs the line between physical and virtual reality, raising ethical questions about how healthcare interactions, diagnoses, and treatments should be conducted (Nagesh, 2017). Ensuring ethical conduct within the virtual healthcare space is essential. Not everyone has equal access to the technology required for the Metaverse. Healthcare disparities can deepen if certain individuals or communities lack access to virtual health services, exacerbating existing inequalities. Existing healthcare regulations may not adequately address the complexities of virtual healthcare in the Metaverse. Healthcare providers and technologists must navigate a complex landscape of legal and regulatory requirements. Achieving interoperability among various virtual healthcare platforms and technologies can be challenging. Ensuring seamless data exchange and communication between different systems is crucial for providing comprehensive care. While the Metaverse offers novel ways to deliver healthcare, ensuring that virtual treatments and interventions are as effective as in-person care is a pressing issue. Validating the efficacy of these new healthcare paradigms is essential. In virtual healthcare, ensuring patient safety is a critical concern. Technology glitches, connectivity issues, or errors in virtual diagnoses and treatments could have real-world consequences. The Metaverse's potential for addiction, isolation, and the blurring of the boundary between the virtual and physical worlds can have implications for mental health and well-being. Managing user-generated content in virtual healthcare spaces is important to prevent misinformation, harmful advice, or abusive behavior. Healthcare professionals need to adapt to the use of virtual healthcare tools and technologies, which may require additional training and skills development. Developing and implementing Metaverse healthcare solutions can be costly (Jain,2022). It's essential to consider how these costs will impact access and affordability for patients. There is a risk that the Metaverse could exacerbate existing health disparities. Ensuring that underserved populations benefit from virtual healthcare is a challenge that needs to be addressed. Determining liability for medical errors or adverse events in virtual healthcare settings can be complex and may require legal clarity. Navigating these issues and challenges in the healthcare Metaverse will require collaboration between healthcare professionals, technologists, policymakers, and ethicists (Gujjar, 2023). Addressing these concerns is crucial to harness the transformative potential of the Metaverse while safeguarding the well-being and rights of patients.

FORWARD-LOOKING PERSPECTIVE

A forward-looking perspective from the Metaverse in healthcare envisions the future of the healthcare industry as it continues to integrate immersive digital technologies, virtual reality, and augmented reality (Srivastava,2023). Telemedicine in the Metaverse is not just about video calls. It's a fully immersive experience where patients and healthcare providers can interact in shared virtual spaces, using lifelike avatars. Patients can receive diagnoses, therapy, and guidance with unprecedented convenience, leading to better access to healthcare services, particularly in remote areas (Shivaraj,2022). The Metaverse, with its vast data capabilities and AI-driven analytics, enables highly personalized healthcare. Treatment plans, medication, and interventions are tailored to an individual's unique genetic makeup, health history, and real-time health data. This level of personalization leads to more effective treatments and preventive care. The healthcare workforce benefits from sophisticated medical training and simulation within the Metaverse. Medical professionals can practice and refine their skills in a safe, immersive environment, leading to better patient outcomes and fewer medical errors. Wearable AR devices and smart clothing continually monitor a person's health. The Metaverse serves as a hub for processing this data, alerting both patients and healthcare providers to any potential health issues in real time. This proactivity can prevent medical emergencies and improve overall health. The Metaverse provides innovative solutions for mental health and wellness. Virtual therapy, support groups, and mindfulness programs help people manage their mental well-being. These services become a crucial part of healthcare, addressing the growing mental health challenges in society. The Metaverse fosters a holistic ecosystem of health and wellness. Users can engage in gamified health activities, fitness routines, and preventive health measures while having fun in immersive virtual environments. A forward-looking perspective ensures that robust ethical frameworks and privacy protections are in place. Regulations and standards address the ethical use of AI, data security, and patient consent, ensuring that healthcare in the Metaverse maintains the highest ethical standards.

REFERENCES

Agarwal, J., Christa, S., Pai, A., Kumar, M. A., & Prasad, G. (2023, January). Machine Learning Application for News Text Classification. In *2023 13th International Conference on Cloud Computing, Data Science & Engineering (Confluence)* (pp. 463-466). IEEE. 10.1109/Confluence56041.2023.10048856

Athar, A., Ali, S. M., Mozumder, M. I., Ali, S., & Kim, H. C. (2023b). *Applications and Possible Challenges of Healthcare Metaverse*. IEEE Xplore. 10.23919/ICACT56868.2023.10079314

Avinash, S., Naveen Kumar, H. N., Guru Prasad, M. S., Mohan Naik, R., & Parveen, G. (2023). Early Detection of Malignant Tumor in Lungs Using Feed-Forward Neural Network and K-Nearest Neighbor Classifier. *SN Computer Science*, 4(2), 195. 10.1007/s42979-022-01606-y

Bansal, G., Rajgopal, K., Chamola, V., Xiong, Z., & Niyato, D. (2022). Healthcare in metaverse: A survey on current metaverse applications in healthcare. *IEEE Access : Practical Innovations, Open Solutions*, 10, 119914–119946. 10.1109/ACCESS.2022.3219845

Bhattacharya, P., Obaidat, M. S., Savaliya, D., Sanghavi, S., Tanwar, S., & Sadaun, B. (2022). Metaverse assisted Telesurgery in Healthcare 5.0: An interplay of Blockchain and Explainable AI. *IEEE Xplore -2022 International Conference on Computer, Information and Telecommunication Systems (CITS)*. IEEE. 10.1109/CITS55221.2022.9832978

Chandrappa, S., Guruprasad, M. S., Kumar, H. N., Raju, K., & Kumar, D. S. (2023). An IOT-Based Automotive and Intelligent Toll Gate Using RFID. *SN Computer Science*, 4(2), 154. 10.1007/s42979-022-01569-0

Chengoden, R., Victor, N., Huynh-The, T., Yenduri, G., Jhaveri, R. H., Alazab, M., Bhattacharya, S., Hegde, P., Maddikunta, P. K. R., & Gadekallu, T. R. (2023b). Metaverse for Healthcare: A survey on potential applications, challenges and future directions. *IEEE Access : Practical Innovations, Open Solutions*, 11, 12765–12795. 10.1109/ACCESS.2023.3241628

Dincelli, E., & Yayla, A. (2022b). Immersive virtual reality in the age of the Metaverse: A hybrid-narrative review based on the technology affordance perspective. *The Journal of Strategic Information Systems*, 31(2), 101717. 10.1016/j.jsis.2022.101717

Dwivedi, Y. K., Hughes, L., Baabdullah, A. M., Ribeiro-Navarrete, S., Giannakis, M., Al-Debei, M. M., Dennehy, D., Metri, B. A., Buhalis, D., Cheung, C. M. K., Conboy, K., Doyle, R., Dubey, R., Dutot, V., Felix, R., Goyal, D., Gustafsson, A., Hinsch, C., Jebabli, I., & Wamba, S. F. (2022). Metaverse beyond the hype: Multidisciplinary perspectives on emerging challenges, opportunities, and agenda for research, practice and policy. *International Journal of Information Management*, 66, 102542. 10.1016/j.ijinfomgt.2022.102542

Farahat, M. A., Darwish, A., & Hassanien, A. E. (2023). The implication of metaverse in the traditional medical environment and healthcare sector: Applications and challenges. In *Studies in big data* (pp. 105–133). Springer. 10.1007/978-3-031-29132-6_7

Gujjar, J. P., Kumar, H. P., & Prasad, M. G. (2023, March). Advanced NLP Framework for Text Processing. In *2023 6th International Conference on Information Systems and Computer Networks (ISCON)* (pp. 1-3). IEEE.

Guru, P. M., Praveen, G. J., Dodmane, R., Sardar, T. H., Ashwitha, A., & Yeole, A. N. (2023, March). Brain Tumor Identification and Classification using a Novel Extraction Method based on Adapted Alexnet Architecture. In *2023 6th International Conference on Information Systems and Computer Networks (ISCON)* (pp. 1-5). IEEE. 10.1109/ISCON57294.2023.10112075

Guru Prasad, M. S., Naveen Kumar, H. N., Raju, K., Santhosh Kumar, D. K., & Chandrappa, S. (2023). Glaucoma detection using clustering and segmentation of the optic disc region from retinal fundus images. *SN Computer Science*, 4(2), 192. 10.1007/s42979-022-01592-1

Kirubasri, G., Sankar, S., Guru Prasad, M. S., Naga Chandrika, G., & Ramasubbareddy, S. (2023). LQETA-RP: Link quality based energy and trust aware routing protocol for wireless multimedia sensor networks. *International Journal of System Assurance Engineering and Management*, ●●●, 1–13.

Koohang, A., Nord, J. H., Ooi, K., Tan, G. W., Al-Emran, M., Aw, E. C., Baabdullah, A. M., Buhalis, D., Cham, T., Dennis, C., Dutot, V., Dwivedi, Y. K., Hughes, L., Mogaji, E., Pandey, N., Phau, I., Raman, R., Sharma, A., Σιγάλα, M., & Wong, L. (2023c). Shaping the Metaverse into Reality: A Holistic Multidisciplinary Understanding of Opportunities, Challenges, and Avenues for Future Investigation. *Journal of Computer Information Systems*, 63(3), 735–765. 10.1080/08874417.2023.2165197

Kukreti, A., Prasad, G., Ram, M., & Naik, P. K. (2023, October). Detection and Classification of Brain Tumour Using EfficientNet and Transfer Learning Techniques. In *2023 International Conference on Computer Science and Emerging Technologies (CSET)* (pp. 1-5). IEEE. 10.1109/CSET58993.2023.10346858

Kumar, H. N. N., Kumar, A. S., Prasad, M. S. G., & Shah, M. A. (2023). Automatic facial expression recognition combining texture and shape features from prominent facial regions. *IET Image Processing*, 17(4), 1111–1125. 10.1049/ipr2.12700

Kumar, M. A., Abirami, N., Prasad, M. G., & Mohankumar, M. (2022, May). Stroke Disease Prediction based on ECG Signals using Deep Learning Techniques. In *2022 International Conference on Computational Intelligence and Sustainable Engineering Solutions (CISES)* (pp. 453-458). IEEE.

Kumar, M. A., Pai, A. H., Agarwal, J., Christa, S., Prasad, G. M., & Saifi, S. (2023, January). Deep Learning Model to Defend against Covert Channel Attacks in the SDN Networks. In *2023 Advanced Computing and Communication Technologies for High Performance Applications (ACCTHPA)* (pp. 1-5). IEEE. 10.1109/ACCTH-PA57160.2023.10083336

Lee, C. W. (2022b). Application of Metaverse Service to Healthcare Industry: A Strategic perspective. *International Journal of Environmental Research and Public Health*, 19(20), 13038. 10.3390/ijerph19201303836293609

Mejia, J. M. R., & Rawat, D. B. (2022b). Recent advances in a medical domain metaverse: status, challenges, and perspective. *2022 Thirteenth International Conference on Ubiquitous and Future Networks (ICUFN)*. IEEE. 10.1109/ICUFN55119.2022.9829645

Musamih, A., Yaqoob, I., Salah, K., Jayaraman, R., Al-Hammadi, Y., Omar, M., & Ellahham, S. (2023b). Metaverse in healthcare: Applications, challenges, and future directions. *IEEE Consumer Electronics Magazine*, 12(4), 33–46. 10.1109/MCE.2022.3223522

Nagesh, H. R., & Prabhu, S. (2017). High performance computation of big data: Performance optimization approach towards a parallel frequent item set mining algorithm for transaction data based on hadoop MapReduce framework. *International Journal of Intelligent Systems and Applications*, 9(1), 75–84. 10.5815/ijisa.2017.01.08

Nagesh, H. R., Prasad, G., Shivaraj, B. G., Jain, D., Puneeth, B. R., & Anadkumar, M. (2022, December). E-Voting System Using Blockchain Technology. In *2022 4th International Conference on Advances in Computing, Communication Control and Networking (ICAC3N)* (pp. 2106-2111). IEEE.

Pai, A., Anandkumar, M., Prasad, G., Agarwal, J., & Christa, S. (2023, January). Designing a Secure Audio/Text Based Captcha Using Neural Network. In *2023 13th International Conference on Cloud Computing, Data Science & Engineering (Confluence)* (pp. 510-514). IEEE.

Pandey, A., Chirputkar, A., & Ashok, P. (2023b). Metaverse: An Innovative Model for Healthcare Domain. *IEEE-2023 International Conference on Innovative Data Communication Technologies and Application (ICIDCA)*. IEEE. 10.1109/ICID-CA56705.2023.10099764

Prabhu, S., Rodrigues, A. P., Prasad, G., & Nagesh, H. R. (2015, March). Performance enhancement of Hadoop MapReduce framework for analyzing BigData. In *2015 IEEE International Conference on Electrical, Computer and Communication Technologies (ICECCT)* (pp. 1-8). IEEE. 10.1109/ICECCT.2015.7226049

Prasad, G., Jain, A. K., Jain, P., & Nagesh, H. R.Nagesh H. R. (2019). A Novel Approach to Optimize the Performance of Hadoop Frameworks for Sentiment Analysis. [IJOSSP]. *International Journal of Open Source Software and Processes*, 10(4), 44–59. 10.4018/IJOSSP.2019100103

Prasad, G., Kumar, A. S., Srivastava, S., Srivastava, A., & Srivastava, A. (2023). An iomt and machine learning model aimed at the development of a personalized lifestyle recommendation system facilitating improved health. In *Dynamics of Swarm Intelligence Health Analysis for the Next Generation* (pp. 162–185). IGI Global. 10.4018/978-1-6684-6894-4.ch009

Prasad, M. G., Agarwal, J., Christa, S., Pai, H. A., Kumar, M. A., & Kukreti, A. (2023, January). An Improved Water Body Segmentation from Satellite Images using MSAA-Net. In *2023 International Conference on Machine Intelligence for GeoAnalytics and Remote Sensing (MIGARS)* (Vol. 1, pp. 1-4). IEEE. 10.1109/MIGARS57353.2023.10064508

Prasad, M. G., Pratap, M. S., Jain, P., Gujjar, J. P., Kumar, M. A., & Kukreti, A. (2022, December). RDI-SD: An Efficient Rice Disease Identification based on Apache Spark and Deep Learning Technique. In *2022 International Conference on Artificial Intelligence and Data Engineering (AIDE)* (pp. 277-282). IEEE. 10.1109/AIDE57180.2022.10060157

Singh, P., Tripathi, V., Singh, K. D., Guru Prasad, M. S., & Aditya Pai, H. (2023, April). A Task Scheduling Algorithm for Optimizing Quality of Service in Smart Healthcare System. In *International Conference on IoT, Intelligent Computing and Security: Select Proceedings of IICS 2021* (pp. 43-50). Singapore: Springer Nature Singapore. 10.1007/978-981-19-8136-4_4

Song, Y., & Qin, J. (2022b). Metaverse and personal healthcare. *Procedia Computer Science*, 210, 189–197. 10.1016/j.procs.2022.10.136

Tan, T. F., Li, Y., Lim, J., Gunasekeran, D. V., Teo, Z. L., Ng, W. Y., & Ting, D. S. (2022). Metaverse and Virtual Health Care in Ophthalmology: Opportunities and Challenges. *Asia-Pacific Journal of Ophthalmology, 11*(3), 237–246. .10.1097/APO.0000000000000537

Turab, M., & Jamil, S. (2023). A comprehensive survey of digital twins in healthcare in the era of Metaverse. *BioMedInformatics*, 3(3), 563–584. 10.3390/biomedinformatics3030039

Ullah, H., Manickam, S., Obaidat, M., Laghari, S. A., & Uddin, M. (2023). Exploring the potential of metaverse technology in healthcare: Applications, challenges, and future directions. *IEEE Access : Practical Innovations, Open Solutions*, 11, 69686–69707. 10.1109/ACCESS.2023.3286696

Wu, T., & Ho, C. B. (2023b). A scoping review of metaverse in emergency medicine. *Australasian Emergency Care (Online)*, 26(1), 75–83. 10.1016/j.auec.2022.08.00235953392

Chapter 4
Emerging Implications of Metaverse in the Healthcare Domain

Praveen Gujjar J.
https://orcid.org/0000-0003-0240-7827
Jain University (Deemed), India

Guru Prasad M. S.
https://orcid.org/0000-0002-1811-9507
Graphic Era University (Deemed), India

Harold Andrew Patrick
https://orcid.org/0009-0004-5349-6799
Jain University (Deemed), India

M. H. Sharieff
Jain University (Deemed), India

Naveen Kumar H. N.
Vidyavardhaka College of Engineering, India

ABSTRACT

The Metaverse, often referred to as the immersive internet, is widely considered the next significant technological disruption on the horizon, with the potential to reshape clinician-patient interactions, enhance the patient experience, transform innovation and research and development processes. The Metaverse is currently in its developmental phase, and the establishment of a definitive framework is an ongoing endeavor. In recent years, the concept of the Metaverse has gained substantial traction and has evolved into a multifaceted virtual universe with limitless possibilities. This chapter

DOI: 10.4018/979-8-3693-2268-0.ch004

Copyright © 2024, IGI Global. Copying or distributing in print or electronic forms without written permission of IGI Global is prohibited.

provides a glimpse into the evolving landscape of healthcare, where the Metaverse's immersive and interconnected experiences have the power to revolutionize how we perceive, access, and deliver healthcare services. From virtual clinics and medical simulations to AI-assisted diagnostics, this chapter explores the multifaceted ways in which the Metaverse is reshaping healthcare and creating new opportunities for improved patient outcomes, education, and research.

INTRODUCTION

The intersection of healthcare and cutting-edge technology has entered an era of unprecedented transformation, with the advent of the Metaverse. The Metaverse, often described as the immersive internet, has rapidly ascended as a concept poised to disrupt, enhance, and revolutionize various sectors of society (Kumar, 2022). In the context of healthcare, the implications of the Metaverse are both ground-breaking and multifaceted, offering innovative solutions for patient care, medical education, telemedicine, and therapeutic interventions. This chapter explores the dynamic landscape where the Metaverse and healthcare converge. As we navigate the uncharted territories of the Metaverse, we embark on a journey that promises to redefine how we perceive, access, and deliver healthcare services. Through immersive and interconnected experiences, the Metaverse has the potential to reshape the healthcare domain, influencing patient outcomes, medical education, and research and development processes (Guru, 2023). It is important to note that the Metaverse is still in its evolutionary phase, and a clear and comprehensive definition framework is a work in progress. In this introductory chapter, we set the stage for an in-depth exploration of the emerging implications of the Metaverse in healthcare. We will delve into the transformative potential it holds for clinicians, patients, educators, researchers, and innovators (Kirubasri, 2023). From virtual clinics to AI-assisted diagnostics, from surgical simulations to cross-collaborations transcending the constraints of time and space, the Metaverse opens a world of possibilities that promise to reshape the healthcare landscape as we know it (Kumar HN, 2023).

LITERATURE REVIEW

The metaverse, a hybrid of augmented and virtual reality, is becoming increasingly popular, especially in the medical field, especially after the pandemic increased the use of telemedicine. Known as the "Cardio Verse," it has the potential to significantly improve medical visits and cardiovascular therapies while also transforming disease education, prevention, and diagnosis. The metaverse has many advantages, but issues with infrastructure, security, and regulations must be resolved before it can be successfully incorporated into healthcare. It can significantly alter how education and medical care are provided (Skalidis et al., 2023).There still needs to be more information about the metaverse in the medical, nursing, public health, childcare, and dental domains. Technologies like social networks, blockchain, augmented reality, virtual reality, artificial intelligence, and avatars are all in the metaverse technology category. Although augmented reality applications have demonstrated potential in critical health scenarios, the influence of metaverse technology on scientific studies and healthcare procedures is still an exciting field of study. A number of noteworthy accomplishments, including the award of the Nobel Peace Prize in physiology and healthcare, and recent developments in metaverse technology point to the possibility of important new developments and applications in this field in the future (Damar, 2022). The use of the metaverse into medicine has the potential to improve mental health services and treat cognitive decline. Numerous uses are possible with it, such as hospital administration, diagnosis, forecasting, preventive, rehabilitation, and companionship. In the fields of immersive consulting, dental care, medical education, and the management of diseases like Parkinson's illness, metaverse technology has already shown promise. The COVID-19 epidemic has led to a rise in the demand for non-face-to-face treatment, and as a result, the metaverse is playing an increasingly important role in healthcare—especially for the elderly—by providing novel perspectives and cutting-edge techniques (Zhou et al., 2022). The metaverse, which uses extended reality technology to provide real-time interactions that occur outside of physical boundaries, is regarded as the next evolution of the Internet. Businesses are realizing how much more profitable the metaverse can be. Insights about possibilities, problems, and future study objectives are provided as this article examines the possible effects of the metaverse in a number of industries, like advertising, the tourism industry, production, management of operations, higher education, retail, banking, healthcare, and management of human resources. The metaverse's entry into these domains is indicative of its revolutionary potential to reshape industries and generate new avenues for engagement and trade (Koohang et al., 2023). As a game-changing technology, the metaverse has attracted a lot of interest from academics and business. In order to improve living circumstances and service quality, the healthcare industry is adopting the metaverse. This study highlights the promise of online anti-aging healthcare in the metaverse, emphasizing how it might enhance patient outcomes, cut expenses, and provide novel healthcare experiences. Through the integration of machine learning, blockchain technology, the Internet of Things, virtual reality, and virtual twins, healthcare providers may deliver customized therapies, safe data ecological systems, and real-time tracking of patients (Kirubasri, 2023). This, in turn, can help accelerate the aging process. These recommendations point towards a route promising for raising healthcare standards and encouraging longer, healthier lives (Mozumder et al., 2023). The swift advancement of digitalization and automation has caused revolutionary expansion in the healthcare industry by presenting novel approaches for economical treatment provision. Healthcare has a bright future thanks to the burgeoning Metaverse, which is being powered by the convergence of technologies like AI, VR, AR, IoT, robots, and quantum computing. This study of the literature offers a thorough investigation of the uses of the Metaverse in healthcare, emphasizing the state of the field today and the technology that makes it possible. It also discusses possible obstacles and suggests future areas of inquiry to optimize the Metaverse's influence on healthcare (Chengoden et al., 2023). The Metaverse is transforming communication and interpersonal relationships by fusing virtual and augmented reality. Its appearance, especially after Mark Zuckerberg's declaration, has attracted a lot of interest in the medical community. In 2022 and 2023, the Metaverse has the potential to revolutionize the healthcare industry and provide profitable opportunities. It can help with a number of healthcare issues, including social connectedness, mental health, regional health access, and virtual health. This assessment of the literature highlights the possible obstacles to the future deployment of the Metaverse while also summarizing its uses and possibilities in the field of healthcare (Athar et al., 2023). Healthcare is investigating how to use the Metaverse to improve patient experiences and accessibility since it has enormous promise for simulating reality. However, there is a dearth of research on practical applications in healthcare. This study focuses on outpatient telemedicine and privacy issues while addressing the state, prospects, and difficulties of the field today (Mejia & Rawat, 2022). The Internet of Things, wearable sensors, 3D modeling, and artificial intelligence have all contributed to the rise in interest in The Metaverse, a virtual environment where users adopt avatars. Given its vital relevance, the field of healthcare appears to be a potential one for Metaverse applications. The pandemic's restrictions on access to healthcare have highlighted the need for creative responses. With an emphasis on digital twins in particular, this article provides an overview of Metaverse-based healthcare by highlighting technologies such as augmented reality (AR), virtual reality (VR), and AR. The suggested methodology promotes the use of digital twins for health assessment and maintenance, emphasizing data completeness, update frequency, and accuracy. Personalized risk factors are used to monitor possible illnesses (Song & Qin, 2022). The COVID-19 epidemic revealed serious flaws in India's healthcare system, including a lack of doctors and necessary supplies. This has led to a group effort to find answers to these problems, making it a crucial matter for experts, public officials, and responsible citizens (Kukreti, 2023). In this regard, the metaverse's transformational potential—which is already well recognized in the gaming and social interaction domains—is being investigated as a potent remedy for healthcare. This essay, which focuses on the healthcare industry, describes the ways in which the Metaverse might improve treatment facilities, learning materials, and other aspects of the industry (Pandey et al., 2023). The 21st century has seen a focus on technology improvement in immersive virtual reality (VR), which has attracted interest from a wide range of fields. However, there have been little research on immersive VR in major IS publications, indicating that the area of information systems (IS) has fallen behind. Advances in immersive virtual reality technology provide novel prospects for both IS researchers and organizations. The present review emphasizes the benefits of immersive virtual reality (VR), including embodiment and interaction, and examines how these affordances have been used in different fields of study. It also emphasizes how IS academics may contribute to the area by doing metaverse research (Dincelli & Yayla, 2022). A dynamic digital universe fashioned by state-of-the-art technology, the Metaverse holds the potential to revolutionize many aspects of everyday life. This article explores the use of the Metaverse in healthcare, providing insightful information about the idea and supporting technology (Singh, 2023). It addresses the obstacles preventing its widespread acceptance in the healthcare industry while examining the vast range of applications, including supply chain management, telemedicine, and medical education. The paper lays the groundwork for future studies that will explore the healthcare industry's potential in using the Metaverse (Musamih et al., 2023). The Metaverse, which makes use of extended reality technology to facilitate distinctive real-time interactions, is a representation of the Internet's future development. This essay investigates its possible effects on a number of industries, including human resource management, marketing, manufacturing, tourism, education, retail, banking, and healthcare. Every industry is examined, with a focus on prospects, difficulties, and suggested study topics. The thorough analysis of the Metaverse's ramifications highlights its transformational potential across several fields (Koohang et al., 2023b). The possibility for immersive experiences in the metaverse is what drives its use, especially in the medical industry (Kumar, 2023). This project uses big data, the Internet of Things, and 5G networks to investigate the use of the Metaverse in acute care. It explores a number of areas, such as education, prehospital and emergency medicine, applications for diagnosis and treatment, and administrative matters, and it shows how widely augmented reality (AR) and virtual reality (VR) may be used in the healthcare industry (Pai, 2023). These results demonstrate how the Metaverse in healthcare is changing and offers insightful information for the future of emergency medicine (Wu & Ho, 2023).

EVOLVING LANDSCAPE OF HEALTHCARE FROM METAVERSE

The metaverse could provide a platform for virtual health consultations and telemedicine. Patients and healthcare providers could interact within immersive virtual environments, enabling more personalized and engaging healthcare experiences. This could be especially beneficial for mental health services and remote monitoring (Avinash, 2023). Healthcare professionals could use the metaverse for medical training and simulations. Surgeons, for example, could practice complex procedures in virtual environments before performing them in real-life, improving their skills and reducing errors. The metaverse can enhance patient education by providing interactive and immersive experiences. Patients could explore 3D models of their own anatomy to better understand their conditions and treatment options (Chandrappa, 2023). Gamified applications could also encourage better adherence to treatment plans and rehabilitation exercises. Researchers from around the world could collaborate in virtual environments to accelerate the pace of medical research. Data sharing and visualization tools within the metaverse could lead to breakthroughs in understanding diseases and developing new treatments. Blockchain technology within the metaverse could be used for secure and decentralized health data management, giving patients more control over their medical records while ensuring privacy and security. Virtual reality (VR) and augmented reality (AR) applications in the metaverse could be used to provide therapeutic interventions for mental health issues such as anxiety and PTSD. Virtual environments could be designed to help individuals relax, manage stress, or confront and overcome their fears. The metaverse could integrate with the Internet of Things (IoT) to provide real-time data on patients' health. Wearable devices and sensors could transmit information to virtual healthcare providers, allowing for proactive healthcare management. Patients with chronic illnesses or specific health challenges could find support and community in the metaverse. They could connect with others facing similar issues, share experiences, and access resources within virtual support groups. The metaverse could offer a platform for pharmaceutical companies to conduct virtual clinical trials, test new drugs, and model the effects of medications on virtual populations. As healthcare and the metaverse converge, there will be ethical and regulatory challenges to address. Ensuring the privacy and security of medical data, maintaining the quality of healthcare services, and navigating liability issues are some of the issues that will need careful consideration.

DEVELOPMENT OF METAVERSE FOR INTELLIGENT HEALTHCARE

The metaverse merges the realms of the physical and virtual, allowing human users and their avatars to engage within a tech-enhanced environment that harnesses high-speed internet, virtual reality, augmented reality, mixed and extended reality, blockchain, digital twins, and artificial intelligence (AI). This convergence, empowered by virtually limitless data, initially appeared in social media and entertainment contexts (Prasad, 2022). Its extension into healthcare has the potential to significantly transform clinical practices and enhance human well-being The development of a metaverse for intelligent healthcare involves creating a virtual and immersive environment that leverages advanced technologies and artificial intelligence (AI) to enhance various aspects of healthcare. The key components and considerations for developing a metaverse for intelligent healthcare are shown in Figure 1.

Figure 1. Metaverse for intelligent healthcare

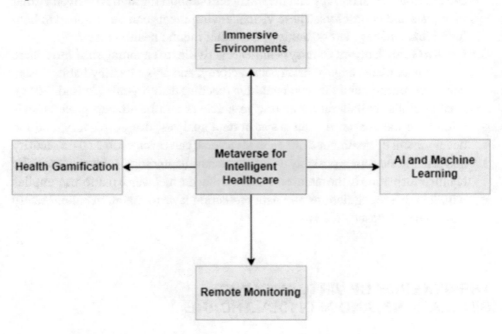

A. **Immersive Environments**: Create immersive virtual environments using technologies like virtual reality (VR), augmented reality (AR), and mixed reality (Nagesh,2017). These environments should be designed to replicate real healthcare settings and allow users, including patients and healthcare professionals, to interact with digital elements and each other (Prabhu,2015). Integrate health data from various sources, including electronic health records (EHRs), wearable devices, and IoT sensors. Use AI to process and analyze this data, providing real-time insights and recommendations for users.

B. **AI and Machine Learning:** Implement AI and machine learning algorithms to provide personalized healthcare solutions. AI can assist in diagnosing medical conditions, predicting health outcomes, and recommending treatment plans (Guru Prasad, 2023). Machine learning models can continuously adapt and improve based on user interactions and data feedback. Offer virtual healthcare consultations within the metaverse. Patients can interact with healthcare providers in real-time, discuss health concerns, receive diagnoses, and develop treatment plans, all within a virtual environment.

C. **Remote Monitoring:** Implementing IoT devices and sensors for real-time re-mote monitoring of patients' health. Use AI to analyze data from these devices, detect anomalies, and trigger alerts when necessary (Prasad, 2022). Metaverse can provide virtual therapy and mental health support through AI-driven virtual therapists and counselors. These virtual environments can be designed to help individuals manage stress, anxiety, and other mental health issues.

D. **Health Gamification:** Gamify healthcare activities to encourage users to adhere to treatment plans, engage in physical activity, and adopt healthy habits. Users can earn rewards and achievements for meeting health goals (Prasad, 2019). Enable global collaboration among researchers and healthcare professionals within the metaverse. AI can assist in data analysis, drug discovery, and the development of treatment strategies. Metaverse can Ensure robust data security and privacy measures, possibly using blockchain technology, to protect sensitive health information in the metaverse. Ensure that the metaverse platform complies with healthcare regulations and data protection laws to maintain patient safety and privacy (Prasad, 2023).

THE SYNERGY OF VIRTUAL CLINICS, SIMULATIONS, AND AI IN HEALTHCARE

The healthcare industry has undergone a profound transformation driven by the convergence of three powerful technologies: virtual clinics, medical simulations, and artificial intelligence (AI). This synergy has the potential to reshape the way healthcare is delivered, medical professionals are trained, and diagnoses are made (Prasad, 2023). It promises to enhance patient care, improve medical education, and revolutionize diagnostic capabilities, ultimately leading to better health outcomes (Agarwal, 2023). The revolution of healthcare access such as virtual clinics, simulations, and AI are shown in Figure 2.

Figure 2. Revolution in healthcare access

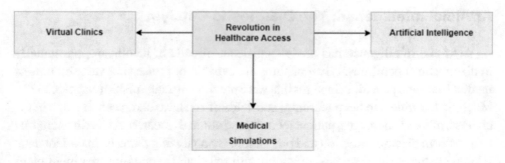

Virtual Clinics: A Revolution in Healthcare Access

Virtual clinics have redefined the accessibility of healthcare services. These digital healthcare platforms allow patients to consult with medical professionals remotely, breaking down geographical barriers and providing care in real-time. Telemedicine, a cornerstone of virtual clinics, connects patients with healthcare providers through high-speed internet and telecommunication technologies. This technology has not only improved patient access to care, especially in remote or underserved areas, but it has also ushered in a new era of patient-centric care. Patients benefit from personalized healthcare experiences that empower them to take control of their health. Virtual clinics are particularly advantageous for managing chronic conditions, providing access to specialists, and offering on-demand healthcare services. For healthcare providers, virtual clinics offer efficient and cost-effective solutions, enabling them to expand their reach, streamline healthcare operations, and deliver more accessible and affordable care.

Medical Simulations

Medical simulations have become a critical component of medical education and training. These simulations provide a safe and controlled environment for medical professionals to practice a wide range of clinical scenarios, from surgery and trauma care to patient interactions. The realism and immersion of these simulations have elevated medical training to new heights. In medical education, simulations are revolutionizing the way future healthcare professionals acquire clinical skills and decision-making abilities. Trainees can engage in hands-on experiences without putting patients at risk. Additionally, medical simulations have expanded to include scenarios that focus on communication skills and empathy, promoting stronger patient-provider relationships and better overall care.

Artificial Intelligence: The Diagnostic Catalyst

Artificial intelligence has made significant inroads in healthcare, particularly in diagnostic capabilities. AI algorithms are capable of processing vast amounts of medical data and providing insights that were previously unattainable (Nagesh,2022). Machine learning and deep learning, subfields of AI, have taken center stage in the analysis of medical images, patient records, and clinical research. AI has the potential to transform disease detection and prediction. By analyzing patterns in patient data, AI can enable early diagnosis, predict health risks, and even tailor treatment plans to individual patients. The real-world applications are impressive, from the early detection of cancer to the management of chronic diseases. However, the integration of AI in healthcare also comes with its own set of challenges, including addressing bias, ensuring fairness, and navigating ethical considerations.

The integration of virtual clinics, medical simulations, and AI creates a synergy that promises to revolutionize healthcare. These technologies complement each other in ways that amplify their individual impacts, resulting in a holistic and patient-centered healthcare experience. For example, in a virtual clinic, a healthcare provider can remotely diagnose a patient's condition while using AI to analyze patient data and medical images, providing a more accurate and timely assessment. In medical education, simulations can incorporate AI-driven patient interactions that adapt to the learner's actions, creating a dynamic and personalized training experience. This synergy is not limited to traditional healthcare settings. The expansion of healthcare accessibility is particularly relevant, as virtual clinics, simulations, and AI are increasingly used to provide care in underserved or remote regions, reducing healthcare disparities. Looking forward, the future of healthcare at the intersection of these technologies is promising. Emerging technologies, such as the development of the metaverse, offer the potential for a fully immersive healthcare experience. The metaverse can enhance telemedicine, provide more realistic simulations, and offer unprecedented opportunities for AI-driven diagnostics and treatments.

CONCLUSION

The metaverse emerges at the intersection of swift and profound technological and social advancements. Within this space, avatars serve as our digital counterparts, replicating various elements of our physical environment, including medical imaging apparatus, and hold the potential to span across multiple fields. Beyond its role in entertainment and social interaction, the metaverse finds applications in professional development, K-12 and higher education, supply chain management, as well as real estate promotion. The metaverse, a concept once relegated to science fiction, is now rapidly becoming a tangible and transformative presence in the healthcare domain. As we explore the emerging implications of the metaverse, it becomes abundantly clear that we stand at the threshold of a paradigm shift in healthcare delivery, training, and diagnostics. This chapter has unearthed the myriad ways in which the metaverse is poised to revolutionize healthcare, ushering in an era of unprecedented possibilities (Gujjar, 2023). Virtual clinics, empowered by the metaverse, offer the promise of democratized healthcare access. Patients can now receive consultations, diagnosis, and even treatment without the constraints of geographical proximity. The virtual clinic model empowers patients, reduces barriers to care, and eases the burden on overburdened healthcare systems. The metaverse is redefining medical education through immersive training and simulations. Healthcare professionals can now practice, refine, and master their skills in safe, risk-free virtual environments. This dynamic training can bridge the gap between theory and practice, enhancing clinical competence, empathy, and effective communication. The metaverse empowers patients to take an active role in their healthcare journey. Patients gain unprecedented access to health information, making informed decisions, and participating in shared decision-making. This shift towards patient-centered care is poised to improve healthcare outcomes and patient satisfaction. The metaverse catalyzes the integration of artificial intelligence into healthcare, facilitating earlier disease detection, predictive analytics, and more personalized care plans. AI-driven virtual assistants provide support to healthcare professionals, streamlining their work and improving patient outcomes. Healthcare's metaverse-driven global collaboration transcends geographical boundaries, enabling researchers and professionals to collaborate in real-time on medical research, drug development, and clinical practice. This transformation has the potential to accelerate the pace of scientific discovery and improve healthcare worldwide.

REFERENCES

Agarwal, J., Christa, S., Pai, A., Kumar, M. A., & Prasad, G. (2023, January). Machine Learning Application for News Text Classification. In *2023 13th International Conference on Cloud Computing, Data Science & Engineering (Confluence)* (pp. 463-466). IEEE. 10.1109/Confluence56041.2023.10048856

Athar, A., Ali, S. M., Mozumder, M. I., Ali, S., & Kim, H. C. (2023). *Applications and Possible Challenges of Healthcare Metaverse*. IEEE Xplore. 10.23919/ICACT56868.2023.10079314

Avinash, S., Naveen Kumar, H. N., Guru Prasad, M. S., Mohan Naik, R., & Parveen, G. (2023). Early Detection of Malignant Tumor in Lungs Using Feed-Forward Neural Network and K-Nearest Neighbor Classifier. *SN Computer Science*, 4(2), 195. 10.1007/s42979-022-01606-y

Chandrappa, S., Guruprasad, M. S., Kumar, H. N., Raju, K., & Kumar, D. S. (2023). An IOT-Based Automotive and Intelligent Toll Gate Using RFID. *SN Computer Science*, 4(2), 154. 10.1007/s42979-022-01569-0

Chengoden, R., Victor, N., Huynh-The, T., Yenduri, G., Jhaveri, R. H., Alazab, M., Bhattacharya, S., Hegde, P., Maddikunta, P. K. R., & Gadekallu, T. R. (2023). Metaverse for Healthcare: A survey on potential applications, challenges and future directions. *IEEE Access : Practical Innovations, Open Solutions*, 11, 12765–12795. 10.1109/ACCESS.2023.3241628

Damar, M. (2022). What the literature on medicine, nursing, public health, midwifery, and dentistry reveals: An overview of the rapidly approaching metaverse. *Journal of Metaverse*, 2(2), 62–70. 10.57019/jmv.1132962

Dincelli, E., & Yayla, A. (2022). Immersive virtual reality in the age of the Metaverse: A hybrid-narrative review based on the technology affordance perspective. *The Journal of Strategic Information Systems*, 31(2), 101717. 10.1016/j.jsis.2022.101717

Gujjar, J. P., Kumar, H. P., & Prasad, M. G. (2023, March). Advanced NLP Framework for Text Processing. In *2023 6th International Conference on Information Systems and Computer Networks (ISCON)* (pp. 1-3). IEEE.

Guru, P. M., Praveen, G. J., Dodmane, R., Sardar, T. H., Ashwitha, A., & Yeole, A. N. (2023, March). Brain Tumor Identification and Classification using a Novel Extraction Method based on Adapted Alexnet Architecture. In *2023 6th International Conference on Information Systems and Computer Networks (ISCON)* (pp. 1-5). IEEE. 10.1109/ISCON57294.2023.10112075

Guru Prasad, M. S., Naveen Kumar, H. N., Raju, K., Santhosh Kumar, D. K., & Chandrappa, S. (2023). Glaucoma detection using clustering and segmentation of the optic disc region from retinal fundus images. *SN Computer Science*, 4(2), 192. 10.1007/s42979-022-01592-1

Kirubasri, G., Sankar, S., Guru Prasad, M. S., Naga Chandrika, G., & Ramasubbareddy, S. (2023). LQETA-RP: Link quality based energy and trust aware routing protocol for wireless multimedia sensor networks. *International Journal of System Assurance Engineering and Management*, ●●●, 1–13.

Koohang, A., Nord, J. H., Ooi, K., Tan, G. W., Al-Emran, M., Aw, E. C., Baabdullah, A. M., Buhalis, D., Cham, T., Dennis, C., Dutot, V., Dwivedi, Y. K., Hughes, L., Mogaji, E., Pandey, N., Phau, I., Raman, R., Sharma, A., Σιγάλα, M., & Wong, L. (2023). Shaping the Metaverse into Reality: A Holistic Multidisciplinary Understanding of Opportunities, Challenges, and Avenues for Future Investigation. *Journal of Computer Information Systems*, 63(3), 735–765. 10.1080/08874417.2023.2165197

Koohang, A., Nord, J. H., Ooi, K., Tan, G. W., Al-Emran, M., Aw, E. C., Baabdullah, A. M., Buhalis, D., Cham, T., Dennis, C., Dutot, V., Dwivedi, Y. K., Hughes, L., Mogaji, E., Pandey, N., Phau, I., Raman, R., Sharma, A., Σιγάλα, M., & Wong, L. (2023b). Shaping the Metaverse into Reality: A Holistic Multidisciplinary Understanding of Opportunities, Challenges, and Avenues for Future Investigation. *Journal of Computer Information Systems*, 63(3), 735–765. 10.1080/08874417.2023.2165197

Kukreti, A., Prasad, G., Ram, M., & Naik, P. K. (2023, October). Detection and Classification of Brain Tumour Using EfficientNet and Transfer Learning Techniques. In *2023 International Conference on Computer Science and Emerging Technologies (CSET)* (pp. 1-5). IEEE. 10.1109/CSET58993.2023.10346858

Kumar, H. N. N., Kumar, A. S., Prasad, M. S. G., & Shah, M. A. (2023). Automatic facial expression recognition combining texture and shape features from prominent facial regions. *IET Image Processing*, 17(4), 1111–1125. 10.1049/ipr2.12700

Kumar, M. A., Abirami, N., Prasad, M. G., & Mohankumar, M. (2022, May). Stroke Disease Prediction based on ECG Signals using Deep Learning Techniques. *In 2022 International Conference on Computational Intelligence and Sustainable Engineering Solutions (CISES)* (pp. 453-458). IEEE.

Kumar, M. A., Pai, A. H., Agarwal, J., Christa, S., Prasad, G. M., & Saifi, S. (2023, January). Deep Learning Model to Defend against Covert Channel Attacks in the SDN Networks. In *2023 Advanced Computing and Communication Technologies for High Performance Applications (ACCTHPA)* (pp. 1-5). IEEE. 10.1109/ACCTHPA57160.2023.10083336

Mejia, J. M. R., & Rawat, D. B. (2022). Recent advances in a medical domain metaverse: status, challenges, and perspective. *2022 Thirteenth International Conference on Ubiquitous and Future Networks (ICUFN)*. IEEE. 10.1109/ICUFN55119.2022.9829645

Mozumder, M. I., Armand, T. P. T., Uddin, S. M. I., Athar, A., Sumon, R. I., Hussain, A., & Kim, H. C. (2023). Metaverse for Digital Anti-Aging Healthcare: An overview of potential use cases based on artificial intelligence, blockchain, IoT technologies, its challenges, and future directions. *Applied Sciences (Basel, Switzerland)*, 13(8), 5127. 10.3390/app13085127

Musamih, A., Yaqoob, I., Salah, K., Jayaraman, R., Al-Hammadi, Y., Omar, M., & Ellahham, S. (2023). Metaverse in healthcare: Applications, challenges, and future directions. *IEEE Consumer Electronics Magazine*, 12(4), 33–46. 10.1109/MCE.2022.3223522

Nagesh, H. R., & Prabhu, S. (2017). High performance computation of big data: Performance optimization approach towards a parallel frequent item set mining algorithm for transaction data based on hadoop MapReduce framework. *International Journal of Intelligent Systems and Applications*, 9(1), 75–84. 10.5815/ijisa.2017.01.08

Nagesh, H. R., Prasad, G., Shivaraj, B. G., Jain, D., Puneeth, B. R., & Anadkumar, M. (2022, December). E-*Voting System Using Blockchain Technology. In 2022 4th International Conference on Advances in Computing, Communication Control and Networking (ICAC3N)* (pp. 2106-2111). IEEE.

Pai, A., Anandkumar, M., Prasad, G., Agarwal, J., & Christa, S. (2023, January). Designing a Secure Audio/Text Based Captcha Using Neural Network. In *2023 13th International Conference on Cloud Computing, Data Science & Engineering (Confluence)* (pp. 510-514). IEEE.

Pandey, A., Chirputkar, A., & Ashok, P. (2023). Metaverse: An Innovative Model for Healthcare Domain. *IEEE-2023 International Conference on Innovative Data Communication Technologies and Application (ICIDCA)*. IEEE. 10.1109/ICIDCA56705.2023.10099764

Prabhu, S., Rodrigues, A. P., Prasad, G., & Nagesh, H. R. (2015, March). Performance enhancement of Hadoop MapReduce framework for analyzing BigData. In *2015 IEEE International Conference on Electrical, Computer and Communication Technologies (ICECCT)* (pp. 1-8). IEEE. 10.1109/ICECCT.2015.7226049

Prasad, G., Jain, A. K., Jain, P., & Nagesh, H. R.Nagesh H. R. (2019). A Novel Approach to Optimize the Performance of Hadoop Frameworks for Sentiment Analysis. [IJOSSP]. *International Journal of Open Source Software and Processes*, 10(4), 44–59. 10.4018/IJOSSP.2019100103

Prasad, G., Kumar, A. S., Srivastava, S., Srivastava, A., & Srivastava, A. (2023). An iomt and machine learning model aimed at the development of a personalized lifestyle recommendation system facilitating improved health. In *Dynamics of Swarm Intelligence Health Analysis for the Next Generation* (pp. 162–185). IGI Global. 10.4018/978-1-6684-6894-4.ch009

Prasad, M. G., Agarwal, J., Christa, S., Pai, H. A., Kumar, M. A., & Kukreti, A. (2023, January). An Improved Water Body Segmentation from Satellite Images using MSAA-Net. In *2023 International Conference on Machine Intelligence for GeoAnalytics and Remote Sensing (MIGARS)* (Vol. 1, pp. 1-4). IEEE. 10.1109/MIGARS57353.2023.10064508

Prasad, M. G., Pratap, M. S., Jain, P., Gujjar, J. P., Kumar, M. A., & Kukreti, A. (2022, December). RDI-SD: An Efficient Rice Disease Identification based on Apache Spark and Deep Learning Technique. In *2022 International Conference on Artificial Intelligence and Data Engineering (AIDE)* (pp. 277-282). IEEE. 10.1109/AIDE57180.2022.10060157

Singh, P., Tripathi, V., Singh, K. D., Guru Prasad, M. S., & Aditya Pai, H. (2023, April). A Task Scheduling Algorithm for Optimizing Quality of Service in Smart Healthcare System. In *International Conference on IoT, Intelligent Computing and Security: Select Proceedings of IICS 2021* (pp. 43-50). Singapore: Springer Nature Singapore. 10.1007/978-981-19-8136-4_4

Skalidis, I., Muller, O., & Fournier, S. (2023). CardioVerse: The cardiovascular medicine in the era of Metaverse. *Trends in Cardiovascular Medicine*, 33(8), 471–476. 10.1016/j.tcm.2022.05.00435568263

Song, Y., & Qin, J. (2022). Metaverse and personal healthcare. *Procedia Computer Science*, 210, 189–197. 10.1016/j.procs.2022.10.136

Wu, T., & Ho, C. B. (2023). A scoping review of metaverse in emergency medicine. *Australasian Emergency Care (Online)*, 26(1), 75–83. 10.1016/j.auec.2022.08.00235953392

Zhou, H., Gao, J., & Chen, Y. (2022). The paradigm and future value of the metaverse for the intervention of cognitive decline. *Frontiers in Public Health*, 10, 1016680. 10.3389/fpubh.2022.101668036339131

Chapter 5
Emerging Implications of Metaverse Healthcare Analysis to the Individual and the Society

Annamalai Selvarajan

https://orcid.org/0000-0001-6336-1194

Jain University (Deemed), India

Sangeetha Nagamani

https://orcid.org/0009-0001-4718-8085

City Engineering College, Bangalore, India

Suresh Kumar A.

https://orcid.org/0000-0001-7145-6337

Jain University (Deemed), India

Tejavarma Dommaraju

Jain University (Deemed), India

Harsha Vardhan Gandhodi

Jain University (Deemed), India

Dimitrios A. Karras

National and Kapodistrian University of Athens, Greece

ABSTRACT

Nowadays, Metaverse continues to be a boon for virtual space. The word Metaverse was coined by Neal Stephenson in his science fiction novel "Snow Crash." It has become the next iteration of the internet. Metaverse is defined as a distinct, ubiquitous, deeply engaged, insistent, 3D virtual space where we can virtually create a life better than the physical world. The real world has evolved tremendously since the COVID-19 pandemic. People have isolated themselves from gatherings and other activities. Organisations began to use new technology for remote work. Metaverse had pushed forward to fix the problem by employing augmented reality (AR), virtual reality (VR), mixed reality (MR) and extended reality (ER). Furthermore, the

DOI: 10.4018/979-8-3693-2268-0.ch005

Copyright © 2024, IGI Global. Copying or distributing in print or electronic forms without written permission of IGI Global is prohibited.

metaverse is regarded as a web of a virtual environment in which avatars interact to provide an immersive experience. Metaverse features include digital avatars, decentralisation, highly effective remote work, security, and privacy.

INTRODUCTION TO METAVERSE HEALTHCARE

Defining the Metaverse in Healthcare

Nowadays, Metaverse continues to be a boon for the Virtual space. The Word Metaverse was coined by Neal Stephenson in his science fiction novel "Snow Crash". It has become the next iteration of the internet. Metaverse is defined as a distinct, ubiquitous, deeply engaged, insistent, 3D virtual space where we can virtually proficient a life better than the physical world. The World has evolved tremendously since the COVID-19 Pandemic. People have isolated themselves from gatherings and other activities. Organisations began to use new technology for remote work. Metaverse had pushed forward to fix the problem by employing Augmented Reality (AR), Virtual Reality (VR), Mixed Reality (MR) and Extended Reality (ER). Furthermore, the metaverse is regarded as a web of a virtual environment in which avatars interact to provide an immersive experience. Metaverse features include digital avatars, decentralisation, highly effective remote work, security, and privacy. Metaverse encompasses multiple novel technologies like Artificial Intelligence, Blockchain technologies, Computer vision, IoTs, Robotics, Cloud Technologies etc. Metaverse promotes tourism wherein tourist starts planning their trip research via 5G and Virtual, augmented metaverse platform. Metaverse is heading online entertainment, which includes online gaming, concerts, sports, and so on and so forth.

Metaverse is one of the backbones of the video game industry. Gaming Firms are initiating substantial R&D investment in order to explore novel, creative and exclusive methods for proposing games to the metaverse. private digital spaces are likely to be the most popular in the metaverse world. New-age digital real estate and online forums would be easily accessible by each and every individual. Metaverse has made a big transformation in the healthcare sector through digital treatments where VR and AR technology enables various medical treatment applications. (Lee, L et al., 2021)

In our upcoming chapters, we are going to deliberate through how Metaverse evolved around the virtual clinics and hospitals and how it is been used by virtual doctors, Nurses and virtual coaches in the medical field. We are going to discuss the experience of the patients in the Metaverse and the social and economic effects of Metaverse healthcare. The additional factor impacting the development of the metaverse is the investment in metaverse development platforms like AR and VR techniques to enhance the medical platforms.

Before we start the context, we shall go through a few terms based on Virtual healthcare.

Telemedicine: We are familiar with the term telehealth, which is also called telemedicine where clinicians provide medical services to patients who are situated remotely. Doctors diagnose, advise, care, monitor and give remainders for the patients regarding their healthcare.

Virtual Visit: It involves virtual two-way conversation with the physicians using audio visual tools. There is no longer a need for the physical visit of the patient to the hospital. Doctors can virtually monitor the patient's health problems and patients in turn can keep an eye on their health conditions too.

Remote Observation: With the help of emerging techniques, virtual setups can be built and patients can be monitored remotely.

MHealth: The term refers to the medical services provided via mobile devices. There are several applications created by various groups to offer patients with individualised treatment.

E-Health: It is referred to as electronic-based health information and services provided by clinicians.

Historical Context and Evolution of Virtual Health Spaces:

In the 1970s, the introduction of communication gadgets such as telegraph and telephone accelerated the practice of telehealth. It helps us to send messages or communicate with health practitioners over large distances. The telegraph was a powerful tool and game-changer in the US Civil War where the first electronic information based on health-related purposes was recorded (Mystakidis, S, 2022).

Timeline of Telemedicine

1905: Introduction of Heart sound transmission by William Einthoven from a hospital to his laboratory.

1910: Electrocardiography was successfully transmitted through cables from the hospital wards to the ECG room.

1920: Two-way communication was introduced to connect the physicians and the mariners for health treatment.

1924: One of the magazines named Radio News initiated the context "RADIO DOCTOR" to express information bounded with the patients, and physicians through telephone or microphone.

1959: Interactive two-way video conversation for Telemedicine in the United States was trailblazed by The University of Nebraska. Doctors share neurological examination data with their medical students on campus using this technique.
1960: NASA's collaboration with the Indian Health Service and Lockheed Corporation inducted Space Technology Applied to Rural Papago Advanced Health Care (STARPAHC) to provide easier access to medications.
1980: Radiology headed up as the first medical speciality to exclusively adopt telemedicine.

Transformation of Telemedicine Through the Internet

The Internet opened up a new era for telehealth by the effective transmission of large amounts of data over a long distance. Thus, the pace and scope of telemedicine improved apparently. Sharing information globally becomes easier due to the digitization of the data.

The COVID-19 pandemic has urged practitioners to provide remote healthcare services. With the help of emerging technologies, a medical physician can perform the medication through video conferencing remotely. The benefits of telemedicine were apparently proved during the pandemic situations. Virtual health care will continue to be a pinnacle for the digital medicine. There are several features which advance virtual health care throughout the world, including digital technologies, faster and cheaper internet facilities and the rising affordability of gadgets. Several international organisations such as WHO i.e. World Health Organisation have advocated for the research of virtual telemedicine techniques to enhance the provision of healthcare (Dionisio, J. D. N., Burns III, W. G., & Gilbert, R. 2013).

EHR Role in Telemedicine

The patient's medical history is maintained over time by the physicians electronically which is otherwise known as Electronic Health Record (EHR). An EHR contains all the clinical information about the person's health care including past medical history, laboratory reports and other information about the medications. The information will help professionals to make better judgements and deliver better treatment since it is timely and readily available.

The key benefits of the EHR are as follows:

1. It reduces duplication of data
2. EHR software provides future planning for diagnosis.
3. It enhances the sharing of health records with consultants.

4.   It provides improvised Quality care.

Introducing Blockchain Technology in the Virtual Health World

Blockchain technology plays a crucial role in the virtual healthcare industry. It is a secure, distributive framework for storing digital data. The blockchain may connect the computers through nodes and it does not require any transactions for building a new block of nodes hence providing a secure transformation of data. A blockchain may develop distinctive cryptocurrency IDs by utilizing its hash function, which is the master key of a blockchain, to add data. The secure immune system of the traditional and previous approach of storing health care data was severely compromised. The cost of virtual health care has grown, causing both patients and doctors to consider it. To make it trustworthy, the stakeholders and the researchers turned towards blockchain technology which provides efficient management of data security at low cost. The confidentiality of the patient's health care information and the data transmission is maintained through data access control and integrity. The data access control privileges are strengthened by blockchain technology which in turn builds trust between the patients and the owners. Numerous investigations have been performed to find out how blockchain prediction might increase the efficiency of healthcare systems (Dwivedi, Y. K et al., 2022).

Major Blockchain Applications in Healthcare Systems:

1.   Maintaining the health information.
2.   Managing the log data.
3.   Digital image sharing.
4.   Patient's monitoring details.

THE CURRENT STATE OF HEALTHCARE IN THE METAVERSE

Although Metaverse has stepped into many sectors like Gaming and entertainment it has more practical applications in health care sectors. Thus far most health care is practicing Extended technologies (XR) which include Virtual reality, mixed reality and Augmented Reality. These technologies are used in various applications and even for diagnosing patients, as well as for conferences and meetings held in remote places. There are several companies that research the storage and management of healthcare data with the help of new emerging technology like Blockchain. Metaverse enhances accuracy, efficiency and the effective results of the patient's imagery. XR enhances access to care in physical therapy and rehabilitation. With freelance treatment therapies, XR can help to reduce the expenditure for the treatment.

Virtual Clinics and Hospitals

The demand for automated healthcare arose as COVID-19 prompted around the world. The requirements of digital healthcare accelerated among all organizations. Virtual clinics enhanced medical services like teleconsultation, emergency nursing points and dispensaries. Teleconsultations include advice on prediabetics, thyroid, weight loss etc. With further empowerment, clinical experts give live reports to patients who have complex problems. The main advantage of virtual clinics is that the waiting time of the patients is significantly reduced and it speeds up the recovery.

Virtual Clinics Instances

1. Initial consultation for the patients
2. Special program for the secondary care patients
3. Virtual Rehabilitation clinics.
4. Digital sessions for therapies

E-clinics have the potential to significantly bridge the rural-urban healthcare gap; nevertheless, more research on important problems including ethical and socioeconomic concerns that have an impact on the standard of treatment and population-level health outcomes is necessary. Metaverse emerged into existence shattering all the constraints of the conventional techniques. Medical professionals can virtually evaluate patients in the metaverse without any restrictions. Healthcare will be more personalized by using metaverse techniques. Training in the metaverse provides healthcare practitioners with a safe and skilled environment to expertise themselves. Complex surgical operations may be practised in realistic, risk-free settings helping the medical trainees to sharpen their abilities. Realistic simulations in training can reduce costs, improve procedural accuracy, and reduce risks. They eliminate in-person labs, conference travel, and surgical equipment. Physicians may plan ahead and increase procedure precision with the use of robotic equipment by controlling them. Metaverse with its XR enhances healthcare service delivery by creating immersive experiences for patients, partners, and employees. The adoption of digital twins in med-tech improves deep learning and patient insights. The metaverse allows stakeholders to test future technologies, forecast patient recovery cycles, and improve treatment response.

Telemedicine and Telehealth in the Metaverse

Various Aspects of Telemedicine in the Metaverse

Metaverse plays various roles in the field of telemedicine. Technologies like digital twins, virtual hospitals, and Blockchain merge into the metaverse to empower medical physicians to provide more unified treatment packages. Metaverse can enhance the patient's reliability and their outcomes using VR and AR technologies. VR can benefit therapy, by providing personalised environments for patients to interact with anxiety-causing situations in safe, closely monitored settings. telemedicine in the metaverse also allows medical care professionals to share the data among themselves and helps in finding out the causes of the illness. In addition to that, Metaverse helps medical students to examine the human body in a realistic approach (Bashshur, R. L. et al., 2011).

Surgeons are utilizing VR, AR, and AI for complex surgeries, with the Metaverse presenting new opportunities for a 360-degree view of patients for better procedure execution. The Metaverse has the ability to transform the mental healthcare of patients by enabling physicians to treat various conditions using immersive technologies. Blockchain in the Metaverse can address patient data security concerns, improving disruption resilience in healthcare. The Metaverse offers a more life-like experience for telemedicine, enhancing the sense of presence compared to traditional video conferencing platforms.

Figure 1. Technologies used

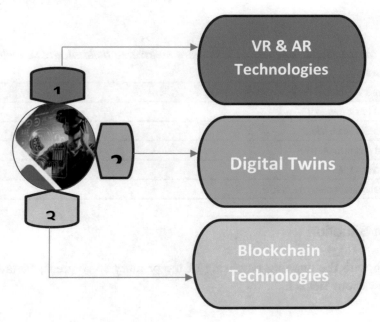

The term Internet of Medical Things (IoMT) refers to the integration of healthcare gadgets and software that are connected through virtual online computer networks and other healthcare IT systems.

IoMT Includes

- monitoring the patients remotely,
- keeping track of the health records,
- Monitoring the whereabouts of the patients,
- Initiating the association between the medical professionals and the ambulances moving towards the hospital
- Medications orders of the patients

IoMT devices connect to the cloud systems to store and examine the collected data from different networks. IoMT provides huge amounts of data to the physicians to understand the patient's health issues more precisely. (Gordon, N. P., & O'Connor, P. J., 2020)

Future Transformation of Metaverse

Table 1. Initial Stage: The key areas where metaverse technologies develop in the near future

Applications Technologies
Surgical Procedures AR
Mental Healthcare VR
Medical treatment AR/VR
Pain therapy VR
Diagnosing and Testing AR/VR

Present Situation

Along with the ongoing practising of the primary stage areas, Metaverse can step into various fields like:

Table 2. Metaverse can step into various fields like the below

Applications Technologies
Eldercare and Impairment AR/VR
Digital clinical treatment AR/VR
Clinical virtual twin XR
Health data Blockchain
Improvised health care data Blockchain

Upcoming Decades

In the following decades, advanced and standardised development in the metaverse techniques can dominate healthcare globally.

Table 3. Upcoming decades

Applications Technologies
Global access to patient's data Blockchain
Robotics Diagnosis XR
Virtual Clinics XR

Healthcare Apps and Services in Virtual Worlds

The metaverse is revolutionizing healthcare by enabling remote patient assessment and consultations through virtual and augmented reality technologies. There are few healthcare apps listed below:

1. Intuitive surgical:

Intuitive Surgical is a leading integrated system that provides support and education to hospitals and medical professionals to lead the way in minimally invasive healthcare.

2. Cable labs:

Cable Labs focuses on innovation in the cable communication sectors. It is now newly stepping into the healthcare in metaverse companies.

3. Microsoft:

Microsoft which is a leading software company is now actively traversing the metaverse in healthcare organisations.

4. **Meta Software**:

Meta software which established social media, now aims to develop virtual environments for people to access healthcare resources using metaverse.

5. 8Chili:

A start-up company called 8chili contributes an AR/VR platform for medical practitioners. It also helps to create and share feasible augmented and virtual reality experiences with medical physicians.

6. **AccuVein**:

AccuVein is a medical instrumental business company which helps in implementing vein lighting technology to benefit medical clinicians in finding veins. AccuVein is now stepping into the metaverse for medical companies.

7. BioflightVR:

BioflightVR is a medical training organisation which offers end-end virtual reality and 360-degree training modules for medical students. It helps in improving the performances and the outcomes of the students.

8. CAE:

A Canadian Business company CAE focuses on the development, manufacturing and distribution of simulation technologies. It also helps in the development of the training projects for the healthcare solutions.

BENEFITS AND ADVANTAGES OF METAVERSE

The metaverse, a concept popularized in science fiction, literature and movies, is a virtual reality world including Augmented reality, Extended reality and block-chain where users interact, create content, and participate in digital events. It has gained attention with the development of virtual worlds like Second Life, VR Chat, Decentral and, allowing users to create avatars, explore virtual environments, and interact with others.

Personal Healthcare and Wellness

Metaverse uses digital twin technology to enhance its personal and healthcare services. In the arena of healthcare, digital Twins can assist patients in updating their health issues and providing them with appropriate actions for their illness. The commonest way to develop digital twins is by using information from multiple resources including sensors that continuously collect information from the body, and centralised health records from the healthcare providers. (Keesara, S., Jonas, A., & Schulman, K., 2020)

The main objective of collecting various data sources is ultimately to improve the quality of life by tracking chronic diseases that are existing and assisting in the detection of prospective illnesses. To accomplish this, real-time sensor data, user input data and EHRs from different healthcare providers are collated and maintained in the digital twin for future research. For efficiency and significance, digital twin data may be inspected on a regular basis in accordance with the risk factors of the significant physical entity. After analysis, the recommendations are delivered to the concerned person either through text messages or multimedia presentations. To attain the goals of digital twins in healthcare, there are technologies like sensor technology, cloud computing and blockchain technology

Sensor Technology

Clinical measuring sensors, like wearable technology, are communicated via wireless sensor networks (WSN) to link virtual and real locations. For coordination, information from various sensors—such as pedometer readings, activity monitoring data, and other relevant data is sent to a digital twin. Digital twins that are more precise and complete can be produced by improving the type and precision of data collected as sensor technology develops. AMON project's wearable telemonitoring system, Toshiba's artificial intelligence system, the telemedicine platform from ST Microelectronics and Mayo Clinic, and a real-time WSN equipped with a pulse oximeter are some couple of instances industry developments.

Blockchain Technology

Since digital twins need the storage of enormous volumes of medical records, data security is crucial for ensuring data integrity. Blockchain data storage is decentralised, making it challenging for hackers to target the pertinent data from digital twins. Hackers must hack every digital twin, which is a very challenging undertaking. Additionally, a digital twin is removed from the blockchain if it is determined to be questionable. (ElHeneidi, S., & Li, S., 2020)

Cloud Computing

Digital twin combined with Cloud computing provides efficient services to the users. Cloud computing provides a new mode of healthcare services by meeting the objectives of decentralised resource collaboration and coordination. It helps in monitoring and analysing the huge amount of data storage. Together, cloud computing and digital twins form CloudDTH, which manages patient health information for extended periods of time. The digital twin's medical data include body temperature, blood pressure, and blood oxygen levels from various medical facilities or digital formats. The healthcare centre's cloud architecture maintains this data. (Zhang, Y., Xu, X., & Liu, Y., 2019)

Remote Monitoring and Diagnostics

In the aftermath of the epidemic, individual healthcare has become more concerned. The advantage of remote health monitoring is readily apparent: although caretakers may need to forego in-person patient interactions, they still require an environment in which all essential data is visible remotely to support diagnosis and treatment. Physicians find it helpful to have remote access to their patients' daily schedules, health records, and direct diagnoses instead of in-person consultations. Remote monitoring includes a collection of patients' health records and consulting the patients remotely based on the patient's records. Some of the benefits of remote monitoring are

1. Overall strengthening of value-based treatment
2. Exploring and enhancing therapy results
3. Direct communication with patients having chronic illness by remote monitoring.
4. The rate of re-admission is reduced.
5. The scarcity of skilled personnel is been overcome.

Remote Monitoring can be classified into three types today

1. Person-Person Monitoring – Important health-related conditions are analysed by face -face meeting with patients and the clinicians
2. Over-Demand Monitoring- The clinicians can keep an eye on the patient's vital conditions from home.
3. Intuitive Monitoring- Accessible, intelligent technology gradually gathers and keep track of the patient's information.

The arena of remote health monitoring is expanding rapidly with new products being introduced regularly and much research is being done frequently. Even if there are plenty of standard solutions available, bespoke ones may be developed to satisfy the specific needs of patients .

Enhanced Education and Training for Healthcare Professionals

In the field of education, Technology has the power to drastically alter education as per the needs of the world. Experts believe that the metaverse follows the best learning factors and can change how the courses are to be taught and how students have to learn. Although the metaverse is still developing, it has new novel possibilities for blending technology in healthcare like edge, cloud computing, Quantum technology, AI, VR and AR, Web 3.0 etc. Doctors and Researchers use Virtual Reality to instruct the medical practitioner. VR provides a 360 view of the patient's health condition or it can provide a replicate of real-world medical operations. The development of the Extended Technologies will be implemented for diagnosis, treatment and it helps in integrating all the technologies like 10G networks, robotics, cloud, edge etc. The healthcare operations utilise metaverse through three main pathways. 1. Tele-Consultation 2. Blockchain 3. Digital Twins. (Smith, A. C et al., 2020)

1. **Tele-Consultations**:

The pandemic has boosted telecommunication services have increased in popularity. Immersive VR and the metaverse in healthcare have improved user experience by raising the feel of presence.

2. Blockchain:

Blockchain is crucial in healthcare for decentralized communities, democratic smart contracts, and digital ownership of digital world items, enhancing the management and security of valuable health data.

3. Digital Twins:

A digital twin is a virtual model created using real-world data to learn about its counterpart, such as a patient's digital twin in the metaverse.

Surgical training affords doctors the information and abilities they need to operate on patients safely and efficiently. The establishment of surgical simulators made possible by the metaverse has made comprehensive operations planning and algorithm development possible.

The revolutionary concept called the Metaverse blends virtual reality with immersive experiences to improve patient care, surgical training, and medical education. It raises the bar for care by enabling individualised training in remote locations. The metaverse communication infrastructure is made to promote global connectedness, which makes real-time interaction and high-precision medical operations possible. It also offers state-of-the-art haptic, augmented, virtual, and AI technology to doctors. By fostering better professional communication, future uses of the metaverse in healthcare will facilitate quicker root cause investigation and easier variable monitoring.

CHALLENGES AND CONCERNS

Data Privacy and Security

Making sure patient data is secure and private is one of the main problems with metaverse healthcare. Data is gathered in a metaverse setting from multiple sources, such as virtual interactions, wearable technology, and sensors. Since this data may contain extremely sensitive information, it's critical to make sure it's shielded from misuse and unwanted access.

There are several strategies to reduce these concerns, including the use of zero-trust security models, block chain technology, and encryption. It's crucial to remember that these technologies are still in their infancy and that there is no assurance that they will be able to completely safeguard patient data in the metaverse.

Ethical Considerations in Virtual Healthcare

There are several moral questions about the application of metaverse technology in the medical field. It is possible, for instance, for people to be forced or abused into taking part in online medical trials or therapies. Furthermore, the employment of metaverse technology raises the possibility of damaging or discriminating virtual healthcare encounters.

Creating moral standards for the application of metaverse technology in healthcare is crucial. These regulations ought to cover topics including the use of artificial intelligence, patient autonomy, and informed consent. Ensuring universal access to metaverse healthcare is crucial, irrespective of an individual's gender, socioeconomic background, race, or ethnicity. (Cohen, I. G., & Mello, M. M, 2018)

Digital Divide and Access Disparities

The possibility of digital gap and access inequalities presents another difficulty for metaverse healthcare. Not everyone has access to the technology required to take part in experiences within the metaverse. This can result in some people losing out on the advantages of metaverse healthcare.

Ensuring universal access to metaverse healthcare is a crucial matter. This might necessitate government action in the form of grants for metaverse software and technology or investments in public-private partnerships to create affordable metaverse healthcare options.

Regulation and Compliance

As metaverse healthcare is a very new and developing sector, its application is not yet governed by any regulations. This brings up several issues, including how to safeguard patients from damage and make sure metaverse healthcare workers are trained and skilled.

The creation of regulatory frameworks for metaverse healthcare is crucial. These frameworks ought to cover matters like patient safety, ethical considerations, and data privacy and security. Ensuring that metaverse healthcare is integrated with current healthcare systems and legislation is also crucial.

- **Implications for the Individual and Society:**

Metaverse healthcare has important new consequences for both individuals and society. Healthcare provided by the metaverse could:

Improve access to healthcare: People may find it simpler to obtain healthcare through metaverse healthcare, irrespective of their financial situation or place of residence.

Enhance the quality of healthcare: Remote patient monitoring and virtual surgery are two examples of cutting-edge healthcare delivery methods that could be made possible via metaverse healthcare.

Reduce healthcare costs: Because metaverse healthcare does not require costly physical infrastructure, it may help save healthcare expenditures.

Improve patient outcomes: Giving patients more individualized and interesting care could assist to improve patient outcomes through metaverse healthcare.

The delivery and receiving of healthcare could be completely transformed by metaverse healthcare. Better patient outcomes as well as increased accessibility, quality, and cost-effectiveness are possible benefits. (Gordon, S. S., & Spetz, J., 2019)

Before metaverse healthcare is extensively used, a number of issues and worries must also be resolved. These include the digital divide, ethical issues, data security and privacy, and legal and regulatory requirements.

Metaverse healthcare has important new consequences for both individuals and society. Healthcare in the metaverse has the potential to improve everyone's access to, cost of, and quality of care. However, before implementing metaverse healthcare on a broad scale, it is crucial to properly evaluate the issues and obstacles surrounding it.

HEALTHCARE AI AND VIRTUAL ASSISTANTS

AI-Driven Virtual Doctors and Nurses

Computer programs that employ artificial intelligence to deliver healthcare services to patients are known as AI-driven virtual physicians and nurses. They can be used for more complex care, such managing chronic ailments or offering mental health support, or for more basic care, like responding to inquiries about symptoms and treatments.

There are several possible advantages for AI-driven virtual physicians and nurses. They are able to:

- Provide 24/7 access to healthcare
- Reduce the burden on human healthcare providers
- Make healthcare more affordable
- Provide personalized care tailored to the individual patient's needs

But there are drawbacks to AI-powered virtual physicians and nurses as well. They might not be able to manage complex medical issues, for instance, or offer the same calibre of treatment as a human healthcare professional. (Verghese, A., & Shah, N. H., 2017)

Virtual Health Coaches

Artificial intelligence is used by virtual health coaches, which are computer programs, to assist people become healthier and happier. They can be utilized to offer assistance with stress management, quitting smoking, weight loss, and other health objectives.

The advantages of virtual health coaches are numerous. They are able to:

- Provide personalized support and motivation
- Help people to track their progress and make necessary adjustments
- Be accessible 24/7
- Be more affordable than human health coaches

For some people, virtual health coaches might not be as beneficial as in-person health coaches. People with complex medical issues or those in greater need of extensive support might benefit more from working with a human health coach.

AI in Healthcare Decision Support

Artificial intelligence (AI) in healthcare decision support is the application of AI to assist healthcare professionals in making more informed decisions on patient care. Artificial intelligence (AI) can be used to examine vast amounts of data, including clinical trials, research studies, and medical records, in order to spot patterns and trends that would be hard or impossible for human healthcare personnel to notice on their own.

Healthcare decision support systems driven by AI may be able to:

- Improve the accuracy of diagnoses
- Identify patients who are at risk of developing complications
- Help healthcare providers to choose the best treatment options for individual patients
- Reduce the cost of healthcare

Virtual assistants and artificial intelligence in healthcare have important new consequences for both individuals and society. Virtual assistants and AI in healthcare have the ability to:

- Improve access to healthcare for people in remote or underserved areas.
- Reduce the cost of healthcare.
- Improve the quality of healthcare by helping healthcare providers to make better decisions.
- Empower individuals to take more control of their own health and well-being.

It is crucial to remember that virtual assistants and artificial intelligence in healthcare are still in their infancy and that a number of issues must be resolved before they can be extensively used. (Morley, J., Machado, C. C., & Silva, C. A, 2020)

Among them are:

- Data privacy and security
- Ethical considerations
- Bias and discrimination
- Regulation and compliance

To guarantee their safe and responsible usage, healthcare AI and virtual assistants require the development of ethical standards and regulatory frameworks. Ensuring universal access to healthcare AI and virtual assistants is crucial, irrespective of an individual's geographic location or financial status.

Healthcare AI and virtual assistants have the ability to completely transform the healthcare industry by increasing patient empowerment, accessibility, quality, and cost-effectiveness, according to metaverse healthcare analysis. Before widespread implementation, nevertheless, bias, ethical issues, data privacy, and regulations need to be addressed.

PATIENT EXPERIENCE IN THE METAVERSE

Patient Communities and Support Groups

Patients can connect with other patients who share similar experiences in a secure and encouraging environment by joining patient communities and support groups in the metaverse. Patients who feel alone or isolated, or who have unusual or chronic illnesses, may find this to be extremely helpful.

Patient communities within the metaverse can provide a range of benefits, including:

- Discussion forums and chat groups
- Virtual events and activities
- Private messaging
- Support groups for specific conditions or needs

These features can help patients to:

- Connect with others who understand their experiences
- Share information and advice
- Reduce feelings of isolation and loneliness
- Get emotional support
- Access resources and information

Virtual Reality for Pain Management

One technology that can be utilized to build immersive virtual environments is virtual reality (VR). Virtual reality (VR) has demonstrated efficacy in pain reduction across multiple contexts, such as clinics, hospitals, and individual homes. (Khan, R., & McDaniel, P., 2019)

Virtual reality (VR) has the potential to enable customized pain management programs for each patient in the metaverse. VR, for instance, can be utilized for:

- Distract patients from their pain
- Provide patients with a sense of control over their pain
- Help patients to learn coping mechanisms for pain
- Reduce patient's reliance on pain medication

Patients with chronic pain may see an improvement in their quality of life with VR pain management programs in the metaverse.

Psychological Well-Being and Mental Health in Virtual Spaces

Enhancing mental and psychological well-being is another benefit of the metaverse. VR, for instance, can be utilized for:

- Treat anxiety and phobias
- Provide exposure therapy for post-traumatic stress disorder (PTSD)
- Help people to manage stress
- Improve social skills
- Promote relaxation and mindfulness

In comparison to conventional therapy, virtual reality (VR) therapies in the metaverse may be more interesting and successful. For patients, they may also be more reasonably priced and easily accessible. The patient experience in the metaverse has important new ramifications for both the person and society.

The metaverse patient experience can potentially:

- Improve the quality of life for patients with chronic or rare diseases.
- Reduce feelings of isolation and loneliness for patients.
- Provide patients with access to resources and support groups that may not be available in their local community.
- Enhance the quality of mental health care for patients with anxiety, phobias, Post-Traumatic Stress Disorder (PTSD), and other mental health conditions.
- Make pain management more efficient and accessible for individuals with chronic pain.

SOCIETAL IMPACTS OF METAVERSE HEALTHCARE

Healthcare Inclusivity and Global Reach

The potential exists for metaverse healthcare to improve accessibility and inclusivity for individuals worldwide. This is due to the fact that metaverse healthcare transcends national borders. Metaverse healthcare services are available to everybody with an internet connection, no matter where they reside. People who live in rural or underdeveloped areas, where access to high-quality healthcare services may be limited, may particularly benefit from this. Reaching out to marginalized or discriminated against groups, including LGBTQ+ individuals or persons with impairments, is another way that metaverse healthcare may help. (McCormick, J. B., & Greenberg, J., 2019)

The concept of healthcare inclusivity and global reach holds that all people, regardless of geography, socioeconomic status, or other circumstances, should have access to high-quality medical care. There's a chance that the metaverse will make healthcare more inclusive and globally accessible. An organized strategy for leveraging the metaverse to improve healthcare accessibility and global reach is as follows:

1. **Expand access to high-quality healthcare in underserved regions:** People who reside in remote or impoverished areas frequently have limited access to this type of care. This gap can be closed by patients receiving therapy from faraway clinicians via the metaverse. For example, a patient in a distant place could use virtual reality to talk to a doctor in a large city.
2. **Lessen the need for hospital stays and travel:** Metaverse healthcare may assist in lessening these requirements, which can be a major obstacle to providing care for those with disabilities and other mobility issues. A patient with limited mobility, for instance, may utilize virtual reality (VR) to take part in physical therapy sessions from the comfort of their own home.
3. **Give patients more individualized and interesting treatment:** Patients may get more individualized and interesting care by using metaverse healthcare. For instance, AR may be used to provide surgeons real-time advice during surgery, and VR can be used to mimic medical procedures so that patients can better understand what to anticipate.
4. **Improve patient education:** By using metaverse healthcare, patients may get more interesting and instructive resources regarding their health and wellbeing. VR may be used, for instance, to educate patients about various medical problems and treatments or to take them on a virtual tour of the human body.

Terms included in the definition of healthcare inclusivity and global reach:

Healthcare inclusivity: The belief that no one should be denied access to high-quality medical treatment because of their financial situation, geography, or other circumstances.

Global reach: The capacity to provide medical treatment to individuals everywhere.

An area that is underserved is one where access to high-quality healthcare is constrained.

Remote provider: A healthcare provider who provides care to patients from a distance.

Mobility impairment: A condition that limits a person's ability to move around. Personalized care is medical attention given specifically to meet each patient's requirements.

Engaging care: Care that is interesting and motivating for the patient. A computer-generated simulation of a medical operation is known as a medical procedure.

Real-time guidance: Information or instruction that is provided immediately, as it is happening.

Patient education: The process of providing patients with information and support so that they can make informed decisions about their health and well-being.

Instances of global reach and inclusion in healthcare inside the metaverse:

- Virtual reality is being used by XRHealth to treat patients in the comfort of their own homes for mental health issues.
- Virtual reality is being used by a startup named Embodied to treat patients with mobility abnormalities and chronic pain via physical therapy.
- A business by the name of High Fidelity is developing a metaverse platform especially for the medical field.
- VR is being used by the University of California, San Francisco (UCSF) to educate surgeons and medical students on intricate operations.

VR is being used by the Mayo Clinic to assist patients in managing their pain.

Implications for Public Health Policy

Public health policy is also affected in a number of ways by metaverse healthcare. Metaverse healthcare, for instance, might be utilized to:

- Promote preventive care and early detection of diseases.
- Provide access to healthcare services for people who are unable to travel to traditional healthcare facilities.
- Develop and evaluate new public health interventions.
- Educate the public about health and disease prevention.

Economic and Social Effects

The economy and society are anticipated to be significantly impacted by metaverse healthcare as well. Metaverse healthcare, for instance, could:

- Create new jobs in the healthcare sector.
- Boost economic activity in the healthcare sector.
- Reduce the cost of healthcare.
- Improve the quality of life of people with chronic illnesses.
- Reduce the burden on healthcare systems.

The ways in which the metaverse can be utilized to enhance public health outcomes and advance health equity are referred to as implications for public health policy in the metaverse.

1. **Collect data on public health trends:** More real-time and thorough data collection on public health trends is possible than ever before because to the metaverse. For instance, AR can be used to monitor the prevalence of chronic diseases and other health issues, while VR can be used to survey people about their health-related behaviors and beliefs.
2. **Develop and test public health interventions:** In a secure setting, the metaverse can be utilized to create and evaluate novel public health initiatives. For instance, AR can be used to teach medical professionals how to deliver a new vaccine, and VR can be used to mimic the effects of a new smoking cessation program on participants.
3. **Educate the public about public health issues:** A more dynamic and engaging approach to educating the public about public health issues is through the usage of the metaverse. For instance, AR can be used to give individuals real-time information on the quality of the air in their neighbourhood, and VR can be used to develop virtual displays about the origins and prevention of cancer.

Terms included in the definition of implications for public health policy:

- **Public health policy:** The application of rules, legislation, and other governmental initiatives to enhance public health.
- **Public health outcomes:** A population's overall health as determined by metrics like disease rates, infant mortality, and life expectancy.
- **Health equity:** The equitable and just allocation of health outcomes among all groups.
- **Real-time data:** Data that is gathered and examined in real time.
- **Public health interventions:** Initiatives include immunization campaigns, smoking cessation programs, and education campaigns that are designed to enhance public health outcomes.

Examples of implications for public health policy in the metaverse:

- To raise awareness of the COVID-19 virus and encourage immunization, the South Korean government is utilizing virtual reality technology.
- The Australian government is assisting smokers in quitting with virtual reality.
- VR is being used by the World Health Organization (WHO) to teach medical personnel how to contain Ebola epidemics.
- VR is being used by the Centers for Disease Control and Prevention (CDC) to inform the public about the risks associated with lead poisoning.

Apart from the aforementioned, the metaverse has promise for tackling an extensive array of public health issues, including:

- Promoting healthy lifestyles
- Preventing chronic diseases
- Improving access to healthcare
- Reducing health disparities
- Responding to public health emergencies

Although the metaverse is still in its infancy, it has the power to completely alter public health practice and policy.

- **Economic and Social Effect**

The term "economic and social effects of the metaverse" describes how society and the economy are predicted to be affected by the metaverse. (Tao, F., 2019)

Economic Effects

The following are some of the predicted major effects of the metaverse on the economy:

- **Creating new jobs and industries:** New sectors of the economy will also be produced by it, including virtual healthcare, virtual education, and virtual tourism.
- **Boosting productivity:** There are several ways that the metaverse might be leveraged to increase productivity. VR can be used, for instance, to replicate difficult work tasks and teach staff member's new abilities. Employees can receive real-time information and direction while working with augmented reality (AR).
- **Reducing costs:** There are several ways that the metaverse might assist businesses in cutting expenses. VR can be utilized, for instance, to have virtual meetings and lessen the need for travel. AR has the potential to increase production and operational efficiency.

Social Effects

The metaverse is also expected to have a significant impact on society, including:

- **Changing the way we interact with each other:** We will engage with one other in new ways as a result of the metaverse, both personally and professionally. For instance, we will be able to interact with individuals from all over the world, attend virtual athletic events and concerts, and work together on projects in a virtual workspace with co-workers.
- **Creating new forms of entertainment and education:** Compared to traditional media, the metaverse will produce new, immersive, and captivating forms of education and entertainment. We will be able to interact with fictional characters and historical individuals, for instance, and explore virtual worlds while learning new skills in a virtual setting.
- **Improving accessibility for people with disabilities:** People with disabilities may find the world easier to navigate thanks to the metaverse. For instance, augmented reality (AR) can help those who are hard of hearing interact with others, and virtual reality (VR) can help those who are visually impaired perceive their surroundings.

Terms Included in the Definition of Economic and Social Effects

- **Economy:** The framework for creating and dispersing products and services within a nation or area.
- **Society:** The entire population of a certain nation or area, taking into account its institutions, laws, and customs.
- **Jobs and industries:** The various jobs that people take on, as well as the companies they work for.
- **Productivity:** The rate at which goods and services are produced.
- **Costs:** The amount of money that is spent on something.
- **Interaction:** The way in which people communicate and behave with each other.
- **Entertainment:** Activities that people do for enjoyment.
- **Education:** The process of learning new skills and knowledge.
- **Accessibility:** The ability of people with disabilities to use something.

Examples of Economic and Social Effects of the Metaverse

- Thousands of new employments are being created as a result of the billions of dollars that the firm Meta is investing in the development of the metaverse.
- NVIDIA is creating hardware and software innovations for the metaverse that are anticipated to increase efficiency and lower expenses across multiple sectors.
- Virtual reality classes covering computer science, business, and the arts are available from the education startup Coursera.
- A new virtual reality platform dubbed Horizon Worlds, being developed by Facebook, would enable users to create and explore virtual worlds with their friends.

Other Societal Impacts

Metaverse healthcare is also likely to have a number of other societal impacts, including:

- **Changes in the way we interact with healthcare providers:** Patients and healthcare professionals will be able to communicate in a more immersive and interesting way in the metaverse. This may result in a more individualized and team-based approach to medical treatment.
- **New ways to learn about health and disease prevention:** Compared to traditional learning methods, the metaverse can be leveraged to generate more

interactive and interesting educational experiences. The public's awareness of health and illness prevention may rise as a result.

- **New ways to connect with other patients:** Patients can connect with others who have experienced similar things by creating support groups and patient communities through the metaverse. Patients with chronic illnesses may have a decrease in emotions of loneliness and isolation as a result, and their quality of life may improve.

Challenges and Concerns

Although metaverse healthcare has the potential to assist people and society in many ways, there are a number of issues and problems that need to be resolved as well. Among them are:

- **Data privacy and security:** A significant amount of personal data will be collected and stored as part of metaverse healthcare. Making sure that this data is shielded from unwanted access and usage is crucial.
- **Ethical considerations:** Before metaverse healthcare is extensively used, there are a number of ethical issues that must be resolved. As an illustration, it's critical to make sure people are not taken advantage of when using metaverse healthcare.
- **Access and equity:** Ensuring universal access to metaverse healthcare is crucial, irrespective of an individual's income or geographic location. Public-private partnerships or government action may be necessary for this.
- **Regulation and compliance:** As metaverse healthcare is a very new and developing field, it is not yet governed by any regulations. Establishing legal frameworks is crucial to ensuring the responsible and safe use of metaverse healthcare.

CONCLUSION

The delivery and receiving of healthcare could be completely transformed by metaverse healthcare. It could improve healthcare accessibility, affordability, and inclusivity. It may also lessen the strain on healthcare systems and enhance the quality of life for those who suffer from chronic illnesses.

Before metaverse healthcare is extensively used, it is crucial to thoroughly evaluate the difficulties and worries surrounding it. Data security and privacy, ethical issues, equity and access, and regulation and compliance are some of these difficulties and worries.

A promising new technology that could enhance healthcare for all is metaverse healthcare. To make sure that metaverse healthcare is created and implemented in a way that benefits people and society at large, collaboration is crucial.

The emergence of Metaverse Healthcare holds great potential to transform the current healthcare landscape and impact society profoundly. Through the use of virtual and augmented reality technology, this innovative paradigm shift enhances patient involvement, medical services, and overall healthcare experiences. The Metaverse enables remote consultations, diagnostics, and even treatments, enabling immersion and customized health interventions. Everyone could have easier access to healthcare as a result, particularly those who reside in rural areas. Furthermore, by encouraging collaborative and interdisciplinary approaches to healthcare, the Metaverse fosters real-time communication and information exchange among healthcare practitioners. (Xie, Y., Xu, X., & Wang, X., 2021)

Therefore, the Metaverse Healthcare not only makes it possible for healthcare to be delivered more effectively, but it also contributes to a more varied and cohesive healthcare ecosystem, ultimately paving the way for a patient-cantered, easily accessible, and efficient healthcare system.

EDUCATION AND TRAINING FOR HEALTHCARE PROFESSIONALS

Ensuring the provision of modern, high-quality healthcare services depends heavily on the education and training of healthcare personnel. Healthcare workers must complete demanding coursework and hands-on training to gain the requisite competences, knowledge, and skills. This program covers a wide range of subjects, such as allied health, medical, nursing, and administrative positions. In order to keep practitioners up to date with changing medical technologies, treatment approaches, and research findings, continuous professional development is highly valued. Furthermore, practical training—which is frequently provided in clinical settings— enables medical professionals to put their theoretical knowledge to use in actual situations, which promotes the growth of their clinical expertise and the provision of high-quality patient care. Given the dynamic nature of medical breakthroughs, lifelong learning is ingrained in the healthcare industry. It ensures that professionals stay up to date and proficient in their respective domains, which ultimately improves patient outcomes and the standard of care. (Mason, D. J., & Jones, D. A., 2021)

Simulation and Training in Virtual Environments

The use of computer-generated simulations to instruct individuals in new techniques or methods is known as simulation and training in virtual environments. Surgical rooms and airplane cockpits are only two examples of the many environments that may be realistically simulated with virtual environments (VEs).

Step-by-Step Explanation of Simulation and Training in Virtual Environments

1. **Identify the skills or procedures to be trained:** Finding the precise techniques or talents that require training is the first step. The following stage after determining the training objectives is to create a simulation that will let students practice these techniques in a secure setting.
2. **Develop the simulation:** Numerous software and hardware tools are available for the development of the simulation. The particular training objectives will determine how complex the simulation is. For instance, a rudimentary manufacturing process simulation might simply need a few simple animations and geometric objects. Complex physics simulations and accurate 3D representations of human anatomy can be needed for a more intricate simulation of a surgical process.
3. **Design the training program:** The goal of the training curriculum should be to facilitate the acquisition of the skills or procedures by the participants. A wide range of activities, including tutorials, simulations, and assessments, should be included in the curriculum.
4. **Deliver the training:** There are numerous ways to give the training, including online, in-person, and hybrid formats. The target audience and the particular training objectives will determine which delivery style is best.

Terms Included in the Definition of Simulation and Training in Virtual Environments

- **Simulation:** A computer-generated model of a real-world process or system.
- **Virtual environment (VE):** A computer-generated simulation of a real-world environment.
- **Training:** The process of teaching someone how to do something.
- **Training objectives:** The specific skills or procedures that need to be trained.
- **Trainee:** A person who is being trained on a new skill or procedure.
- **Assessment**: A test or evaluation of a trainee's skills or knowledge.

Examples of Simulation and Training in Virtual Environments

- Before operating actual aircraft, pilots receive training in flight simulators.
- Before doing actual surgeries, surgeons practice in virtual reality simulators.
- Before using actual machinery, factory workers receive training in virtual reality simulators.
- Before entering battle, soldiers rehearse in virtual reality simulators.
- Teachers instruct pupils in a variety of topics, including math, science, and history, using virtual reality.

Benefits of Simulation and Training in Virtual Environments

- **Safety:** VEs can provide a safe environment for trainees to practice new skills or procedures without the risk of injury or damage to equipment.
- **Cost-effectiveness:** VEs can be more cost-effective than traditional training methods, such as on-the-job training or classroom instruction.
- **Efficiency:** VEs can help trainees learn new skills or procedures more efficiently than traditional training methods.
- **Effectiveness:** VEs have been shown to be effective in training people on a wide range of skills and procedures.

Continuous Medical Education in the Metaverse

The method via which medical personnel stay current on the newest medical information and abilities is known as continuous medical education (CME). Maintaining one's expertise and offering patients top-notch treatment are imperative for healthcare workers. The metaverse has the power to completely transform CME by improving its usability, effectiveness, and accessibility. (Nair, S., & Choi, K. S., 2021)

The following is a methodical approach to utilizing the metaverse for ongoing medical education:

1. **Develop virtual learning environments (VLEs):** Clinical environments, including operation rooms, patient rooms, and examining rooms, can be realistically simulated using VLEs. Healthcare workers can learn about new medical procedures, treatments, and medications by creating interactive learning modules with VLEs.
2. **Use virtual reality (VR) and augmented reality (AR) to create immersive learning experiences:** With the use of virtual reality (VR), medical personnel can be transported into virtual clinical environments and practice new techniques in a secure setting. By superimposing digital data onto the physical world, aug-

mented reality (AR) can help medical personnel learn about human anatomy and physiology and offer them real-time guidance during medical procedures.

3. **Create social learning experiences:** Healthcare workers can work together and gain knowledge from one another's experiences by creating social learning environments using the metaverse. Healthcare practitioners, for instance, can take part in online seminars, workshops, and conferences by using VLEs. They can mentor and coach one another as well as create virtual study groups using VLEs.

Terms included in the definition of continuous medical education in the metaverse:

● Continuous Medical Education (CME): The process that keeps medical personnel abreast of the most recent developments in medicine.
● Virtual learning environments (VLEs): Training and educational tools that utilize computer-generated models of actual surroundings.
● Virtual reality (VR) refers to an immersive computer-generated simulation of a real-world environment that the user can experience.
● AR stands for augmented reality, a technique that superimposes digital data on the physical world.
● Social learning experiences: These are educational opportunities where students collaborate and interact with one another.

Real-time examples of continuous medical education in the metaverse:

● The business XRHealth is creating a virtual reality (VR) platform for continuing medical education (CME) that will enable medical practitioners to practice procedures in a virtual setting.
● Immerse is a business that is creating an AR platform for CME that can be used to teach medical professionals about new drugs and procedures.
● The American Medical Association (AMA) is in the process of creating a metaverse platform for continuing medical education (CME) that will facilitate communication among medical professionals, enable them to attend virtual conferences, and engage in online learning modules.

These are but a few instances of the modern applications of the metaverse for ongoing medical education. We may anticipate seeing even more ground-breaking and inventive uses of this technology in the healthcare industry as the metaverse grows.

The metaverse holds the potential to transform ongoing medical education by improving its effectiveness, accessibility, and engagement. Healthcare workers will be able to work together more readily and engage in more immersive and interactive learning experiences when acquiring new medical information and abilities. In the end, this will result in better patient care.

FUTURE TRENDS AND EMERGING TECHNOLOGIES

A lot of things in our lives could entirely alter as a result of emerging trends and technologies. Many cutting-edge innovations are becoming popular in a range of sectors, such as artificial intelligence and healthcare. Advanced automation and artificial intelligence are expected to revolutionize businesses by enhancing human capabilities and streamlining processes. Personalized therapies are made possible by precision medicine and genetics in healthcare, and applications of virtual and augmented reality are transforming our understanding of education and healthcare delivery. The Internet of Things (IoT) is enabling a more connected world by enhancing communication and productivity through smart devices. Quantum computing has the potential to transform science and problem-solving, and it may also bring forth significant advances in data processing techniques. These tendencies all point to the future, when technology will likely permeate every aspect of our life and present both opportunities and obstacles for technological innovation. (Binns, R., & Gillett, G., 2021)

Augmented Reality (AR) in Healthcare

A computer-generated image is superimposed on a user's perspective of the real world using augmented reality (AR) technology to create a composite view. The application of AR in healthcare has the potential to completely change how we identify, treat, and manage illnesses.

Step-by-step explanation of augmented reality in healthcare:

1. **Identify the clinical problem that AR can solve:** Finding a specific clinical issue that AR can address is the first step. AR has the potential to enhance surgical precision, assist individuals with long-term illnesses in managing their symptoms, and educate medical personnel.
2. **Develop an AR application:** Creating an augmented reality application that can address the clinical problem comes next. Numerous software and hardware technologies are available for the development of augmented reality applications. The particular clinical issue that the AR application is attempting to resolve will determine how difficult it is.

3. **Evaluate the AR application:** After the AR application has been created, it is crucial to assess it to make sure it is reliable and secure. It is best to test the AR application on actual patients in a healthcare environment.
4. **Deploy the AR application:** The AR application can be made available to patients and healthcare practitioners when it has been tested and determined to be secure and efficient.

Terms included in the definition of augmented reality (AR) in healthcare:

- Augmented reality (AR) is a technology that creates a composite vision by superimposing a computer-generated image over a user's perspective of the real world.
- A clinical problem is any ailment or problem in medicine that needs to be diagnosed, treated, or managed.
- AR application: A software program that makes use of augmented reality to address a medical issue.
- A medical facility is the clinical setting where patients receive diagnosis and treatment.
- A person licensed to provide healthcare services, such as a physician, nurse, or pharmacist, is referred to as a healthcare provider.

Real-time examples of augmented reality in healthcare:

- Nurses and physicians utilize the AccuVein AR gadget to visualize veins under the skin, which facilitates the initiation of intravenous (IV) lines.
- Stroke neurologists use the Viz.ai AR platform to diagnose strokes rapidly and precisely, which can result in more efficient and swift treatment.
- Surgeons can enhance surgical precision and safety by using the Stryker AR platform to view the patient's anatomy in real time.

Benefits of augmented reality (AR) in healthcare:

- **Improved accuracy:** AR can improve the accuracy of medical procedures, such as surgery and biopsies.
- **Reduced risk of complications:** AR can help to reduce the risk of complications during medical procedures.
- **Faster treatment:** AR can help healthcare professionals to diagnose and treat patients more quickly.
- **Improved patient experience:** AR can make medical procedures less stressful and more comfortable for patients.

- **Reduced costs:** AR can help to reduce the costs of healthcare by making medical procedures more efficient and effective.

Holographic Telemedicine

A form of telemedicine known as holographic telemedicine makes use of holographic technology to provide a three-dimensional, real-time interactive image of a physician or other healthcare provider. This eliminates the need for patients to travel to a hospital or doctor's office in order to obtain medical care from a distance. (Ahsan, M. N., & Kamal, M. M., 2021)

Although holographic telemedicine is still in its infancy, it has the potential to completely transform the way that medical treatment is provided. The following are a few possible advantages of holographic telemedicine:

- **Increased access to healthcare:** People living in remote or underserved locations may find it easier to get healthcare with the help of holographic telemedicine. It can also be utilized to give healthcare to those who have mobility issues or disabilities.
- **Improved quality of care:** Patient's care can be provided with higher quality thanks to holographic telemedicine. Holographic telemedicine, for instance, can be utilized to give patients more individualized care and to educate them about their diseases and available treatments.
- **Reduced costs:** By minimizing the need for travel and improving the effectiveness of medical care, holographic telemedicine can lower healthcare expenses.

Here are some real-time case studies of holographic telemedicine:

- A patient in rural California received care from the University of California, San Francisco (UCSF) in 2021 through the use of holographic telemedicine. The physician was physically hundreds of miles away, yet the patient was able to view and communicate with him in real time.
- In 2022, a patient with Parkinson's disease received care from the Mayo Clinic via holographic telemedicine. The patient was able to take part in physical therapy sessions from the convenience of their own home because to holographic telemedicine.
- Holographic telemedicine, as proposed by XRHealth, will enable patients to get mental health therapy in the comfort of their own homes starting in 2023. Patients can see and communicate with a therapist in real time using

XRHealth's holographic telemedicine platform, even if the therapist is physically located elsewhere.

The delivery of healthcare could be completely changed via holographic telemedicine. Accessible, reasonably priced, and individualized healthcare can be achieved using holographic telemedicine. Additionally, it may contribute to raising the standard of treatment that patients receive.

Block Chain and Healthcare Data in the Metaverse

A distributed ledger technology called block chain can be used to exchange and store data in a transparent and safe manner. It might completely change how medical data is stored and accessed in the metaverse. (Zhao, G. et al., 2020)

Benefits of using blockchain to manage healthcare data in the metaverse:

- Enhanced security: By making healthcare data harder to hack or tamper with, blockchain technology can assist to increase security.
- Enhanced transparency: By offering a tamper-proof record of every transaction, blockchain can contribute to the improvement of healthcare data transparency.
- Enhanced interoperability: By facilitating data sharing across various healthcare organizations and providers, blockchain can help to enhance the interoperability of healthcare data.
- Increased patient control: By letting individuals decide who can access and use their data, blockchain can help give patients more control over the information about their healthcare.

Here are some real-time case studies of blockchain and healthcare data in the metaverse:

- A framework for managing healthcare data based on blockchain was introduced in 2021 by MediLedger. Through the platform, patients can securely and transparently exchange their medical information with other organizations as well as healthcare practitioners.
- HealthToken introduced a blockchain-driven clinical trial management platform in 2022. Pharmaceutical companies may effectively and safely handle the data gathered during clinical trials with the help of this platform.
- The startup Gem introduced a blockchain-based technology for patient record management in 2023. Through the platform, patients can securely and trans-

parently share their medical records with other organizations and healthcare practitioners, as well as access and control their own records.

Blockchain has the power to completely change how healthcare data is stored and managed in the metaverse. Blockchain technology has the potential to enhance healthcare data security, transparency, interoperability, and patient control. Both lower expenses and better patient care may result from this. (Zarefsky, J., & Kogan, S., 2022)

CASE STUDIES AND SUCCESS STORIES

XRHealth

A firm called XRHealth uses virtual reality (VR) to treat mental health issues. Despite the therapist's actual location being elsewhere, patients may view and communicate with them in real time thanks to XRHealth's virtual reality platform.

Hospitals and clinics all over the world utilize XRHealth to offer patients mental health treatments. For instance, the Veterans Health Administration (VA) uses XRHealth to treat veterans' mental health issues.

AccuVein

A firm called AccuVein creates augmented reality (AR) tools for the medical field. The AR gadgets from AccuVein facilitate the easier initiation of intravenous (IV) lines by enabling medical professionals to see veins beneath the skin.

Hospitals and clinics all across the world are using AccuVein's AR devices to increase the precision and effectiveness of IV-line placement. For instance, the Mayo Clinic uses AR devices from AccuVein to enhance the patient experience during IV-line installation.

These are only two of the numerous ways that metaverse technology is now being applied to enhance healthcare. We may anticipate seeing even more ground-breaking and inventive uses of this technology in the healthcare industry as the metaverse grows.

REFERENCES

Ahsan, M. N., & Kamal, M. M. (2021). A survey on encryption techniques for secure healthcare data transmission. *Health Information Science and Systems*, 9(1), 1–12.33235709

Ball, M. (2022). *The Metaverse: And How It Will Revolutionize Everything*. Liveright. 10.15358/9783800669400

Bashshur, R. L., Shannon, G. W., Krupinski, E. A., & Grigsby, J. (2011). The empirical foundations of telemedicine interventions for chronic disease management. *Telemedicine Journal and e-Health*, 17(6), 484–516. 10.1089/tmj.2011.010321718114

Binns, R., & Gillett, G. (2021). Ethical frameworks for virtual health technologies: Addressing issues of equity and access. *Health Care Analysis*, 29(4), 463–475.

Cohen, I. G., & Mello, M. M. (2018). Ethical and legal issues in virtual health care. *The Journal of Law, Medicine & Ethics*, 46(2), 245–259.

Dionisio, J. D. N., Burns, W. G.III, & Gilbert, R. (2013). 3D Virtual Worlds and the Metaverse: Current Status and Future Possibilities. *ACM Computing Surveys*, 45(3), 1–38. 10.1145/2480741.2480751

Dwivedi, Y. K., Hughes, L., Baabdullah, A. M., Ribeiro-Navarrete, S., Giannakis, M., Al-Debei, M. M., & Jamal, A. (2022). Metaverse beyond the hype: Multidisciplinary perspectives on emerging challenges, opportunities, and agenda for research, practice and policy. *International Journal of Information Management*, 66, 102527. 10.1016/j.ijinfomgt.2022.102542

ElHeneidi, S., & Li, S. (2020). Blockchain-based healthcare data security and privacy: A review. *Journal of Healthcare Engineering*, 2020, 1–13.

Gordon, N. P., & O'Connor, P. J. (2020). The impact of the Internet on telehealth: Data transmission and service delivery. *Journal of Telemedicine and Telecare*, 26(5), 267–273.

Gordon, S. S., & Spetz, J. (2019). Regulatory issues and compliance for virtual health care: A review. *Journal of Telemedicine and Telecare*, 25(6), 335–341.

Keesara, S., Jonas, A., & Schulman, K. (2020). COVID-19 and health care's digital revolution. *The New England Journal of Medicine*, 382(23), e82. 10.1056/NEJMp200583532240581

Khan, R., & McDaniel, P. (2019). Sensor-based healthcare monitoring system: A review of recent advances. *Sensors (Basel)*, 19(10), 2290.31108994

Lee, L., Braud, T., Zhou, P., Wang, L., Xu, D., Lin, Z., & Hui, P. (2021). All One Needs to Know about Metaverse: A Complete Survey on Technological Singularity, Virtual Ecosystem, and Research Agenda. *arXiv preprint arXiv:2110.05352.*

Mason, D. J., & Jones, D. A. (2021). Bridging the digital divide: Strategies for improving access to healthcare technology. *Journal of Nursing Scholarship*, 53(2), 129–138.

McCormick, J. B., & Greenberg, J. (2019). Ethical considerations in the use of telehealth technologies. *Telemedicine Journal and e-Health*, 25(10), 939–944.

Morley, J., Machado, C. C., & Silva, C. A. (2020). The ethics of artificial intelligence in healthcare: A review. *Health and Technology*, 10(6), 1029–1038.

Mystakidis, S. (2022). Metaverse. *Encyclopedia*, 2(1), 486–497. 10.3390/encyclopedia2010031

Nair, S., & Choi, K. S. (2021). Frameworks for compliance in emerging virtual health care environments. *Health Law Journal*, 28(4), 304–317.

Smith, A. C., Thomas, E., Snoswell, J. A., Haydon, H., & Caffery, L. J. (2020). Telehealth for patients with chronic disease: A review of the evidence. *Journal of Telemedicine and Telecare*, 26(5), 283–293.32196391

Stephenson, N. (1992). *Snow Crash*. Bantam Books.

Tao, F., Zhang, M., Liu, Y., & Nee, A. Y. C. (2019). Digital twin-driven smart manufacturing: Connotation, reference model, applications and research issues. *Robotics and Computer-integrated Manufacturing*, 61, 101–112.

Verghese, A., & Shah, N. H. (2017). Virtual care and the future of medicine: A review of telemedicine. *Health Affairs*, 36(12), 2182–2188.

Xie, Y., Xu, X., & Wang, X. (2021). A survey on data privacy and security issues in virtual healthcare environments. *Journal of Medical Systems*, 45(8), 1–12.

Zarefsky, J., & Kogan, S. (2022). Privacy and security concerns in the metaverse healthcare: A systematic review. *Healthcare Informatics Research*, 28(1), 54–63.

Zhang, Y., Xu, X., & Liu, Y. (2019). Cloud computing for digital twins in healthcare: A review and future research directions. *Future Generation Computer Systems*, 98, 220–237.

Zhao, G., Xu, X., Li, B., & Liu, W. (2020). Blockchain technology for digital twins: A review and future directions. *Journal of Cleaner Production*, 275.

Chapter 6
Aiding in Prognosis of Fibromyalgia Syndrome Utilizing MCDM TOPSIS Method in Fusion With Fuzzy Logic

Raghavendra M. Devadas

Department of Information Technology, Manipal Institute of Technology Bengaluru, Manipal Academy of Higher Education, Manipal, India

Vani Hiremani

Symbiosis Institute of Technology, Symbiosis International University (Deemed), India

Praveen Gujjar J.

https://orcid.org/0000-0003-0240-7827

Faculty of Management Studies, Jain University (Deemed), India

ABSTRACT

The study addresses the complexity of Fibromyalgia syndrome (FMS) by integrating multi-criteria decision-making (MCDM) TOPSIS with fuzzy logic for accurate prognosis. A comprehensive set of criteria, including clinical, psychological, and physiological factors, is employed. Fuzzy logic models uncertainties and subjective expert opinions. The method systematically evaluates and ranks FMS prognoses, contributing to transparency in decision-making. Incorporating sensitivity analysis with small variations enhances reliability. Considering symptoms, patients, and expert ratings, the study identifies patient 5 as more likely to have FMS (closeness

DOI: 10.4018/979-8-3693-2268-0.ch006

Copyright © 2024, IGI Global. Copying or distributing in print or electronic forms without written permission of IGI Global is prohibited.

coefficient 0.881), while patient 1 is less prone (closeness coefficient 0.088).

INTRODUCTION

Fibromyalgia (FM) is a long-term condition that causes muscle and joint pain. The most common symptoms of this condition include muscle and joint stiffness, sleeplessness, fatigue, mood disturbances, cognitive impairment, anxiety and depression, sensitivity, and difficulty performing daily activities (Gerdle, 2008; Bennett, 2007). FM has also been linked to certain illnesses, including infections, diabetes, and rheumatic diseases, as well as neurological disorders (Bellato et al., 2012). Following the identification of areas of extreme sensitivity referred to as "pain points", the term "Fibromyalgia" was subsequently developed (Smythe, H. A., & Moldofsky, H, 1977). As per the American College of Rheumatology, diagnosis of FM is based on two factors: (a) bilateral pain at or above the waist (centralized pain); and (b) chronic, generalized pain lasting at least 3 months (pain on palpation at or above 11 of 18 specified body sites) (Galvez-Sánchez et al., 2020). The prevalence of FM is estimated to affect approximately 5% of the global population. Women are more likely to develop FM than men, and the average age at which FM is present is between the ages of 30 and 35 (Wolfe et al., 1995). Accurate and early diagnosis is essential for providing timely treatment and improving the quality of life for individuals suffering from Fibromyalgia. Traditionally, Fibromyalgia diagnosis has relied on clinical judgment, which introduces subjectivity and may result in misdiagnosis or delayed diagnosis. However, advancements in computational and decision-making methodologies offer promising avenues for enhancing the diagnostic process. One of the methods that has been proposed for diagnosing Fibromyalgia is based on Fuzzy Multi-Criteria Decision Making (FMCDM). FMCDM is a technique that can handle uncertainty and vagueness in the decision-making process by using fuzzy sets and linguistic variables. Fuzzy sets are mathematical models that can represent imprecise or incomplete information, such as the degree of severity or frequency of symptoms. Linguistic variables are words or phrases that can express qualitative judgments, such as mild, moderate, or severe. One of the FMCDM methods that has been applied to diagnose Fibromyalgia is the fuzzy technique for order preference by similarity to the ideal solution (TOPSIS). In this context, the Fuzzy Technique for Order of Preference by Similarity to Ideal Solution (Fuzzy TOPSIS) emerges as a powerful tool for aiding healthcare professionals in the precise and systematic diagnosis of Fibromyalgia. Fuzzy TOPSIS is a multi-criteria decision-making method that accommodates the inherent uncertainty and vagueness often associated with medical diagnoses. It provides a structured framework for evaluating multiple criteria, each represented as fuzzy linguistic variables, to rank and select the most suitable diagnosis among a set of alternatives. Fibromyalgia is a complex condition characterized by a range of symptoms, and choosing the right criteria is crucial for an accurate diagnosis. Here are some important criteria to consider,

- **Pain Symptoms:** One of the hallmark symptoms of Fibromyalgia is widespread pain that affects all four quadrants of the body. Assessing the location, intensity, and duration of pain is crucial. The presence and sensitivity of tender points at specific anatomical locations can be indicative of Fibromyalgia.
- **Fatigue and Sleep Disturbances:** Evaluate the severity and persistence of fatigue, which is a common symptom in Fibromyalgia. Assess sleep patterns and disturbances, such as insomnia, restless legs, or sleep apnea, which are often associated with Fibromyalgia.
- **Psychological Symptoms:** Consider the presence and severity of mood disorders, as Fibromyalgia is frequently accompanied by depression and anxiety. Evaluate cognitive function, including memory, concentration, and mental clarity.
- **Stress and Trauma History:** Inquire about significant life stressors or traumatic events, as these can contribute to the onset or exacerbation of Fibromyalgia symptoms.
- **Physical Examination Findings:** As mentioned earlier, the presence and sensitivity of tender points upon physical examination are important diagnostic criteria. Evaluate the degree of muscle stiffness and restricted range of motion.
- **Duration of Symptoms:** Consider the duration of symptoms. Fibromyalgia is typically diagnosed when symptoms have been present for at least three months.
- **Other Symptoms:** Irritable Bowel Syndrome (IBS): Assess the presence of gastrointestinal symptoms like abdominal pain, bloating, and irregular bowel movements, which are common in Fibromyalgia patients. Evaluate the frequency and intensity of headaches or migraines. Assess sensitivities to light, noise, temperature, and other sensory stimuli.
- **Quality of Life and Functional Impairment:** Assess the impact of symptoms on the patient's quality of life and daily functioning. This can include the ability to work, engage in physical activities, and perform routine tasks.

When using Fuzzy TOPSIS for Fibromyalgia diagnosis, each of these criteria should be transformed into fuzzy linguistic variables to account for the inherent uncertainty in symptom descriptions and assessments. Moreover, the selection and weighting of these criteria should involve collaboration with medical experts who have experience in diagnosing Fibromyalgia to ensure the model's accuracy and clinical relevance. By incorporating the expertise of medical professionals and considering diverse diagnostic criteria, Fuzzy TOPSIS empowers clinicians to make more informed and consistent diagnostic decisions, ultimately benefiting patients. This research paper aims to explore the application of Fuzzy TOPSIS in the diagnosis of Fibromyalgia disease. By defining relevant diagnostic criteria, converting them into fuzzy linguistic variables, and integrating expert opinions, this paper intends to develop a robust diagnostic model that can assist healthcare providers in identifying Fibromyalgia with greater accuracy. Through a comprehensive literature review and empirical analysis, this study will demonstrate the potential of Fuzzy TOPSIS as a valuable tool in the diagnosis of Fibromyalgia.

Motivation for the Study

Complexity of Fibromyalgia Syndrome (FMS)

FMS is a complex and multifaceted disorder characterized by various symptoms such as widespread pain, fatigue, and cognitive impairments. The intricate nature of FMS poses challenges for accurate prognosis and individualized treatment planning.

Subjectivity in Clinical Assessments

Clinical assessments of FMS often involve subjective elements, including patient-reported symptoms and expert opinions. Integrating a systematic decision-making approach can enhance the objectivity of prognosis, leading to more reliable outcomes.

Need for Personalized Medicine

The variability in symptoms and responses to treatments among FMS patients underscores the importance of personalized medicine. Aiding in prognosis using advanced methodologies can contribute to tailoring treatment plans to individual patient needs.

Research Gaps

Limited Decision Support Systems for FMS Prognosis

There is a gap in the availability of comprehensive decision support systems specifically designed to aid in the prognosis of FMS. Existing methods may not adequately capture the complexity and uncertainty inherent in FMS cases.

Integration of MCDM and Fuzzy Logic in FMS Prognosis

The literature lacks research that integrates Multi-Criteria Decision-Making (MCDM) methods, such as TOPSIS, with fuzzy logic for FMS prognosis. This fusion has the potential to address both objective clinical data and subjective assessments effectively.

Transparent and Explainable Decision-Making

Many existing models lack transparency and explainability in the decision-making process. There is a need for methodologies that not only provide accurate prognoses but also offer insights into the factors influencing the decisions, promoting trust among healthcare professionals and patients.

Contributions of This Study

- The research contributes by proposing a comprehensive set of criteria that considers clinical, psychological, and physiological factors relevant to FMS. This holistic approach provides a more thorough evaluation of prognosis.
- The fusion of MCDM TOPSIS with fuzzy logic allows for a more nuanced representation of uncertainty and linguistic assessments, the result is a decision-support architecture that scales with the ever-evolving nature of FMS.
- The proposed methodology aims to enhance transparency in the decision-making process, offering clear insights into how prognoses are determined. Additionally, the personalized nature of the approach ensures that individual patient needs and experiences are taken into account.
- The research contributes by presenting preliminary results of applying the proposed methodology to a sample of FMS cases. These initial findings indicate promising outcomes, demonstrating the potential effectiveness of the integrated MCDM TOPSIS and fuzzy logic approach.
- Sensitivity analysis is performed to ensure that the integrated MCDM TOPSIS and fuzzy logic model can adapt to evolving conditions, making it a valuable tool for personalized and adaptive decision-making in the context of Fibromyalgia prognosis

In summary, the research addresses critical gaps in FMS prognosis methodologies, introducing an innovative approach that combines MCDM TOPSIS with fuzzy logic to provide a holistic, transparent, and personalized decision support system. This paper is organized into the following sections, in section 2 literature review is presented, section 3 represents the theoretical background of this study, section 4 represents methodology followed along with an empirical study and section 5 concludes this paper.

LITERATURE REVIEW

Several investigations have utilized fuzzy TOPSIS in the identification of Fibromyalgia based on various criteria and data origins. For instance, (Akram, M et al. 2019) employed bipolar fuzzy TOPSIS and bipolar fuzzy ELECTRE-I methodologies to diagnose Fibromyalgia considering 18 symptoms and 10 diseases. They utilized bipolar fuzzy sets to express both positive and negative facets of symptoms and diseases. A comparison with other FMCDM approaches revealed the superior credibility and accuracy of their techniques. (Ahmad, S. A., & Mohamad, D, 2017) applied fuzzy TOPSIS and simplified fuzzy TOPSIS for diagnosing Fibromyalgia based on 11 symptoms and 5 diseases. Triangular fuzzy numbers were used to indicate symptom severity and criterion weights. Their methodologies exhibited greater consistency and robustness compared to crisp TOPSIS. FMCDM (Fuzzy Multi-Criteria Decision Model) is employed to determine the optimal site considering a blend of factors, while FTOPSIS (Fuzzy Techniques of Order Preference Using Similarities to the Perfect Solution) is utilized to rank potential alternative sites (Al Mohamed et al., 2023). Pal et al. (2019) conducted a study aiming to establish connections between SBI, depression, Fibromyalgia, and chronic fatigue syndrome (CFS) among rheumatologists in a clinical environment. Naeem, K et al. (2021) focused on predicting PCOS alongside mental health using fuzzy inference and SVM. An Integrated Hesitant Fuzzy Language MCDM (HFL) approach assesses smart health technologies based on research (Büyüközkan, G, 2020) employing hesitant fuzzy linguistic MCDM techniques. Another research (Bhaskar, 2020) implements a fuzzy embedded TOPSIS methodology to tackle MCDM-related issues. A case study with experimental datasets was presented to enhance the understanding of the proposed method. Kutlu Gündoğdu (2019) introduces an intuitionistic fuzzy TOPSIS methodology for selecting the appropriate sustainable supplier, encompassing nine criteria and 30 sub-criteria, for manufacturers of automotive spare parts. A novel approach for choosing an advanced manufacturing system involves integrating AHP with TOPSIS using spherical fuzzy sets (Mathew, M, 2020). Some of the noted works based on fuzzy logic include (Devadas, R. M et al., 2023) and (Devadas, Raghavendra and G. N. Srinivasan, 2019).

THEORETICAL BACKGROUND

In this section, theoretical basis of all the methods used in this study are illustrated.

Multi-Criteria Decision-Making

MCDM, or Multi-Criteria Decision-Making, is a dynamic field in decision science that strives to support decision-makers in their process of assessing and choosing between alternatives by taking into account various criteria or goals (Hwang, C. L., & Yoon, K, 1981). Its key goals include supplying a well-defined method for decision-making, addressing a diverse range of criteria, and simplifying the discovery of optimal solutions in intricate decision scenarios. Some of the MCDM techniques are detailed below:

- **Analytic Hierarchy Process (AHP):** AHP is a structured method for hierarchically decomposing complex decisions (Saaty, T. L, 1980). It employs pairwise comparisons to derive criteria weights and has been widely used in fields like project selection and resource allocation.
- **ELECTRE**: ELECTRE methods focus on outranking relations to compare alternatives (French, S, 1996). These methods accommodate imprecise data and have found applications in areas such as environmental management and project evaluation.
- **Weighted Sum Model:** The weighted sum model aggregates criteria scores using predefined weights (Keeney, R. L., & Raiffa, H, 1976). It is straightforward and widely applicable, particularly when the decision-maker can articulate the position of each criterion.
- **Fuzzy Decision-Making**: Fuzzy decision-making integrates fuzzy set theory to handle uncertainties inherent in decision problems (Zadeh, L. A, 1965). It can be used to represent abstract or qualitative data and is helpful in cases where exact numerical information may not be available.

Some of the real-world applications of MCDM methods are illustrated below:

- **Systematic Evaluation:**
    - o   Objective: Develop a systematic approach for evaluating alternatives based on multiple criteria.
    - o   Example: In selecting a new manufacturing process, consider factors like cost, efficiency, environmental impact, and safety simultaneously.
- **Handling Diverse Criteria:**

o   Objective: Address decision problems with diverse and often conflicting criteria.

o   Example: In urban planning, evaluate potential locations for a new park considering criteria such as accessibility, environmental impact, and community engagement.

- **Optimal Solution Identification:**
  o   Objective: Facilitate the identification of optimal solutions aligned with decision-makers' preferences.
  o   Example: Choose the most suitable supplier by considering criteria like cost, reliability, and delivery time in procurement decisions

- **Trade-off Analysis:**
  o   Objective: Enable decision-makers to analyze trade-offs between competing criteria.
  o   Example: When selecting a transportation mode, weigh factors such as cost, speed, and environmental impact to make informed trade-offs.

- **Preference and Priority Setting:**
  o   Objective: Allow decision-makers to express preferences and set priorities among criteria.
  o   Example: In healthcare resource allocation, prioritize criteria like patient outcomes, cost-effectiveness, and accessibility.

- **Handling Uncertainty:**
  o   Objective: Address uncertainty in decision problems.
  o   Example: In investment decisions, account for uncertainties by using fuzzy logic to model imprecise data related to market conditions.

- **Adaptive Decision-Making:**
  o   Objective: Develop methodologies for adaptive decision-making in dynamic environments.
  o   Example: In supply chain management, adapt decision criteria and weights based on changes in market conditions, demand, and supplier performance.

Recent developments in MCDM include:

- **Integration with Machine Learning (ML):** Researchers are exploring the integration of ML techniques, such as neural networks and clustering algorithms, to enhance the predictive capabilities of MCDM models and automate decision processes.
- **Dynamic Decision-Making**: New methodologies address dynamic decision environments where criteria or preferences evolve over time. Adaptive

MCDM approaches are crucial for real-world scenarios with changing conditions

- **Interdisciplinary Applications:** MCDM has expanded its reach into interdisciplinary domains such as sustainability, healthcare, and finance. Researchers are developing tailored MCDM frameworks to address specific challenges in these diverse fields.
- **Advanced Sensitivity Analysis:** Sensitivity analysis in MCDM is evolving to provide more nuanced insights into the influence of variations in criteria weights and data on decision outcomes.

TOPSIS Method

The TOPSIS is a multi-criteria decision-making technique that was developed in the early 1980s. Since then, it has become a widely used tool for decision making in many industries, such as business, engineering and environmental sciences, to choose the best option from a wide range of alternatives based on a variety of factors. The TOPSIS method is one of the widely used MCDM techniques that assists decision-makers in ranking alternatives by considering their proximity to both the ideal and anti-ideal solutions. TOPSIS incorporates the concept of relative closeness to ideal solutions, making it especially suitable for situations where multiple conflicting criteria are involved. It balances the trade-offs between maximizing the benefits of the chosen alternative and minimizing deviations from the ideal values for each criterion. Here's an introduction to TOPSIS along with the key equations involved:

Definition 1: Decision Matrix (A)

$$A = [a_{ij}]$$

The above matrix represents the original data matrix containing the performance values of alternatives on different criteria. Each element a_{ij} denotes the performance of alternative i on criterion j.

Definition 2: Normalized Decision Matrix

$$n_{ij} = \frac{a_{ij}}{\sqrt{\Sigma_{i=1}^{m}(a_{ij})^2}} \tag{1}$$

Normalizes the decision matrix (A) to bring all criteria to a common scale. The normalized matrix n_{ij} ensures that no single criterion dominates the decision-making process.

Definition 3: Weighted Normalized Decision Matrix (W)

$$w_{ij} = n_{ij} \times b_j \qquad (2)$$

Reflects the relative importance of each criterion by applying weights to the normalized matrix (N). The weighted matrix w_{ij} considers both the importance of each criterion and the performance of each alternative.

Definition 4: Ideal Solution (I+)

$$i_j^+ = max(w_{ij}), \textit{ for all } i = 1, 2, ..., m \qquad (3)$$

The eqn (3) identifies the best performance on each criterion by finding the maximum value in each column of the weighted matrix (W). The ideal solution i_j^+ represents the most desirable value for criterion j.

Definition 5: Anti-Ideal Solution (I-)

$$i_j^- = min(w_{ij}), \textit{ for all } i = 1, 2, ..., m \qquad (4)$$

The above eqn identifies the worst performance on each criterion by finding the minimum value in each column of the weighted matrix (W). The anti-ideal solution i_j^- represents the least desirable value for criterion j.

Definition 6: Distance to Ideal Solution (D+)

$$d_i^+ = \sqrt{\Sigma_{j=1}^n \left(w_{ij} - i_j^+ \right)^2} \qquad (5)$$

Eqn (5) measures the distance of each alternative to the ideal solution. d_i^+ calculates the Euclidean distance between the performance of alternative i and the ideal solution across all criteria.

Definition 7: Distance to Anti-Ideal Solution (D-)

$$d_i^- = \sqrt{\Sigma_{j=1}^n \left(w_{ij} - i_j^- \right)^2} \qquad (6)$$

Eqn (6) measures how close each alternative is to the anti-ideal solution. d_i^- calculates the Euclidean distance between the performance of alternative i and the anti-ideal solution across all criteria.

Definition 8: Relative Closeness (C)

$$c_i = \frac{d_i^-}{d_i^+ + d_i^-} \qquad (7)$$

The above eqn calculates the relative closeness of each alternative to the ideal solution. c_i represents the proportion of the distance to the anti-ideal solution compared to the total distance (sum of distances to ideal and anti-ideal solutions) for alternative i. A higher c_i indicates a more favorable ranking.

These equations collectively constitute the TOPSIS method, providing a systematic approach to multi-criteria decision-making by considering both the positive and negative aspects of each alternative relative to ideal and anti-ideal solutions.

Fuzzy Logic

Fuzzy logic is a mathematical framework for dealing with uncertainty, imprecision, and vagueness in data and decision-making. Unlike classical or Boolean logic, which operates in binary terms of true or false, fuzzy logic allows for the representation of partial truth or membership in a gradual and continuous manner. Fuzzy logic is based on the concept of fuzzy sets, which were introduced by [17] in the 1960s. Fuzzy sets extend classical set theory by allowing elements to belong to a set to varying degrees, rather than in an all-or-nothing fashion. This degree of membership is represented by a value between 0 and 1, where 0 indicates no membership, 1 indicates full membership, and values in between signify partial membership. Fuzzy logic provides a framework for dealing with linguistic variables and rules. It is especially well-suited for systems and problems where exact numerical values are difficult to determine or where human expertise and natural language are involved. Fuzzy logic has been widely applied in various fields, including control systems, artificial intelligence, decision-making, and pattern recognition.

Fuzzy TOPSIS Method

Fuzzy TOPSIS (Technique for Order Preference by Similarity to Ideal Solution) is an extension of the classic TOPSIS method, specifically designed to handle decision-making problems where the criteria and data involve uncertainty, imprecision, or ambiguity represented using fuzzy sets. It is a powerful tool in multi-criteria decision-making (MCDM) that allows for the inclusion of linguistic assessments and fuzzy data.

The steps involved in the Fuzzy TOPSIS method are as follows:

Definition 1: Fuzzy Decision Matrix (X)

The fuzzy decision matrix (X) represents the alternatives evaluated against multiple criteria using fuzzy linguistic terms. Each row corresponds to an alternative, and each column corresponds to a criterion. The matrix is represented as follows,

	C1	C2	C3	...	Cm
A1	$(T1, \mu1)$	$(T2, \mu2)$	$(T3, \mu3)$	...	$(Tk, \mu k)$
A2	$(T1, \mu1)$	$(T2, \mu2)$	$(T3, \mu3)$	...	$(Tk, \mu k)$
A3	$(T1, \mu1)$	$(T2, \mu2)$	$(T3, \mu3)$	...	$(Tk, \mu k)$
...	...	...	...	...	...
An	$(T1, \mu1)$	$(T2, \mu2)$	$(T3, \mu3)$	...	$(Tk, \mu k)$

$$(8)$$

Where,

n = number of alternatives

m = number of criteria

$(Ti, \mu i)$ = fuzzy linguistic term and its membership degree for the i-th alternative and j-th criterion.

Definition 2: Fuzzy Weights (W)

Assign fuzzy weights (W) to each criterion to represent their relative importance. Fuzzy weights are typically represented using fuzzy linguistic terms.

Definition 3: Normalized decision matrix

The relation between the positive ideal solutions and the negative ideal solutions can be used to calculate the normalized decision matrix as per below equations (2) and (3).

Positive ideal solution:

$$\tilde{r}_{ij} = \left(\frac{u_{ij}}{w_j^*}, \frac{v_{ij}}{w_j^*}, \frac{w_{ij}}{w_j^*}\right); c_j^* = \max_i c_{ij} ; \tag{9}$$

Negative ideal solution:

$$\tilde{r}_{ij} = \left(\frac{u_j^-}{w_{ij}}, \frac{u_j^-}{v_{ij}}, \frac{u_j^-}{u_{ij}}\right); u_j^- = \min_i u_{ij} ; \tag{10}$$

Definition 4: Design the Weighted Normalized Decision Matrix

Since each criterion has a different weight, the weighted normed decision matrix is calculated by multiplying each criterion's weight in the normalized fuzzy decision matrix by the following formula:

$$\tilde{d}_{ij} = \tilde{r}_{ij} . \tilde{w}_{ij} \tag{11}$$

Where $\tilde{w}_{ij}$ represents weight of criterion c_j

Definition 5: Identify the fuzzy positive ideal solution (FPIS, I*) and the fuzzy negative ideal solution (FNIS, I^-)

The FPIS and FNIS of the alternatives can be defined as follows:

$$I^* = \{\tilde{d}_1^*, \tilde{d}_2^*, ..., \tilde{d}_n^*\} = \left\{ \left(\max_j d_{ij} \Big| i \in M \right), \left(\min_j d_{ij} \Big| i \in N \right) \right\}$$

$$I^- = \{\tilde{d}_1^-, \tilde{d}_2^-, ..., \tilde{d}_n^-\} = \left\{ \left(\min_j d_{ij} \Big| i \in M \right), \left(\max_j d_{ij} \Big| i \in N \right) \right\}$$

Where $\tilde{d}_i^*$ is the max value of i for all the alternatives and $\tilde{d}_1^-$ is the min value of i for all the alternatives. M and N represent the positive and negative ideal solutions, respectively.

Definition 6: Determine the distance from each of the alternatives to the ideal fuzzy positive I* and the distance from each alternative to the ideal fuzzy negative I^-.

$$Z_i^* = \sum_{j=1}^{n} di(\tilde{d}_{ij}, \tilde{d}_j^*) i = 1, 2, ..., m \tag{14}$$

$$Z_i^- = \sum_{j=1}^{n} di(\tilde{d}_{ij}, \tilde{d}_j^-) i = 1, 2, ..., m \tag{15}$$

The *di* distance between two triangular fuzzy numbers, a(u1, v1, w1) and b(u2, v2, w2), can be calculated as:

$$di_d(\overline{M}_1, \overline{M}_2) = \sqrt{\frac{1}{3}\left[(u_1 - u_2)^2 + (v_1 - v_2)^2 + (w_1 - w_2)^2\right]} \tag{16}$$

Where, $di\left(\tilde{d}_{ij}, \tilde{d}_j^*\right)$ and $di\left(\tilde{d}_{ij}, \tilde{d}_j^-\right)$ are crisp numbers

Definition 7: Rank the alternatives according to the closeness coefficient as per equation (17)

The degree of similarity between the two alternatives can be determined by calculating the closeness coefficient.

$$CLC_i = \frac{Z_i^-}{Z_i^+ + Z_i^-} \tag{17}$$

PROPOSED METHODOLOGY

The proposed methodology is represented in Figure 1.

Figure 1. Proposed methodology

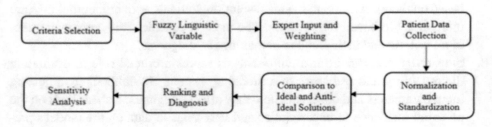

The following are the steps performed:

1. **Criteria Selection:** The process begins with identifying and selecting relevant criteria that can help in the diagnosis of Fibromyalgia. These criteria include patient-reported symptoms, physical examination findings, laboratory test results, and possibly even psychological assessments.
2. **Fuzzy Linguistic Variable:** The next step is to convert the selected criteria into fuzzy linguistic variables to represent the uncertainty and vagueness associated with Fibromyalgia diagnosis. For instance, symptoms like "widespread pain" and "fatigue" can be quantified using linguistic terms such as "mild," "moderate," and "severe".
3. **Expert Input and Weighting:** Here the inputs from a panel of medical experts who are experienced in diagnosing Fibromyalgia are gathered. These experts can assign weights to each criterion based on their clinical significance and relevance in the diagnosis process. Fuzzy linguistic variables can be used to express these weights.
4. **Patient Data Collection:** Collect patient data, including symptom severity scores, clinical examination results, and any relevant laboratory test values. The data is transformed into fuzzy linguistic variables to account for uncertainty.
5. **Normalization and Standardization:** Normalize and standardize the fuzzy linguistic variables to ensure that they are on a common scale for comparison. This step is essential to eliminate biases introduced by different measurement units.

6. **Comparison to Ideal and Anti-Ideal Solutions:** Calculate the distance between each patient's data and the ideal solution (representing a "healthy" state) and the anti-ideal solution (representing the worst-case scenario). Fuzzy TOPSIS will consider both criteria that should be maximized (e.g., symptom severity reduction) and criteria that should be minimized (e.g., misclassification risk).

7. **Ranking and Diagnosis:** Apply the Fuzzy TOPSIS method to rank patients based on their proximity to the ideal solution. Patients with higher rankings are more likely to have Fibromyalgia. The method considers the combined effect of all criteria and their weights in making the diagnosis.

8. **Sensitivity Analysis:** Sensitivity analysis serves a crucial role in evaluating the reliability and resilience of a model or system. By deliberately adjusting input parameters and observing how they affect outcomes, it sheds light on the potential influence of uncertainties and variations in data on the model's predictions and decisions. In essence, it offers valuable insights into the stability and effectiveness of a model.

In the following table, the high-level pseudocode is presented.

Algorithm 1. FibromyalgiaFuzzyTOPSIS

Input:
- Decision Matrix A (m x n)
- Criteria Weights B (1 x n)
- Fuzzy Logic Components (Normalized Decision Matrix N, Weighted Normalized Decision Matrix W, Ideal Solution I+, Anti-Ideal Solution I-)
- Number of Alternatives m
- Number of Criteria n
Output:
- Ranked list of alternatives based on TOPSIS with Fuzzy Logic
Procedure:
1. Apply fuzzy logic to model linguistic assessments in the Decision Matrix A.
For i = 1 to m
For j = 1 to n
Apply fuzzy logic to convert A[i][j] into linguistic assessments
End For
End For
2. Normalize the Decision Matrix A to obtain the Normalized Decision Matrix N.
For i = 1 to m
For j = 1 to n
Calculate: N[i][j] = A[i][j] / sqrt(sum(A[k][j]^2, for k=1 to m))
End For
End For

continued on following page

Algorithm 1. Continued

---

3. Weight the Normalized Decision Matrix N to obtain the Weighted Normalized Decision Matrix W.
For i = 1 to m
For j = 1 to n
Calculate: W[i][j] = N[i][j] * B[j]
End For
End For

---

4. Sensitivity Analysis:
a. Identify the Ideal Solution I+ and Anti-Ideal Solution I- for the original matrix.
For j = 1 to n
Calculate: I+[j] = max(W[i][j], for i=1 to m)
Calculate: I-[j] = min(W[i][j], for i=1 to m)
End For
b. Introduce small variations (+0.05 and -0.05) to the original matrix.
c. Repeat step 4a for the varied matrices.

---

5. Calculate the Euclidean distances to the Ideal Solution D+ and Anti-Ideal Solution D- for each alternative.
For i = 1 to m
Calculate: D+[i] = sqrt(sum((W[i][j] - I+[j])^2, for j=1 to n))
Calculate: D-[i] = sqrt(sum((W[i][j] - I-[j])^2, for j=1 to n))
End For

---

6. Calculate the Relative Closeness C for each alternative.
For i = 1 to m
Calculate: C[i] = D-[i] / (D+[i] + D-[i])
End For

---

7. Rank the alternatives based on the Relative Closeness C in descending order.
Output the ranked list of alternatives.
End Algorithm

The FibromyalgiaFuzzyTOPSIS algorithm integrates fuzzy logic into the TOPSIS method for enhanced prognosis in FMS. It begins by applying fuzzy logic to model linguistic assessments in the original decision matrix, subsequently normalizing it and obtaining a weighted normalized decision matrix. The algorithm then incorporates sensitivity analysis, introducing small variations to assess the stability of the model. Ideal and Anti-Ideal Solutions are identified for both the original and varied matrices, and Euclidean distances are computed. The Relative Closeness for each alternative is determined, leading to the ranking of alternatives based on their closeness coefficients. This algorithm combines the benefits of fuzzy logic and sensitivity analysis to provide a robust and nuanced approach to FMS prognosis. Algorithm 2 describes the sensitivity analysis performed.

Algorithm 2. *Fuzzy TOPSIS with sensitivity analysis*

Function FuzzyTOPSISWithSensitivityAnalysis(originalMatrix):
1. Normalize the decision matrix
2. Apply fuzzy logic to model linguistic assessments
3. Calculate fuzzy weighted normalized decision matrix
4. Identify positive (+0.05) and negative (-0.05) variations for sensitivity analysis
5. Initialize empty arrays for original and varied ranks
6. Loop for each variation (+0.05, -0.05):
a. Apply TOPSIS to the original and varied matrices
b. Calculate Closeness Coefficient and ranks for each patient
c. Append the ranks to the corresponding array
7. Display original and varied ranks for sensitivity analysis
8. Assess stability of ranks by comparing original and varied results
9. Output sensitivity analysis summary
End Function

The FuzzyTOPSISWithSensitivityAnalysis function initiates by normalizing the decision matrix and incorporating fuzzy logic to model linguistic assessments. It calculates the fuzzy weighted normalized decision matrix, followed by the identification of positive and negative variations for sensitivity analysis. Arrays for original and varied ranks are initialized, and a loop is executed for each variation, applying TOPSIS and calculating Closeness Coefficients. The function displays original and varied ranks, assessing the stability by comparing the results. The output includes a summary of sensitivity analysis, providing insights into the robustness of the TOPSIS method under small variations in input data.

Empirical Study

This study considers five patients in the form of alternatives and four criterions which are the symptoms to be looked in the course of Fibromyalgia syndrome and are ranked based on FUZZY TOPSIS method. Table 1 shows the type of criterion and weight assigned to each criterion. Table 2 depicts the fuzzy scale used in this paper.

Table 1. Criterion with weights

Name	Weight
Pain	(1.500,1.500,3.500)
Fatigue	(1.500,3.500,5.500)
Sleep Disturbance	(3.500,5.500,7.500)
Tender Points	(5.500,7.500,9.500)

Table 2. Fuzzy scale

Linguistic terms	L	M	U
Low Pain	0	0	0.5
Medium Pain	0	0.5	1
High Pain	0.5	1	1.5
Low Fatigue	1	1.5	2
Medium Fatigue	1.5	2	2.5
High Fatigue	2	2.5	3
Low Sleep Disturbance	2.5	3	3.5
Medium Sleep Disturbance	3	3.5	4
High Sleep Disturbance	3.5	4	4.5
Low Tender Points	4	4.5	5
Medium Tender Points	4.5	5	5.5
High Tender Points	5	5.5	6

Step 1: This paper considers three medical experts who provide weights in linguistic terms and the same is tabulated in tables [3-5]. The mean of all three experts' decisions is tabulated in Table 6.

Table 3. 1ˢᵗ expert's decision matrix

	Pain	Fatigue	Sleep Disturbance	Tender Points
Patient_1	1	4	9	10
Patient_2	1	4	7	11
Patient_3	3	5	8	10
Patient_4	2	6	8	12
Patient_5	1	6	9	12

Table 4. 2ⁿᵈ expert's decision matrix

	Pain	Fatigue	Sleep Disturbance	Tender Points
Patient_1	1	4	7	10
Patient_2	1	5	8	11
Patient_3	1	5	8	11
Patient_4	3	6	9	10
Patient_5	3	6	7	12

Table 5. 3rd expert's decision matrix

	Pain	Fatigue	Sleep Disturbance	Tender Points
Patient_1	3	4	7	10
Patient_2	2	5	8	10
Patient_3	1	4	9	11
Patient_4	1	6	8	12
Patient_5	3	6	7	11

Table 6. Mean decision matrix

	Pain	Fatigue	Sleep Disturbance	Tender Points
Patient_1	(0.16,0.33,0.83)	(1.00,1.50,2.00)	(2.83,3.33,3.83)	(4.00,4.50,5.00)
Patient_2	(0.00,0.16,0.66)	(1.33,1.83,2.33)	(2.83,3.33,3.83)	(4.33,4.83,5.33)
Patient_3	(0.16,0.33,0.83)	(1.33,1.83,2.33)	(3.16,3.66,4.16)	(4.33,4.83,5.33)
Patient_4	(0.16,0.50,1.00)	(2.00,2.50,3.00)	(3.16,3.66,4.16)	(4.66,5.16,5.67)
Patient_5	(0.33,0.66,1.16)	(2.00,2.50,3.00)	(2.83,3.33,3.83)	(4.83,5.33,5.83)

Step 2: In this step normalized decision matrix is tabulated as per eqns (2) and (3) and is shown in Table 7.

Table 7. Normalized decision matrix

	Pain	Fatigue	Sleep Disturbance	Tender Points
Patient_1	(0.14,0.28,0.71)	(0.33,0.50,0.66)	(0.68,0.80,0.92)	(0.68,0.77,0.85)
Patient_2	(0.00,0.14,0.57)	(0.44,0.61,0.77)	(0.68,0.80,0.92)	(0.74,0.82,0.91)
Patient_3	(0.14,0.28,0.71)	(0.44,0.61,0.77)	(0.76,0.88,1.00)	(0.74,0.82,0.91)
Patient_4	(0.14,0.42,0.85)	(0.66,0.83,1.00)	(0.76,0.88,1.00)	(0.80,0.88,0.97)
Patient_5	(0.28,0.57,1.00)	(0.66,0.83,1.00)	(0.68,0.80,0.92)	(0.82,0.91,1.00)

Step 3: The weight of each criterion in a normalized fuzzy decision matrix is multiplied by the weight of the normed decision matrix as per eqn (4) and is tabulated in Table 8.

Table 8. Weighted normalized matrix

	Pain	Fatigue	Sleep Disturbance	Tender Points
Patient_1	(0.21,0.42,2.49)	(0.50,1.75,3.67)	(2.38,4.39,6.89)	(3.77,5.78,8.14)
Patient_2	(0.00,0.21,2.00)	(0.66,2.13,4.27)	(2.38,4.39,6.89)	(4.08,6.21,8.68)
Patient_3	(0.21,0.42,2.49)	(0.66,2.13,4.27)	(2.66,4.84,7.50)	(4.08,6.21,8.68)

continued on following page

Table 8. Continued

	Pain	Fatigue	Sleep Disturbance	Tender Points
Patient_1	**(0.21,0.42,2.49)**	**(0.50,1.75,3.67)**	**(2.38,4.39,6.89)**	**(3.77,5.78,8.14)**
Patient_4	(0.21,0.64,2.99)	(1.00,2.91,5.50)	(2.66,4.84,7.50)	(4.40,6.64,9.23)
Patient_5	(0.42,0.85,3.50)	(1.00,2.91,5.50)	(2.38,4.39,6.89)	(4.55,6.85,9.50)

Step 4: Fuzzy positive ideal solution (FPIS, I*) and the fuzzy negative ideal solution ($FNIS, I^-$) are calculated as per eqns (5) and (6) and is depicted in Table 9.

Table 9. Positive and negative ideal solutions

	I*	I^{I^-}
Pain	(0.428,0.857,3.500)	(0.000,0.215,2.000)
Fatigue	(1.000,2.917,5.500)	(0.500,1.750,3.667)
Sleep Disturbance	(2.660,4.840,7.500)	(2.380,4.399,6.899)
Tender Points	(4.557,6.857,9.500)	(3.772,5.786,8.143)

Step 5: The distance between each alternative and FPIS besides the distance among each alternative and FNIS are correspondingly calculated as per eqns(7) and (8) and are tabulated in Table 10.

Table 10. Distance from I and I^- solutions*

	Distance from I*	Distance from I^-
Patient_1	3.485	0.336
Patient_2	2.95	0.867
Patient_3	2.158	1.663
Patient_4	0.556	3.264
Patient_5	0.46	3.357

Step 6: In this step closeness coefficient and ranking of the alternatives as per eqn(10)

The most suitable alternative is the one that is the closest to the I* and the most distant from the I^-. The closeness ratio of each alternative, as well as its ranking order, is presented in Table 11. The closeness coefficient graph is depicted in Figure 2.

Table 11. Closeness coefficient

	CLC_i	Rank
Patient_1	0.088	5

continued on following page

Table 11. Continued

	CLC_i	Rank
Patient_2	0.227	4
Patient_3	0.435	3
Patient_4	0.854	2
Patient_5	0.88	1

As per Table 11. Patient number 5 ranks first which infers that he/she is more suspected of possessing Fibromyalgia and a treatment plan has to be initiated, further patient number 1 ranks number 5 and has the least possibility of possessing Fibromyalgia syndrome.

Figure 2. Closeness coefficient graph

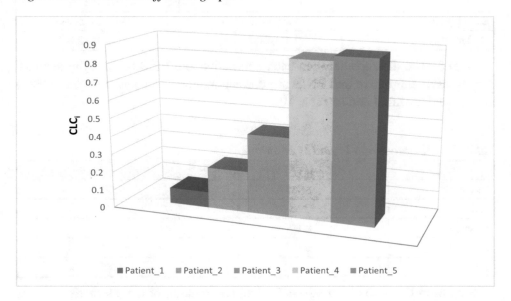

Sensitivity Analysis

As per algorithm 2, sensitivity analysis is incorporated to assess the impact of small variations on the Ideal Solution I+ and Anti-Ideal Solution I- for the original and varied matrices. This step helps evaluate the stability of the TOPSIS method in the face of uncertainties or variations in input data. The normalized matrix from Table 7 is considered and variations of (+0.05) and (-0.05) is added which is tabulated in Tables 12-13.

Table 12. Positive variation (+0.05)

	Pain	Fatigue	Sleep Disturbance	Tender Points
Patient_1	**(0.19,0.33,0.76)**	**(0.38,0.55,0.71)**	**(0.73,0.85,0.97)**	**(0.73,0.82,0.90)**
Patient_2	(0.05,0.19,0.62)	(0.49,0.66,0.82)	(0.73,0.85,0.97)	(0.79,0.87,0.96)
Patient_3	(0.19,0.33,0.76)	(0.49,0.66,0.82)	(0.81,0.93,1.05)	(0.79,0.87,0.96)
Patient_4	(0.19,0.47,0.90)	(0.71,0.88,1.05)	(0.81,0.93,1.05)	(0.85,0.93,1.02)
Patient_5	(0.33,0.62,1.05)	(0.71,0.88,1.05)	(0.73,0.85,0.97)	(0.87,0.96,1.05)

Table 13. Negative variation (-0.05)

	Pain	Fatigue	Sleep Disturbance	Tender Points
Patient_1	**(0.09,0.23,0.66)**	**(0.28,0.45,0.61)**	**(0.63,0.75,0.87)**	**(0.63,0.72,0.80)**
Patient_2	(-0.05,0.09,0.52)	(0.39,0.56,0.72)	(0.63,0.75,0.87)	(0.69,0.77,0.86)
Patient_3	(0.09,0.23,0.66)	(0.39,0.56,0.72)	(0.71,0.83,0.95)	(0.69,0.77,0.86)
Patient_4	(0.09,0.37,0.80)	(0.61,0.78,0.95)	(0.71,0.83,0.95)	(0.75,0.83,0.92)
Patient_5	(0.23,0.52,0.95)	(0.61,0.78,0.95)	(0.63,0.75,0.87)	(0.77,0.86,0.95)

The Coefficient and Ranks were recalculated using the original (Table 11) and the two varied matrices, the fuzzy TOPSIS method, and the results are tabulated in Tables 14 and 15.

Table 14. Positive variation (+0.05) closeness coefficient and ranks

	CLC_i	Rank
Patient_1	0.090	5
Patient_2	0.228	4
Patient_3	0.436	3
Patient_4	0.855	2
Patient_5	0.881	1

Table 15. Negative variation (-0.05) closeness coefficient and ranks

	CLC_i	Rank
Patient_1	0.086	5
Patient_2	0.225	4
Patient_3	0.432	3
Patient_4	0.851	2
Patient_5	0.877	1

The original fuzzy TOPSIS method ranks patients based on their Closeness Co-efficient, with Patient_5 being the most preferred and Patient_1 the least preferred. The positive variation results in slight increases in the Closeness Coefficient for all patients, leading to minimal changes in rankings. The negative variation results in slight decreases in the Closeness Coefficient for all patients, again leading to minimal changes in rankings. The sensitivity analysis plot is illustrated in Figure 3.

Figure 3. Sensitivity analysis result

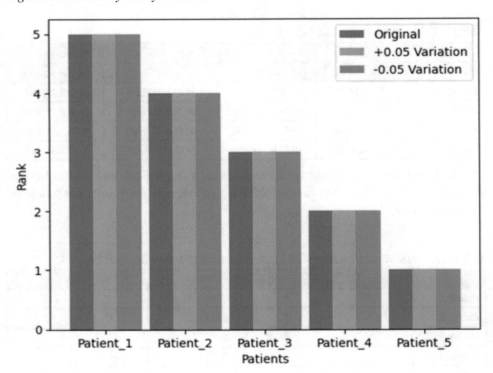

The provided plot visually represents the changes in ranks for each patient with both positive (+0.05) and negative (-0.05) variations applied to the normalized de-cision matrix in the fuzzy TOPSIS method. The plot illustrates that the introduced variations have a limited impact on the overall ranking of patients, confirming the stability of the original ranking.

CONCLUSION

In conclusion, this research successfully employed the Multi-Criteria Decision-Making (MCDM) Technique for Order Preference by Similarity to Ideal Solution (TOPSIS) method, fused with fuzzy logic, to enhance the prognosis of Fibromyalgia Syndrome (FMS). The comprehensive set of criteria, spanning clinical, psychological, and physiological factors, was rigorously evaluated using fuzzy logic to account for the inherent uncertainty in clinical assessments. The application of the MCDM TOPSIS method resulted in the following notable outcomes: The original fuzzy TOPSIS analysis identified Patient 5 with the highest Closeness Coefficient of 0.880 as more likely to be detected with FMS, while Patient 1, with a Closeness Coefficient of 0.088, was considered less prone to the syndrome. The sensitivity analysis introduced small variations of +0.05 and -0.05 to the normalized decision matrix. However, the impact on ranks was minimal, indicating the stability of the original prognosis. Despite the successful application of the methodology, limitations should be acknowledged: The study lacked external validation, and the model's performance was not tested on an independent dataset. Future studies should consider external validation to assess the generalizability of the proposed approach, explore the integration of biomarkers and advanced imaging techniques to enhance the objectivity of clinical data and further refine the prognostic model, investigate the integration of machine learning algorithms to enhance the predictive capabilities of the model leveraging a broader range of data sources.

REFERENCES

Ahmad, S. A., & Mohamad, D. (2017). A comparative analysis between fuzzy topsis and simplified fuzzy topsis. *AIP Conference Proceedings*, 040072. 10.1063/1.4995904

Akram, M., Shumaiza, , & Arshad, M. (2019). Bipolar fuzzy TOPSIS and bipolar fuzzy ELECTRE-I methods to diagnosis. *Computational & Applied Mathematics*, 39(1), 7. 10.1007/s40314-019-0980-8

Al Mohamed, A. A., Al Mohamed, S., & Zino, M. (2023). Application of fuzzy multicriteria decision-making model in selecting pandemic hospital site. *Future Business Journal*, 9(1), 14. 10.1186/s43093-023-00185-5

Bellato, E., Marini, E., Castoldi, F., Barbasetti, N., Mattei, L., Bonasia, D. E., & Blonna, D. (2012). Fibromyalgia syndrome: Etiology, pathogenesis, diagnosis, and treatment. *Pain Research and Treatment*, 426130, 1–17. 10.1155/2012/42613023213512

Bennett, R. M., Jones, J., Turk, D. C., Russell, I. J., & Matallana, L. (2007). An internet survey of 2,596 people with Fibromyalgia. *BMC Musculoskeletal Disorders*, 8(1), 27. 10.1186/1471-2474-8-2717349056

Bhaskar, A. S., Khan, A., & Patre, S. R. (2020). Application potential of fuzzy embedded TOPSIS approach to solve MCDM based problems. *Intelligent Manufacturing*, 99-121. .10.1007/978-3-030-50312-3_5

Büyüközkan, G., & Mukul, E. (2020). Evaluation of smart health technologies with hesitant fuzzy linguistic MCDM methods. *Journal of Intelligent & Fuzzy Systems*, 39(5), 6363–6375. 10.3233/JIFS-189103

Devadas, R., & Srinivasan, G. N. (2019). Review Of Different Fuzzy Logic Approaches for Prioritizing Software Requirements. *International Journal of Scientific & Technology Research.*, 8(09), 296–298.

Devadas, R. M., Hiremani, V., Bidwe, R. V., Zope, B., Jadhav, V., & Jadhav, R. (2023). Identifying factors in congenital heart disease transition using fuzzy DEMATEL. *International Journal of Advanced Computer Science and Applications*, 14(12). 10.14569/IJACSA.2023.0141218

French, S. (1996). Multicriteria Methodology for Decision Aiding. *The Journal of the Operational Research Society*, 48, 1257–1258.

Galvez-Sánchez, C. M., & Reyes Del Paso, G. A. (2020). Diagnostic Criteria for Fibromyalgia: Critical Review and Future Perspectives. *Journal of Clinical Medicine*, 9(4), 1219. 10.3390/jcm904121932340369

Gerdle, B., Björk, J., Cöster, L., Henriksson, K., Henriksson, C., & Bengtsson, A. (2008). Prevalence of widespread pain and associations with work status: A population study. *BMC Musculoskeletal Disorders*, 9(1), 102. 10.1186/1471-2474-9-10218627605

Hwang, C., & Yoon, K. (1981). Methods for multiple attribute decision making. *Multiple Attribute Decision Making,* 58-191. Springer. .10.1007/978-3-642-48318-9_3

Hwang, C., & Yoon, K. (2012). *Multiple attribute decision making: Methods and applications a state-of-the-Art survey.* Springer Science & Business Media.

Keeney, R. L., & Raiffa, H. (1976). *Decisions with multiple objectives: Preferences and value tradeoffs.* Cambridge University Press.

Kutlu Gündoğdu, F., & Kahraman, C. (2019). Spherical fuzzy sets and spherical fuzzy TOPSIS method. *Journal of Intelligent & Fuzzy Systems*, 36(1), 337–352. 10.3233/JIFS-181401

Mathew, M., Chakrabortty, R. K., & Ryan, M. J. (2020). A novel approach integrating AHP and TOPSIS under spherical fuzzy sets for advanced manufacturing system selection. *Engineering Applications of Artificial Intelligence*, 96, 103988. 10.1016/j.engappai.2020.103988

Naeem, K., Riaz, M., & Karaaslan, F. (2021). A mathematical approach to medical diagnosis via pythagorean fuzzy soft TOPSIS, VIKOR and generalized aggregation operators. *Complex & Intelligent Systems*, 7(5), 2783–2795. 10.1007/s40747-021-00458-y

Pal, M., Arora, H. D., Kumar, V., & Kumar, D. S. (2019). Application of TOPSIS in the Diagnosis of Vector Borne Diseases. *International Journal of Engineering and Advanced Technology*, 8(6), 5217–5223. 10.35940/ijeat.F8585.088619

Saaty, T. L. (1988). The analytic hierarchy process, (2nd ed). New York: McGraw-Hill.

Wolfe, F., Ross, K., Anderson, J., Russell, I. J., & Hebert, L. (1995). The prevalence and characteristics of Fibromyalgia in the general population. *Arthritis and Rheumatism*, 38(1), 19–28. 10.1002/art.17803801047818567

Zadeh, L. A. (1965). Fuzzy Sets. *Information and Control*, 8(3), 338–353. 10.1016/S0019-9958(65)90241-X

Chapter 7
Applications, Requirements, Architectures, Security Issues and Emerging Motivation for Smarter Healthcare

S. Radha
https://orcid.org/0000-0002-7296-2132
Vivekanandha College of Engineering for Women, India

C. Visali
https://orcid.org/0009-0009-3052-0166
Vivekanandha College of Engineering for Women, India

C. Aparna
Sengunthar Engineering College, India

C. Aarthi
https://orcid.org/0000-0002-6000-2812
Sengunthar Engineering College, India

R. Logambal
Vivekanandha College of Engineering for Women, India

ABSTRACT

The healthcare industry has witnessed significant advancements in recent years, driven

DOI: 10.4018/979-8-3693-2268-0.ch007

Copyright © 2024, IGI Global. Copying or distributing in print or electronic forms without written permission of IGI Global is prohibited.

by the integration of technology and data analytics. Smarter healthcare systems aim to enhance the quality of patient care, improve efficiency, and reduce costs through the intelligent use of technology. This chapter explores existing models, proposes a new model, discusses the requirements and architectures for smarter healthcare systems, addresses security issues, and highlights the emerging motivations for adopting these solutions. One prominent model is the electronic health record (EHR) system, which enables the digital storage and sharing of patient medical records. Additionally, wearable devices and mobile health applications empower individuals to track their health, collect data, and receive personalized insights. A proposed model for smarter healthcare is the integration of artificial intelligence (AI) and machine learning (ML) algorithms. These technologies can analyze vast amounts of medical data, identify patterns, and provide accurate predictions and diagnoses.

INTRODUCTION

The population is growing at an exponential rate, making urbanization more challenging. Because of this, management of the following sectors is crucial: education, transportation, energy, healthcare, etc. Better administrative decision-making and implementation involve transparency, reliability, optimization, and monitoring.

Within a short period of time, healthcare technology has improved. In particular for communities, adult healthcare is crucial. For the community's older residents, Tomita et al. (2010) suggested integrating healthcare with smart homes. This method takes care of all the healthcare resources for older persons who remain at home. A sensor-enabled strategy for remote health condition monitoring was proposed by Aziz et al. (2016). Remote data transmission is possible with wireless sensors that assess temperature and blood pressure. The concerned medical professionals and teams can then review the information to look for ways to prevent sickness. The doctor will be informed right away if the data collected exceeds the worrying level. The healthcare study on disease detection was analyzed by Chui et al. (2017).

Technological advancements appear to be changing the healthcare. With the help of artificial intelligence and big data analysis heath care systems provide effective services in smart cities. The human condition necessitates the provision of healthcare. To facilitate the assessment of a patient's health, sensor-enabled IoT devices can be utilized. These devices can be used to analyze the patient's heart-bit rate and blood pressure value, as well as their oxygen saturation levels. Historical patient information can aid in a precise diagnosis. The location of doctors and nurses can be determined using sensors and paging devices, which can aid in the dispatch of emergency medical teams. Data generated by sophisticated medical and healthcare devices will be substantial. Because medical data is so sensitive, data security and privacy must be improved.

Existing Smart Healthcare Technologies

Smart healthcare is a broad term encompassing a variety of applications and technologies that are designed to enhance patient care, streamline processes, and enable healthcare providers to make more informed decisions. It is also referred to as digital healthcare or eHealth, and is characterized by the incorporation of technology and data into healthcare systems in order to enhance efficiency, access, and quality. The following are some of the key concepts associated with smart healthcare:

1. Electronic Health Record:
    - Electronic health records (EHRs) are the data that a patient has about themselves. They have all the info they need, like their medical history, what their diagnosis was, what medications they're taking, how they're being treated, when they got their immunizations, if they have any allergies, what radiology images they're seeing, and even their lab results.
    - Health reports facilitate the sharing of information among healthcare providers, which leads to better coordination of care.
2. Telemedicine and Telehealth:
    - These technologies enable remote consultation and monitoring of patients, as well as allowing for diagnoses report over a distance using telecommunications technology.
    - Video consultations, remote monitoring devices, and mobile health apps fall under this category.
3. Wearable Devices:
    - Patient-worn devices are utilized to monitor a variety of health indicators, as well as physical activity and sleep patterns.
    - Wearables devices can be utilized for ongoing monitoring and early identification of health conditions.
4. Health Information Exchange (HIE):
    - HIE provides a secure platform for healthcare providers to exchange patient data electronically, facilitating improved coordination of care, reducing duplicate tests, and enhancing patient safety.
5. Artificial Intelligence and Machine Learning:
    - They are used in healthcare for tasks like image recognition, natural language processing, predictive analytics, and personalized treatment planning.

- They are able to analyze a vast amount of data to recognize patterns and make deductions, resulting in more precise diagnoses and treatment plans.
6. Healthcare IoT:
   - IoT devices in healthcare include smart medical devices like connected insulin pumps, blood glucose monitors, and other devices that can communicate with each other and with healthcare providers.
7. Remote Patient Monitoring:
   - This involves using technology to collect and monitor patient data outside of traditional healthcare settings. Especially for identifies the patients chronic conditions.
8. Block chain in Healthcare:
   - Block chain technology can be used to secure and streamline the sharing of patient records, ensuring privacy and security.
9. Predictive Analytics and Population Health Management:
   - These technologies use data to identify patterns, trends, and potential health risks in populations. They enable healthcare providers to proactively address health issues.
10. Robotic Process Automation (RPA):
    - Using software robots to take care of tedious tasks in healthcare administration like billing, setting up appointments, and handling claims.
11. Personalized Medicine:
    - Smart healthcare technologies can facilitate the personalized treatment plans and suggested previous medical history.

Healthcare systems are provides patient-centric, efficient technology and also gives authenticated access to the users who can benefit from these technologies.

Requirements for Intelligent Computing

The utilization of cutting-edge technologies through the use of intelligent computing is essential for the advancement of smart healthcare and data-driven approaches to enhance various aspects of healthcare delivery. There are many reasons why intelligent computing is essential in the context of smart healthcare:

1. Data Analytics and Predictive Modelling: Intelligent computing systems can process and analyze vast amounts of healthcare information, including electronic health records, medical imaging, and wearable device data. By applying machine learning and data analytics techniques, these systems can identify patterns, trends, and anomalies in the data.

2. Remote Patient Monitoring: Smart healthcare relies on intelligent computing to monitor patients remotely using connected devices and sensors. Intelligent algorithms can then analyse and identify the early warning signs of health issues and notify healthcare providers or patients themselves, facilitating timely interventions and reducing hospital readmissions.

3. Personalized Treatment Plans: Intelligent computing are facilitates for the patient treatment records based on their medical history and lifestyle. By leveraging machine learning algorithms, healthcare providers can tailor interventions, medications, and therapies to each patient's unique needs, maximizing treatment efficacy and minimizing adverse effects.

4. Clinical Decision Support: Intelligent computing systems can provide clinical decision support to healthcare professionals by offering evidence-based recommendations and guidelines at the point of care. These systems can help doctors make more accurate diagnoses, choose appropriate treatments, and avoid medication errors.

5. Efficient Resource Management: In healthcare facilities, intelligent computing can optimize resource allocation, such as staffing levels, bed availability, and equipment utilization. Predictive analytics can help hospitals anticipate patient admissions and discharges, ensuring that resources are allocated efficiently to meet demand.

6. Telemedicine and Telehealth: Telemedicine relies heavily on intelligent computing technologies for virtual consultations, diagnostic support, and remote monitoring. It enables healthcare access for patients in remote areas and provides convenience for both patients and healthcare providers.

7. Healthcare Fraud Detection: The utilization of intelligent computing technology can be utilized to identify fraudulent practices in healthcare billing and insurance claims. Machine learning algorithms are used to analyse the data suspicious patterns, and also reduces the fraud activities.

8. Drug Discovery and Development: Intelligent computing, particularly in the form of computational biology and bioinformatics, accelerates drug discovery by simulating and analyzing molecular interactions. This can lead to the identification of potential drug candidates more quickly and cost-effectively.

9. Public Health Surveillance: Intelligent computing helps monitor and respond to public health threats, such as disease outbreaks and bioterrorism events. The process involves examining data from various sources like social media and environmental information.

10. Intelligent Computing can facilitate patient engagement by delivering tailored health advice, notifications, and educational material via mobile applications and other digital channels. This can enable individuals to become more proactive in their health management.

Here are some specific examples of how intelligent computing is being used in smart healthcare today:

- AI-powered drug discovery is helping to develop new and more effective treatments for diseases.
- ML-based algorithms are being used to diagnose diseases such as cancer and Alzheimer's disease more accurately and efficiently than traditional methods.
- The use of wearable devices and mobile applications is enabling the collection of real-time patient health information, enabling the monitoring of patient health status and the early detection of potential issues.
- Telemedicine platforms are using video conferencing and other technologies to enable patients to consult with doctors and other healthcare professionals remotely.

Overall, intelligent computing systems are used to transforming data into the healthcare industry through automating tasks, analysing data, and providing insights. Intelligent computing can enhance the quality, effectiveness, and accessibility of healthcare service for all patients.

Healthcare-Driven Intelligent Computing Paradigms

To develop popularity of human life has improved with new innovations and techniques. Latest innovation of urban growth has to develop and evolve in technological aspects in human Healthcare. Intelligent computing provides human health development and security in every smart city. For growing population, chronical diseases and demographical changes are plays vital role in healthcare system especially in smart cities.

Healthcare-based intelligent computing solutions address these issues by leveraging some of the technologies, like healthcare IoT, data analytics, Artificial Intelligence in telemedicine and block chain (blockchain) methods. This paradigms are transformative and reforming the urban health care systems. Healthcare-driven intelligent computing paradigms plays vital role in secure futuristic smart cities by analyzing and exploring the health based research in human life. By achieving and evolving urban well beings health care sector can contribute their smart work (Tripathi et al., 2020).

Based on this smart work, health-care driven paradigm exposes their benefits, application statuaries, key technologies and challenges within the context of futuristic smart cities. Using various strategies, components and techniques this research can provide health based considerations, secure and sustainable urban environments. This research can contribute various methods and techniques also investigate health care paradigms followed by healthcare application system. The work mainly focused on growing population along with their secure urban well beings.

Healthcare IoT

Healthcare IoT has a powerful tool for healthcare application like patient care, remote monitoring device, activity awareness and fitness (Rong et al., 2020). This research also proposed new technologies for health monitoring remote systems which includes the key aspects are wearable health monitor, IoT enabled medical devices, and data collection and analysis.

A wearable health monitor serves as a unit for the collection of data. The data acquisition process is employed to acquire information regarding blood pressure, heart health, and body temperature. Medical devices that are enabled by IoT technology, whereas, collect the information from sensors to transmit through communication and networking. The collection and analysis of data includes the processing and analysis of the data (Khoo, 2011).

The health monitoring system architecture outlined in Figure 1 is composed of five stages: initial data collection, data retention, data administration, data analysis, and data visualization for the purpose of further investigation. Using IoT healthcare system provides innovation solution and also improves the overall efficiency within futuristic smart cities.

Wearable Health Monitors

Wearable health monitors one of the prime examples of health care systems, which is mainly designed for gathering real time heath relevant data and informed to the healthcare takers, patients and care providers. Recent day's different type of wearable monitors are available in human life such as smart watches, continuous glucose monitors, fitness monitor etc., each one are developed for health monitoring purposes.

Wearable health monitors are mainly collect and capture different type of health metrics which includes activity duration, heart bitrate, body blood pressure, human records, and electrocardiogram readings. Remote monitoring system plays vital role in human's life in case of abnormal situation through real time data and allowing real-time intervention. Health monitoring devices are developed mainly for elderly people and patient purpose. Which is care about patient health records and body fitness features like their active timing, step count, calories reading and proceed some of the personal healthcare ideas.

IoT- Enabled Medical Devices

IoT- enabled medical devices are essential forefront of patients, public healthcare services and elderly persons to enhance their quality of life. They performing self-care as well as providing automating data collection and transmission, enhanced outcome, reduced cost of care and enabling healthcare professional to make decision promptly using data driven records. IoT-enabled medical devices include smart thermometers, ingestible sensors, patient monitoring device and smart infusion pumps etc., however, evolving medical technology expose the nature of medical data, protect the patient information and incorporate robustness of the security measures.

Data Collection and Analysis

Data collection and analysis mainly focused on several features such as real-time data streams, data integration, big data analytics etc., A real-time data streams ensure data security and reliable transformation to its receiver such as cloud platform or electronic health records. Similarly, data integration provides holistic layout of a patient health details in comprehensive basis for their further treatment and consultation. In advanced method of predictive and machine learning modeling in big data analytics are identify the treads, optimized patient care, patterns, methods, anomalies and earliest stage of diagnoses.

IoT in healthcare system consist of wearable health monitors, IoT-enabled medical devices, and data collection and analysis has advanced and essential part in the health care industry. These innovations are mainly focused on patient outcomes, data-driven health care decisions, continuous patient monitoring progress as well as enhanced healthcare updating within the futuristic smart cities. However, they ensure the secure and privacy concerns for every individuals.

Big Data Analytics in Healthcare

The Internet of Things (IoT) is a rapidly developing technology in the field of smart city research, and it necessitates the utilization of large-scale data analytics in order to make them operational. This technology will generate a vast amount of data, which can be utilized to create and implement a variety of services in future-oriented smart cities. Big data analytics has evolve the tools and techniques which needed to analyze a lot of health related information and data efficiency. Big data is a major part of interconnecting public service, people in local governance to promote cooperation. Big data analytics plays a vital role in healthcare industry by improving patient health care, predicting disease outbreaks, and optimizing resource allocation. Figure 2 shows workflow of big data analytics which includes Health Data Processing, Disease Outbreak Prediction and Resource Allocation.

Health Care Data Processing

The primary purpose of health data processing is to reduce the occurrence of health-related disorders or illnesses in individuals. The primary components of this process are health professionals and health facilities, which are supported by systems such as medical imaging, laboratories, and e-health records. This is the foundation of big data analytics (Zhang et al., 2014).

Electronic health record (EHR) consists of million and more sample details related to healthcare systems. There are many components are available in this processing such as Electronic medical records store the patients clinical and medical information and patient personal health records. Over the next few years, an electronic health record (EHR) will collect, store and analyze medical imaging data as well as social-behavioral data and environmental data to enhance service, quality and cost effectiveness.

The big data in healthcare system categorize into three key aspects such as data integration, data cleaning and normalization and data warehousing. This method can generate alters message and share health related data. Data cleaning and normalization techniques are finds the errors and missing information in their records and normalize the data to give accurate and quality format.

Similarly, data warehouse stored huge volume of patient information, where as to improve the health outcomes and cost-effectiveness. With the help of data warehouse patient have easily access or retrieve data for further research.

Disease Outbreak Prediction

Using of big data in healthcare is to predict disease outbreaks especially in futuristic smart cities. Big data analytics has to analyze historical health data with the help of epidemiological models in real-time data and also helps to predicting the spread of disease, whether it is an infectious disease or a chronic illness, within an urban population. These systems can use different sources, such as hospital admissions and social media, as well as environmental factors. Early warnings can help healthcare authorities take preventative measures. The predictive analytics to better allocate resources as well as it can help hospitals and healthcare facilities prepare for a surge in patient admissions, and then allocate resources more efficiently.

Resource Allocation

Big data analytics provides quality healthcare in smart cities by optimizing resource allocation. It helps healthcare institutions plan for patient surges, forecast demand for services, and optimize staff scheduling. A healthcare system has to manage inventory and respond quickly in case of emergencies. Big data analytics aim to improve patient care, public health, and contribute to the overall health and wellbeing of urban residents. It is the foundation of modern healthcare. And enables healthcare providers and health authorities to analyze and process large amounts of data, anticipate disease events, and manage resources effectively.

Artificial Intelligence in Healthcare

Artificial intelligence (AI) technologies react like human a related mechanism that includes learning, thinking, adapting, engaging and sensing. It plays vital role in human's life for interpreting and decision making process. AI healthcare have the potential to transform many aspects of patient care, administrative process, and pharmaceutical organization. There are huge research proposal are implemented in AI healthcare where AI can perform better than humans at all key aspect task especially in diagnosing diseases (Kumar et al., 2023).

The utilization of healthcare applications, AI has experienced a surge in popularity and advancement due to the increasing computational capabilities of modern computers and the vast amount of data that can be collected and utilized. Artificial Intelligence (AI) has a variety of applications in medicine that can be leveraged across a broad spectrum of medical disciplines and critical areas where it has a significant impact on clinical decision-making and disease diagnosis, as well as the analysis and reporting of large volumes of data across a variety of modalities to diagnose disease and inform clinical decisions.

Medical Diagnosis and Imaging

AI has revolutionized in healthcare monitoring system mainly focused on medical diagnosis and imaging field. AI can analyze medical images with a lot more precision and speed than ever before, which helps doctors detect diseases like cancer earlier and make more accurate assessments. AI systems are act as a pattern recognition, which can spot anomalies and changes in medical images that can identify the diagnose conditions like cancer, fractures, and heart disease. AI model also assess patients care and identifies, if they're at risk for certain diseases, which can help doctors to personalized treatment plans.

AI-powered with catboats and virtual assistants used to access medical information, so that patients can get quick answers to their questions, set up appointments, and get basic medical advice instantly. Artificial Intelligence (AI) methodology used in a clinical trial to evaluate an artificial intelligence (AI) technology for medical use, particularly in the form of high-dimensional (or over-dimensional) diagnostic or predictive models using artificial deep neural networks, primarily from the perspectives of Clinical Epidemiology and Biostatistics.

Robotic Surgery

Artificial Intelligence (AI) has revolutionized research and development in the field of robotic surgery, transforming human initiated actions into a personalized surgical plan based on pre-surgical digital segmentation. Deep learning is a powerful AI application that has attracted a great deal of interest from numerous companies, leading to the development of intelligent robots. This text outlines the key steps in the processing and analysis of large-scale data to construct, define, and use deep-learning models to construct autonomous robots.

AI-powered robotic surgery is a revolutionary way of using AI in healthcare to make surgical procedures more precise and less invasive. Robotic systems, powered by AI algorithms have to delicate and complex tasks with minimal risk of complications and faster recovery times. Surgeons can get real-time feedback from the systems and adjust their capabilities if needed. AI-powered robotic surgery systems can be used in smart cities to help remote surgeons operate on patients in remote areas, which is especially useful in emergency situations or remote areas.

Predictive Analytics

Predictive analytics encompasses statistical models that are ranging from analytical to machine learning technique, whereas to create a historical data sets and make prediction about future or previously unknown events. AI is involved in the development of health care systems and providers' quality metrics for mortality, which require continuous monitoring and understanding of patient performance to determine if interventions to improve outcomes have been successful. "Big data" are generally large and complex data, which is complicated in traditional data processing applications or on-site database management tools.

Artificial Intelligence (AI) is a powerful tool in the healthcare sector in smart cities. Predictive analytics powered by AI, disease outbreak prediction, patient risk stratification, and resource allocation, healthcare services can be adapted to the requirements of metropolitan populations. An Artificial Intelligence-based model must be able to detect individuals, who are at a heightened risk for certain health conditions allowing healthcare providers to offer tailored preventive care and interventions to improve patient outcomes. This information can also be used to allocate resources during pandemics and other healthcare crises. The integration of AI into healthcare promises to provide improved accuracy, efficiency, and accessibility, leading to improved public health management and a greater sense of security for residents.

Metaverse

The Metaverse is now referred to as the Internet's future. Bansal et al. (2022) presented an exploration of the potential of Metaverse developments in the medical sector, which included the integration of telemedicine and clinical therapy, as well as medical education and mental health. Despite of benefits, some issues are needed to resolve before the use of Metaverse. These technologies necessitate high computer expenses, real-time service response, and the processing of enormous amounts of data. In order to be more cost-effective, the hardware should be made smart, adaptable, and tiny.

Privacy and Security

The utilization of user data for the collection and processing of information may pose a risk to the security and privacy of users, as evidenced by numerous research studies (Chen & Zhang, 2022; Zhao et al., 2022). We consider privacy and security to be one of the most essential requirements for the implementation of the Metaverse especially in healthcare sector. In real world, privacy and security concerns could cause havoc if they are not fully addressed. The hijacking of clones in the Metaverse makes it possible for criminals to carry out crimes, spread false information, or take the identities of users. Thus, judgments made in the virtual world may affect the people in real world (Slater et al., 2020).

Digital Currencies and Payments: There will be billions of users on this global online market, and consumers will be able to conduct quick and easy transactions using fiat money and cryptocurrencies. It will be difficult to guarantee the security of online transactions, though (Slater et al., 2020).

Block Chain for Health Data Security

Block chain technology has a prominent sector in healthcare system. This is used to protect sensitive and streamline data from the public sector. Main constrain of this block chain model is to provide a framework of smart cities also ensure data privacy and security. Block chain has been adopted by a wide range of stakeholders and technologies and is utilized in a wide range of contexts. Its provide platform for conducting business with simple and scalability also much easier one (Jing et al., 2014).

Block chain serves as a means of storage and preservation that facilitates the utilization of the immutable. This will allowed for secure and sensitive data storage in an off-chain repository for each patient. It contains various databases so that data encryption and integrity plays vital role in block chain healthcare security. The integration of Block chain with public cloud technologies will guarantee uniform Performance and data consistency. Furthermore, this integration will facilitate data transparency and even provide backward traceability to validate the data stored in off-chain repositories (Radha & Babu, 2018).

The implementation of a block chain healthcare system has been demonstrated in Figure 3. Data analytics is conducted on health care report to generate output that is enrolled in the block chain. Result are distributed to all participants in the network, such as the patient, physician, etc., through a decentralized virtual network, and is verified and validated by all nodes in the system. The output block is linked to chain, for further proceeding to form an unchangeable record.

Secure Health Records

Secure health records ensure security and confidentiality data. Block chain is used to create patients' health records in tamper-proof and immutable. Each system maintain immutable ledger for each patient. Once a record is created then this model cannot allowed either alter or delete options. Health care data is distributed across the network.

Data can be decentralized to protect unauthorized person to access or manipulate the information are challenging task. One of the important techniques in this process is cryptographic hashing, if anyone can alter the data that may reflect to other subsequent blocks. It is creating a reliable and secure audit trail. Using data integration and data security also monitor unauthorized access to patient records is nearly impossible due to block chain's encryption and decentralized nature. Block chain can sharing of health data between different healthcare providers using interoperability technique.

Data Privacy

Evolving the new technologies in healthcare industry, main two factors are provides cost-effective solutions: safety and privacy. Healthcare is narrow system, whereas the decision made in patient care carries potentially life-altering consequences. So guiding principle in medicine remains "do not harmful". When patient considering the safety, then another complicated concern is data privacy of their personal information. Whereas providing care is a core principle in this industry that includes digital foot print, data extraction and exploitation etc., so prevent the data healthcare systems ensure the safety measures.

Block chain technology plays vital role in health care industry. A block chain method allows anyone to access the data, but does not permit the data control to be written or altered. Only authorized users may access the data. Therefore this technology is more reliable and very secure in an immutable and decentralized network. In a healthcare system data sharing is common whereas retained the privacy and security is challenging task. Some of the key factors can enhance patient data privacy and security in healthcare industry.

Data Security and Immutability

Block chain is used to store an immutable data in secure way. Once the data is recorded on a block chain then it's impossible to alter or delete. Patient records are tamper proof secure, which helps to prevent counterfeiting and also their medical history are remain safe and secure on medi-ledger. This ledger uses in distributed to record entire medical product history from its manufacture.

Patient Ownership and Control

Patient care is an essential part in healthcare service delivery. Block chain can empower patients has to control over their health data. Patients can use cryptographic keys for access and revoke their records, even they have own control in patientory. It provides huge control access over their privacy and data.

Secure Data Sharing

MedRec is a decentralized platform that enables healthcare providers to securely share medical records with each other. Multidisciplinary patient management relies on the sharing of patient data among different specialists. Blockchain allows for the decentralisation of data sharing, allowing for temporary access to patient records when needed, as well as the audit trail to ensure transparency about who has access to the patient's records and when. MedRec stores patient records on a distributed ledger, which helps to ensure that only those who need the data have access to it and that it is kept safe.

Consent Management

Medical chain is a consent management platform that facilitates the automation of consent management through the use of block chain-enabled smart contracts. Through this platform, patients can establish rules for the use of their medical data, and healthcare providers can grant access to the data through smart contracts. This system ensures that data usage is in accordance with the patient's wishes, and that proper consent is sought and enforced when research or clinical trials require the patient's data.

Interoperability

Healthcare systems are often hindered by data silos, which impede the efficient exchange of information. Through the use of block chain technology, interoperability can be achieved by creating a single platform where multiple healthcare providers can access patient data in a secure manner. This can result in a more comprehensive level of care without compromising the privacy of data. Hyper ledger Fabric, a block chain platform, is designed to facilitate the development of interoperable healthcare records, which are stored on a distributed ledger and accessible to authorized healthcare providers.

Ultimately, the utilization of block chain technology in the medical field is in line with the pressing need to protect patient privacy. Block chain provides a secure platform for the exchange of data, the management of patient consent, and the creation of decentralized identity solutions, while also allowing for the efficient provision of healthcare services and medical research. The argument for data protection through block chain is compelling, as it offers a new way of managing healthcare data that places security and patient autonomy at the forefront. Nevertheless, its successful adoption necessitates collaboration between stakeholders, the assistance of regulatory authorities, and the refinement of the technology to ensure that it meets the specific needs of healthcare.

Challenges in Smart Healthcare System

Implementing smart healthcare technologies can offer numerous benefits, including improved patient care, reduced costs, and increased efficiency. However, there are several challenges associated with their implementation:

1. Data Security and Privacy: Healthcare systems deal with patient information, making them vulnerable to cyberattacks. Defending patient details from data breaches and adhering to data privacy regulations is a persistent challenge.

2. Interoperability: Smart healthcare technologies often involve a variety of devices and systems that need to communicate with each other. Ensuring seamless interoperability between different platforms, vendors, and data formats can be complex and costly.
3. Data Integration: Healthcare data is typically fragmented across various systems and formats. Integrating this data into a unified and usable format for analysis and decision-making is a significant challenge.
4. Regulatory Compliance: Healthcare technologies are subject to a variety of regulatory and compliance requirements, which may differ from one state to another. Maintaining up-to-date with changing regulations and adhering to compliance requirements can be time-consuming and expensive.
5. Resource Constraints: Many healthcare providers, especially smaller facilities, may lack the resources (financial, technical, or human) to implement and maintain smart healthcare technologies effectively.
6. User Adoption: Healthcare professionals may resist adopting new technologies due to concerns about usability, workflow disruption, or fear of job displacement. Ensuring that users are comfortable with and trained in using these technologies is crucial.
7. Accuracy and Reliability: The utilization of smart healthcare technologies, including wearables and remote monitoring devices, may raise concerns regarding the accuracy and dependability of data generated. Misinterpretation of data or false alarms can lead to unnecessary interventions or neglect of genuine issues.
8. Ethical Concerns: The utilization of AI and ML in healthcare may raise ethical issues, including the potential for algorithmic bias, lack of transparency in the decision-making process, and the possibility for automation to take the place of human judgement.
9. Costs: Implementing smart healthcare technologies can be expensive, and the return on investment may not be immediate. Healthcare organizations must carefully consider the costs and benefits.
10. Infrastructure and Connectivity: Reliable infrastructure, including high-speed internet and network connectivity, is necessary for the effective functioning of smart healthcare technologies. Rural or underserved areas may lack the necessary infrastructure.
11. Patient Trust: Patients need to trust that their data will be handled securely and used for their benefit. Building and maintaining patient trust in smart healthcare technologies is essential.
12. Health Disparities: The adoption of smart healthcare technologies can be uneven, resulting in inequalities in healthcare access and results. Some patients may lack access to the technology or the necessary skills to effectively utilize it.

13. Data Overload: The proliferation of data from smart healthcare technologies can overwhelm healthcare professionals. There's a need for tools and systems that can effectively filter and prioritize data for decision-making.
14. Long Implementation Timelines: Implementing smart healthcare technologies can be a time-consuming process, involving planning, vendor selection, customization, and training. Delays in implementation can hinder the realization of benefits.

In order to address these issues, there is a need for collaboration between providers, technology providers, policy makers, and regulatory authorities to foster an environment conducive to the successful deployment of intelligent healthcare technologies. Furthermore, continuous monitoring and adaptation of these technologies is necessary to ensure that they remain relevant to the ever-changing requirements of health care systems and patients.

Smart Healthcare Security

Security in smart healthcare systems is a multifaceted concern that involves protecting sensitive patient information, ensuring the integrity of medical devices, and safeguarding against potential cyber threats. Here are some critical security aspects in smart healthcare:

1. Patient Data Privacy and Confidentiality:
   - Encryption: Enforce End-to-End Encryption (E2E) for Data in Transit and at Rest to prevent Unauthorized Access.
   - Access Controls: Eliminate access to non-authorized personnel through the implementation of robust authentication and role based access control.
   - Data Minimization: Collect only necessary patient data and ensure that it is used for legitimate purposes.
2. Regulatory Compliance:
   - Compliance with Regulations: Enforce healthcare data protection legislation such as the Health Insurance Portability and Accountability Act (HIPAA) in the United States, the General Data Protection Regulation (GDPR) in the European Union, as well as local data protection acts.
3. Secure Communication:
   - Secure Protocols: It is recommended to utilize secure communication protocols such as HTTPS (secure connection protocol), SSL/TLS (secure standard layer 2.0), and secure messaging standards.
4. Device Security:

- Secure Boot Process: Ensure that medical devices have a secure boot process to prevent unauthorized firmware modifications.
- Regular Updates and Patching: It is recommended to implement security updates and patches for medical devices in order to address known security vulnerabilities.
- Device Authentication: In order to prevent unauthorized access to medical devices, it is necessary to implement robust authentication mechanisms.

5. Network Security:
   - Firewalls and Intrusion Detection Systems (IDS): Use firewalls for traffic control and identity and access control (IDS) to identify and address suspicious activity.
   - Network Segmentation: Separate networks to isolate sensitive data and systems from less secure areas.

6. Identity and Access Management (IAM):
   - Multi-Factor Authentication (MFA): Enforce the utilization of Macro Financial Assistance (MFA) for healthcare professionals who have access to sensitive systems or data.

7. Incident Response and Recovery:
   - Incident Detection and Reporting: Establish mechanisms to promptly detect and report security incidents.
   - Response Plan: Establish a comprehensive incident response strategy to reduce the impact of security incidents.
   - Data Backup and Recovery: It is important to ensure that critical data is regularly backed up and that a comprehensive recovery plan is in place in the event of data loss.

8. Physical Security:
   - Access Controls: Physical access to the data centre, server rooms, and medical equipment to authorized personnel only.
   - Surveillance and Monitoring: Monitor access to restricted areas through the use of security cameras and monitoring systems.

9. Security Audits and Assessments:
   - Regular Audits: Utilize security testing, penetration testing, and vulnerability testing to detect and resolve vulnerabilities.

By addressing these security aspects, smart healthcare systems can better protect patient information maintain the integrity of medical devices, cyber threats and breaches. Where as to adopt a holistic and proactive approach to security in order to effectively safeguard the healthcare ecosystem.

CONCLUSION

This chapter provides an overview of the current state-of-the-art technologies of Internet of Things (IoT), cloud computing and edge computing to enable more effective healthcare services. This technology monitors in-critical condition patients that necessitate continuous monitoring as opposed to the traditional manual monitoring system. Healthcare-Driven technology provides an advanced method for future scope. Many researches evolve exact solution for both public and private healthcare industries as well as existing technologies.

This chapter highlighted the recent updates and techniques are used also discussed important role for making health care development in urban smart cities. Security constraints are challenging task in this field. Secure monitoring system provides data privacy and reliability for patient records also gives alert where the patient conditions are changed abnormal case. These systems continuously capture patient health wise analytics and prediction using deep- leaning techniques.

After discharged from hospital the patient can be monitored through some IoT devices. This IoT and big data models are generally, cost effective and reliable one. In addition, patient data can be maintained in a repository for future healthcare references, and prescriptions. As an extension, health care research gives exact prototype for patient data analytics it can be helpful for any new emerging technologies.

Opportunities

Smart cities are focused to design and face different kind of challenges and opportunities also create unique impact on urban living. Data management in healthcare system had a huge amount of data collection so managing and maintaining of this data to be scalable and secured. Integrating numerous technologies and various health related systems from various vendors can be challenging and complex task. Ensure the system should be face interoperability and salability. Forming a digital and conventional infrastructure in a smart city, health care system can ensure the requirement and investments are the challenging issue. Similarly, these are less cost effective.

Huge amounts of healthcare data protection are being gathered allowed to share, which raises important concerns about data security. A continuous focus is on making is sure that healthcare information is insulated from cyber-attacks and illegal users. Enormous amounts of public health care information protection. Information can be obtained and communicated, which increases significant problems with the security of health records from cyber-attacks of health records from cyber-attacks and malicious access is a massive problem.

Numerous varieties of healthcare applications and devices are frequently used in urban smart cities. It can be challenging to attain flawless interoperability and integration in these components. Application Programming Interfaces are used to create standard data and file format in the network interoperability system. In data generation process in healthcare system must be reliable and accurate, whereas patient should take decision according to this data. Make sure quality of data is a challenging issue in a real world environment. Machine learning algorithms, data verification and validation process are used to improve data quality.

Using some new innovation is creating technical advancement a path between public and private sector through eco system. Sustainable investments can reduce environmental impact and cost. Also provide energy efficiency and renewable energy resources. Implementation of this smart city planning can help mitigate infrastructure challenges.

Smart cities can improve the medical accessibility with the help of IoT device, telemedicine and monitoring system. Similarly, advanced healthcare devices are easily identify early stages of disease and optimize the resource allocations etc., Data-driven technologies are used to analyze also improve the patient outcomes. Smart cities can serve hub for creating new innovation and health related researches.

Healthcare-driven intelligent computing paradigms in smart cities are offers number of opportunities and challenges that are related to privacy, integrity for the public trust policy. They also give varieties of health related decision making, data accessibility and privacy. So these challenges and opportunities can lead and maintain some innovative technologies in sustainable way.

REFERENCES

Kumar, , SKose, , USharma, , SKumar, , J. (2023). *Dynamics of Swarm Intelligence Health Analysis for the Next Generation*. IGI Global.

Aziz, K., Tarapiah, S., Ismail, S. H., & Atalla, S. (2016). Smart real-time health-care monitoring and tracking system using GSM/GPS technologies. *2016 3rd MEC International Conference on Big Data and Smart City (ICBDSC)*. IEEE. 10.1109/ICBDSC.2016.7460394

Bansal, G., Rajgopal, K., Chamola, V., Xiong, Z., & Niyato, D. (2022). Healthcare in Metaverse: A Survey on Current Metaverse Applications in Healthcare. *IEEE Access : Practical Innovations, Open Solutions*, 10, 119914–119946. 10.1109/ACCESS.2022.3219845

Chen, D., & Zhang, R. (2022). Exploring research trends of emerging technologies in health metaverse: A bibliometric analysis. SSRN *Electron. J*. 10.2139/ssrn.3998068

Chui, K., Alhalabi, W., Pang, S., Pablos, P., Liu, R., & Zhao, M. (2017). Disease diagnosis in smart healthcare: Innovation, technologies and applications. *Sustainability (Basel)*, 9(12), 2309. 10.3390/su9122309

Jing, Q., Vasilakos, A. V., Wan, J., Lu, J., & Qiu, D. (2014). Security of the internet of things: Perspectives and challenges. *Wireless Networks*, 20(8), 2481–2501. 10.1007/s11276-014-0761-7

Khoo, B. (2011). RFID as an Enabler of the Internet of Things: Issues of Security and Privacy. *Internet of Things (iThings/CPSCom),International Conference on and 4th International Conference on Cyber, Physical and Social Computing*. IEEE. 10.1109/iThings/CPSCom.2011.83

Radha, S., & Babu, C. (2018). An Enhancement of Cloud Based Sentiment Analysis and BDAAs Using SVM Based Lexicon Dictionary and Adaptive Resource Scheduling. *Journal of Computational and Theoretical Nanoscience*, 15(2), 437–445. 10.1166/jctn.2018.7107

Rong, G., Mendez, A., Bou Assi, E., Zhao, B., & Sawan, M. (2020). Arnaldo Mendez, Elie Bou Assi, Bo Zhao, Mohamad Sawan: Artificial Intelligence in Healthcare: Review and Prediction Case Studies, Elsevier. *Engineering (Beijing)*, 6(3), 291–301. 10.1016/j.eng.2019.08.015

Slater, M., Gonzalez-Liencres, C., Haggard, P., Vinkers, C., Gregory-Clarke, R., Jelley, S., Watson, Z., Breen, G., Schwarz, R., Steptoe, W., Szostak, D., Halan, S., Fox, D., & Silver, J. (2020). The Ethics of Realism in Virtual and Augmented Reality. *Frontiers in Virtual Reality*, 1, 1. 10.3389/frvir.2020.00001

Tomita, R. M., Russ, S. L., Sridhar, R., & Naughton, M. B. J. (2010). Smart home with healthcare technologies for community-dwelling older adults. *Smart Home Systems.*, 1, 139–158. 10.5772/8411

Tripathi, G., Abdul Ahad, M., & Paiva, S. (2020). SMS: A Secure Healthcare Model for Smart Cities. *Electronics (Basel)*, 9(7), 1135. 10.3390/electronics9071135

Zhang, Z.-K., Cho, M. C. Y., Wang, C.-W., Hsu, C.-W., Chen, C.-K., & Shieh, S. (2014). IoT security: ongoing challenges and research opportunities. *2014 IEEE 7th International Conference on Service-Oriented Computing and Applications*. IEEE. 10.1109/SOCA.2014.58

Zhao, R., Zhang, Y., Zhu, Y., Lan, R., & Hua, Z. (2022). Metaverse: Security and Privacy Concerns. arXiv, arXiv:2203.03854.

Chapter 8
Integration of Computer Vision Techniques, UAV, and Metaverse Analysis to Uplift Healthcare Services

Naveen Kumar H. N.
Vidyavardhaka College of Engineering, India

Guru Prasad M. S.
https://orcid.org/0000-0002-1811-9507
Graphic Era University (Deemed), India

Chandrappa S.
Jain University (Deemed), India

Praveen Gujjar J.
https://orcid.org/0000-0003-0240-7827
Jain University (Deemed), India

Suresh Kumar A.
https://orcid.org/0000-0001-7145-6337
Jain University (Deemed), India

ABSTRACT

Unmanned aerial vehicles (UAVs) play a vital role in healthcare applications, specifically in rural and isolated regions. The metaverse, a collective virtual shared place, offers a one-of-a-kind platform for immersive and collaborative healthcare

DOI: 10.4018/979-8-3693-2268-0.ch008

Copyright © 2024, IGI Global. Copying or distributing in print or electronic forms without written permission of IGI Global is prohibited.

data analysis. Improved patient outcomes and healthcare efficiency can be achieved by the widespread adoption of computer vision (CV) tools and techniques in clinical settings. The synergy between CV, metaverse analysis, and UAV communication offers a transformative approach to healthcare delivery. This study investigates the incorporation of computer vision methodologies and strategies into the metaverse framework to augment healthcare services provided by UAV communication. UAVs with extensive communication capabilities act as a link between the physical and metaverse, allowing for seamless data flow and analysis. This multidisciplinary approach offers real-time, immersive insights that improve diagnosis, decision-making, and overall patient care, and it has the potential to completely transform the way healthcare is delivered.

INTRODUCTION

Personal health is indispensable for fulfilment, productivity, and pleasure. Physical health, mental well-being, longevity, academic and professional achievement, and interpersonal connections are all significantly influenced. It promotes community well-being, contributes to economic expansion, and decreases healthcare expenditures. India has made significant advancements in the health sector during the past few decades. The life expectancy at birth has been increased from 62.1 years in 2000 to 70.8 years in 2019. The average lifespan has surpassed 67 years, while the mortality rates of infants are decreasing. Several diseases, including polio, guinea worm disease, yaws, and tetanus, have been eliminated (WHO, 2019). Despite these advancements, it is anticipated that communicable illnesses will remain a significant public health issue in the ensuing decades, endangering both national and global health security. India is currently facing a severe lack of healthcare workforce.

In 2016, Low-Income and Middle-Income Countries (LMICs) reported an excess of 15.6 million fatalities due to 61 ailments. After removing deaths that may be averted through public health interventions, 8.6 million additional deaths were amenable to health care, with 5.0 million estimated to be related to poor-quality care and 3.6 million due to non-use of health care. Poor health care quality was a substantial cause of excess mortality across a wide range of ailments, including cardiovascular disease and accidents, as well as neonatal and communicable diseases. A lack of healthcare professionals, transportation obstacles, socioeconomic inequality, and restricted access to facilities are just a few of the particular difficulties faced by rural communities. Based on the study, the annual mortality rate attributable to substandard care in India is approximately 122 per 100,000 individuals. This figure places India behind South Africa (93) and Brazil (74), Russia (91), China (46) and Nepal (93), as well as its neighbouring countries of Sri Lanka (51) and Pakistan (119).

The mortality toll from substandard care surpasses that of inadequate healthcare accessibility. Poor care quality claimed the lives of 1.6 million Indians in 2022, which is nearly double the number of deaths among those who did not utilise healthcare services (Kruk M E, 2018). The predicted shortage of health care workers by 2030 with respect to WHO thresholds is depicted in Figure 1 (WHO, 2022).

Figure 1. Estimates of health worker shortages (in million) by 2030 at WHO thresholds

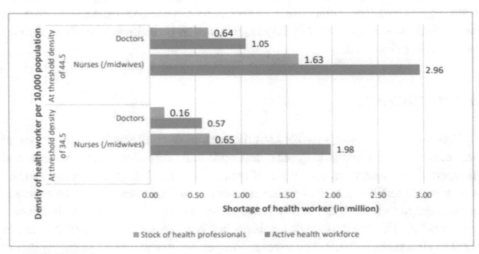

(WHO, 2022)

Approximately 75% of health infrastructure, medical personnel, and other resources are concentrated in metropolitan regions, where 27% of the population resides. The rural population in particular continues to be a significant source of concern regarding the health status of the Indian populace. Both at the macro (national and state) and micro (district and regional) levels, the issue of rural health must be addressed in order to improve the prevailing situation. The present imperative is a paradigm shift from the prevailing "biomedical model" to a "sociocultural model," which ought to bridge the gaps and uplift quality of rural life (Ashok Vikhe Patil, 2022).

Personalised healthcare, an increasingly prominent area, seeks to customise medical treatments and interventions to suit the unique requirements of individual patients. Following the COVID-19 pandemic, there was a significant surge in the demand for virtual and non-face-to-face treatment modalities (Kotiyal A, 2023). The convergence of Metaverse analysis, Unmanned Aerial Vehicle (UAV), and Computer Vision (CV) is introducing a novel era of personalised medical solutions. This multidimensional approach not only addresses existing healthcare concerns, but also lays the path for disruptive solutions that improve patient care, optimise operational efficiency, and close accessibility gaps. This chapter extensively explores the revolutionary possibilities that these technologies possess (Prasad M G, 2023).

By harnessing the capabilities of Machine Learning (ML) and Artificial Intelligence (AI), CV methods empower healthcare professionals to derive significant knowledge from medical videos and images. This allows for faster & more accurate diagnostics, resulting in earlier disease detection and treatment (Prasad G, 2023). When effectively combined with UAVs, these technologies expand their coverage to distant or underdeveloped regions, enabling rapid response to crises, transportation of medical resources, and even offering telemedicine services to unreachable locations. The Metaverse is an immersive virtual realm that blends components of Augmented Reality (AR), Virtual Reality (VR), & the internet, adding a new layer to healthcare studies. Healthcare workers can communicate in real time by building a shared digital platform that transcends geographical borders. Metaverse analysis also enables advanced medical training, simulation, and research, encouraging a collaborative environment that overcomes previous constraints.

COMPUTER VISION TECHNIQUES IN SMART HEALTH CARE

Computer vision (CV) encompasses a wide range of applications through the utilization of advanced technologies. Convolutional neural networks and other deep learning algorithms are redefining the way that CV technologies operate in recent times. CV applications are not entirely unfamiliar to the healthcare sector. To a certain extent, computer vision technologies are incorporated into X-rays, CT scans, and magnetic resonance imaging systems. Over the course of many years, medical professionals have been utilizing software to perform imaging scan analysis, diagnose patients, and prescribe subsequent treatments. On the other hand, generative artificial intelligence significantly improves the accuracy of CV, making it possible to use it in areas that were previously inaccessible (Gao J, 2018).

Deep learning models can be trained with large amounts of image data, which allows CV systems to achieve an accuracy rate of up to 99%. In comparison to the charting accuracy of 50% that was achieved by legacy computer vision systems, this achieved a significant improvement. Through this breakthrough, strong motivations have been provided for the discovery of novel use cases for vision-aided techniques in the healthcare industry (Angelica C, 2021).

Taking into consideration the increasing significance of computer vision in the field of medical imaging, Nvidia has introduced Clara-AGX (Madhavanunni A N, 2023). The fifth point is a computing architecture that is scalable and supports real-time image processing for medical applications. While this is going on, Medtronic offers an app that is powered by artificial intelligence and enables surgeons to digitally prepare and practice procedures. By introducing solutions that are both intelligent and efficient, computer vision is playing a significant role in the revolutionizing of the healthcare industry. A comprehensive summary on the ongoing efforts to address the issues that usually arise in this field is reported (Gao J, 2018). The capability of Deep Learning algorithms in classification of diseases based on medical data is analysed (Roth M, 2019). Some of the CV techniques that are used in smart healthcare are illustrated in Figure 2.

Figure 2. Computer vision techniques in smart healthcare

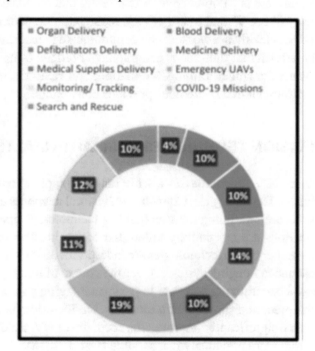

Medical Imaging Analysis

The application of computer vision in the field of medicine is particularly important for medical imaging analysis. For the purpose of diagnosis, treatment planning, and monitoring a variety of medical conditions, it involves the utilization of algorithms and techniques for the purpose of analyzing and interpreting medical images while providing valuable insights (Bayoudh K, 2022). The prime aspects in medical imaging analysis are represented in Figure 3.

- **MRI and CT Scan Analysis:** In the process of interpreting magnetic resonance imaging (MRI) and computed tomography (CT) scans, computer vision algorithms can be of assistance. This can be of great assistance in the detection and diagnosis of a variety of conditions, including tumors and abnormalities.
- **X-ray and Radiography:** For the purpose of assisting in the identification of fractures, abnormalities, and other medical conditions, computer vision techniques can be utilized to automate the analysis of X-ray and radiographic images (Avinash S, 2023).

Figure 3. Medical imaging analysis

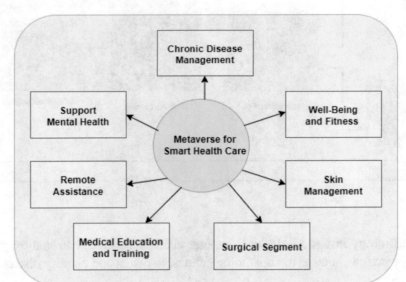

Analysis of medical images makes a significant contribution to the enhancement of the effectiveness and precision of diagnostic procedures in the healthcare industry, which ultimately results in improved patient outcomes. Research that is currently being conducted continues to investigate new approaches to improve the capabilities of computer vision in the field of medicine as technology continues to advance (Guru Prasad M S, 2023).

Disease Detection and Diagnosis

The use of computer vision for disease detection and diagnosis is a game-changing application that makes use of sophisticated algorithms to analyze medical images and provide assistance to medical professionals in recognizing and describing a variety of diseases. The application of CV in disease detection and diagnosis is graphically presented in Figure 4.

Figure 4. Disease detection and diagnosis through CV

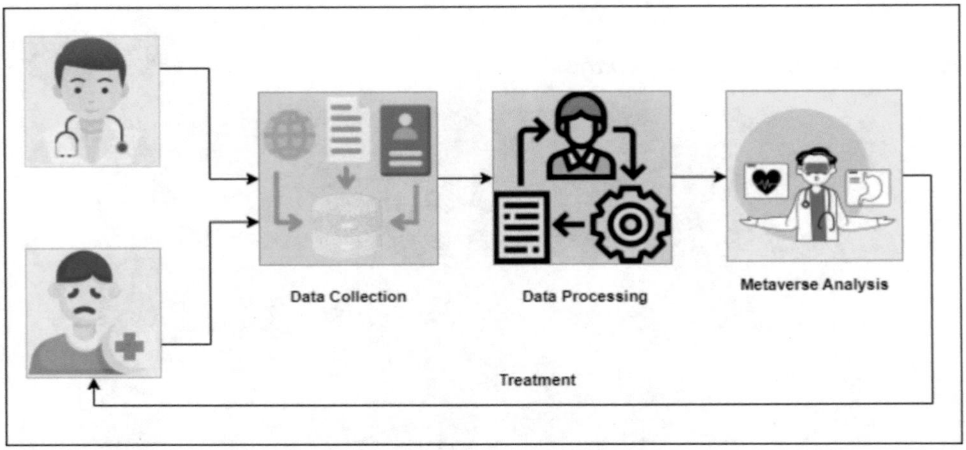

- **Pathology Image Analysis:** Computer vision algorithms can analyze pathology images, such as histopathology slides, to detect and classify diseases like cancer.
- **Skin Lesion Analysis:** Image analysis can be used to identify and classify skin lesions, assisting in the early detection of skin cancers.

In addition to improving the efficiency of workflows in the healthcare industry, disease detection and diagnosis through computer vision also contribute to earlier and more accurate diagnoses, which ultimately lead to better outcomes for patients. The capabilities of these applications are continually fine-tuned and expanded thanks to on-going research and development, which is continually advancing technology (Chandrappa S, 2019).

Remote Patient Monitoring

In order to monitor patients' health and activities from a distance, a technique known as remote patient monitoring (RPM) via computer vision makes use of cameras and various other sensors. Technology like this makes it possible for medical professionals to collect data in real time, evaluate the conditions of their patients, and take prompt action when it is required.

Figure 5. The key aspects of remote patient monitoring through computer vision

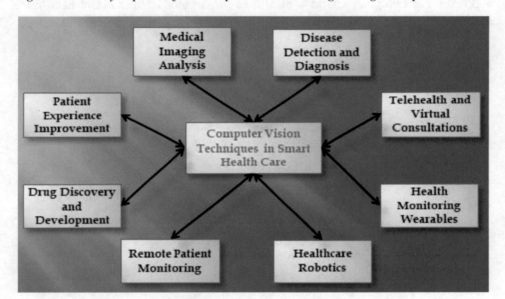

- **Activity Recognition:** Computer vision can be employed to monitor patients' activities remotely. This includes tracking movements, detecting falls, and ensuring that patients are following prescribed rehabilitation exercises.
- **Vital Signs Monitoring:** Using cameras and computer vision, vital signs such as heart rate, respiratory rate, and temperature can be monitored without physical contact, providing a non-intrusive method for continuous health assessment.

It is especially beneficial for people who have chronic conditions, the elderly, or those who are recovering from surgery to have remote patient monitoring through computer vision. This type of monitoring enables proactive care, early intervention, and improved overall patient outcomes. In addition to this, it brings about a reduction in the frequency of hospital visits, which contributes to healthcare solutions that are both cost-effective and patient-centered (Chandrappa S, 2022).

Healthcare Robotics

The field of healthcare robotics refers to the incorporation of robotic systems and automation technologies into various aspects of healthcare in order to improve patient care, enhance surgical procedures, and increase overall efficiency. The application of computer vision is of critical importance in the field of healthcare robotics because it enables robots to perceive and engage with their surroundings.

Figure 6. The overview of healthcare robotics

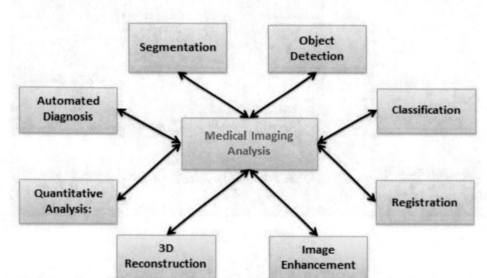

- **Surgical Assistance:** Computer vision can be integrated into robotic surgery systems to provide real-time feedback to surgeons, enabling more precise and minimally invasive procedures.
- **Assistive Robots:** Robots equipped with computer vision can assist patients with tasks, such as medication reminders, monitoring daily activities, and providing companionship.

As the field of healthcare robotics continues to advance, the incorporation of computer vision technologies is enhancing the capabilities of these robotic systems. This makes them more adaptable, intelligent, and capable of providing patients with personalized care (Kolpashchikov D, 2022).

Patient Experience Improvement

Computer vision technologies play a significant role in improving various aspects of patient care and satisfaction, which is an essential component of healthcare. Additionally, improving the patient experience is an essential aspect of healthcare.

Figure 7. Quality care through CV

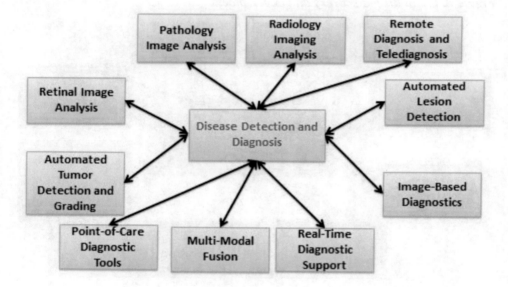

- **Facial Expression Analysis:** Computer vision can analyze facial expressions to assess patients' pain levels or emotional states, providing valuable information to healthcare providers.
- **Gesture Recognition:** Gesture-based interfaces can be employed in healthcare settings to improve communication and interaction with patients, especially those with limited mobility.

By incorporating computer vision technologies into various aspects of patient care, healthcare providers are able to create a more streamlined, individualized, and positive experience for patients, which ultimately contributes to increased patient satisfaction and improved outcomes altogether (Mascagni P, 2022).

Drug Discovery and Development

Researchers are able to examine complicated biological data, discover potential drug candidates, and improve the drug development process with the assistance of computer vision, which plays an essential role in the process of drug discovery and development.

Figure 8. CV in drug discovery and development

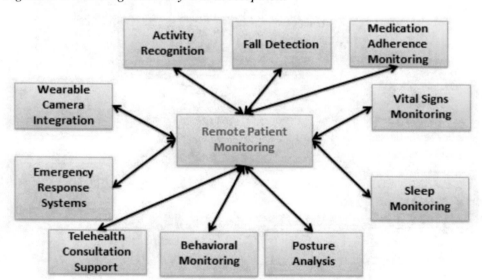

- **Cellular Image Analysis:** Computer vision is used in the analysis of microscopic images to study cellular structures, aiding in drug discovery and development processes.

Researchers are able to speed up the process of identifying potential drug candidates, improve the efficiency of the drug development process, and improve the likelihood of success in delivering new and effective therapies to patients when they make use of computer vision in the process of drug discovery and development.

While these applications demonstrate the potential of computer vision in healthcare, it's essential to address privacy concerns, regulatory compliance, and ensure the ethical use of such technologies in patient care (Dara S, 2022).

UAVS IN SMART HEALTHCARE

Amidst the ever-evolving healthcare environment of the twenty-first century, emergent technologies remain instrumental in revolutionising conventional methodologies and augmenting the results for patients. Drones, or Unmanned Aerial Vehicles (UAVs), are new, cutting-edge technologies that might dramatically alter the way people get medical treatment. UAVs have the potential to expand access to healthcare to underserved areas by quickly and easily navigating difficult terrains and covering great distances. UAVs are at the vanguard of the technological revolution that is reshaping healthcare by enabling telemedicine services in remote areas and facilitating the rapid transport of medical supplies. This advancement is characterised by enhanced efficiency, accessibility, and responsiveness. The generalized smart health architecture employing UAV is depicted in Figure 9. A Body Area Network (BAN) is a specialised network topology that is specifically engineered to connect implantable and wearable sensors. Its purpose is to establish a unified system that enables the devices to monitor, collect data, and communicate in real-time. Real-time monitoring of vital signs through BANs aids in detection of anomalies at the early stage. BANs use wireless technology to build seamless networks within & outside the human body. UAVs acquire patient's information through BANs and communicate the same to the doctor, medical servers. UAVs play an important role in optimising the healthcare supply chain by transporting key drugs and aiding emergency response in remote places.

Figure 9. UAV enabled generalized smart healthcare

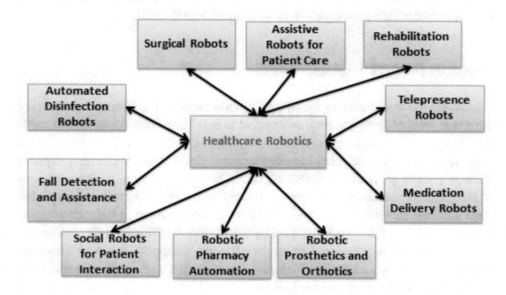

Internet of Medical Things (IoMT) is used to acquire vital signs of patient in smart healthcare systems (Shankar N, 2022). The remote health monitoring system is proposed by integrating of IoMT and UAVs. This combination has the potential to address several key issues in the health care domain. The system measures blood pressure, heart rate, temperature, humidity, and SpO2; the data is stored on the UAV. The model utilises UAVs to transport data in challenging communication environments, such as hills and islands. This study examines data transfer by combining two or three autonomous units with a built-in health monitoring system. UAVs can facilitate post-analysis therapy by transporting medicines to remote regions.

The proposed system is suitable to both developed and developing countries, reducing the transmission of COVID-19 by minimising person-to-person interaction and promoting smart healthcare (Munawar H S, 2021). AI-driven UAV-based sample collection procedure is employed involving the delivery of self-collection equipment to prospective patients and the subsequent retrieval of the samples for analysis. Diverse test cases are executed utilising a fictitious case study of Islamabad, Pakistan, in which the paths of UAVs are optimised utilising four key algorithms—greedy, intra-route, inter-route, and tabu—in order to reduce carbon emissions and save time associated with alternative transportation methods. The best optimized path is derived from the tabu algorithm. The study offers a first step towards managing COVID-19 and other pandemics in underdeveloped nations in a way that minimises person-to-person interaction and lowers the risk of illness transmission. For underdeveloped nations that find it difficult to regulate such emissions, the lower carbon footprints of these UAVs provide an additional benefit.

The UAV-powered architecture uses drones to reliably and efficiently collect data from BANs (Ullah, S, 2019). The UAV arranges the nodes in a star topology network and allocates resources via wakeup radio in the proposed architecture. Path planning, tracking accuracy, maximizing coverage, and handoffs are found to be the significant issues in employing UAVs. The study aims to evaluate the cost-effectiveness of using UAV with Automated External Defibrillators (AED) during Out-of-Hospital Cardiac Arrests (OHCAs) (Bauer J, 2021). A location allocation analysis was used to build three UAV networks that cover 80%, 90%, or 100% of rural areas without timely access to EMS (i.e., time-to-defibrillation: >10 min).

Delivery of Medical Supplies

UAVs have the potential to transport AEDs, laboratory test samples, pathology specimens, and HIV therapies. Delft University of Technology conducted research to provide solutions for AED delivery missions. UAVs are also employed in delivering organ, and blood. The constraints of ground transportation are circumvented by using UAVs to deliver organs for transplantation. Organ transplantation is a time-sensitive procedure that necessitates prompt delivery in order to reduce ischemia durations. UAVs make transportation swift and efficient, improving the likelihood of organ transplant success and saving lives. UAVs are efficient blood and plasma carriers in emergency/disaster situations or in isolated locations with inadequate infrastructure. The distribution of UAVs in the health care sector is depicted in Figure 10 (Merei A, 2023). A promising "lab-on-a-drone" proof-of-concept and numerous pilot studies demonstrating the advantages of drone use in infectious disease epidemiology and surveillance were recently reported. Drones have a lot of potential applications in epidemiology, infectious illnesses, and clinical microbiology. Drone implementation in medicine is expected to increase in the next 5 years due to cost reductions, speed, convenience, and the growing drone industry. Drones' broad use is hindered by considerations such as national airspace legislation, legal medical difficulties, geography and climate variances, and community acceptance across cultures and societies (Poljak M, 2020).

Figure 10. The distribution of UAVs in the health care sector

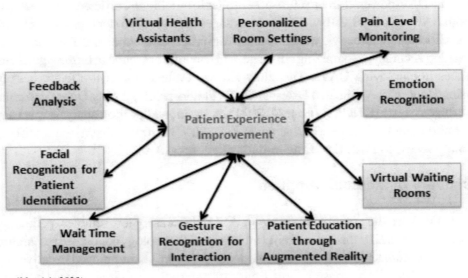

(Merei A, 2023)

Subsequently, drones have been utilised to transport small relief supplies to areas hit by significant natural disasters, such as the 2010 Haitian earthquake, the 2012 Atlantic hurricane Sandy, the 2015 Vanuatu category 5 cyclone Pam, and the 2015 Nepal earthquake. In Papua New Guinea, 'Doctors Without Borders' employed drones to transfer mock tuberculosis (TB) test samples from a rural settlement to a major coastal city. The United Nations Children's Fund (UNICEF) used drones to transport HIV testing kits in Malawi, Africa, shortening the time needed to test infants living in remote regions (Balasingam M, 2017).

METAVERSE FOR SMART HEALTH CARE

Several digital healthcare treatments and methods might be explored and engaged with in the metaverse, which could serve as a virtual environment. For instance, by experimenting with virtual versions of themselves, individuals may see the effects of various dietary and exercise habits on their physical and mental well-being. Looking forward to seeing how this technology evolves in the years to come, the metaverse's potential in healthcare is quite promising (Kumar, 2022). Future applications of digital healthcare in the metaverse will be covered in this section. Potential use cases for smart healthcare inside the metaverse are shown in Figure 11.

Figure 11. Use cases for Metaverse smart health care

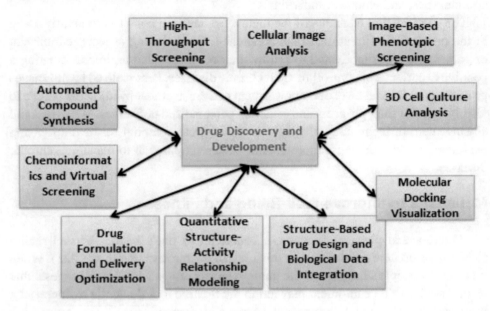

Metaverse-Based Chronic Disease Management

A chronic illness is one that either permanently affects a person's ability to do everyday tasks or needs ongoing medical treatment (Kirubasri,2013). Chronic diseases are defined as those that have persisted for one year or more and may have several causes, including but not limited to cigarette smoking and second-hand smoke exposure, unhealthy eating habits, lack of physical exercise, and excessive alcohol use (Prabhu, 2015). A novel platform for revolutionising chronic illness management is offered by the metaverse, an ever-expanding world of digital interaction. People dealing with long-term health issues may find a comprehensive healthcare solution in this online space. Users are able to join in support groups, see health indicators via connected devices, and have consultations all inside a visually engaging and interactive virtual healthcare service, made possible by immersive technology. The metaverse might revolutionise the conventional doctor-patient interaction by bringing together the real and virtual worlds in a way that is easy for everyone to understand and use (Prasad, 2019). It could also increase accessibility, strengthen communities, and empower individuals.

The gamification elements of the metaverse have the potential to greatly assist in the promotion of treatment plan adherence. By including aspects reminiscent of games, users are motivated to follow their recommended regimens, creating a positive experience of controlling their chronic diseases. Personalised health spaces provide an additional level of empowerment and engagement by allowing people to visibly monitor their progress and establish personalised objectives. With the rapid advancement of technology, the metaverse has great potential for revolutionising healthcare by introducing a more patient-centered approach to managing chronic diseases.

Metaverse to Improve Well-Being and Fitness

Wellness and physical fitness are beneficial to one's health. Virtual reality (VR) opens up new possibilities in this field in the metaverse (Guru, 2023). When it comes to people's happiness, the game sector is crucial. Evidence suggests that virtual reality (VR) equipment may aid in the treatment of dementia by increasing brain activity. Through the metaverse, people with dementia are able to access other realities, relive past experiences, and communicate with loved ones far away. Many opportunities for physical fitness are available in the metaverse as well (Gujjar,2023). Fitness streaming is among their most played fitness games, and it was inspired by the game Fortnite. Despite scepticism from some, the fitness metaverse is already looking like one of the most exciting and groundbreaking prospects in the fitness industry (Prasad, 2023).

Metaverse technology has the potential to revolutionise the fitness and wellness industry by enabling smarter, more individualised training programmes led by virtual trainers (Agarwal, 2023). People living with mental illness or dementia might also benefit from exercising in virtual reality. The virtual reality headsets deliver engaging virtual experiences that have the potential to improve one's mood and give constructive mental exercises. Organisations vying for market share and profits are increasingly focusing on VR-based fitness. The first health and fitness metaverse, FitnessVR, which was formally launched in Dubai in March 2022, was powered by blockchain technology. The 'Alo Sanctuary,' a virtual health area for yoga and meditation, was revealed by Alo Yoga and Roblox in February 2022. More and more individuals are likely to use virtual reality (VR) into their health and wellness routines as their knowledge and ability to pay grow.

Metaverse for Skin Management

The exciting new frontier of revolutionary skin management treatments is the metaverse, with its one-of-a-kind combination of virtual experiences and real healthcare solutions (Kumar, 2023). Here in this virtual space, people may find a variety of apps that aim to improve skin health and solve dermatological issues. Users might be able to communicate with virtual physicians to get individualised recommendations and treatment strategies during virtual skincare consultations, which could eventually become the norm (Pai, 2023). With the use of integrated augmented reality (AR) capabilities, users can see how different skincare treatments and regimens may look before committing to them.

In addition, people may have access to sophisticated dermatological treatments in a simulated environment via virtual skincare clinics that can be hosted in the metaverse. Included in this category are interactive skincare demos, real-time monitoring of skin issues, and virtual skin examinations (Nagesh,2017). Integrating gamification components into skincare regimens might make them more engaging, transforming the process of maintaining skin health into an exciting and informative adventure. Users have the option to design their own avatars with realistic skin simulations, giving them a head start when it comes to trying out treatments and goods before actually applying them. With its interactive and comprehensive approach that blends virtual experiences with real-world solutions, the metaverse has the potential to reshape skincare management in the future of technology.

Metaverse to Support Mental Health

One of the fastest-growing issues in modern society is mental health. A person's mental health is significantly impacted by a number of circumstances, such as stressful situations and hectic daily routines (Prasad,2023). Multiple comorbid disorders develop as a result of it over time. In the mid-1990s, virtual reality (VR) began to be used as a tool for the treatment of mental health issues. Mood and behaviour may be directly affected by digital experiences in the Metaverse, which can provide brief pleasure and respite from stress. The mental health treatment scene is set to undergo a transformation because to the efforts of many firms operating in the metaverse. Metaverse therapy has the potential to alleviate symptoms of a wide range of mental health conditions, including but not limited to: ADHD, phobias, post-traumatic stress disorder (PTSD), other anxiety-related diseases, hallucinations, and delusions. The Food and Drug Administration (FDA) approved the use of a virtual reality (VR) game developed by Akili Interactive called EndeavorRX in June 2020 to treat attention deficit hyperactivity disorder (ADHD) in youngsters.

Nevertheless, mental health may be directly affected by excessive digital usage. The individual may exhibit altered behaviour patterns and develop an addiction in some instances. Depression, irritability, stress, paranoid thoughts, physical symptoms, and psychoses are among the many problems that may arise from it. Furthermore, it may wreak havoc on a person's mental, emotional, monetary, and social health (Nagesh,2022).

The Metaverse for the Provision of Remote Assistance to Critical Patients

The digital health plays a crucial role in helping patients by continuously tracking their health status. Rapid, risk-free health improvement is possible with the help of metaverse-based monitoring and therapy apps. Medical professionals use it to treat a variety of illnesses. With the patient's information in hand, the healthcare professional may outline the precise goal of the necessary therapy. The creation of a 3D virtual environment begins with the usage of various software and hardware to generate 3D virtual data. The most efficient method is used to build and identify the necessary medical data's metaverse VR and AR. Both the treatment planning and the actual therapy may benefit from this process (Prasad,2022). Figure 12 shows a sample of a monitoring strategy. In this scenario, the doctor records and sends the patient feedback after analysing the patient's data, which allows them to discuss the results with other specialists for accurate interpretation and treatment suggestions.

Figure 12. Remote assistance using metaverse

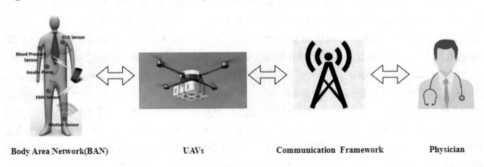

Metaverse to Revolutionize the Medical Education and Training

The ideal setting for actual processes, as opposed to just disseminating information, is provided by AR. By replicating real-world processes and allowing cellular level detail of the human body, virtual reality (VR), augmented reality (AR), mixed reality (MR), and artificial intelligence (AI) are already being used by many organisations and hospitals to train physicians and medical workers. Right now, pre-operative training and diagnosis are where augmented and virtual reality technologies are really shining (Singh,2023). More accurate visualisations and the adoption of novel approaches are probable outcomes of the more sophisticated technological forms.

The 8chili team is hard at work developing an augmented reality (AR) and virtual reality (VR) platform for use in healthcare. They're also creating platforms for remote collaboration and surgical training, with applications in patient engagement, medical student education, and healthcare skill training. When it comes to medical issues, the metaverse can give you a bird's-eye perspective and even simulate actual surgeries. With its emphasis on teamwork and complete immersion, Metaverse has all the makings of a game-changing surgical teaching tool for medical schools and hospitals. It will be difficult to evaluate the metaverse programmes at this time as they are still in the experimental phase. Metaverse research has the potential to lead to more cutting-edge medical discoveries as technology continues to improve.

Rise of Metaverse in Surgical Segment

The current prevalence of surgical robots opens up new possibilities for the data that virtual reality and augmented reality may collect and utilise to create a metaverse platform that will allow for more intricate surgical operations. Startup in the medical field By projecting a vein map onto the skin, Accuvein simplified routine medical operations including injecting medication, drawing blood, and placing intravenous drips. In a similar vein, a surgeon from Johns Hopkins performed the first spinal neuro-navigation operation in 2020 using an Augmedic startup's xvision augmented reality equipment (Kukreti, 2023).

Metaverse procedures call for a deeper familiarity with anatomy and physiology as well as the use of tools with enhanced dexterity in handling delicate objects. In a similar vein, it should be more customisable for each user. From basic procedures like removing malignant tumours to complex spinal surgeries, the future holds a wide variety of possibilities. But the surgeons may become better at doing complicated procedures as time goes on and they get more training. As medical technology develops, the metaverse will likely find use in a variety of surgical and clinical contexts, from routine treatments to more difficult ones, such as the removal of tumours and the execution of intricate spine surgeries. Furthermore, the metaverse might enhance augmented reality pre- and post-operative inspections and results. It has the potential to improve surgical results by providing a detailed data breakdown. It has the potential to be a fantastic resource for remote surgeons looking to enhance teamwork and patient care.

CONCLUSION

Computer vision technologies have had a profound impact on many parts of healthcare, including diagnosis, imaging, surgery, and patient care. Computer vision algorithms have proven to be extremely useful in medical image analysis, anomaly detection, and the improvement of physicians' ability to make accurate and timely diagnoses. UAVs have several common medical uses, such as conducting disaster assessments in areas with limited access, transporting medical supplies to remote areas, delivering aid packages, medicines, vaccines, blood, and more, and even potentially facilitating the rapid delivery of automated external defibrillators to patients experiencing cardiac arrest. Drones have the potential to improve geriatric medicine by offering mobility support to the elderly through robot-like technologies. In healthcare, metaverse analysis not only makes realistic simulations easier for medical students to practise on, but it also builds immersive environments for mental health, therapy, and rehabilitation. The Metaverse facilitates a cooperative environment wherein healthcare professionals from various disciplines can convene virtually to deliberate on cases, exchange insights, and make contributions towards offering patients care that is more comprehensive and unified. The integration of computer vision, unmanned aerial vehicles, and the metaverse not only enhances the quality of care but also transforms the healthcare delivery system, making it more technologically sophisticated, efficient, and inclusive.

The medical applications of drones are vast and potentially transferable on a global scale. National regulations, climatic zones and topography, medicolegal and licensure concerns, as well as community acceptability and reception in various countries, are all obstacles that these applications must overcome. It is imperative that stakeholders in the medical and drone sectors, in addition to manufacturers, insurance providers, legislative bodies, and government agencies, collaborate to tackle these challenges. The research shall focus on designing edge-edge, edge-cloud, and edge-end collaboration mechanisms to enhance the security and privacy of the Metaverse in healthcare. The development of an energy-efficient consensus protocol and a new Metaverse architecture with green edge-cloud computing is needed to enable green networking and computing in the Metaverse for healthcare.

REFERENCES

Agarwal, J., Christa, S., Pai, A., Kumar, M. A., & Prasad, G. (2023, January). Machine Learning Application for News Text Classification. In *2023 13th International Conference on Cloud Computing, Data Science & Engineering (Confluence)* (pp. 463-466). IEEE. 10.1109/Confluence56041.2023.10048856

Angelica, C., Purnama, H., & Purnomo, F. (2021, October). Impact of computer vision with deep learning approach in medical imaging diagnosis. In *2021 1st International Conference on Computer Science and Artificial Intelligence (ICCSAI)* (Vol. 1, pp. 37-41). IEEE.

Avinash, S., Naveen Kumar, H. N., Guru Prasad, M. S., Mohan Naik, R., & Parveen, G. (2023). Early Detection of Malignant Tumor in Lungs Using Feed-Forward Neural Network and K-Nearest Neighbor Classifier. *SN Computer Science*, 4(2), 195. 10.1007/s42979-022-01606-y

Balasingam, M. (2017). Drones in medicine—The rise of the machines. *International Journal of Clinical Practice*, 71(9), e12989. 10.1111/ijcp.1298928851081

Bauer, J., Moormann, D., Strametz, R., & Groneberg, D. A. (2021). Development of unmanned aerial vehicle (UAV) networks delivering early defibrillation for out-of-hospital cardiac arrests (OHCA) in areas lacking timely access to emergency medical services (EMS) in Germany: A comparative economic study. *BMJ Open*, 11(1), e043791. 10.1136/bmjopen-2020-04379133483448

Bayoudh, K., Knani, R., Hamdaoui, F., & Mtibaa, A. (2022). A survey on deep multimodal learning for computer vision: Advances, trends, applications, and datasets. *The Visual Computer*, 38(8), 2939–2970. 10.1007/s00371-021-02166-734131356

Chandrappa, S., Dharmanna, L., & Basavaraj, A. (2022). A novel approach for early detection of neovascular glaucoma using fractal geometry. *Int J Image Graph Signal Process*, 14(1), 26–39. 10.5815/ijigsp.2022.01.03

Chandrappa, S., Dharmanna, L., & Neetha, K. I. R. (2019, July). Automatic elimination of noises and enhancement of medical eye images through image processing techniques for better glaucoma diagnosis. In *2019 1st International Conference on Advances in Information Technology (ICAIT)* (pp. 551-557). IEEE. 10.1109/ICAIT47043.2019.8987312

Dara, S., Dhamercherla, S., Jadav, S. S., Babu, C. M., & Ahsan, M. J. (2022). Machine learning in drug discovery: A review. *Artificial Intelligence Review*, 55(3), 1947–1999. 10.1007/s10462-021-10058-434393317

Gao, J., Yang, Y., Lin, P., & Park, D. S. (2018). Computer vision in healthcare applications. *Journal of Healthcare Engineering*, 2018.29686826

Gujjar, J. P., Kumar, H. P., & Prasad, M. G. (2023, March). Advanced NLP Framework for Text Processing. In *2023 6th International Conference on Information Systems and Computer Networks (ISCON)* (pp. 1-3). IEEE.

Guru, P. M., Praveen, G. J., Dodmane, R., Sardar, T. H., Ashwitha, A., & Yeole, A. N. (2023, March). Brain Tumor Identification and Classification using a Novel Extraction Method based on Adapted Alexnet Architecture. In *2023 6th International Conference on Information Systems and Computer Networks (ISCON)* (pp. 1-5). IEEE. 10.1109/ISCON57294.2023.10112075

Guru Prasad, M. S., Naveen Kumar, H. N., Raju, K., Santhosh Kumar, D. K., & Chandrappa, S. (2023). Glaucoma detection using clustering and segmentation of the optic disc region from retinal fundus images. *SN Computer Science*, 4(2), 192. 10.1007/s42979-022-01592-1

Kirubasri, G., Sankar, S., Guru Prasad, M. S., Naga Chandrika, G., & Ramasubbareddy, S. (2023). LQETA-RP: Link quality-based energy and trust aware routing protocol for wireless multimedia sensor networks. *International Journal of System Assurance Engineering and Management*, 1–13.

Kolpashchikov, D., Gerget, O., & Meshcheryakov, R. (2022). *Robotics in healthcare. Handbook of Artificial Intelligence in Healthcare* (Vol. 2). Practicalities and Prospects.

Kotiyal, A., Kumar, D. S., Prasad, M. G., Manjunath, S. R., Chandrappa, S., & Prabhu, B. A. (2023, June). Real-Time Drowsiness Detection System Using Machine Learning. In *International Conference on Advanced Communication and Intelligent Systems* (pp. 49-58). Cham: Springer Nature Switzerland. 10.1007/978-3-031-45121-8_5

Kruk, M. E., Gage, A. D., Joseph, N. T., Danaei, G., García-Saisó, S., & Salomon, J. A. (2018). Mortality due to low-quality health systems in the universal health coverage era: A systematic analysis of amenable deaths in 137 countries. *Lancet*, 392(10160), 2203–2212. 10.1016/S0140-6736(18)31668-430195398

Kukreti, A., Prasad, G., Ram, M., & Naik, P. K. (2023, October). Detection and Classification of Brain Tumour Using EfficientNet and Transfer Learning Techniques. In *2023 International Conference on Computer Science and Emerging Technologies (CSET)* (pp. 1-5). IEEE. 10.1109/CSET58993.2023.10346858

Kumar, M. A., Abirami, N., Prasad, M. G., & Mohankumar, M. (2022, May). Stroke Disease Prediction based on ECG Signals using Deep Learning Techniques. In *2022 International Conference on Computational Intelligence and Sustainable Engineering Solutions (CISES)* (pp. 453-458). IEEE.

Kumar, M. A., Pai, A. H., Agarwal, J., Christa, S., Prasad, G. M., & Saifi, S. (2023, January). Deep Learning Model to Defend against Covert Channel Attacks in the SDN Networks. In *2023 Advanced Computing and Communication Technologies for High Performance Applications (ACCTHPA)* (pp. 1-5). IEEE. 10.1109/ACCTH-PA57160.2023.10083336

Madhavanunni, A. N., Kumar, V. A., & Panicker, M. R. (2023). A Portable Ultra-sound Imaging Pipeline Implementation with GPU Acceleration on Nvidia CLARA AGX. *arXiv preprint arXiv:2311.00482.*

Mascagni, P., Alapatt, D., Sestini, L., Altieri, M. S., Madani, A., Watanabe, Y., & Hashimoto, D. A. (2022). Computer vision in surgery: From potential to clinical value. *npj. Digital Medicine*, 5(1), 163.36307544

Merei, A., Mcheick, H., & Ghaddar, A. (2023). Survey on Path Planning for UAVs in Healthcare Missions. *Journal of Medical Systems*, 47(1), 79. 10.1007/s10916-023-01972-x37498478

Munawar, H. S., Inam, H., Ullah, F., Qayyum, S., Kouzani, A. Z., & Mahmud, M. P. (2021). Towards smart healthcare: Uav-based optimized path planning for delivering COVID-19 self-testing kits using cutting edge technologies. *Sustainability (Basel)*, 13(18), 10426. 10.3390/su131810426

Nagesh, H. R., & Prabhu, S. (2017). High performance computation of big data: Performance optimization approach towards a parallel frequent item set mining algorithm for transaction data based on hadoop MapReduce framework. *International Journal of Intelligent Systems and Applications*, 9(1), 75–84. 10.5815/ijisa.2017.01.08

Nagesh, H. R., Prasad, G., Shivaraj, B. G., Jain, D., Puneeth, B. R., & Anadkumar, M. (2022, December). E-Voting System Using Blockchain Technology. In *2022 4th International Conference on Advances in Computing, Communication Control and Networking (ICAC3N)* (pp. 2106-2111). IEEE.

Pai, A., Anandkumar, M., Prasad, G., Agarwal, J., & Christa, S. (2023, January). Designing a Secure Audio/Text Based Captcha Using Neural Network. In *2023 13th International Conference on Cloud Computing, Data Science & Engineering (Confluence)* (pp. 510-514). IEEE.

Patil, A. V., Somasundaram, K. V., & Goyal, R. C. (2002). Current health scenario in rural India. *The Australian Journal of Rural Health*, 10(2), 129–135. 10.1111/j.1440-1584.2002.tb00022.x12047509

Poljak, M., & Šterbenc, A. J. C. M. (2020). Use of drones in clinical microbiology and infectious diseases: Current status, challenges and barriers. *Clinical Microbiology and Infection*, 26(4), 425–430. 10.1016/j.cmi.2019.09.01431574337

Prabhu, S., Rodrigues, A. P., Prasad, G., & Nagesh, H. R. (2015, March). Performance enhancement of Hadoop MapReduce framework for analyzing BigData. In *2015 IEEE International Conference on Electrical, Computer and Communication Technologies (ICECCT)* (pp. 1-8). IEEE. 10.1109/ICECCT.2015.7226049

Prasad, G., Gujjar, P., Kumar, H. N., Kumar, M. A., & Chandrappa, S. (2023). Advances of Cyber Security in the Healthcare Domain for Analyzing Data. In *Cyber Trafficking, Threat Behavior, and Malicious Activity Monitoring for Healthcare Organizations* (pp. 1-14). IGI Global.

Prasad, G., Jain, A. K., Jain, P., & Nagesh, H. R. (2019). A Novel Approach to Optimize the Performance of Hadoop Frameworks for Sentiment Analysis. [IJOSSP]. *International Journal of Open Source Software and Processes*, 10(4), 44–59. 10.4018/IJOSSP.2019100103

Prasad, G., Kumar, A. S., Srivastava, S., Srivastava, A., & Srivastava, A. (2023). An iomt and machine learning model aimed at the development of a personalized lifestyle recommendation system facilitating improved health. In *Dynamics of Swarm Intelligence Health Analysis for the Next Generation* (pp. 162–185). IGI Global. 10.4018/978-1-6684-6894-4.ch009

Prasad, M. G., Agarwal, J., Christa, S., Pai, H. A., Kumar, M. A., & Kukreti, A. (2023, January). An Improved Water Body Segmentation from Satellite Images using MSAA-Net. In *2023 International Conference on Machine Intelligence for GeoAnalytics and Remote Sensing (MIGARS)* (Vol. 1, pp. 1-4). IEEE. 10.1109/MIGARS57353.2023.10064508

Prasad, M. G., Kumar, D. S., Pratap, M. S., Kiran, J., Chandrappa, S., & Kotiyal, A. (2023, June). Enhanced Prediction of Heart Disease Using Machine Learning and Deep Learning. In *International Conference on Advanced Communication and Intelligent Systems* (pp. 1-12). Cham: Springer Nature Switzerland. 10.1007/978-3-031-45121-8_1

Prasad, M. G., Pratap, M. S., Jain, P., Gujjar, J. P., Kumar, M. A., & Kukreti, A. (2022, December). RDI-SD: An Efficient Rice Disease Identification based on Apache Spark and Deep Learning Technique. In *2022 International Conference on Artificial Intelligence and Data Engineering (AIDE)* (pp. 277-282). IEEE. 10.1109/AIDE57180.2022.10060157

Roth, M. (2019). *Computer vision in healthcare–current applications*.

Shankar, N., Nallakaruppan, M. K., Ravindranath, V., Senthilkumar, M., & Bhagavath, B. P. (2022). Smart IoMT Framework for Supporting UAV Systems with AI. *Electronics (Basel)*, 12(1), 86. 10.3390/electronics12010086

Singh, P., Tripathi, V., Singh, K. D., Guru Prasad, M. S., & Aditya Pai, H. (2023, April). A Task Scheduling Algorithm for Optimizing Quality of Service in Smart Healthcare System. In *International Conference on IoT, Intelligent Computing and Security: Select Proceedings of IICS 2021* (pp. 43-50). Singapore: Springer Nature Singapore. 10.1007/978-981-19-8136-4_4

Ullah, S., Kim, K. I., Kim, K. H., Imran, M., Khan, P., Tovar, E., & Ali, F. (2019). UAV-enabled healthcare architecture: Issues and challenges. *Future Generation Computer Systems*, 97, 425–432. 10.1016/j.future.2019.01.028

World Health Organization. (2019). *World health statistics overview 2019: monitoring health for the SDGs, sustainable development goals (No. WHO/DAD/2019.1)*. World Health Organization.

World Health Organization. (2022). *Health workforce in India: where to invest, how much and why?* WHO.

Chapter 9
UAV Communication for Metaverse Intelligent Systems With Blockchain Technology

M. Vasim Babu

https://orcid.org/0000-0001-6896-6344

MIT, Anna University, India

S. Ramprabhu

MIT, Anna University, India

Ramesh Sekaran

Jain University (Deemed), India

ABSTRACT

In the not-so-distant future, the confluence of cutting-edge technologies such as artificial intelligence (AI), telemedicine, and blockchain is transforming the way we perceive and interact with the world. A pivotal component of this paradigm shift is the use of unmanned aerial vehicles (UAVs) to enable seamless communication within the Metaverse, where physical and digital realms blend harmoniously. This chapter delves into the intricate web of UAV communication, exploring its applications, challenges, and potential for shaping the metaverse of tomorrow.

DOI: 10.4018/979-8-3693-2268-0.ch009

Copyright © 2024, IGI Global. Copying or distributing in print or electronic forms without written permission of IGI Global is prohibited.

INTRODUCTION

The concept of the Metaverse, a term coined in science fiction and popularized in recent years, represents a fascinating and transformative shift in how humans perceive and interact with the digital and physical worlds. Often depicted as a fully immersive digital universe where users can interact, socialize, work, and even play, the Metaverse is a realm where the boundaries between the real and the virtual blur into an interconnected digital reality. As we delve into this concept, it becomes clear that the Metaverse is on the brink of becoming a ubiquitous and transformative part of our lives, offering a host of opportunities and challenges (Bhutta et al., 2021).

At its core, the Metaverse is a convergence of various technologies and platforms, driven by advancements in artificial intelligence, augmented reality, virtual reality, blockchain, and more. These technologies combine to create a digital realm where users can create, explore, and interact with a rich tapestry of experiences. The Metaverse's rise is a testament to humanity's enduring fascination with merging the tangible and intangible, the physical and digital.

One of the most exciting aspects of the Metaverse's ascent is the potential for it to revolutionize how we interact with information, entertainment, and each other. It offers a platform for creativity, collaboration, and exploration that transcends the limitations of the physical world. The following discussion highlights some key facets of the Metaverse's rise (Deepa et al., 2022).

The Metaverse, often portrayed in science fiction, is a collective digital universe where humans can interact, socialize, work, and even play in a virtual environment. With advancements in AI, Telemedicine, and Blockchain, this concept is swiftly becoming a reality. Within the Metaverse, users engage in both synchronous and asynchronous experiences that require a complex web of communication. UAVs are emerging as a crucial link in facilitating this communication.

In a world where physical gatherings can be constrained by geography and circumstance, the Metaverse offers a compelling alternative. Virtual gatherings, meetings, and events enable people to connect regardless of their physical locations. It's a space for both casual interactions and professional collaborations (Zhang, Li, Wang et al, 2021).

Artificial intelligence (AI) plays a pivotal role in shaping the Metaverse. It powers the virtual environments, creating lifelike NPCs (non-playable characters) and enhancing user experiences. AI also enables dynamic content generation, adapting the Metaverse to individual users and making it feel more realistic and responsive.

Augmented reality (AR) and virtual reality (VR) technologies are instrumental in making the Metaverse immersive. AR overlays digital content on the real world, while VR transports users to entirely virtual environments. These technologies provide the sensory experiences that make the Metaverse engaging and captivating (Kumar et al., 2021).

Blockchain technology underpins the Metaverse's economic ecosystem. It facilitates secure and transparent transactions, enabling the creation and exchange of digital assets, including cryptocurrencies and non-fungible tokens (NFTs). Blockchain also safeguards the ownership and provenance of digital goods, such as virtual real estate or art.

Robust and high-speed internet connectivity is a fundamental requirement for the Metaverse. It allows users to interact seamlessly and access content without interruption. Emerging technologies like 5G and beyond are poised to enhance the Metaverse's connectivity, enabling smoother interactions and real-time experiences.

UAVS AND THEIR ROLE

Unmanned Aerial Vehicles (UAVs), also commonly known as drones, have come a long way from their military origins to become an essential component of the emerging Metaverse. The Metaverse, a digital realm where the boundaries between the real and the virtual blur, offers users a seamless blend of experiences, interactions, and opportunities. UAVs, with their remarkable capabilities, are poised to play a pivotal role in shaping and enhancing the Metaverse in various ways, bridging the gap between the physical and digital worlds.

The Versatile Roles of UAVs in the Metaverse

Surveillance and Security

One of the fundamental roles of UAVs in the Metaverse is surveillance and security. In this interconnected digital universe, the need for safeguarding digital assets and ensuring the privacy of users is paramount. UAVs equipped with advanced sensors and AI-driven analytics have become integral to the task of monitoring and securing the Metaverse. They provide real-time data, tracking activities, identifying potential threats, and ensuring a safe and secure environment for users. In essence, UAVs act as digital sentinels, patrolling the digital realm, and maintaining order (Jabbar et al., 2020).

Telemedicine and Healthcare

Telemedicine is revolutionizing healthcare in the Metaverse, and UAVs are at the forefront of this transformation. Through AI-driven algorithms and precise navigation, UAVs can deliver essential medical supplies, provide rapid response to emergencies, and even facilitate remote surgeries within the digital realm. Teleoperated surgical systems, guided by expert surgeons, can perform intricate procedures through the Metaverse, while UAVs ensure seamless real-time communication and data transfer during these critical operations. In the context of healthcare, UAVs act as lifelines, providing access to healthcare services and life-saving interventions (Belchior et al., 2021).

Virtual Shopping

Commerce in the Metaverse is another domain where UAVs play a pivotal role. Blockchain technology ensures secure, transparent transactions, and UAVs become the delivery agents for products purchased in virtual stores. With the assistance of AI, UAVs optimize delivery routes and schedules to enhance the user experience. They're not just delivery vehicles; they are personalized shopping assistants, making recommendations based on user preferences, and ensuring the timely arrival of virtual and physical goods in the Metaverse.

Infrastructure Maintenance

Maintaining and nurturing the digital assets and infrastructure of the Metaverse is essential to provide a seamless experience for users. UAVs equipped with AI-powered sensors and maintenance capabilities inspect and repair digital assets regularly. Their autonomous operations, guided by AI, ensure the efficiency and reliability of digital infrastructure within the Metaverse. These aerial maintenance workers contribute to the overall stability and performance of the digital world, all while adhering to the transparency and traceability provided by the blockchain.

THE INTEGRATION OF AI IN UAV COMMUNICATION

The efficient functioning of UAVs in the Metaverse heavily relies on Artificial Intelligence (AI). The combination of UAVs and AI in the Metaverse leads to the following capabilities:

In the dynamic and interconnected world of the Metaverse, the ability to adapt to changing network conditions is crucial. UAVs, empowered by AI algorithms, can seamlessly switch between various communication protocols, ensuring uninterrupted connections in a highly populated and interconnected digital realm. AI's adaptive communication algorithms help UAVs maintain a reliable and efficient network, delivering services and data in real time (Yang, 2022).

UAVs in the Metaverse require the ability to make autonomous decisions. AI plays a pivotal role in this aspect, guiding UAVs in making decisions related to routing, resource allocation, and network management. These decisions are based on real-time data analysis, ensuring optimal performance and minimal latency in the Metaverse. AI-driven decision-making ensures that UAVs can navigate the complexities of the digital realm, making split-second choices to provide users with the best possible experience.

For seamless communication within the Metaverse, UAVs need to understand and respond to user queries and commands. AI models, such as Natural Language Processing (NLP), enable UAVs to interpret user intentions expressed in natural language and convert them into actions. In essence, UAVs act as personal assistants, facilitating interactions and transactions in a manner that feels natural to users. Through NLP, they can understand context, engage in conversations, and execute tasks as directed, enhancing the overall user experience.

Surveillance and Security in the Metaverse

One of the primary roles of UAVs in the Metaverse is surveillance and security, and AI is at the forefront of this function. The digital realm demands robust security measures, and UAVs, coupled with AI, provide critical support.

AI-powered UAVs collect and analyze real-time data in the Metaverse, identifying potential security threats, monitoring user activities, and ensuring a safe environment. This dynamic surveillance helps maintain order and security in the digital ecosystem, protecting users and digital assets.

UAVs equipped with AI algorithms excel in threat detection and mitigation. AI-driven image and video analysis can identify suspicious behavior or activities, and UAVs can respond swiftly to potential threats. Whether it's preventing digital breaches or maintaining privacy, AI-powered UAVs play a crucial role in ensuring security within the Metaverse.

In the event of crises or emergencies within the Metaverse, UAVs with AI-driven decision support systems act as first responders. They can reach remote locations swiftly, deliver life-saving aid, and provide essential services. This capacity to respond autonomously and efficiently to emergencies has a significant impact on the safety and well-being of Metaverse users (Chengoden et al., 2022).

Telemedicine and Healthcare in the Metaverse

The integration of telemedicine and UAVs powered by AI has profound implications for healthcare in the Metaverse, enabling access to medical services and interventions like never before.

UAVs in the Metaverse facilitate remote medical consultations, allowing users to connect with healthcare professionals, specialists, and general practitioners. AI supports these interactions by capturing and transmitting medical data in real-time, ensuring accurate diagnoses and informed treatment decisions. Remote medical consultations become a standard practice within the Metaverse, offering convenient and accessible healthcare services.

AI-driven UAVs equipped with medical supplies play a pivotal role in emergency medical response. In critical situations, these autonomous UAVs can reach remote locations and deliver life-saving medical aid. The combination of AI and UAV technology ensures rapid response, improving the chances of survival for individuals in need of immediate medical assistance.

One of the most remarkable applications of AI in the Metaverse is surgical support. Expert surgeons, guided by AI, can control surgical robots remotely. These robots, located within the digital realm, are equipped with precision instruments and perform complex procedures with incredible precision. The AI ensures real-time communication and responsiveness, making remote surgeries within the Metaverse a reality. The implications for telemedicine and healthcare are profound, enabling expert medical procedures to be performed regardless of geographical boundaries.

BLOCKCHAIN AND SECURE COMMUNICATION

Blockchain technology, a revolutionary and disruptive innovation, is playing a pivotal role in reinforcing the security and transparency of communication within the Metaverse. The Metaverse, a digital realm where the real and virtual worlds merge, relies on secure and transparent communication to provide users with a seamless and trustworthy experience. Blockchain, with its decentralized ledger and cryptographic protocols, addresses fundamental challenges within the Metaverse, ensuring the integrity of transactions, the safeguarding of digital assets, and the protection of user privacy.

The Metaverse represents a vision of an interconnected digital universe where individuals and digital entities coexist and interact. Within this expansive digital landscape, users traverse a multitude of virtual environments, from bustling cities and serene landscapes to imaginative realms that defy physical laws. It is a space where users can engage in diverse activities, from entertainment and commerce to social interactions and education. In this complex and dynamic environment, secure and transparent communication is the cornerstone of trust and reliability (Ning et al., 2021).

Blockchain technology, originally designed to support cryptocurrencies like Bitcoin, has evolved into a transformative force that extends beyond finance. At its core, blockchain is a decentralized and immutable ledger that records transactions across a network of computers. This ledger is secured through cryptographic algorithms, ensuring that once data is recorded, it cannot be altered. These features make blockchain a perfect fit for the Metaverse, where trust and transparency are paramount.

Reinforcing Security Within the Metaverse

Security within the Metaverse is a multifaceted challenge. Users interact with digital assets, engage in financial transactions, and share personal information, all of which must be protected from unauthorized access and malicious actors. Blockchain technology addresses these security concerns comprehensively:

Encryption and Data Protection

Blockchain uses advanced cryptographic techniques to encrypt data, rendering it indecipherable without the proper decryption keys. This encryption ensures that sensitive user information, such as financial data and personal details, remains secure and confidential.

Immutable Transactions

Once data is recorded on the blockchain, it is virtually impossible to alter or delete. This immutability safeguards transactions, asset ownership, and contractual agreements within the Metaverse. Users can have confidence that their digital assets and transactions are protected from fraud or manipulation.

Decentralization

Blockchain operates on a decentralized network of nodes, meaning that there is no single point of control. This decentralization mitigates the risk of a single point of failure and makes it exceptionally challenging for malicious actors to compromise the system. The absence of a central authority enhances the security of the Metaverse's communication infrastructure.

ENSURING TRANSPARENCY

Transparency is fundamental in the Metaverse. Users must be able to verify the authenticity and provenance of digital assets, and ensure that their interactions occur as expected. Blockchain technology enforces transparency in several key ways:

Public Ledger

The blockchain ledger is public and accessible to all participants within the network. This transparency allows users to verify the accuracy of transactions, ensuring that they are conducted honestly and as intended. Users can view the history of transactions related to digital assets, offering a complete and verifiable record.

Digital Asset Ownership

Digital assets within the Metaverse, such as virtual real estate or digital art, are tokenized and represented on the blockchain. This tokenization ensures clear ownership, and the ownership records are transparent and publicly accessible. Users can confidently verify their ownership of digital assets within the Metaverse.

Smart Contracts

Smart contracts, self-executing agreements with the terms of the contract directly written into code, ensure transparency in contractual interactions. These contracts automatically execute when predefined conditions are met, and their code is publicly available on the blockchain, making the terms and execution of agreements transparent and verifiable.

In conclusion, the fusion of UAV communication, AI, Telemedicine, and Blockchain technology is transforming the Metaverse into a dynamic, interconnected digital realm. As this technology matures, it has the potential to revolutionize various aspects of our lives, from healthcare to commerce and beyond. However, a thoughtful approach that considers ethics, regulation, and infrastructure development is essential to ensure that these advancements benefit society as a whole. The future of the Metaverse is exciting, but it must also be mindful of the challenges it faces (Jeon et al., 2022).

RESEARCH DIRECTION IN UAV COMMUNICATION FOR METAVERSE INTELLIGENT SYSTEMS

Research in the field of UAV (Unmanned Aerial Vehicle) communication for Metaverse Intelligent Systems is an exciting and rapidly evolving area. As the Metaverse gains prominence and its applications become more diverse, the role of UAVs in supporting communication and infrastructure within this digital realm is of increasing importance. Here are some promising research directions in this domain:

Investigate methods to enhance the security and privacy of data transmitted through UAVs within the Metaverse. Research should focus on encryption methods, data protection, and secure communication protocols to ensure that users' information and transactions remain confidential and protected from cyber threats. Explore how AI can further optimize UAV communication within the Metaverse. Investigate the use of machine learning algorithms to enhance adaptive communication, autonomous decision-making, and natural language processing for UAVs. Develop AI models that can anticipate user needs and provide proactive assistance.

Study the integration of blockchain technology to enhance the security and transparency of UAV communication. Research should focus on the development of blockchain-based solutions for transaction verification, digital asset ownership, and identity verification within the Metaverse. Investigate the design and optimization of network infrastructure to support UAV communication within the Metaverse. Research should address the scalability challenges associated with the growing number of users, devices, and digital assets in the Metaverse. Develop innovative solutions to ensure robust, high-speed, and low-latency connectivity. Examine the development of regulatory and ethical frameworks specific to UAV communication within the Metaverse. Research should explore how regulations can ensure user safety, data protection, and ethical conduct. Address issues related to surveillance, data ownership, and digital asset transactions.

Investigate how to ensure inclusive access to UAV communication within the Metaverse, considering factors such as affordability, digital literacy, and accessibility for individuals with disabilities. Explore strategies to bridge the digital divide and make the Metaverse accessible to a diverse and global user base. Research the use of UAVs for emergency response and healthcare applications within the Metaverse. Investigate how UAVs can deliver medical supplies, provide remote medical consultations, and support telemedicine. Develop AI-driven systems that enable UAVs to act as first responders in crisis situations (Huo et al., 2022).

Study the application of blockchain technology to ensure transparent and verifiable ownership of digital assets within the Metaverse. Explore how blockchain can be used to establish and maintain the provenance of digital art, virtual real estate, and other unique digital assets. Investigate methods to maintain data integrity and transparency within the Metaverse. Explore how blockchain and AI can be used to safeguard critical data, such as medical records and surveillance data. Develop protocols to ensure that data remains unaltered and accessible to authorized parties.

Research the design and development of user-friendly interfaces and interaction methods for controlling UAVs within the Metaverse. Investigate the use of augmented and virtual reality interfaces, gesture control, and voice commands to make UAV interaction more intuitive and immersive. Explore sustainable power sources and energy-efficient technologies for UAVs within the Metaverse. Investigate renewable energy options, battery optimization, and power management to reduce the environmental impact of UAV operations. Research the use of UAVs for entertainment purposes within the Metaverse. Explore how UAVs can enhance the delivery of immersive content, such as virtual concerts, sports events, and interactive storytelling experiences. Investigate the cultural and societal impacts of UAV communication within the Metaverse. Examine how this technology affects identity, community building, and social interaction in the digital realm. Consider the implications of digital ownership and representation in the Metaverse.

Research the collaborative potential of UAVs and AI systems in the Metaverse. Investigate how UAVs can work alongside AI-driven virtual entities to provide enhanced services and experiences to users. Explore how UAVs can be used in educational and training contexts within the Metaverse. Investigate the development of immersive virtual environments for learning, skill development, and professional training, utilizing UAVs as tools for experiential education.

Research in UAV communication for Metaverse Intelligent Systems is a multidisciplinary field that spans artificial intelligence, blockchain technology, network infrastructure, ethics, and numerous application domains. These research directions offer opportunities to advance our understanding of how UAVs can enhance the Metaverse's communication ecosystem and contribute to the development of secure, transparent, and inclusive digital environments.

The following table shows the comparison of various UAV communication methods for Metaverse Intelligent Systems requires a comprehensive breakdown of parameters. This table offers a simplified comparison of three UAV communication methods of WiFi, 5G, and Satellite Communication.

Table 1. The comparison of various UAV communication methods for metaverse intelligent systems requires a comprehensive breakdown of parameters

Parameter	WiFi	5G	Satellite Communication
Latency	Low	Very Low	High
Bandwidth	Moderate	High	Very High
Coverage Area	Limited	Moderate	Global
Network Density	Low to Moderate	High	High
Reliability	Subject to Interference	High	High
Cost	Low	Moderate to High	High
Energy Efficiency	Moderate	High	Moderate
Scalability	Limited	High	High
Security	Vulnerable	High	High
Mobility Support	Limited	High	High
Spectrum Availability	Shared and Congested	Dedicated Spectrum	Licensed Bands
Use Cases	Short-range, indoor	Diverse Applications	Remote and Rural Areas
Data Intensive Applications	Online Gaming, Streaming	AR/VR, IoT	Remote Sensing, Data Transfer
Privacy Concerns	Potential for Eavesdropping	Stronger Privacy	Data Encryption Required
Accessibility in Remote Areas	Limited	Limited	Available, but costly
Deployment Complexity	Low	Moderate	High
Regulatory Challenges	Local Regulations	Spectrum Allocation	Licensing and Compliance

UAV COMMUNICATION FOR METAVERSE INTELLIGENT SYSTEMS WITH BLOCKCHAIN TECHNOLOGY

The Metaverse, a digital universe of interconnected virtual worlds and augmented realities, is fast becoming a critical component of our digital existence. In this emerging landscape, Unmanned Aerial Vehicles (UAVs) are playing a pivotal role, bridging the virtual and physical worlds by facilitating various applications such as surveillance, delivery, and exploration. However, this integration poses a set of unique challenges, especially in the domain of UAV communication, including issues related to reliability, security, and data integrity. To address these challenges, this research proposal outlines a comprehensive study on leveraging blockchain technology for UAV communication within the Metaverse.

The Metaverse, sometimes described as a collective virtual shared space, is expanding rapidly. It is anticipated that it will become an integral part of various industries, from entertainment and gaming to education and commerce. Within this digital realm, UAVs are utilized for tasks like real-time data acquisition, surveillance, virtual goods delivery, and much more. To ensure the seamless operation of UAVs in the Metaverse, robust and secure communication systems are essential. These systems need to cope with the unique challenges of this digital frontier, including real-time data synchronization, network congestion, and the safeguarding of sensitive information (Duan et al., 2021).

Blockchain technology, famous for its security and data integrity features, has the potential to address these issues. Blockchain is a distributed ledger that records data in a decentralized, immutable, and transparent manner. It has been successfully applied in various domains, including finance, supply chain, and healthcare, for data security, transparency, and trust. Integrating blockchain into UAV communication within the Metaverse may provide solutions to data integrity, security, and real-time synchronization challenges.

The generic steps to design a model for Metaverse Intelligent Systems with Blockchain Technology in UAV Communication

- Develop and implement a blockchain-based framework for UAV communication in the Metaverse.
- Enhance the reliability and real-time synchronization of data between UAVs and Metaverse servers.
- Strengthen data security and privacy to protect UAV communication from potential cyber threats.
- Investigate the impact of blockchain integration on UAV communication performance within the Metaverse.

The Systematic block diagram for designing a model for Metaverse Intelligent Systems with Blockchain Technology in UAV Communication is shown below. The communication system of the Unmanned Aerial Vehicle (UAV). It includes components such as UAV transceiver, antennas, signal processing units, and data encryption modules. The intelligent system that operates in the metaverse environment. It includes components such as machine learning algorithms, computer vision modules, decision-making systems, and natural language processing units. The blockchain system consists of components like distributed ledger, consensus mechanism, smart contracts, and encryption algorithms. In the data Collection phase, the process of collecting data from various sources such as sensors, cameras, and communication channels. The collected data is preprocessed to remove noise, outliers, and irrelevant information. It may also involve data fusion techniques to combine information from multiple sources (Xi et al., 2022).

The blockchain provides a decentralized and secure infrastructure for storing and accessing data. The data can be shared between multiple UAVs and other entities in the network, allowing for collaborative decision-making and intelligent system operation. the intelligent analysis and decision-making process based on the collected and preprocessed data. The machine learning algorithms, computer vision modules, and decision-making systems analyze the data to extract valuable insights, classify objects, detect anomalies, and make informed decisions. The distributed nodes in the network verify and validate the transactions, ensuring the integrity and security of the data stored in the blockchain. Consensus algorithms such as Proof of Work (PoW) or Proof of Stake (PoS) are used to reach a consensus on the validity of transactions. Cryptographic techniques such as encryption, digital signatures, and secure channels are used to protect the confidentiality, authenticity, and integrity of the communication. The system continuously monitors its performance, collects feedback from the environment, and updates its models and algorithms accordingly. This feedback loop helps in improving the accuracy, efficiency, and adaptability of the intelligent system.

Figure 1. This feedback loop helps in improving the accuracy, efficiency, and adaptability of the intelligent system

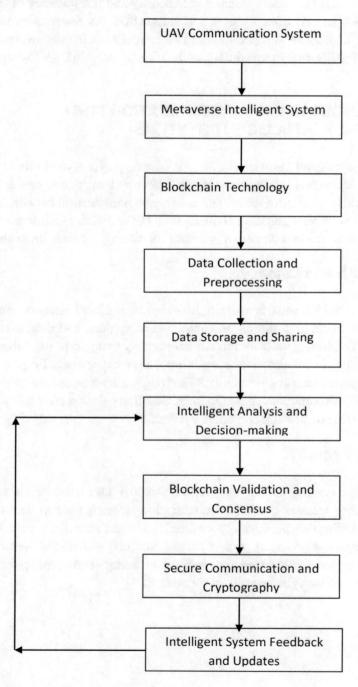

In this model, UAVs play a critical role in facilitating communication within the Metaverse while blockchain technology ensures data integrity and trust. Decentralized identity and smart contracts enhance the security and transparency of the system, and analytics and AI offer insights and automation. It's essential to design each component with security, scalability, and user experience in mind to create a robust Metaverse Intelligent System with Blockchain Technology in UAV Communication.

CHALLENGES IN UAV COMMUNICATION FOR METAVERSE INTELLIGENT SYSTEMS

Unmanned Aerial Vehicles (UAVs), or drones, play a pivotal role in the development of Metaverse Intelligent Systems. These systems aim to create immersive virtual worlds and require robust and reliable communication between UAVs and the Metaverse. Five significant challenges in UAV communication for Metaverse Intelligent Systems and discusses potential solutions to address these challenges.

Bandwidth and Latency

UAVs in the Metaverse demand high bandwidth and low latency communication. They must stream high-definition video, telemetry data, and user interactions in real-time. Traditional network infrastructures may struggle to meet these requirements, leading to latency issues and a poor user experience. Employ advanced communication technologies such as 5G and edge computing to provide low-latency, high-bandwidth communication. Optimize data transmission protocols for efficient use of available bandwidth and latency reduction.

Network Security

Metaverse systems collect and transmit sensitive user data, which requires rigorous security measures. UAV communication is susceptible to various security threats, including data breaches, cyber-attacks, and unauthorized access. Implement strong encryption protocols, robust access controls, and regular security audits. Utilize blockchain technology for secure data storage and identity management. Train personnel on cybersecurity best practices.

Reliability and Redundancy

Ensuring the reliability of UAV communication is essential. UAVs may operate in remote or challenging environments where network disruptions can occur. A single point of failure in the communication infrastructure could be detrimental. Design a communication network with built-in redundancy and failover mechanisms. Utilize mesh networking to ensure that UAVs can communicate with multiple peers and access points. Implement autonomous route planning for UAVs to adapt to network failures (Zhang, Zhang, Wang et al, 2021).

Regulatory Compliance

UAV operations are subject to strict regulations imposed by aviation authorities and data protection agencies. Compliance with these regulations is mandatory, and it can be complex within the Metaverse, which blurs the lines between real and virtual worlds. Collaborate with regulatory bodies to establish UAV communication guidelines specific to the Metaverse. Develop compliance protocols and monitoring systems to ensure adherence to these guidelines. Educate UAV operators and Metaverse users on the importance of regulatory compliance.

Integration With Blockchain

Integrating blockchain technology for data integrity and trust introduces performance and scalability challenges. Blockchain networks can become slow and costly as more data is stored and processed. Utilize advanced consensus mechanisms like Proof of Stake (PoS) or sharding to enhance blockchain scalability. Explore off-chain solutions for data storage and management, while using the blockchain for critical trust-related functions like transaction verification.

CONCLUSION

The transformational potential of the Metaverse is propelled by the seamless integration of cutting-edge technologies such as Artificial Intelligence, Telemedicine, and Blockchain. These innovations are at the forefront of reshaping our interactions with the world, and they form the foundation for a dynamic and immersive digital future.

A central element of this transformation is the strategic utilization of Unmanned Aerial Vehicles (UAVs) to facilitate communication within the Metaverse. This chapter has delved into the intricate web of UAV communication, elucidating its manifold applications, formidable challenges, and the vast potential it holds in shaping the Metaverse of tomorrow.

As we look ahead to the not-so-distant future, the fusion of these technologies and UAV communication promises to redefine our concept of reality, creating a space where physical and digital worlds harmoniously coexist. The implications are profound, ranging from revolutionizing healthcare and education to enhancing entertainment, commerce, and beyond. However, the journey towards this vision is not without its hurdles, including bandwidth constraints, security concerns, regulatory complexities, and the need for innovative solutions to integrate UAVs seamlessly into the Metaverse.

In the face of these challenges, it is evident that interdisciplinary collaboration, innovative problem-solving, and a commitment to regulatory compliance will be instrumental in realizing the full potential of UAV communication in the Metaverse. As we embark on this transformative journey, it is clear that the evolution of the Metaverse will continue to be a captivating story of technological ingenuity, pushing the boundaries of what we can achieve in the digital realm.

REFERENCES

Belchior, R., Vasconcelos, A., Guerreiro, S., & Correia, M. (2021). A survey on blockchain interoperability: Past, present, and future trends. *ACM Computing Surveys*, 54(8), 1–41. 10.1145/3471140

Bhutta, M. N. M., Khwaja, A. A., Nadeem, A., Ahmad, H. F., Khan, M. K., Hanif, M. A., Song, H., Alshamari, M., & Cao, Y. (2021). A survey on blockchain technology: Evolution, architecture and security. *IEEE Access : Practical Innovations, Open Solutions*, 9, 61048–61073. 10.1109/ACCESS.2021.3072849

Chengoden, R., Victor, N., Huynh-The, T., Yenduri, G., Jhaveri, R. H., Alazab, M., Bhattacharya, S., Hegde, P., Maddikunta, P. K. R., & Gadekallu, T. R. (2022). *Metaverse for healthcare: A survey on potential applications, challenges and future directions.* arXiv preprint arXiv:2209.04160.

Deepa, N., Pham, Q.-V., Nguyen, D. C., Bhattacharya, S., Prabadevi, B., Gadekallu, T. R., Maddikunta, P. K. R., Fang, F., & Pathirana, P. N. (2022). A survey on blockchain for big data: Approaches, opportunities, and future directions. *Future Generation Computer Systems*, 131, 209–226. 10.1016/j.future.2022.01.017

Duan, H., Li, J., Fan, S., Lin, Z., Wu, X., & Cai, W. (2021). Metaverse for social good: A university campus prototype. *Proceedings of the 29th ACM International Conference on Multimedia*, (pp. 153–161). ACM. 10.1145/3474085.3479238

Huo, R., Zeng, S., Wang, Z., Shang, J., Chen, W., Huang, S., Wang, T., Yu, F., & Liu, Y. (2022). A comprehensive survey on blockchain in industrial internet of things: Motivations, research progresses, and future challenges. *IEEE Commun. Surv. Tutor.* IEEE.

Jabbar, R., Fetais, N., Krichen, M., & Barkaoui, K. (2020). Blockchain technology for healthcare: Enhancing shared electronic health record interoperability and integrity. *IEEE International Conference on Informatics, IoT, and Enabling Technologies (ICIoT)*, (pp. 310–317). IEEE.

Jeon, H.-j., Youn, H.-c., Ko, S.-m., & Kim, T.-h. (2022). Blockchain and AI meet in the metaverse. In *Advances in the Convergence of Blockchain and Artificial Intelligence* (p. 73). BoD–Books on Demand. 10.5772/intechopen.99114

Kumar, P., Kumar, R., Srivastava, G., Gupta, G. P., Tripathi, R., Gadekallu, T. R., & Xiong, N. N. (2021). PPSF: A privacy-preserving and secure framework using blockchain-based machine-learning for IoT-driven smart cities. *IEEE Transactions on Network Science and Engineering*, 8(3), 2326–2341. 10.1109/TNSE.2021.3089435

Ning, H., Wang, H., Lin, Y., Wang, W., Dhelim, S., Farha, F., Ding, J., & Daneshmand, M. (2021). A survey on metaverse: the state-of-the-art, technologies, applications, and challenges, , arXiv preprint arXiv:2111.09673.

Xi, N., Chen, J., Gama, F., Riar, M., & Hamari, J. (2022). The challenges of entering the metaverse: An experiment on the effect of extended reality on workload. *Information Systems Frontiers*, 1–22. 10.1007/s10796-022-10244-x35194390

Yang, D. (2022). *Expert consensus on the metaverse in medicine*. Clinical eHealth.

Zhang, L., Li, F., Wang, P., Su, R., & Chi, Z. (2021). A blockchain-assisted massive IoT data collection intelligent framework. *IEEE Internet of Things Journal*.

Zhang, L., Zhang, Z., Wang, W., Jin, Z., Su, Y., & Chen, H. (2021). Research on a covert communication model realized by using smart contracts in blockchain environment. *IEEE Systems Journal*.

Chapter 10
Impact of UAV Communication in the Healthcare Sector on IoT Framework

M. Sathiya

Vivekanandha College of Arts and Sciences for Women (Autonomous), India

A. Gayathiri

Vivekanandha College of Arts and Sciences for Women (Autonomous), India

P. Sumitra

Vivekanandha College of Arts and Sciences for Women (Autonomous), India

S. Sabitha

Vivekanandha College of Arts and Sciences for Women (Autonomous), India

G. Sathya

Vivekanandha College of Arts and Sciences for Women (Autonomous), India

George Ghinea

Brunel University, Brunei

ABSTRACT

Unmanned aerial vehicles (UAV) are appropriate as viable instruments in communication systems. The concept of the unmanned aerial vehicle fits with the internet of things (IoT), which frequently deploys an outsized number of sensors across a large area. To deliver wireless communications, UAVs have been employed as an airborne communication platform. To show the idea's viability, the authors present a UAV-based architecture for communicating with BANs in a dependable and power-efficient manner. The design that has been suggested employs the wakeup-radio-based communication paradigm between a UAV and plenty BANs.

DOI: 10.4018/979-8-3693-2268-0.ch010

Copyright © 2024, IGI Global. Copying or distributing in print or electronic forms without written permission of IGI Global is prohibited.

The authors examine the proposed protocol's performance in terms of throughput and latency by designating different priority to hubs and gateways. The authors also highlight outstanding research topics and obstacles for building effective procedures for UAV-based data collecting in smart healthcare systems.

INTRODUCTION

A medical drone is a form of unmanned aerial vehicle (UAV) that healthcare practitioners use to transfer medicinal goods and communicate with patients from a distance. In most situations, healthcare providers employ drones for ferrying goods from health professionals and offices to patients, lab partners, and garbage removal centre.

Drones are becoming increasingly trustworthy and less pricey making them a promising developing technology for both catastrophe and non-emergency medical professionals. As a result, it's not shocking that the medical drone sector is exploding. According to one estimate, the overall medical drone market will be worth $643 million by 2027.

The more common popular word "drone" evolved because the loud and cadenced sound of vintage clothing military unmanned target aircraft reminded that of a male bee. The Navy developed a radio-controlled drone that carried a torpedo in 1942. Nowadays the drone is poised to become a significant disruptor in shipping. UAVs have been around for almost a century, dating back to World War I **(Chen, Yeh, Chamberland, huff, 2019)**. While UAVs were originally designed for use in combat, they are today employed for a wide range of purposes. A few weeks ago, the US military employed a drone commanded from the US to target an Iranian official in Baghdad.

Drones are becoming increasingly popular in healthcare for transporting medicines and other medical supplies to rural as well as disadvantaged areas. Zipline, the premier designer and manager of drones for shipment located in the United States, recently secured multiple collaborations around Africa to transport vaccinations, blood products, and other healthcare supplies to rustic and isolated places.

What Impact May Drones Have on Healthcare?

Drones, also referred to as unmanned aerial vehicles, were originally developed for military tasks in the United States and the United Kingdom amid World War I. Drone technology is currently exploited in today's world to increase its applicability in other critical industries, including healthcare.

With the advent of tele health and virtual care, it is now feasible to make credible judgments and deliver healthcare remedies to patients who are difficult to reach. The biggest barriers to widespread use of tele health include the supply of medications (Zhao, Wu, Wen, Liu, Wu, 2019), vaccinations, and other medical supplies to remote places, as well as the collection of biological samples for laboratory testing. Drones have shown enormous potential in overcoming these challenges.

Drones may be used to carry resources quickly and with great care. This has the potential to reduce injury to organs during transit. Drones can be used to transport medical supplies to those living in rural places as well as those afflicted by natural disasters or calamities at a low cost.

Drones can also be used inside hospitals to transport biological samples or medications from one level to the next or from one building to the next. Poor GPS signals or radio frequencies, on the other hand, could serve as an impediment to successful indoor drone operations. The Bluetooth protocol may be able to circumvent this barrier in part.

Drones can also be used for medical monitoring. Drones with integrated cameras can shoot movies or photographs of on-ground circumstances in densely populated places with a high frequency of infectious illnesses, assisting healthcare specialists in identifying and limiting the variables which contribute to rapid spread of illness.

Figure 1. Scope of communication technology with drones

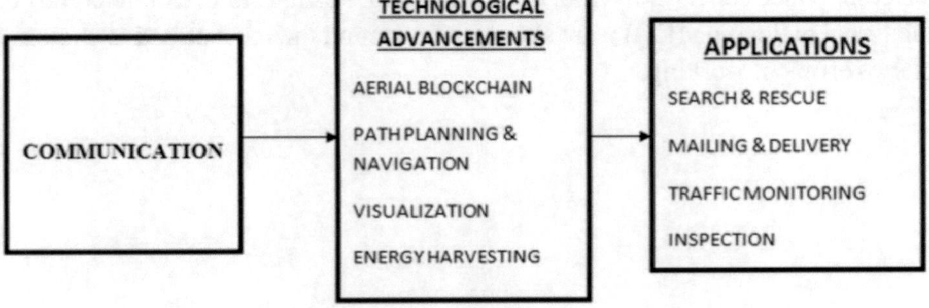

Tiny, unmanned aircraft with gripper arms can be used to deliver medications to elderly people and assist them with daily duties like as picking things up off the floor or sorting clothes. Robotics is quite crucial in this sort of job. When designing robotic vehicles for the elderly, two major factors must be considered: safety and dependability.

It just took three minutes for the drone to deliver AED to the patient. Such quick delivery is especially important for keeping the dying person's brain alive, as this fragile organ can only survive under perfused circumstances (constant blood flow). Any disruption in the circulatory system might cause serious destruction of brain tissue.

IOT-ENABLED UAV COMMUNICATION SYSTEM

Drones are unable to conduct computationally intensive tasks because to limited processing capability and onboard storage. Drone integration with the IoT (**Fotouhi, Ding, Hassan, 2017**) and the cloud is envisioned as a feasible solution to this problem. A service-oriented cloud-based management system, or Drone Planner, communicates via the MAVLink protocol and provides a simple yet efficient API for developing drone applic*ations (**Zen,Zeng, Zhang, 2017**). A machine-type multicast service (MtMS) for facilitating concurrent data transfer to MTC devices. Its architecture and methods were created to minimise latency while also reducing energy usage and control overhead. Several articles investigating IoT utilisation in end-to-end systems have revealed considerable outcomes.

The tradeoffs between turning agility, flying speed, and battery life have been explored using these parameters and varied experiments. The AidLife mobile infrastructure, which leverages an existing public transit system to build an adaptable system for trustworthy communication during a crisis. Physical collisions, the selection of IoT equipment, communication technologies, smart UAV-networking, and compliance concerns have all been addressed. Furthermore, cloudlets and computational offloading (CO) were shown to be around the most effective choices for energy-efficient working.

OVERVIEW ON UAVS AS MEMBERS OF IOT

UAVs for Wireless Networks

One of the most intriguing uses of the associated technology is the utilization of UAVs **(Gupta, Jain, Vazkun, 2016)** since important entity in next-generation wireless networks. A selection of promising application cases is provided below.

- UAV-borne base stations comprise fragmented 5G transmission networks in order to increase the coverage and capacity of existing wireless access technologies.
- Unmanned aerial vehicle (UAV)-based aerial networks that provide dependable, adaptive, and rapid wireless communication in public-safety settings.
- UAVs that assist earth's networks in disseminating knowledge while improving connectivity.
- Unmanned aerial vehicles (UAVs) as on-demand flying antennas for mmWave communications, massive MIMO, and 3D network MIMO.
- Unmanned aerial vehicles (UAVs) that provide reliable and renewable IoT uplink connection.
- Unmanned aerial vehicles (UAVs) that act as backhaul for terrestrial networks, enabling quick, dependable, cost-effective, and high-speed communication.
- UAVs that can store popular content and successfully serve mobile users by monitoring their mobility habits.
- UAVs that use wireless infrastructure for surveillance, remote sensing, virtual reality, and package delivery.
- In a smart-city the circumstances, unmanned aerial vehicles (UAVs) acquire huge amounts of municipal data and/or increase wireless coverage.

UAV–IoT Frameworks

As a result of their incredible agility, UAVs are already widely seen as promising members, if not educators, of the IoT vision. They may offer new value-added IoT services and stock a variety of MTMC devices. In accordance to the IoT idea, "things" are meant to be able to connect anywhere **(Ouahouah, Taleb, Song, Benzaid, 2017)**, at any time, and perform any service. UAVs can satisfy these requirements due to their autonomy, flexibility, and programmability. In this sector, a number of

UAV-enabled IoT frameworks covering a variety of applications in the real world have been proposed.

UAV-based crowd surveillance IoT platform **(Qin, Dong, Dai, Xu, 2019)**. Given a UAV's **(Zen, Zhang, 2017)** restricted computational electrical and battery capacity, its appropriate platform employs and leverages facial recognition techniques, as well as optimal multimedia processing offloading to a Mobile Edge Computing (MEC) node. The developed test bed takes video surveillance footage and utilizes facial recognition technology to identify individuals that are suspects using the Local Binary Pattern Histogram (LBPH) approach from the Open-Source Computer Vision (OpenCV) toolkit. In the proposed platform, a system orchestrator is employed to centrally control a fleet of UAVs.

A communication architecture for unmanned aerial vehicles (UAVs) in urban IoT scenarios **(Sanchez-Aguero, Valera, Vidal, Tipantuna, Hesselbach, 2020)**. It develops a multipath multihop architecture for connecting unmanned aerial vehicles to terrestrial control centres. According to real-world experiments, the given design significantly enhances control efficacy and dependability in the face of local congestion. Apparently to the researchers, the work was inspired by the DARPA Hackfest on Software Defined Radios.

5G and IoT Sensor Technologies for UAVs

5G technology will probably enhance mobile internet connections (European Commission, 2024), facilitate ultra-reliable networks with very low latency and very high availability, improve traffic safety and control, and support industrial applications such as inaccessible industrialized, guidance, surgical procedure, logistics, track, and task force management. It will be utilized for smart agriculture, precision farming, smart buildings, smart metering, 4K/8K UHD broadcasting (Jaziri, Nasri, Chahed, 2016), virtual and augmented reality, and other applications with no range constraints, such as residences, businesses, and huge events. This type of device communication may be integrated with normal Human-sort Communications (HTC) in the framework of a 5G infrastructure via proper gateways.

Figure 2. Unmanned aerial vehicle (UAV)-enhanced 5G-enabled IoT services

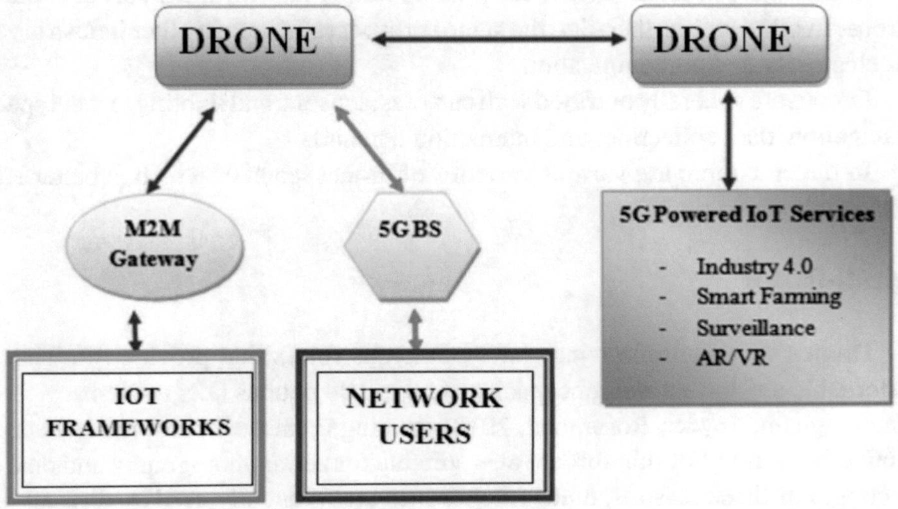

Security for UAVs Over IoT

Security in UAVs as part of an IoT (Sun, Duo, Wang, Zin, Gao, 2019) setting is a tough task that requires the right integration of several approaches linked to various aspects of IoT networking and UAV operation. The security and privacy implications of such an Endeavour are thoroughly discussed in the next two subsections. All strategy's fundamental concept is to add UAV-specific security extensions to various IoT technologies and security methodologies, allowing for the necessary cooperation.

Protection for UAVs

Some of the largest and most challenging challenges in developing the architecture of coordinated projects using several UAVs (Multi-UAVs) is the establishment of a network capable of connecting the various types of aircraft used while also protecting the vehicles and the fleet mission from failure. Since an outcome, it is vital to protect a fleet's lifetime by

(a) constructing and maintaining flexible aerial networks
(b) implementing proper fleet-management procedures.

TYPES OF DRONES DO MEDICAL PROVIDERS USE

Considering its name, a medical drone is simply like any other sort of economic drone. In other words, these are the same sorts of crafts seen in other industries such as electricity and communication.

Drones are generally outfitted with cameras, sensors, and lighting to meet specific navigation, data collecting, and interaction demands.

In the end, there are various varieties of drones, each of which is better suited for certain use cases.

Multi-Rotor

Drones with multiple wings have numerous rotors that provide lift. They are affordable and have a weight capacity of 50 to 100 pounds (Zègre-Hemsey, Bogle, Cunningham, Snyder, Rosamond, 2018), making them perfect for modest surgical deliveries. Drones of this sort are also suitable for aerial photography and data collecting. For those reasons, multi-rotor drones are frequently used by disaster relief organizations to assist in rescue missions.

Single Rotor

Single-rotor drones, as the name implies, feature only one rotor and are designed similarly to helicopters. The devices are far more efficient than multi-rotor drones in terms of operation and can fly for extended periods of time. Someone happen to be frequently heavier, significantly more sophisticated, and more costly.

Fixed-Wing Drones

Some medical providers are increasingly deploying fixed-wing aerial vehicles that look like aero planes, as well as fixed-wing hybrids that combine wings and rotors. These drones are better suited for extended distances flight.

Passenger Ambulance Drones

A few companies are now testing passenger ambulance drones, which can carry patients and medical personnel from one location to an additional one via the sky. To be sure, these sorts of aircraft will take some time to become economically viable. However, they have the potential to alter catastrophe medical reaction in the decades to come.

Benefits of Medical Drones

A medical unmanned aircraft offers several advantages to healthcare practitioners, making them more popular. Through that in mind, let's take a look at some of the benefits of employing medical drones for research.

Safe to Use

Medical drones do not need aeroplane pilots, making them far safer to conventional methods of transportation such as autos, helicopters, and aeroplanes. Radio frequency interference and probable theft are two of the most serious risks to drones. Before deploying UAVs in the field, medical teams are highly recommended to observe FAA requirements and monitor local meteorological conditions.

Fly Long Distances

The latest developments in beyond visual line of sight (BVLOS) technology allow drones to fly more safely than ever before. As a consequence, drones can transfer sensitive things to partners who are located outside of the local vicinity.

Save Money

Drone prices might vary based on models and dimension. Drones, in general, have lower capital and expenses for operation than traditional modes of transportation. Commercial drones can range in price from $500 to $5,000, depending on the manufacturer and type.

Drones have been developed to navigate to rural communities and hospitals in Taiwan, Nepal, and other nations. Zipline's drone delivery programmed will be expanded to remote towns in Maryland, Nevada, and Washington, as well as several Native American reservations. Condoms and birth control pills have been distributed to women across Ghana by drone. In Papua New Guinea, Médecins Sans Frontières tested the use of drones for carrying samples of stool for TB testing in 2014. Drones enable quick and cost-effective access to critical diagnosing methods in laboratories.

DRONES IN HEALTHCARE: SOME USE CASES

UAVs have a wide range of potential uses in healthcare. They are organised as follows: (1) Prehospital Emergency Care, (2) Accelerated The lab Diagnostic Testing, and (3) Surveillance services Presently, UAVs have been demonstrated to transport vaccinations (Shaikh, Baidya, Levorato, 2018), haemoglobin, and automatic the outside cardiac arrest machines. Furthermore, they are being employed as a public health monitoring method to identify mosquito habitats and drowning victims on shoreline.

The Indian Scenario

In India, the National Disaster Management Authority (NDMA) (Motlagh, Bagaa, Taleb, Song, 2017) has begun to use drones for disaster relief and rescue. Similarly, during elections in Chhattisgarh, the Central Reserve Police Force employed UAVs (Zen, Zhang, 2016) to monitor a 40,000-square-kilometer region and provide round-the-clock surveillance. The Uttar Pradesh government employed drones to ensure peace and order during the Kumbh Mela event in Allahabad, as did the Mumbai police during the spectacular Ganpati festival. Drones are being used in solar power facilities by the National Thermal Power Corporation for predictive maintenance, monitoring, and intrusion detection. A single unit of blood was successfully carried by UAV from a distant primary health care facility in Uttarakhand's Tehri district.

Drones might be game changers in areas that are especially challenging to reach regionally. A trial project is set to begin in Pune and Nandurbar. The launch will be funded by a grant from the Serum Institute of India, the world's largest vaccine maker (Qin, Dong, Wang, Xu, 2019). Telangana's authority, in partnership with Apollo Hospitals and the World Economic Forum, has finalized plans for a six-month trial programme named 'Pharmaceutical products from the Sky' to begin in 2020. The project's goal is to investigate the use of drones to improve access to healthcare for communities throughout Telangana.

DRONE REGULATIONS IN INDIA

Drones might be game changers in locations that are very difficult to reach economically. A pilot project would be launched in Pune and Nandurbar. The Serum Institute of India, the world's largest vaccine manufacturer, will support the launch. Telangana's government has approved preparations for a six-month pilot initiative called 'Pharmaceutical Products from the Sky,' which will begin in 2020 in collaboration with Apollo Hospitals and the World Economic Forum. The project's purpose is to explore possibilities at using drones to increase access to healthcare for people across Telangana.

Policy Development Considerations

The Indian Ministry of Civil Aviation published an in-depth regulations for the use of unmanned aerial systems (UAS), often known as drones, in December 2018. The following would allow commercial usage of drones inside Visual Line of Sight (VLOS) (Gettinger,2017). For licenced activities, travelling a drone would need manual controls and an operator permission. Technical guidance for policy-compliant production is additionally published.

The Ministry of Civil Aviation issued the Drone Ecosystem Policy Roadmap in February 2019, proposing transit of new kinds of airfreight, acknowledged vendors of services for the skies deconfliction and permission (Digital Sky), and the ability to fly drones beyond visual line of sight (BVLOS). These legislative changes are essential to adopt drone delivery solutions for medical and other purposes, as BVLOS flying needs to occur to make drone deployment commercially viable. Drone delivery is not permitted under present regulations, however firms may apply to the DGCA for an exception.

Technical Issues Specifications

Drone designs have grown more competent, inexpensive, and readily accessible as a result of the development of microminiaturization and mass manufacture of underlying technologies like as processors, micro electrical mechanical systems (MEMS) sensors, and batteries for smart devices. Fixed-wing, rotary-wing, multi-rotor, and hybrid designs are the most frequent. Infrared heat multicolored, and hyper spectral imaging instruments are available. Drones are usually made up of an airframe, a propulsion system, and a navigational system.

Automation, robotics, miniaturization, materials science, spectral and thermal imaging, and light detection and ranging advancements have resulted in drone-enabled methods in sectors that are as varied as the farming industry, power, buildings, and communication, as well as gather and disaster management. Drones will become even more adaptable as a dizzying array of technologies—Wi-Fi connectivity, rechargeable batteries, compact high-resolution digital cameras, GPS receiver chips, accelerometer chips, and other miniaturized electronics—become available.

Drones allow for the delivery of blood, vaccinations, birth control, snake bite serum, and other medical supplies to remote regions, as well as the capacity to reach patients who require rapid medical treatment under a few minutes, which can be the difference between life and death in some circumstances. They may transfer medicine within hospital boundaries, transmit blood between hospital buildings, and provide elderly patients with gadgets to help them age in situ. UAS (Wang, Bai, Zhang, Guan, Chen, 2012) provide the health care business with a plethora of intriguing options, including the ability to save money as well as lives. The prospects exist, which is why researchers, businesses, and non-profit organizations are looking to UAS to deliver implementations that increase efficiency and therapeutic outcomes.

Transporting Blood and Hazardous Compounds

Toxic materials ought to be consistently carried properly and in conformity with approved biohazard regulations (Lien, Chen, Lin, 2011). Because it is an established practice, this use case does not necessarily address an unmet need in the medical field. However, it is frequently exceedingly expensive and, in certain cases, time-sensitive.

Drones are revolutionizing blood and hazardous materials deliveries in the healthcare sector by delivering faster, more efficient, and dependable delivery choices. Listed below are some examples of how drones are affecting this field:

- Improved delivery time
- Increased accessibility
- Enhanced safety
- Cost-effective

Different organizations and businesses have been investigating the use of drones for medical delivery in recent years. Zipline, a California-based startup, for example, utilises drones to carry health care supplies, such as blood and vaccinations, to distant places in Rwanda and Ghana. Vayu, another startup, is collaborating with the Indian government to distribute vaccinations and healthcare goods to outlying parts of the nation as well.

Vaccine and Medicine Delivery

Drones are also assisting in the delivery of vaccinations and medications in the medical industry. Access to healthcare services and medical supplies is limited in many places of the world owing to a lack of infrastructure or tough terrain (Zègre-Hemsey, Bogle, Cunningham, Snyder, Rosamond, 2018). This is especially true in rural and distant locations, where getting immunizations and medications can be difficult. Drones provide a solution to this problem by distributing medical supplies such as vaccinations and medications in a timely, dependable, and cost-effective manner.

Drones (**Yang, Cao, Yin, Xiao, Xi, Wu, 2017**) were utilized to transport medical supplies, including COVID-19 test kits, personal protective equipment (PPE), and vaccinations, in various regions of the world in 2020, during the COVID-19 pandemic. Furthermore, the World Health Organization (WHO) has recognized the use of drones for vaccination distribution as a critical priority in achieving universal health coverage, particularly in remote locations.

Diagnostics

One of the primary purposes for drones is diagnosing. When the patient's specimen is obtained, it must be sent to the lab, and the analysis must be performed within a particular time frame, which might be as short as two hours because certain diagnostic procedures are temperature and time-sensitive. Alienated populations play a key role here, and UAVs have a growing and rising market.

Because the same methods for diagnosing may not be available at every institution, clinic, or even chemist, shuttles are regularly deployed between healthcare providers **(Condoluci, Araniti, Mahmoodi, Dohler, 2016)**. A drone's great range, dexterity, and capacity allow it to perform tests that are diagnostic under time restrictions, and it has the potential to significantly boost patient results by delivering medical samples for testing and analysis in a more timely and secure manner.

Organ Transfers

Given the confined time frame for delivering transplanted from donor to recipient, which is normally between 4-36 hours subject to the donated organ type, the need for extremely speedy conveyance, such as private aeroplane charter or helicopter, is critical. Drones can make transplant transportation easier, more effective, and also more inexpensive. Getting an organ to a patient in need promptly might be difficult in certain rural or rural regions. Drones have the potential to shorten transit times and improve the success rate of donor organs.

For example, the University of Maryland Medical Centre used a drone to carry a kidney for transplantation in 2019. The organ was delivered to the recipient after the drone flew 2.8 miles hauling it in a temperature-controlled package.

Among the numerous benefits of drones in healthcare, there are certain issues that must be faced. One of the most significant obstacles is the lack of legislation and standards controlling the use of drones in healthcare. Proper training and certification of drone pilots and operators, as well as the establishment of safety standards, are also required.

Transporting Blood and Other Supplies

Flirtey, a drone company, just performed the first ship-to-shore drone delivery in the United States. In accordance to a news release, the assignment, which was undertaken in collaboration with the John Hopkins University School of Medicine and the nonprofit Field Innovation Team (FIT), demonstrated how UAS may convey relief like as medications and water during a catastrophe situation. During the demonstration, the drones transported medical samples for emergency testing, flying between an on-site medical relief camp in Cape May, New Jersey, and a test laboratory on a vessel off the coast of New Jersey. In addition, the drones ferried medical supplies from the ship to the onshore surgical camp.

This is not the first time Flirtey has accomplished a successful mission for the medical industry. In the summer of 2016, the company participated in the Let's Fly Wisely event in Wise **(Cordeiro, Ishihara, Ferreira, 2020)**, Va., where they collaborated with the Remote Area Medical Clinic (RAM), the Mid-Atlantic Aviation Partnership at Virginia Tech (MAAP), and NASA to bring the medical packages to volunteers on the ground, who in turn ensured that overlooked attendees were provided with the packages—the first time a UAS delivered medical supplies and medicinal products in the US.

Stan Brock, the founder and president of RAM, a charity organization that offers medical treatment to rural locations, became interested in the deployment of delivery drones a few years ago. At the time, the organization had just recently begun air ambulance operations to deliver medication and vaccinations to remote areas of the upper Amazon rain forest. Manned fixed-wing helicopters fly every two days to provide immunizations, snakebite serum, and other medical supplies to outlying settlements, which is a more expensive and difficult operation than employing UAS.

Aside from last year's presentation, RAM has been working with Dennis Strege, owner of MasterFlight Inc., to develop a drone prototype specifically for this use. The aircraft he's upgrading, initially designed for power line inspections, will be able to fly 150 nautical miles with a cargo of 55 pounds. The UAS will be able to make repeated deliveries throughout the day despite terrible weather conditions that would leave manned aircraft grounded. Strege characterized the vehicle as appropriate for a RAM programme launched recently in the Philippines, where medication must be delivered over extensive expanses of water.

Hospital Deliveries

Nowadays, much of the research involving health-care drones focuses on distribution to remote places, but that isn't the only way UAS may help this business. Will Stavanja, founder of consulting firm Wilstair, is one of several researching how UAS may be utilised in hospitals.

One method is to transfer blood samples and drugs from floor to floor or building to building rather than making such deliveries on foot or using the pressurized tube systems commonly used in hospitals, according to Stavanja. This can be very beneficial for expanding hospitals. Expansion of a pneumatic tube system is an expensive undertaking, but deploying a drone instead allows hospitals to move experiments and drugs from floor to main floor at a minimal cost.

Plenty of people who are hesitant to utilize drones within hospitals are concerned that it may cost them their jobs, according to Stavanja. However, he claims that it will allow them to spend more time with patients and focus on other activities. Persons are additionally required to give flight routes and control the drones to guarantee the proper cargo is transported at the right temperature to the right spot.

"Based on an application for smart phones, physicians are able to say that they want a certain item delivered in Room X and the aerial vehicle can be automatically established to do so," she added. "This also allows organizations to use their current employees to do other jobs while helping with other medical centre demands." Drones can perform some of the minor tasks, such as transporting medications from floor over floor. This results in improved treatment for sufferers."

Flight Conditions

Each drone deployment device will always have operational limitations. Weather has a huge impact on the whole aviation industry, posing special difficulties in addition to typical weather-related issues. Flight time, payload capacity, and safe flying altitudes may all be affected by air volume, transpiration, and heat. In contrast to manned aviation, where graphic and instrument regulations determine what operations are permitted based on current weather conditions, drone operations are primarily limited by visibility conditions (e.g., haze, fog, low clouds), with operators having the final say on precipitation, temperature, and other factors. Future study will be needed to determine how well medical drones perform in various weather and illumination conditions.

CONCLUSION

Drones are increasingly being examined for medical applications all around the world. It is a supplement to current transportation networks that provides benefit over conventional techniques in certain conditions. Drones' appropriate placement in health-care systems is still being explored, and will be influenced by local requirements and resources. Projects trying bi-directional drone transport are currently researching potential, developing technologies that and gaining hands-on knowledge. Drone usage has the potential to improve medical services, especially among faraway and/or disadvantaged locations, by reducing lab testing turnaround times, enabling just-in-time lifesaving medical supply/device delivery, and lowering urban pharmaceutical care costs. Robotics provide a huge chance for tackling the supply chain for healthcare inadequacies, decreasing running out and waste. Deaths caused by infections such as the dengue virus, ailments such as newborn hemorrhaged loss of blood due to incidents, and even time-critical organ transplantation may be managed with faster answers, higher-quality goods, and improved availability. By implementing modern logistical systems in the sky, wellness deficiencies, particularly those felt in remote places suffering from a lack of facility and predicted expansion that outpaces investment, can be addressed and lives avoided.

FUTURE WORK

Future studies should investigate human-drone interactions in real-world scenarios. While surveys and simulation studies show that the majority of bystanders would be comfortable interacting with medical drones, more research is needed to understand how this might work in practice, particularly in the context of communication with 9-1-1 dispatchers along with partnership with working in CPR as well as employing an AED, both of and these are notoriously difficult and call for educating the public on their own. The general public may have different perspectives on these new drone capabilities. When drones become extensively deployed, however, they may generate public concerns about safety, privacy, and financial expenses.

ACKNOWLEDGEMENT

The author would like to express to the management for providing the opportunity to use our college's facilities for this chapter.

REFERENCES

Chen, Z., Yeh, S., Chamberland, J. F., & Huff, G. H. (2019). A Sensor-Driven Analysis of Distributed Direction Finding Systems Based on UAV Swarms. *Sensors (Basel)*, 19(12), 2659. 10.3390/s1912265931212836

Condoluci, M., Araniti, G., Mahmoodi, T., & Dohler, M. (2016). Enabling the iot machine age with 5g: Machine-type multicast services for innovative real-time applications. *IEEE Access, 4.*

Cordeiro, T. F. K., Ishihara, J. Y., & Ferreira, H. C. (2020). A Decentralized Low-Chattering Sliding Mode Formation Flight Controller for a Swarm of UAVs. *Sensors (Basel)*, 20(11), 3094. 10.3390/s2011309432486183

Fotouhi, A., Ding, M., & Hassan, M. (2017). Understanding autonomous drone maneuverability for internet of things applications. *A World of Wireless, Mobile and Multimedia Networks (WoWMoM), IEEE 18th International Symposium*. IEEE.

Gettinger, D. (2017). *Drones at Home: Public Safety Drones*. Center for the Study of the Drone at Bard College.

Gupta, L., Jain, R., & Vaszkun, G. (2016). Survey of important issues in UAV communication networks. *IEEE Communications Surveys and Tutorials*, 18(2), 1123–1152. 10.1109/COMST.2015.2495297

ICT-317669 METIS Project. Scenarios, Requirements and KPIs for 5G Mobile and WirelessSystem.Availableonline:https://cordis.europa.eu/docs/projects/cnect/9/317669/080/deliverables/001-ETISD11v1pdf.pdf

Jaziri, A., Nasri, R., & Chahed, T. (2016). *Congestion mitigation in 5G networks using drone relays*. In *Proceedings of the 2016 International Wireless Communications and Mobile Computing Conference (IWCMC)*, Paphos, Cyprus. 10.1109/IWCMC.2016.7577063

Lien, S. Y., Chen, K. C., & Lin, Y. (2011). Toward ubiquitous massive accesses in 3GPP machine-to-machine communications. *IEEE Communications Magazine*, 49(4), 66–74. 10.1109/MCOM.2011.5741148

Ma, X., Liu, T., Liu, S., Kacimi, R., & Dhaou, R. (2020). Priority-Based Data Collection for UAV-Aided Mobile Sensor Network. *Sensors (Basel)*, 20(11), 3034. 10.3390/s2011303432471092

Motlagh, N. H., Bagaa, M., & Taleb, T. (2017). UAV-based IoT platform: A crowd surveillance use case. *IEEE Communications Magazine*, 55(2), 128–134. 10.1109/MCOM.2017.1600587CM

Motlagh, N. H., Bagaa, M., Taleb, T., & Song, J. (2017). Connection steering mechanism between mobile networks for reliable UAV's IoT platform. In *Proceedings of the 2017 IEEE International Conference on Communications (ICC)*, Paris, France. 10.1109/ICC.2017.7996718

Motlagh, N. H., Taleb, T., & Arouk, O. (2016). Low-Altitude Unmanned Aerial Vehicles-Based Internet of Things Services: Comprehensive Survey and Future Perspectives. *IEEE Internet of Things Journal*, 3(6), 899–922. 10.1109/JIOT.2016.2612119

Motlagh, N., Taleb, T., & Arouk, O. (2016). Low-altitude unmanned aerial vehicles-based internet of things services: Comprehensive survey and future perspectives. *IEEE Internet of Things Journal, 3*(6).

Mozaffari, M., Saad, W., Bennis, M., & Debbah, M. (2016). Unmanned Aerial Vehicle With Underlaid Device-to-Device Communications: Performance and Tradeoffs. *IEEE Transactions on Wireless Communications*, 15(6), 3949–3963. 10.1109/TWC.2016.2531652

Narang, M., Liu, W., Gutierrez, J., & Chiaraviglio, L. (2017). A cyber physical buses-and-drones mobile edge infrastructure for large scale disaster emergency communications. *2017 IEEE 37th International Conference on Distributed Computing Systems Workshops (ICDCSW)*. IEEE.

Ouahouah, S., Taleb, T., Song, J., & Benzaid, C. (2017). *Efficient offloading mechanism for UAVs-based value added services*. In *Proceedings of the 2017 IEEE International Conference on Communications (ICC)*, Paris, France. 10.1109/ICC.2017.7997362

Qin, Z., Dong, C., Wang, W., & Xu, Z. (2019). Trajectory Planning for Data Collection of Energy-Constrained Heterogeneous UAVs. *Sensors (Basel)*, 19(22), 4884. 10.3390/s1922488431717421

Qin, Z., Li, A., Dong, C., Dai, H., & Xu, Z. (2019). Completion Time Minimization for Multi-UAV InformationCollection via Trajectory Planning. *Sensors (Basel)*, 19(18), 4032. 10.3390/s1918403231540537

Sanchez-Aguero, V., Valera, F., Vidal, I., Tipantuna, C., & Hesselbach, X. (2020). Energy-Aware Management in Multi-UAV Deployments: Modelling and Strategies. *Sensors (Basel)*, 20(10), 2791. 10.3390/s2010279132422970

Shaikh, Z., Baidya, S., & Levorato, M. (2018). Robust Multi-Path Communications for UAVs in the Urban IoT. In *Proceedings of the 2018 IEEE International Conference on Sensing, Communication and Networking (SECON Workshops)*, (pp. 1–5). IEEE. 10.1109/SECONW.2018.8396356

Sun, H., Duo, B., Wang, Z., Lin, X., & Gao, C. (2019). Aerial Cooperative Jamming for Cellular-Enabled UAV Secure Communication Network: Joint Trajectory and Power Control Design. *Sensors (Basel)*, 19(20), 4440. 10.3390/s1920444031614986

Wang, D., Bai, L., Zhang, X., Guan, W., & Chen, C. (2012). Collaborative relay beamforming strategies for multiple destinations with guaranteed QoS in wireless machine-to-machine networks. *International Journal of Distributed Sensor Networks*, 8(8), 525640. 10.1155/2012/525640

Yang, P., Cao, X., Yin, C., Xiao, Z., Xi, X., & Wu, D. (2017). Proactive Drone-Cell Deployment: Overload Relief for a Cellular Network Under Flash Crowd Traffic. *IEEE Transactions on Intelligent Transportation Systems*, 18(10), 2877–2892. 10.1109/TITS.2017.2700432

Zègre-Hemsey, J. K., Bogle, B., Cunningham, C. J., Snyder, K., & Rosamond, W. (2018). Delivery of automated external defibrillators (AED) by drones: Implications for emergency cardiac care. *Current Cardiovascular Risk Reports*, 12(11), 25. 10.1007/s12170-018-0589-230443281

Zeng, Y., & Zhang, R. (2017). Energy-Efficient UAV Communication With Trajectory Optimization. *IEEE Transactions on Wireless Communications*, 16(6), 3747–3760. 10.1109/TWC.2017.2688328

Zeng, Y., Zhang, R., & Lim, T. J. (2016). Throughput Maximization for UAV-Enabled Mobile Relaying Systems. *IEEE Transactions on Communications*, 64(12), 4983–4996. 10.1109/TCOMM.2016.2611512

Zhang, J., Zeng, Y., & Zhang, R. (2017). Spectrum and energy efficiency maximization in UAV-enabled mobile relaying. In *Proceedings of the 2017 IEEE International Conference on Communications (ICC)*, Paris, France. 10.1109/ICC.2017.7997208

Zhao, H., Wu, S., Wen, Y., Liu, W., & Wu, X. (2019). Modeling and Flight Experiments for Swarms of High Dynamic UAVs: A Stochastic Configuration Control System with Multiplicative Noises. *Sensors (Basel)*, 19(15), 3278. 10.3390/s1915327831349676

Chapter 11
UAV Communication for Various Learning Approaches in Metaverse Healthcare Analysis Using Cloud Computing

Akshay Bhuvaneswari Ramakrishnan
https://orcid.org/0009-0000-1578-0984
SASTRA University, India

S. Srijanani
Velammal Engineering College, India

Mukunth Madavan
SASTRA University, India

R Manikandan
https://orcid.org/0000-0001-6116-2132
SASTRA University, India

S. Magesh
https://orcid.org/0000-0003-2876-7337
Dr. M.G.R Educational and Research Institute, India

ABSTRACT

The revolutionary integration of unmanned aerial vehicle (UAV) communication, metaverse technology, learning techniques, and cloud computing in the healthcare industry is investigated in this chapter. Unmanned aerial vehicles (UAVs) are capable

DOI: 10.4018/979-8-3693-2268-0.ch011

Copyright © 2024, IGI Global. Copying or distributing in print or electronic forms without written permission of IGI Global is prohibited.

of collecting a wide variety of data, which can then be viewed in the metaverse. In order to detect illnesses at an earlier stage, machine learning is powered by cloud computing. At the same time that ethical concerns and regulatory problems are being highlighted, the necessity of international collaboration is being emphasized. Applications in the real world illustrate a future in which medical care is not limited by geographic boundaries; it will be possible to receive treatment remotely and receive medical education on a global scale. The chapter is a representation of a collective aspiration to make healthcare a fundamental human right, so rewriting the history of human compassion and the advancement of medical technology.

INTRODUCTION

Unmanned Aerial Vehicles (UAVs) that are fitted with sophisticated sensors have emerged as an essential component in the process of data collection within the healthcare industry (A Román et al.,2024). Unmanned Aerial Vehicles (UAVs) are able to circumvent geographical limitations and collect important life signs and environmental data in real time, which is essential for medical study. These vehicles take on the role of data couriers by utilizing unmanned aerial vehicle (UAV) connectivity, thereby bridging the gap between remote places and medical professionals (Saunders ., et al.,2024). The technological complexities of unmanned aerial vehicle (UAV) communication and the revolutionary influence it has on the accessibility of healthcare data are discussed in this chapter. Concurrently, the manifestation of the metaverse as a revolutionary space for the depiction of healthcare is taking place. Through the use of the metaverse, which functions as a dynamic canvas, raw data may be transformed into interactive simulations, which in turn makes intensive medical study possible. In order to fully realize the promise of the metaverse for use in healthcare applications, it is essential to address technical factors such as data rendering, user interaction, and integration with data obtained by unmanned aerial vehicles (UAVs). Within the scope of this chapter, the technological complexities of utilizing the metaverse for the purpose of healthcare visualization and analysis are investigated. The central focus of this investigation is on the interactions between unmanned aerial vehicle (UAV) communication, metaverse technology, a variety of learning approaches, and cloud computing. In this context, the focus shifts to technical elements, such as the incorporation of cloud platforms and machine learning techniques. The purpose of this chapter is to analyze the technical aspects of unmanned aerial vehicle (UAV) communication (Al-lQubaydhi, N ., et al.,2024) in conjunction with learning strategies within the metaverse (Zhang, X., et al.,2024), and to investigate how cloud computing enhances the synergy between these two aspects. Using a technical perspective, this chapter envisions a future in which healthcare analysis is not only accurate and data-driven, but also broadly accessible, transcending the restrictions that have traditionally been associated with it.

UAV COMMUNICATION IN HEALTHCARE

When it comes to the integration of unmanned aerial vehicles (UAVs) and the collecting of data in the healthcare industry, UAVs that are outfitted with sophisticated sensors act as messengers between the actual and virtual domains of healthcare (Gad.G, et al.,2024). The landscape of remote medical interventions is being reimagined by these unmanned vehicles, which are able to transmit data in real time (Vijitha Ananthi, J., et al.,2023). They offer prompt, data-driven assistance to medical personnel in both routine and emergency situations. Figure 1 illustrates the technological complexities of unmanned aerial vehicle (UAV) communication, which highlight the importance of ensuring the safe and rapid transmission of real-time data. This part navigates the complications and promises of unmanned aerial vehicle (UAV) communication in the context of changing healthcare accessible (Khaer, A., et al.,2023). From guaranteeing interoperability standards to resolving challenges connected to data security and privacy, this section covers all of these topics.

Figure 1. UAV communication infrastructure in healthcare

When it comes to sending medical expertise to locations that are inaccessible or remote, unmanned aerial vehicles (UAVs) serve as crucial conduits in addition to transmitting data. Healthcare personnel are able to remotely analyze medical issues, provide advice, and organize emergency actions by utilizing communication channels that operate in real time (Budiyono, A., et al., 2023). The adaptability of unmanned aerial vehicle (UAV) communication extends beyond the realm of emergency situations, making it possible to carry out normal healthcare interventions, health monitoring, and preventative measures in areas with limited infrastructure. Important aspects of this technological integration include the interoperability of data gathered by unmanned aerial vehicles (UAVs) and the smooth integration of that data into processes in the healthcare industry. It is of the utmost importance to establish secure communication protocols in order to guarantee the confidentiality and privacy of patient information when UAV data is being transmitted between devices (Tedeschi, P., et al., 2023). Furthermore, in order to build a cohesive healthcare ecosystem, the technological standards that govern the communication of unmanned aerial vehicles (UAVs) need to be aligned with the Electronic Health Records (EHRs) and health information systems that are already in place. This section elucidates how unmanned aerial vehicle (UAV) communication emerges as a transformational force, not only democratizing healthcare accessible but also boosting the precision and timeliness of data-driven medical analysis

METAVERSE SIMULATIONS AND DATA VISUALIZATION

The power of real-time rendering is harnessed by metaverse simulations, which enables the creation of interactive environments that provide medical practitioners with an in-depth and all-encompassing perspective of complex medical problems (Chengoden, R., et al.,2023). The information that is gathered by unmanned aerial vehicles (UAVs) is instantaneously analyzed in these dynamic virtual domains, where it is transformed into lively simulations that react in real time. The immediacy of this information (Qu, Q., et al., 2024) not only improves the interpretability of healthcare data but also makes it easier for multiple people to work together to explore and analyze it (Li, K., et al., 2022). This information is being rapidly transmitted to the metaverse, which is represented by symbols that are symbolic of virtual reality. Arrows illustrate this transmission. Within the metaverse, healthcare scenarios are brought to life, presenting simulations that offer engaging experiences. This visual encapsulation represents the transformative process in which data generated by unmanned aerial vehicles (UAVs) evolves into immersive metaverse scenarios. It also highlights the essential role that integration plays in defining future healthcare experiences.. The technical complexities lie in the seamless integration of data collected by UAVs, which ensures that the virtual representation continues to be synchronized with the information that is continually evolving in the real world. These simulations go beyond the conventional methods of data visualization by providing a platform that is both responsive and immersive. This platform allows medical professionals to traverse, dissect, and comprehend complex medical problems with an unprecedented level of detail and interactivity. As an additional benefit, this real-time rendering capabilities acts as a bridge between the physical and virtual realms, bridging the gap for improved healthcare analysis and decision-making.

CLOUD COMPUTING AND MACHINE LEARNING

The combination of Machine Learning (ML) and Cloud Computing (CC) has a powerful impact on the merging of healthcare and technology (Gao, JK., et al.,2020). These technologies are crucial in harnessing the complete capacity of healthcare data, specifically data gathered by Unmanned Aerial Vehicles (UAVs) (Aazam, M., et al., 2021). The workflow commences with unmanned aerial vehicles (UAVs) outfitted with state-of-the-art sensors, crossing geographical boundaries to acquire up-to-the-minute healthcare data. However, the full potential is realized when this data is transmitted to the cloud. Cloud systems, due to their intrinsic ability to scale and analyze large volumes of data, function as dynamic centers where extensive healthcare data is utilized (Prawiyogi, A.G., et al.,2022). Machine learning algorithms, located within these cloud platforms, undertake a process of analysis and interpretation. They analyze the complexities of data collected by UAVs, discovering patterns that may be difficult for humans to perceive. Cloud computing goes beyond simple storage and serves as a central platform where machine learning algorithms analyze intricate datasets, providing early indications of illness and revealing trends in healthcare needs.This combination marks the beginning of a new era in healthcare analytics. Utilizing the vast computational power of the cloud, machine learning algorithms convert unprocessed data into practical and useful information. Envision a situation in which predictive analytics form the fundamental basis for medical decision-making, providing a proactive approach to healthcare. As algorithms progress, precision medicine transforms from a mere idea to a concrete reality, influencing healthcare solutions customized to the unique profiles of specific patients (Mir, M.H., et al.,2021). This paradigm change extends beyond exclusive institutions and is a significant step towards making healthcare accessible to all. Now, let's examine a particular scenario that demonstrates how the integration of UAV data gathering with cloud-based analytics and predictive insights might profoundly transform healthcare procedures.

ETHICAL AND MORAL CONSIDERATIONS

It is vital that a critical investigation into the ethical and moral dimensions of this technological transformation be carried out in the midst of the confluence of unmanned aerial vehicle (UAV) communication, metaverse technology, and machine learning in the healthcare industry (Cawthorne, D., et al., 2020). The protection of patient privacy is of the utmost importance in light of the fact that information is moving between the physical world and the metaverse in a seamless manner (Wang, N., et al., 2021). As a result of the merging of realities, questions about permission, data security, and the construction of rigorous ethical frameworks are becoming more prevalent. Furthermore, the increasing sophistication of machine learning algorithms presents ethical difficulties (Wang, N., 2021), particularly in sensitive medical contexts. This phenomenon shines a light on the ethicality of algorithmic conclusions and the potential biases that are embedded within them.

REGULATORY CHALLENGES AND INTERNATIONAL COLLABORATION

Not only does the incorporation of unmanned aerial vehicle (UAV) communication, metaverse technology, and advanced machine learning in the healthcare industry undergo a transformation in medical procedures, but it also presents complex issues for regulatory frameworks (Ali, M., et al., 2023). The purpose of this part is to look into the dual role that regulatory systems play, which is to encourage innovation while also protecting against the possibility of misuse. In order to successfully navigate this delicate balance, worldwide collaboration is required. Because unmanned aerial vehicles (UAVs) are able to cross national lines, international cooperation is becoming increasingly necessary in order to fully exploit the promise of the metaverse (Dwivedi, Y.K., et al., 2022). A strong emphasis is placed on the complexity involved in formulating rules and regulations that foster innovation while also maintaining ethical and legal integrity. Specifically, this part places an emphasis on the necessity of collective intelligence on a worldwide scale in order to formulate policies that are responsible in their support of innovation. There is a graphic depiction of the real-world uses of this integration, which demonstrates a future in which the traditional limitations of time and geography will no longer be able to restrict the delivery of medical treatment. With the potential to have far-reaching effects, the potential influence ranges from remote medical oversight to worldwide medical education cooperation.

IMPLEMENTATIONS IN THE REAL WORLD

The real-world applications of combining unmanned aerial vehicle (UAV) communication, metaverse technology, and machine learning in healthcare provide a vivid picture of a future that is unrestricted by old barriers. This transition from theoretical exploration to practical implications involves the use of these technologies. Imagine the possibility of a scenario in which a medical professional located in a metropolitan hub is able to successfully bridge geographical divides by utilizing real-time data sent by unmanned aerial vehicles (UAVs) to coordinate a complex therapy. Imagine a group of medical students from different continents working together to do a virtual dissection within the metaverse. This would allow them to get a comprehensive understanding of the subject matter. Visualize a future in which individuals suffering from uncommon diseases are able to connect with one another through the use of metaverse-based virtual support groups, thereby establishing a sense of belonging. Within this part, concrete views into the revolutionary possibilities of these interconnected technologies are provided. These glimpses illustrate a future in which healthcare transcends temporal and spatial restrictions, giving solutions that are both equitable and inventive to a wide range of medical concerns.

Disaster Response and Relief Efforts

In the context of disaster response and relief activities, the integrated application of unmanned aerial vehicle (UAV) communication, metaverse technology, and machine learning appears as a transformational potential force (Ozturkcan, S., 2023) . The use of unmanned aerial vehicles (UAVs) that are fitted with sophisticated sensors allows them to swiftly traverse impacted areas following natural disasters, thereby obtaining real-time data that is essential for making educated decisions. When it comes to disaster preparedness, metaverse simulations are an extremely important component since they enable first responders to mimic a variety of scenarios and ultimately improve their response techniques.Rapid data processing is ensured by the seamless integration of cloud computing, which enables immediate analysis of massive datasets. The quick identification of affected locations, the assessment of infrastructure damage, and the evaluation of possible dangers are all made easier by this capability. In the process of processing this data, machine learning algorithms detect patterns that are symptomatic of emerging problems such as outbreaks of disease or shortages of resources of various kinds. The application of this predictive analytics technique improves the effectiveness of relief efforts and makes it possible to take preventative measures.

Telemedicine and Continuous Monitoring

The convergence of unmanned aerial vehicle (UAV) communication, metaverse technology, and machine learning reshapes the landscape of telemedicine, enabling opportunities for continuous monitoring and individualized healthcare solutions that have never been seen before. Under this model, patients who are outfitted with wearable gadgets become active participants in the management of their own health.The data obtained by unmanned aerial vehicles (UAVs) serves as the basis for continuous monitoring, with sensors capturing (Bibri, S.E., et al., 2023) important health measures in real time. A continuous feedback loop between patients and healthcare providers is established as a result of the seamless transfer of this data through communication channels on unmanned aerial vehicles (UAVs). Through the use of metaverse simulations, telemedicine experiences can be elevated to the level of interactive virtual consultations. It is possible for medical experts to remotely examine patients, discuss symptoms, and adapt interventions through the use of this virtual connection, which is made possible by metaverse technology.

Precision Medicine and Personalized Therapies

The combination of unmanned aerial vehicle (UAV) communication, metaverse technology, and machine learning represents a revolutionary step forward in the field of healthcare, notably in the areas of precision medicine and individualized therapies. Unmanned Aerial Vehicles (UAVs) that are fitted with sophisticated sensors are able to collect an unprecedented amount of varied health data, which includes everything from ambient elements to real-time patient vitals (Hemachandran, K., et al., 2023).Computing in the cloud emerges as the primary facilitator, providing the infrastructure necessary to store, process, and analyze this enormous dataset. When this occurs, metaverse simulations come into action, thereby generating interactive environments in which medical personnel are able to investigate intricate medical situations. The synergy with machine learning algorithms that are working within the cloud environment makes it possible to recognize subtle patterns and correlations that may be difficult for humans to observe.It is possible to tailor medical interventions to the specific characteristics of each individual patient through the utilization of this integrated strategy. According to the information presented in this part, precision medicine is not a theoretical concept but rather a concrete reality in which therapies are precisely adjusted to match the specific requirements of each individual patient. Integration goes beyond traditional diagnostic procedures, providing a proactive healthcare paradigm that recognizes early indicators of diseases and adjusts to the genetic composition of the individual, lifestyle circumstances, and medical history of the patient.Precision medicine and personalized therapies, which are driven by the convergence of unmanned aerial vehicle (UAV) communication, metaverse technology, and machine learning, represent a paradigm shift in the healthcare industry. This shift represents a future in which healthcare is not only timely but also intricately aligned with the intricate specifics of each patient's health journey.

Global Medical Education Collaborations

Through the use of unmanned aerial vehicle (UAV) communication, metaverse technology, and machine learning, the revolutionary power of this technology is extended to the field of medical education. This forward-thinking strategy envisions a future in which geographical borders will no longer be a barrier to the interchange of medical knowledge and skills. Because they provide a dynamic platform for participatory learning experiences, metaverse simulations play a vital role in the collaborative educational landscape that we are currently experiencing. As seen in the integrated scenario, medical students from different continents participate in activities within the metaverse, such as doing virtual corpse dissections. An abundant flow of knowledge, viewpoints, and insights is fostered by this immersive environment, which transcends the restrictions that are traditionally associated with it. By gathering data from the actual world, unmanned aerial vehicles (UAVs) that are fitted with sophisticated sensors provide a contribution to this environment for collaborative learning. Students are able to engage with genuine and varied healthcare scenarios because to the incorporation of this data, which is communicated through UAV communication channels. This data becomes an intrinsic part of the teaching experience. The cloud computing platform, which offers a safe and scalable environment for the storage and processing of massive datasets, is the essential component that underpins this integration solution. Through the analysis of medical data and the presentation of insights that contribute to a full understanding of a variety of medical diseases, machine learning algorithms further enrich the educational experience.

In the future of education, this integrated approach to medical education will redefine what it means to study. It establishes a worldwide collaborative environment in which medical students from all parts of the world are able to communicate with one another, acquire new knowledge, and contribute to a pool of information that is shared all together. The vision that is presented in this section goes beyond the traditional confines of education, paving the way for a future in which the next generation of healthcare professionals will be trained through an educational landscape that is internationally integrated and technologically enhanced.

CONCLUSION

In conclusion, the incorporation of unmanned aerial vehicle (UAV) communication, metaverse technology, a variety of learning methodologies, and cloud computing into the healthcare industry is a significant step toward changing the very essence of medical practice. As we make our way through the intricacies, ethical conundrums, and practical applications that are discussed in this chapter, it becomes abundantly clear that we are not passively observing the growth of technology; rather, we are actively engaging in the process of rewriting the story of human compassion, resilience, and advancement. The future that is envisioned is one in which healthcare is not limited by geographic, socioeconomic, or educational constraints; rather, it is created as a universal right that is accessible to all individuals. This chapter propels us into a future in which breakthrough technologies effortlessly intersect, converting healthcare into a domain that is individualized, data-driven, and accessible on a global scale. This is accomplished by dissecting the complexities, facing ethical problems, and visualizing the practical applications. The more we accept these breakthroughs, the more we not only achieve great strides in medical research, but we also go on a communal adventure to rewrite the history of human compassion. This will pave the way for a healthcare environment that is inclusive, innovative, and deeply human-centered.

REFERENCES

Aazam, M., Zeadally, S., & Flushing, E. F. (2021). Task offloading in edge computing for machine learning-based smart healthcare. *Computer Networks*, 191, 108019. 10.1016/j.comnet.2021.108019

Al-lQubaydhi, N., Alenezi, A., Alanazi, T., Senyor, A., Alanezi, N., Alotaibi, B., Alotaibi, M., Razaque, A., & Hariri, S. (2024). Deep learning for unmanned aerial vehicles detection: A review. *Computer Science Review*, 51, 100614. 10.1016/j.cosrev.2023.100614

Ali, M., Naeem, F., Kaddoum, G., & Hossain, E. (2023). Metaverse communications, networking, security, and applications: Research issues, state-of-the-art, and future directions. *IEEE Communications Surveys and Tutorials*.

Bibri, S. E., & Jagatheesaperumal, S. K. (2023). Harnessing the potential of the metaverse and artificial intelligence for the internet of city things: Cost-effective XReality and synergistic AIoT technologies. *Smart Cities*, 6(5), 2397–2429. 10.3390/smartcities6050109

Budiyono, A., & Higashino, S. I. (2023). A Review of the Latest Innovations in UAV Technology. Journal of Instrumentation. *Automation and Systems*, 10(1), 7–16.

Cawthorne, D., & Robbins-van Wynsberghe, A. (2020). An ethical framework for the design, development, implementation, and assessment of drones used in public healthcare. *Science and Engineering Ethics*, 26(5), 2867–2891. 10.1007/s11948-020-00233-132578062

Chengoden, R., Victor, N., Huynh-The, T., Yenduri, G., Jhaveri, R. H., Alazab, M., Bhattacharya, S., Hegde, P., Maddikunta, P. K. R., & Gadekallu, T. R. (2023). Metaverse for healthcare: A survey on potential applications, challenges and future directions. *IEEE Access : Practical Innovations, Open Solutions*, 11, 12765–12795. 10.1109/ACCESS.2023.3241628

Dwivedi, Y. K., Hughes, L., Baabdullah, A. M., Ribeiro-Navarrete, S., Giannakis, M., Al-Debei, M. M., Dennehy, D., Metri, B., Buhalis, D., Cheung, C. M., Conboy, K., Doyle, R., Dubey, R., Dutot, V., Felix, R., Goyal, D. P., Gustafsson, A., Hinsch, C., Jebabli, I., & Wamba, S. F. (2022). Metaverse beyond the hype: Multidisciplinary perspectives on emerging challenges, opportunities, and agenda for research, practice and policy. *International Journal of Information Management*, 66, 102542. 10.1016/j.ijinfomgt.2022.102542

Gad, G., Farrag, A., Aboulfotouh, A., Bedda, K., Fadlullah, Z. M., & Fouda, M. M. (2024). Joint Self-Organizing Maps and Knowledge Distillation-Based Communication-Efficient Federated Learning for Resource-Constrained UAV-IoT Systems. *IEEE Internet of Things Journal*, 11(9), 15504–15522. 10.1109/JIOT.2023.3349295

Gao, J., Wang, H., & Shen, H. (2020). Machine learning based workload prediction in cloud computing. In *2020 29th international conference on computer communications and networks (ICCCN)* (pp. 1-9). IEEE. 10.1109/ICCCN49398.2020.9209730

Hemachandran, K., & Rodriguez, R. V. (Eds.). (2023). *The Business of the Metaverse: How to Maintain the Human Element Within this New Business Reality*. CRC Press.

Khaer, A., Sarker, M. S. H., Progga, P. H., Lamim, S. M., & Islam, M. M. (2023). UAVs in Green Health Care for Energy Efficiency and Real-Time Data Transmission. In *International Conference on Intelligent Sustainable Systems* (pp. 773-788). Singapore: Springer Nature Singapore. 10.1007/978-981-99-1726-6_60

Li, K., Cui, Y., Li, W., Lv, T., Yuan, X., Li, S., Ni, W., Simsek, M., & Dressler, F. (2022). When internet of things meets metaverse: Convergence of physical and cyber worlds. *IEEE Internet of Things Journal*, 10(5), 4148–4173. 10.1109/JIOT.2022.3232845

Mir, M. H., Jamwal, S., Islam, S., & Khan, Q. R. (2021). Machine learning techniques and computing technologies for IoT based smart healthcare (COVID-19 case study). In *2021 3rd International Conference on Advances in Computing, Communication Control and Networking (ICAC3N)* (pp. 2089-2095). IEEE.

Ozturkcan, S. (2023). Technology and disaster relief: The Türkiye-Syria earthquake case study. In L. Aldieri (Ed.), *Innovation-Research and development for human, economic and institutional growth.*

Prawiyogi, A. G., Purnama, S., & Meria, L. (2022). Smart Cities Using Machine Learning and Intelligent Applications. *International Transactions on Artificial Intelligence*, 1(1), 102–116. 10.33050/italic.v1i1.204

Qu, Q., Hatami, M., Xu, R., Nagothu, D., Chen, Y., Li, X.E., Blasch, E., Ardiles-Cruz, E. & Chen, G. (2024). *Microverse: A Task-Oriented Edge-Scale Metaverse.*

Román, A., Heredia, S., Windle, A. E., Tovar-Sánchez, A., & Navarro, G. (2024). Enhancing Georeferencing and Mosaicking Techniques over Water Surfaces with High-Resolution Unmanned Aerial Vehicle (UAV) Imagery. *Remote Sensing (Basel)*, 16(2), 290. 10.3390/rs16020290

Saunders, J., Saeedi, S., & Li, W. (2024). Autonomous aerial robotics for package delivery: A technical review. *Journal of Field Robotics*, 41(1), 3–49. 10.1002/rob.22231

Tedeschi, P., Al Nuaimi, F. A., Awad, A. I., & Natalizio, E. (2023). Privacy-Aware Remote Identification for Unmanned Aerial Vehicles: Current Solutions, Potential Threats, and Future Directions. *IEEE Transactions on Industrial Informatics*.

Vijitha Ananthi, J., & Subha Hency Jose, P. (2023). Optimal design of artificial bee colony based UAV routing (ABCUR) algorithm for healthcare applications. *International Journal of Intelligent Unmanned Systems*, 11(2), 285–295. 10.1108/IJIUS-08-2021-0099

Wang, N. (2021). "As it is Africa, it is ok"? Ethical considerations of development use of drones for delivery in Malawi. *IEEE Transactions on Technology and Society*, 2(1), 20–30. 10.1109/TTS.2021.3058669

Wang, N., Christen, M. & Hunt, M. (2021). *Ethical Considerations Associated with "Humanitarian Drones": A Scoping*. Springer.

Zhang, X., Zhang, H., Sun, K., Long, K., & Li, Y. (2024). Human-Centric Irregular RIS-Assisted Multi-UAV Networks with Resource Allocation and Reflecting Design for Metaverse. *IEEE Journal on Selected Areas in Communications*, 42(3), 603–615. 10.1109/JSAC.2023.3345426

Chapter 12
Incorporation of Computer Vision and Metaverse Analysis Using UAV Communications for Healthcare Applications

Mukunth Madavan
SASTRA University, India

Akshay Kumar R.
TL Consulting Group, Australia

Akshay Bhuvaneswari Ramakrishnan
https://orcid.org/0009-0000-1578-0984
SASTRA University, India

Manikandan R.
https://orcid.org/0000-0001-6116-2132
SASTRA University, India

S. Magesh
https://orcid.org/0000-0003-2876-7337
Dr. M.G.R. Educational and Research Institute, India

ABSTRACT

The integration of computer vision, unmanned aerial vehicles (UAVs), and metaverse analysis has potential to transform healthcare and offers solutions to geographical challenges. Emphasizing real-world applications, it details how computer vision aids

DOI: 10.4018/979-8-3693-2268-0.ch012

Copyright © 2024, IGI Global. Copying or distributing in print or electronic forms without written permission of IGI Global is prohibited.

in real-time patient monitoring and disease detection, while the metaverse enables immersive medical simulations and remote patient monitoring. Unmanned aerial vehicles help break the geographical barriers and give people access to healthcare services. The synergy between computer vision and metaverse analysis facilitates revolutionary data analysis and has multiple applications. Augmented reality (AR) and virtual reality (VR) tools enhance user engagement, enabling remote patient monitoring and medical simulations. The integration of metaverse analysis with UAVs introduces applications such as remote operation, telemedicine, propelling healthcare into a new era.

INTRODUCTION

The healthcare industry is constantly evolving with engineers and doctors working together to leverage the power of advanced technologies to solve the complex problems in healthcare. In recent years, the focus on this combination has led to several innovations in the healthcare industry, transforming traditional practices into efficient and scalable modern solutions. The fusion of multiple technologies allows us to construct systems that have fewer disadvantages since the fusion masks the negative impact of each technology individually.

In recent years, the field of Artificial Intelligence(AI) has been revolutionizing medical research (Alowais S.A et al.,2023), providing a more efficient way to extract knowledge from large amounts of data and analyse it quickly. There are different types of machine learning algorithms which can be implemented based on the type of data used in the problem. Similarly, there are different subfields of Artificial intelligence like Natural Language Processing(NLP), Cognitive computing, Computer Vision, Deep learning and Machine Learning which provide a wide variety of options for us to tackle even the most complex of the problems (Priyadarshini, S. B. B., et al., 2020).

These state of art technologies which are constantly evolving can be used to fuel medical research, which leads to better healthcare services being provided for the patients. Most of the research in the medical field is patient centric which involves developing drugs that are more efficient in curing the disease and cost effective as it makes the drug accessible to everybody (Maizes, V et al., 2009). On the other side, there is an aspect of healthcare which involves making the medical services available even in remote areas. There is also a need for emergency medical services in inaccessible locations where transport to these areas is either time consuming or not feasible.

Telemedicine acts as a perfect solution to these problems (Stanberry, B., 2000). It is a recent trend in healthcare which at its heart uses various online communication tools such as video calls to provide healthcare services remotely. It allows doctors to diagnose patients remotely and provide consultation. The demand for telemedicine services increased exponentially during the COVID-19 pandemic to avoid the spread of infection and to reduce the crowd present in hospitals. Several applications were released which allows users to book an online consultation with a specific doctor and get their queries cleared (Srivastav, A., et al.,2022). Even though the online mode is not the best way to provide medical services it is really beneficial in emergency and pandemic situations.

This chapter delves into the key aspects of integrating Computer Vision, Metaverse Analysis, and UAV Communications to transform the healthcare landscape. It briefly discusses the role of Computer Vision in medical image analysis, surgical assistance, and patient monitoring. Furthermore, it investigates the applications of Metaverse Analysis in medical training, telemedicine, and collaborative research and development. The chapter also explores the use of UAV Communications for establishing connectivity in remote areas, facilitating emergency response, and enabling seamless information exchange. Additionally, it proposes a synergistic integration of these three technologies to create a virtual healthcare ecosystem, transcending geographical barriers.

Moreover, the chapter discusses the challenges and future directions associated with the proposed integrated approach, including data security, privacy concerns, and regulatory considerations. Through this comprehensive examination, the chapter aims to contribute to the ongoing efforts in enhancing healthcare accessibility, efficiency, and quality, ultimately improving patient outcomes and saving lives.

THE FOUNDATION

This section provides a comprehensive description of the three pillars Computer vision, Metaverse analysis and UAV communications which forms the foundation of our integrated approach. Each of the technologies play a vital role in achieving the final goal and vision. The amalgamation of these technologies has a huge potential to revolutionize the telemedicine sector.

Computer Vision

Computer vision is a very interesting and a widely used technology which comes under the family of Artificial Intelligence (Szeliski, R., 2022). It gives machines the ability to load images and use various machine learning algorithms to extract specific features from the images.

Machines will be able to view and understand images and extract data from it which then be used effectively based on the problem in focus.

The main advantage of this technology is the ability to scan through and analyse a dataset that may be terabytes in size, containing lakhs of images evaluating each image pixel by pixel and work on efficiently computing all the necessary values for various use cases of computer vision such as pattern detection, image context generator, abnormality detection (Chen, X., 2022). The time it takes to analyse all the images is the prime factor for computer vision as the entire process of analysing is computationally intensive, hence the algorithms used in computer vision are generally focussed on efficiency and throughput.

Computer vision has been really beneficial in assisting doctors in making decisions. It provides the doctor with data which are derived from analysing the live feed or in some medical images or videos. The computer vision system designed for medical purposes is designed carefully considering all the edge cases and failure points, as the system will be used in conditions where the patient's life may be at risk. So there is lots of effort and time put into the development of medical computer vision systems so that they are failure proof. Most of the work is done in the pre-development phase where they consider all cases which the system might work in and make sure the working logic of the system provides accurate and error free results.

There are multiple scenarios in which these computer vision systems are extremely useful. Let us discuss some of them:

Medical Visual Data Analysis

This is one of the widely known use cases of computer vision. Utilizing the power of computer vision to be able to interpret visual data used in healthcare such as X-ray, MRI and CT scans. There are specialized image recognition algorithms which minutely scans the image and finds anomalies (Stalling, D.,et al., 2005). There are some details which cannot be detected by the naked eye, but the machine never misses the details and helps for early identification of diseases.

Surgery Assistance and Monitoring

Computer vision has been recently transforming medical surgery procedures. Generally, surgical procedures involve making complex and intricate movements and every single movement during this procedure matters a lot (Sherlaw-Johnson, C. et al., 2004). Additionally there are other details such as the body temperature, blood pressure and heart rate which should be simultaneously monitored by the surgeon. Assisted surgeries involve computer vision constantly guiding the surgeons with all the vital information into the field of view of the doctor. It can also display how accurate the surgeon is and what the next steps in the procedure are. This is very helpful for the surgeons to make accurate cuts during surgery and hence reducing the risks involved.

Patient Monitoring

There are algorithms in computer vision which do computationally intensive tasks and are used for classification and regression problems. On the other hand, computer vision has excellent monitoring and anomaly detection capabilities. Patient monitoring is one of those use cases where there might be input user data including audio, video and other health medical data which may be extracted from specialized medical instruments or from digital wearable devices. Let us take an example where a system is fed a real time video stream of a patient from a camera set above the patient bed and the system also receives the heart rate and blood pressure from the vital signs monitor setup beside the patient (Malasinghe, L. P., et al., 2019). Now the system can be set to alert the doctor or the duty nurses whenever there is a sudden heavy movement from the patient or if the blood pressure or heart rate goes above or below a certain threshold. This provides all day surveillance and keeps record of how the patient behaves throughout the day. Sleep monitoring is another additional feature which can be implemented.

These are just some popular use cases of computer vision. There has been a lot of funding for research in computer vision healthcare applications to extract more information and design specialized algorithms for solving complex medical problems. Deep learning based algorithms have the potential to detect even the smallest error which is not possible for a doctor to diagnose.

The use of computer vision also comes with its own set of challenges. The two big problems that we are facing are accuracy of the computer vision algorithms and the second one is medical data security and privacy.

The accuracy of the predictions is the most important factor especially in the field of healthcare as the life of the patient is at risk and we cannot rely on systems which do not provide accurate results. Developers follow guidelines while developing the systems for healthcare so that they will be able to develop a system which is error free and the data used for training these systems is very diverse to make sure the system behaves properly to a wide range of input.

Medical data of a patient is considered as personal and should be used and processed securely. Any other party involved which is utilizing the medical data should strictly adhere to the ethical guidelines to prevent data leaks and unauthorized access of the patient's medical history and data.

Metaverse Analysis

The metaverse is an advanced technology that combines the physical and virtual worlds together and provides the user an immersive experience (Davis, A. et al.,2009). It allows the user to transcend into a completely new world and interact with them and see changes simultaneously. The metaverse analysis can be used in multiple industries such as Communication, Digital shopping, Entertainment, Gaming and many more. There are more and more products which are focussed on metaverse as many believe that metaverse is the next big step in technology which will help humans break geographical barriers and create a shared virtual environment based on the requirement.

Metaverse comprises multiple technologies like Virtual Reality(VR) and Augmented Reality (AR) (MacCallum, K. et al., 2019) which allows us to enter into these dynamic virtual worlds and interact with others. The users can explore the world as characters or commonly called as avatars. They can explore a wide variety of landscapes which are completely designed by the developers and constantly feed input into the world by making those movements in the real world. For example a user doing a specific hand movement will be recorded and will be reflected in the virtual world.

This interesting technology has limitless possibilities and has potential to revolutionize the way humans interact completely. Top tech companies have been already working on products for metaverse and the support for these products in the market has been outstanding. Let us now discuss some of the products that are currently available in the market.

Meta which is formerly known as Facebook is at the forefront of the Metaverse technology and has been one of the early investors into this technology. They have an entire product line like Oculus VR headsets which provides the users an immersive experience (Parisi, T., 2015). Meta uses the metaverse technologies to host Horizon Workrooms which allows employees from different geographical locations to work together by utilizing the metaverse. This is one of the examples. Different types of virtual worlds are being developed and used from the Horizon Worlds which allows the users to explore a wide range of worlds with different scenarios and characters.

Another tech giant that is worth mentioning is Microsoft who is currently integrating metaverse tools to their already existing Azure cloud platform. Azure cloud services has been the biggest product of Microsoft for so many years offering a wide range of services from storage to hosting to computing facilities. A new addition to the list is a platform named Mesh which allows for creating a virtual environment to conduct virtual gatherings and collaborations and hence transforming the way people communicate.

Roblox, one of the widely known platforms and a favourite for many gamers, allows people to play user generated games. They are also stepping into the metaverse trend and started allowing users to delve into user generated worlds experiencing superior gaming experience and better gameplay. Similarly Google, even though not predominant in the Metaverse field, are launching multiple initiatives like Google ARCore to develop innovative products using metaverse and hence contributing to the cause of improving the technology.

The investment and the research made by these tech giants is huge and the audience for the metaverse products are rapidly increasing. A recent trend in the metaverse is trade of virtual objects. Users can now buy and sell goods and services in the virtual world and interact with people interested in the trade, and this allows for users to become rightful owners of virtual goods.

Now let us focus on metaverse analysis which involves extraction of information and carrying out systematic studies in the virtual world. There are a wide range of tools used and are being developed for metaverse analysis. Virtual and dynamic environments which allows the users to interact and learn various activities and provides the opportunity to analyse and make decisions upon them which can be implemented in either the physical or virtual world.

Some of the popular use cases of Metaverse in healthcare are:

Medical Training

This is one of the use cases where Metaverse can be used to transform the way students learn new things. Medical students who are learning to make surgeries or basic healthcare practices can now utilize metaverse by creating virtual worlds which is similar to the hospital environment where students practice (Coles, T. R et al., 2010). These worlds act as a virtual lab receiving inputs from the students in the real world and carrying out complex medical procedures. This allows for a superior experience for students and hence, better learning outcomes. There can be virtual worlds created for any similar type of problems like biotechnology engineers who have to build complex compounds and visualize it. So metaverse will play a huge role in the field of education in the upcoming years.

Telemedicine

As discussed in the previous section, telemedicine is rapidly growing and the remote consultations can be carried out in metaverse with the doctor able to view data about the patient from smart wearable devices recording health data of the patient (Murala, D. K., et al., 2023) as depicted in figure 1. This mode of consultation makes the interaction between the doctor and the patient, more closer to real life communication.

Figure 1. Virtual medical consultations

Another advantage of using metaverse for consultations is the doctor can use 3D representations of human anatomy or an organ related to the disease in the metaverse and explain about the diagnosis of the disease more easily in this case. Doctors can educate the patients easily in the metaverse which is not possible over a normal video call.

Collaborative Research and Development

Visualizing data and presenting it to others is one of the best features of metaverse. Researchers from different geographical locations can collaborate without the need of travelling to a specific place (Suzuki, S. N. et al.,2020). Using this platform, a group of researchers can now visualize and pitch their ideas to fellow researchers and simultaneously interact and apply changes to the proposed solution. This leads to a more efficient research flow and breaks geographical barriers and brings together the best minds of the world to solve the most complex scientific problems.

Even though the metaverse has a lot of features and can be used in different industries it also comes with its own set of challenges. The two main problems will be developing these virtual worlds and the second one is preventing misuse of the virtual world. The virtual world that is designed for a specific requirement involves a very big process of meticulously deciding how each and every part of the metaverse reacts to the user and generally takes a lot of time. So it is not possible to develop these virtual worlds as quickly as a mobile or desktop application. Responsible use of the metaverse technology and the way the users follow the ethical guidelines while interacting with the data in the metaverse is also important for a safer environment as most of these environments are shared by multiple users.

UAV Communications

We as humans have witnessed tremendous growth in communication techniques. From using wired communication like landline to 5G it is a very big leap and all of this is possible because of the constant search to find new ways to communicate or improve the existing communication system.

Unmanned Aerial vehicles commonly referred to as drones are being used for communication and this is one of the new trends in the communication sector (Zeng, Y. et al., 2016). UAVs have been used for decades as they have excellent surveillance capabilities and also used to collect data from a certain remote location. Drones have been used in the military for delivering goods during emergency operations and also for surveillance. Recently they have also been used for delivering food to customers.

The nature of UAVs allow it to be more mobile and often act as relays in remote areas to establish a stable connection. By acting as a relay they fly to a remote area which is in between two distant cell towers and act as a bridge between them temporarily. This is used when mobile coverage is required for some period of time in a very remote area.

There are different types of Unmanned aerial vehicles and drones are designed specifically for the situation it will be used in. For example, an emergency monitoring node will be designed to be fast and agile whereas a drone used for delivering food in affected areas will be designed such that the frame of the drone is able to carry heavy weight. (Gao, J., et al., 2024) briefly discusses efficient use of UAV communication to improve Internet of Medical Things. The Similarly surveillance drones are made to last longer in a single trip and are equipped with high quality cameras and are also made to produce very less noise.

Let us discuss some of the applications of Unmanned Aerial Vehicles:

Connectivity in Remote Areas

UAVs can act as a cell tower temporarily over a specific area which does not have the infrastructure for the traditional mode of communication. So the coverage from the UAVs which will be flying over a remote area can then be used to access voice and data services. This is also very useful in disaster affected areas where the existing infrastructure might be damaged, so a fleet of drones can be deployed to provide reliable communication services to the people in the disaster affected area.

Forest and Agriculture Management

The ability of the drone to provide a bird eye's view to the user is simply out-standing and can be used by farmers to collect data about the growth patterns of the crops and which areas are performing well and which areas are not. This allows the farmer to make informed decisions to improve the crop yield. Similarly forest officials can use drones which will fly over the entire forest collecting data about the types of plants, animals and the ecosystem present in the forest.

Security Surveillance

Initially drones were designed to fly over a region and report visual or audio data about the area. The police force has been using this for decades to monitor certain locations which are not quickly accessible. Similarly it takes less time for the drone to be launched and fly to the surveillance location compared to a police officer going to the location. It is also used to prevent any form of attacks in large public gatherings (Paucar, C. et al., 2018). The live video feed from the drones are constantly analysed to detect any movement that may possess a threat.

Communication Relay Networks

A fleet of drones have the capacity to cover kilometres of area and if these drones are interconnected and form a chain they can act as a relay network or an ad-hoc network allowing for information exchange (Xie, L.,et al., 2024). The ability of drones to conquer even the hardest of the terrains is one of the important features of communications based on UAVs.

Emergency Services

The ability of drones to swiftly fly to a high altitude is very useful in emergency situations. There are small drones which are designed to be extremely fast and rigid. These drones are often used inside buildings for monitoring purposes. For example, in an emergency situation where a tall building is on fire. While the fire service team gets inside to every house and saves people, drones can be deployed outside and inside the building to find out how many people are trapped and collect their exact locations. This information can then be communicated to the officers who can rescue the victims more quickly.

Along with the benefits, there are a lot of restrictions for flying a drone. Every country has a maximum threshold height for flying drones and it may depend on several factors like whether it is a city or a town, the type of buildings present in the location. Additionally there are airspace regulations which are to be followed in private property and military zones. Apart from the ethical problem, the drone design should be sufficient to satisfy the power and performance constraints required for a task.

Medical Logistics

A fleet of drones can be employed for the rapid and efficient transportation of medical samples, such as blood or tissue specimens, between healthcare facilities and laboratories, significantly reducing the time required for diagnosis and treatment.Moreover, UAVs can be seamlessly integrated into the medical supply chain, facilitating the faster and more efficient transportation of medical equipment, pharmaceuticals, and other supplies between hospitals, clinics, and distribution centers. This streamlined logistics process empowered by UAVs has the potential to revolutionize the healthcare industry.

INTEGRATION OF COMPUTER VISION AND METAVERSE ANALYSIS

The amalgamation of these two cutting edge technologies enhances the virtual experience with the computer vision able to decipher and process visual data which will be a guiding force in the dynamic and immersive worlds of metaverse. This combination offers a myriad of possibilities which can be used in several domains changing the way we interact with digital environments.

Computer vision plays a huge role in this integration by providing more output for the characters or objects in the metaverse. It makes the virtual world more interesting and brings it closer to the physical world. Computer vision can be used to accurately detect body movements, facial gestures and body language and replicate these features of the person in the digital world. Apart from the simple inputs given to the metaverse avatars (Hamilton, S., 2022), the inputs provided by the computer vision algorithm can make better replicas of the humans in the physical world. Hence, creating a seamless bridge between the physical and digital world.

The healthcare sector will be hugely benefited from this combination of technologies as computer vision analysing visual data which may be live video stream or medical images allows for a better representation of healthcare data in the metaverse. It is also easy for making better simulations for diagnosis. Similarly, computer vision can be used to provide a more immersive experience when the students are learning in medical training situations.

Another situation where this integration is really helpful is in the case of User Personalization. For example computer vision can be used to detect a player's behaviour patterns and make personalization according to that data in the metaverse game. This will provide a better user experience for gamers who use metaverse for gaming.

Virtualization of real world locations can be done using computer vision. Normally whenever a virtual world is created there are thousands of developers who work tirelessly for designing the world visually and developing it through code. The designing process can be made simple by using computer vision. For example, for making a virtual world containing the Eiffel tower, a high quality camera system which is using computer vision algorithms in the background to detect every minute detail from cars to small objects present in that location can be detected and then provided as an input for the designing process of the metaverse. Hence this will lead to faster development rate and hence saves a lot of time and financial resources for companies who create metaverse related products. Virtual tourism which allows people to experience famous tourist locations by exploring the virtual worlds which are exact replicas of the real world locations is one of the businesses that is made possible because of this integration.

There are several difficulties and limitations involved when developing products using this integration. The main concern is how to securely use the data collected using computer vision in the metaverse. Similarly replicating real world locations have their own problems with people claiming ownership and copyright of places and images

EXPLORING METAVERSE TOOLS FOR HEALTHCARE

There are several cutting edge technologies which are used for experiencing the metaverse. The tools which are researched the most are Augmented reality(AR) and Virtual reality(VR). These two tools act as the forefront in terms of the products used for experiencing metaverse. They have a transformative potential to change the way the healthcare industry works. They are not just changing the way we approach healthcare but rather alters the way diagnostics, treatment and patient engagement is done in present day hospitals.

Virtual reality(VR) completely changed the perspective of people when it comes to enjoying an immersive experience (Ullah, H.,et al.,2023). It uses VR headsets which also have its own set of controllers which covers the entire vision of the user and takes them to a completely new virtual world. It achieves this using a high quality display designed specifically for this purpose which comes with accurate motion tracking. There are several VR headsets like Apple vision Pro, Oculus and HTC which are currently the top selling VR headsets in the market.

VR has been used in multiple domains such as gaming where gamers are experiencing completely dynamic and action filled virtual worlds with amazing gameplay and it is popularly used as an alternative for online video meetings which can now be made more realistic by using VR headsets. Similarly students can now practice for their laboratory experiments in virtual labs which replicate the real life lab practical experience.

While VR is focussed on taking the users to a completely new world, Augmented reality(AR) is focussed on enhancing the physical world with an overlay of information on the user's field of view. AR often uses a combination of camera and sensors to showcase specific data or holographic images on the user's field of view. Overall this gives the user a blended reality where the system adjusts to the reality of the user instead of taking the user to a completely new reality. Another advantage of Augmented reality is that it is more affordable (Amer, A., et al ., 2014) to implement compared to Virtual reality. There are thousands of AR applications released in the market. Snapchat is a very popular example. It is a social media mobile application which allows users to communicate and the focus of the app is to use images in conversation. It allows the users to use filters which add graphics to the current camera live stream. Users can choose from a wide range of filters with each having a different holographic experience. Similarly AR is being implemented in online shopping applications by introducing virtual try on where the live camera input of the user's phone combined with AR gives an image of the user wearing a dress that they want to try out. AR does this by detecting the user's body and shape and overlaying the image of the dress on the image of the user. This is one of the very interesting applications of Augmented reality.

When it comes to healthcare both VR and AR have been really useful for providing better medical services to the patients. It is used to give better education by providing immersive training and simulation worlds for medical students. It is also used in telemedicine to easily provide remote consultations. Doctors will be able to explain to the patients more easily by using AR headsets to display simulations and other medical information.

Even though this technology has been in the market for several years, there is a lot to improve, starting from making hardware which allows the headsets to be much smaller and that will provide a better user experience to the customers.

DISASTER RESPONSE ACROSS THE SKIES: A CASE STUDY

In the previous sections, we have discussed the three pillars Computer Vision, Metaverse Analysis and UAV Communications and how integration between each pillar of our approach is possible and what are its applications. The proposed approach beautifully integrates each of the technologies to leverage the strengths of each technology to build a synergistic integration which solves several complex problems in healthcare.

To understand the proposed approach clearly we will use a case study which will explain how the amalgamation of the three technologies solves the problem of disaster response. Each technology used has a vital role and serves an important part in providing emergency medical services to inaccessible locations.

Let us take a situation where there is a large landslide where there is a sudden movement in the slope of the mountain wiping out all man made infrastructure built upon the slopes. This completely stops any mode of transport to the disaster affected areas because damaged roads and landslides severely affects the existing communication infrastructure such as cell towers which is necessary for audio and data services.

This situation traps the people in the disaster affected area without any help from other areas. There will be a high demand for doctors and other medical services during these situations. But unfortunately the repair of the roads takes a lot of time and finding another route to the disaster affected location is also time consuming and hence there are no feasible options to provide emergency medical services to the people who were injured in the landslide.

Our proposed approach can be used in this situation to quickly provide the medical services to the patients through the metaverse. There are several steps involved in this process. Let us discuss each of the steps in detail.

Establishing Aerial Connectivity

The first step in this process involves deploying a fleet of Unmanned Aerial Vehicles (UAV) also called Drones into the disaster affected areas. The fleet of drones will be uniformly covering the entire area and each of the drones will be fitted with miniature cell towers capable of providing mobile coverage up to a certain range.

Figure 2. Internet connectivity using unmanned aerial vehicles

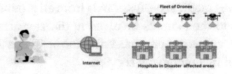

An advantage of using drones is that it will be able to fly to inaccessible locations easily and travel for longer distances (Yanmaz, E., 2022). It can easily reach locations which do not have proper roads or the roads are damaged because of the disaster. Now the chain of drones acts as a bridge connecting people from the disaster affected areas to the medical professionals.

Virtual Triage Through Computer Vision

The disaster affected zone will have hospitals and doctors but doctors will not be able to provide medical service to all as the number of patients who are injured because of the disaster might be very high. Hence the disaster affected area will be facing a shortage of healthcare professionals. This is where they will receive support from the doctors around the world through Computer vision and Metaverse Analysis.

In these situations, hospitals which have a proper camera setup can be centres of telemedicine through metaverse. Hospitals which have proper camera setup in operation theatres and in general medical rooms coupled with Computer vision algorithms which has unlimited potential and detects even the minute movements and accurately replicates them in the metaverse. These systems will utilize the data and mobile services provided by the Unmanned Aerial vehicles as depicted in figure 2. As discussed in the previous section each of the technologies is essential to make the whole proposed solution work. If UAV communications are not available then there is no use of the computer vision cameras as doctors from the areas not affected by the disaster will not be able to provide their services.

Virtual Medical Consultation Beyond Broken Roads

The next step involves medical professionals from all around the globe providing their medical services to the patients involved in disaster affected areas. The live feed from the computer vision systems present in the hospitals feeds data into virtual worlds made for providing emergency services.

There are two types of services that can be provided here. One is direct medical consultations where the doctor provides consultations to the patients directly by analysing the problem and all their health data. This can be done under the supervision of nurses and direct consultations are done only for cases which are less severe. The second case is Medical assistance. As the doctors are less in number they definitely need assistance in diagnosis and also in surgery.

In emergency situations, the doctors have to do a specialized surgery but currently might not have some of the equipment for those surgery and similarly specialized doctors might not be available at the hospital. Delivery Drones which are designed to handle heavy weight can be used to deliver the specialized equipment. Specialized doctors can provide assistance to the doctors in the hospital through metaverse. The operation theatres are fitted with high resolution cameras which replicate every movement made by the surgeon in the metaverse.

This integrated approach helps doctors around the world to collaborate and assist the doctors in the disaster affected areas and provide immediate feedback during the surgery. Hence it makes sure that life saving surgeries can be done with precision regardless of the physical distance from the doctors to the disaster site.

NAVIGATING THE DATA SECURITY AND PRIVACY MAZE

The integration of Computer vision, Metaverse analysis and UAV communications revolutionizes the dynamic landscape of healthcare. This approach provides endless opportunities to transform patient care. However as we move towards an approach that is more interconnected and data driven, handling the data securely is a major concern.

Healthcare data are being used throughout the process starting from using computer vision to detect data to representing the medical data in the metaverse. All of this data comes under sensitive information and it is a law to handle the patient data securely and follow all the ethical guidelines whenever using the data for any purpose. This ensures that the patient trusts the system. There are several challenges that we face when implementing this approach such as reliability of the UAV communications (Nawaz, H.,et al., 2021), Interoperability, Data security and privacy, Cost and Resource allocation etc. The main challenge that we will focus on is Data security and privacy.

Sensitive information about the patient such as medical images and videos are used by the computer vision algorithms. Both personally identifiable information (PII) and protected health information (PHI) are used in this process. The metaverse is used to represent all the healthcare data which is shared by people, mostly doctors. The bridge connecting both which is UAV communications which is responsible for sharing all the healthcare data is also prone to attacks. So, we have to establish frameworks to establish data security in both physical and virtual worlds.

Figure 3. Methods for data security and privacy

To overcome this challenge we have to implement several safety measures as depicted in figure 3. The first step towards secure communication is Encryption. In the proposed approach data is continuously being transmitted between UAV communications, Computer vision systems and the Metaverse. To avoid unauthorized access we can use end to end encryption. In the previous sections, the disadvantage of UAV communications and one of them is it being prone to attacks. But after implementing end to end encryption even if the hacker gets data from the communication line they cannot make any sense out of it as it is ciphered and only visible to the sender and the receiver.

Access Control mechanisms should be implemented with each person having a certain amount of access to the healthcare data (Samarati, P., et al., 2000). This method is known as Role based Access control. For example, a doctor will have complete access to all the data whereas an accounts staff working in a hospital does have access to only those details needed for managing the hospital. The accountant does not have the access to view patient images or similar sensitive data. This prevents sensitive data being shared to everyone.

Regulatory adherence is a must to establish a system that needs to communicate securely. A set of guidelines which need to be followed by any party involved in this system. Government should implement data governance frameworks which involve regular audits so that the involved parties follow the rules properly.

A dynamic consent model should be set up in the system to ensure that the patients give consent for their data to be used. The system should be transparent and the patient should have the option to limit the access for their data. The patients will now know where and for what purpose their data are being used and have control over them. This consent model ensures that the patients and their family trust the healthcare system and our approach.

There are several privacy preserving technologies that can be implemented to ensure data privacy. These technologies allow for the people who use the data to extract meaningful data without directly using the raw data. One of those technologies is Homomorphic encryption which is very interesting as it carries out computations on the encrypted data such that during the analysis phase only the required information is extracted and the raw data is still untouched. This allows for the identities of the patients to be hidden which is one of the goals of data privacy. There are other similar methods such as Federated learning which helps us to extract data while upholding the data privacy standards.

The above mentioned technologies can be implemented to make the existing system secure. On the other hand whenever a new system is developed, the security aspect should always be considered as one of the foundational principles. The developers who will be implementing this integrated approach should create an ethical design where we keep in mind the security and privacy of the data in every step of the design and implementation process as it is always better to develop a system with security in mind rather than adding security after developing the system.

CONCLUSION

In the culmination of our exploration into the Incorporation of Computer vision and Metaverse analysis to transform the healthcare industry with the UAV communications as the backbone we have seen the limitless potential of this approach and the challenges that it poses. Innovation in the healthcare industry is important as unlike any other industry, the healthcare industry saves human lives. So new developments which lead to the betterment of the industry and the healthcare practitioners are always invited. The pages of this book chapter delves into how technology can be utilized to make healthcare accessible to every person and every location irrespective of the physical distance.

The foundations of the approach are Computer vision, Metaverse analysis and UAV communications. Each one of these technologies equally contribute to the proposed approach and comes with its own set of strengths and weaknesses. The convergence of the three technologies unveils a glimpse into the future where traditional healthcare frameworks are transformed into a completely new virtual and more connected system embracing both the physical and virtual worlds and bringing out the best of both.

Several applications of the technologies used in this chapter and the case study discussed in this chapter acts as a tiny spark which embodies hope for a better future where healthcare services are available even in the direst of situations. Hence this is not the finale, rather the starting point of a journey to a better future where technology and healthcare intertwine seamlessly.

REFERENCES

Alowais, S. A., Alghamdi, S. S., Alsuhebany, N., Alqahtani, T., Alshaya, A. I., Almohareb, S. N., Aldairem, A., Alrashed, M., Bin Saleh, K., Badreldin, H. A., Al Yami, M. S., Al Harbi, S., & Albekairy, A. M. (2023). Revolutionizing healthcare: The role of artificial intelligence in clinical practice. *BMC Medical Education*, 23(1), 689. 10.1186/s12909-023-04698-z37740191

Amer, A., & Peralez, P. (2014, October). Affordable altered perspectives: Making augmented and virtual reality technology accessible. In *IEEE global humanitarian technology conference (GHTC 2014)* (pp. 603-608). IEEE.

Coles, T. R., Meglan, D., & John, N. W. (2010). The role of haptics in medical training simulators: A survey of the state of the art. *IEEE Transactions on Haptics*, 4(1), 51–66. 10.1109/TOH.2010.1926962955

Davis, A., Murphy, J., Owens, D., Khazanchi, D., & Zigurs, I. (2009). Avatars, people, and virtual worlds: Foundations for research in metaverses. *Journal of the Association for Information Systems*, 10(2), 1. 10.17705/1jais.00183

Gao, J., Xu, X., Qi, L., Dou, W., Xia, X., & Zhou, X. (2024). Distributed Computation Offloading and Power Control for UAV-Enabled Internet of Medical Things. *ACM Transactions on Internet Technology*, 3652513. 10.1145/3652513

Hamilton, S. (2022). Deep Learning Computer Vision Algorithms, Customer Engagement Tools, and Virtual Marketplace Dynamics Data in the Metaverse Economy. *Journal of Self-Governance and Management Economics*, 10(2), 37–51.

MacCallum, K., & Parsons, D. (2019, September). Teacher perspectives on mobile augmented reality: The potential of metaverse for learning. In *World Conference on Mobile and Contextual Learning* (pp. 21-28). IEEE.

Maizes, V., Rakel, D., & Niemiec, C. (2009). Integrative medicine and patient-centered care. *Explore (New York, N.Y.)*, 5(5), 277–289. 10.1016/j.explore.2009.06.00819733814

Malasinghe, L. P., Ramzan, N., & Dahal, K. (2019). Remote patient monitoring: A comprehensive study. *Journal of Ambient Intelligence and Humanized Computing*, 10(1), 57–76. 10.1007/s12652-017-0598-x

Murala, D. K., Panda, S. K., & Dash, S. P. (2023). MedMetaverse: Medical Care of Chronic Disease Patients and Managing Data Using Artificial Intelligence, Blockchain, and Wearable Devices State-of-the-Art Methodology. *IEEE Access : Practical Innovations, Open Solutions*, 11, 138954–138985. 10.1109/ACCESS.2023.3340791

Nawaz, H., Ali, H. M., & Laghari, A. A. (2021). UAV communication networks issues: A review. *Archives of Computational Methods in Engineering*, 28(3), 1349–1369. 10.1007/s11831-020-09418-0

Parisi, T. (2015). *Learning virtual reality: Developing immersive experiences and applications for desktop, web, and mobile.* O'Reilly Media, Inc.

Paucar, C., Morales, L., Pinto, K., Sánchez, M., Rodríguez, R., Gutierrez, M., & Palacios, L. (2018). Use of drones for surveillance and reconnaissance of military areas. In *Developments and Advances in Defense and Security: Proceedings of the Multidisciplinary International Conference of Research Applied to Defense and Security (MICRADS 2018)* (pp. 119-132). Springer International Publishing. 10.1007/978-3-319-78605-6_10

Priyadarshini, S. B. B., Bagjadab, A. B., & Mishra, B. K. (2020). A brief overview of natural language processing and artificial intelligence. *Natural Language Processing in Artificial Intelligence*, 211-224.

Samarati, P., & de Vimercati, S. C. (2000). Access control: Policies, models, and mechanisms. In *International school on foundations of security analysis and design* (pp. 137–196). Springer Berlin Heidelberg.

Sherlaw-Johnson, C., Gallivan, S., Treasure, T., & Nashef, S. A. M. (2004). Computer tools to assist the monitoring of outcomes in surgery. *European Journal of Cardio-Thoracic Surgery*, 26(5), 1032–1036. 10.1016/j.ejcts.2004.07.02615519199

Srivastav, A., & Sharma, A. (2022). *Healthcare Platform for Online Consultation.*

Stalling, D., Westerhoff, M., & Hege, H. C. (2005). Amira: A highly interactive system for visual data analysis. *The visualization handbook, 38,* 749-67.

Stanberry, B. (2000). Telemedicine: Barriers and opportunities in the 21st century. *Journal of Internal Medicine*, 247(6), 615–628. 10.1046/j.1365-2796.2000.00699. x10886483

Suzuki, S. N., Kanematsu, H., Barry, D. M., Ogawa, N., Yajima, K., Nakahira, K. T., Shirai, T., Kawaguchi, M., Kobayashi, T., & Yoshitake, M. (2020). Virtual Experiments in Metaverse and their Applications to Collaborative Projects: The framework and its significance. *Procedia Computer Science*, 176, 2125–2132. 10.1016/j.procs.2020.09.249

Szeliski, R. (2022). *Computer vision: algorithms and applications.* Springer Nature. Chen, X., & Konukoglu, E. (2022). Unsupervised abnormality detection in medical images with deep generative methods. In *Biomedical Image Synthesis and Simulation* (pp. 303–324). Academic Press.

Ullah, H., Manickam, S., Obaidat, M., Laghari, S. U. A., & Uddin, M. (2023). Exploring the Potential of Metaverse Technology in Healthcare: Applications, Challenges, and Future Directions. *IEEE Access : Practical Innovations, Open Solutions*, 11, 69686–69707. 10.1109/ACCESS.2023.3286696

Xie, L., Su, Z., Xu, Q., Chen, N., Fan, Y., & Benslimane, A. (2024). A Secure UAV Cooperative Communication Framework: Prospect Theory Based Approach. *IEEE Transactions on Mobile Computing*, 1–16. 10.1109/TMC.2024.3367124

Yanmaz, E. (2022). Positioning aerial relays to maintain connectivity during drone team missions. *Ad Hoc Networks*, 128, 102800. 10.1016/j.adhoc.2022.102800

Zeng, Y., Zhang, R., & Lim, T. J. (2016). Wireless communications with unmanned aerial vehicles: Opportunities and challenges. *IEEE Communications Magazine*, 54(5), 36–42. 10.1109/MCOM.2016.7470933

Chapter 13
Blockchain in Healthcare Department:
Blockchain in Healthcare Data Management

Daksh Srivastava
VIT-AP University, India

Nandini Mahanag
VIT-AP University, India

ABSTRACT

Blockchain technology is revolutionizing healthcare data management by introducing unprecedented levels of security, privacy, and interoperability. It provides a tamper-resistant, decentralized ledger for storing patient records and enables secure, transparent sharing of medical data among healthcare providers and patients. With blockchain, patients have more control over their data, ensuring their privacy while enhancing data accuracy. Moreover, healthcare institutions can streamline administrative processes and reduce fraud. This innovative approach promises to improve patient care, reduce costs, and reshape the healthcare industry's data management landscape. The Department of Health and Human Services keeps track of and posts the data breaches. The battle against the COVID-19 pandemic highlighted the importance of the blockchain technology.

DOI: 10.4018/979-8-3693-2268-0.ch013

Copyright © 2024, IGI Global. Copying or distributing in print or electronic forms without written permission of IGI Global is prohibited.

INTRODUCTION TO BLOCKCHAIN

The development of information and communication technology (ICT) has ushered in a new era where every neccesity can be fulfilled just by a single click. Every area of human life, including agriculture, smart cities, industrial automation, smart homes, healthcare, etc., depends on these new technologies and control systems. The most significant of these applications is healthcare, which is one of a person's basic needs. Electronic health records (EHRs) and control systems are the main components of Internet of Things (IoT) applications in healthcare. Control systems aid in supplying control techniques, and electronic health records (EHRs) play a big part in offering medical services that are quick, affordable, and easy to use.

Blockchain technology is one of the innovation that falls under information and communication technology (ICT) which is a broad term that encompasses technologies used for data manipulation, storage, retrieval, transmission, and exchange of information. It relies on networks of computers (nodes) to maintain and update the blockchain ledger, uses cryptographic techniques to secure data and transactions, and involves the storage and retrieval of information in a distributed manner.(Sharma, 2022)

Blockchain is a revolutionary technology that has transformed the way we think about data, transactions, and trust in the digital age. It was originally introduced as the underlying technology behind the digital cryptocurrency Bitcoin, but its applications have since expanded far beyond just cryptocurrencies. Imagine a digital ledger or record book that is duplicated and distributed across a network of computers, also known as nodes. Each new transaction or piece of data is grouped into a block. Once a block is filled with transactions, it is linked to the previous block in chronological order, forming a chain of blocks - hence the name "**blockchain**."

Blockchain is recasting the technology worldwide providing the stable data integrity and security. Countries such as Saudi Arabia is one such example, former correspondent to healthcare executives' perception and the internet connection, Saudi Arabia's pharmacuetical businesses are being prevented from using blockchain technology due to economic imbalance and lack of cooperation. blockchain technology in the pharmacuetical industries, Saudi Arabia were found as system robustness, increased data safety and decentralization, need for enhanced supply chain management and interoperability, and government laws and policies.(Kumar, 2020)

DEFINITION OF BLOCKCHAIN

It is a sequential chain of blocks, where each block contains a set of transactions, and these blocks are linked together in a way that ensures the integrity and immutability of the recorded data.

Key concepts and features of blockchain technology include:

Decentralization: Blockchain is a decentralized system, unlike traditional centralized systems that have a single entity in charge of the database. The ledger is maintained collectively by the network participants.

Transparency: All participants in the network can see all transactions recorded on the blockchain. This transparency helps ensure trust among participants and prevents fraud.

Security: Each block in the blockchain is linked to the previous block using cryptographic hashes. This linkage makes it extremely difficult to alter any information in a block providing a high level of security against tampering.

Immutability: Once a block is added to the blockchain, it is nearly impossible to alter the information within it. This immutability makes blockchain particularly suitable for recording critical data, such as financial transactions or identity records.

Consensus Mechanisms: Blockchain networks use various consensus mechanisms to agree on the validity of transactions and to ensure that all participants have a consistent view of the ledger.

Smart Contracts: Smart contracts are self-executing contracts with the terms of the agreement directly written into code. They automatically execute and enforce agreements when predefined conditions are met.

Public vs. Private Blockchains: Public blockchains are open and accessible to anyone. Private blockchains, on the other hand, they are limited to specific individuals and are frequently utilized in business settings to maintain privacy.

Use Cases: Applications in various industries such as supply chain management, healthcare, finance, voting systems, real estate, and more. Its unique features make it a powerful tool for addressing trust and security issues in the digital world. Logically, a blockchain can be seen as consisting of several layers:[24]

- infrastructure (hardware)
- networking (node discovery, information propagation[25] and verification)
- consensus (proof of work, proof of stake)
- data (blocks, transactions)
- application (smart contracts/decentralized applications, if applicable)

Figure 1. Blockchain formation

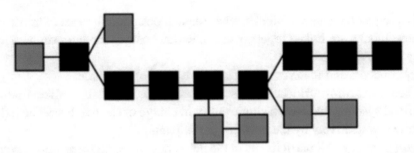

Blockchain formation. The main chain (black) consists of the longest series of blocks from the genesis block (green) to the current block. Orphan blocks (purple) exist outside of the main chain. (source: wiki)

HISTORY OF BLOCKCHAIN

Cryptographer David Chaum first proposed a blockchain-like protocol in his 1982 thesis "Computer Systems Established, Maintained, and Trusted by Mutual Suspicious Groups". Further work on cryptographically secure blockchains was described in 1991 by Stuart Haber and W.Scott Stornetta. They wanted to implement a system where the document timestamps could not be tampered with. In 1992, Haber, Stornetta and Dave Bayer incorporated the Merkle tree into the design, which improved its performance by allowing multiple document certificates to be collected in a single block. Under the management of the company Surety, their document certificate hashes have been published in The New York Times weekly since 1995.

o   In 2008 Satoshi Nakamoto, an individual (or group of individuals).By timestamping blocks without requiring them to be signed by a third party, Nakamoto significantly enhanced the architecture. He also added a difficulty parameter to control the rate at which blocks are added to the chain.

o   In August 2014, the size of the bitcoin blockchain file, which contains a history of every transaction that has ever taken place on the network, hit 20 GB (gigabytes).

o   From January 2016 to 2017, The size of the bitcoin blockchain increased from roughly 30 GB in January 2015 to 50 GB and 100 GB . By the start of 2020, the ledger size had surpassed 200 GB. Blockchains reportedly reached the early adopters phase with a 13.5% acceptance rate within the financial services sector, according to Accenture's application of the diffusion of innovations theory. The Chamber of Digital Commerce launched the Global Blockchain Forum, an initiative of industry trade groups (Deka, 2021).

DIFFERENCES BETWEEN CONVENTIONAL SECURITY MECHANISMS AND BLOCKCHAIN

Data Centralization vs. Decentralization

Conventional: Traditional healthcare systems often use centralized databases to store patient records. This centralization can make the system a target for hackers. A breach in one location could compromise a large volume of sensitive data. Capece, G., & Lorenzi, F. (2020).

Blockchain: Blockchain operates on a decentralized network of nodes. Patient data is stored across multiple nodes, making it highly resilient against single points of failure. Even if one node is compromised, the entire system remains secure due to the distributed nature of the data.(Fusco, 2020)

Data Centralization:

1. Single Point of Control: In a centralized system, all data is stored, managed, and controlled by a single entity or authority, often referred to as the central database or server.
2. Efficiency: Centralized systems can be more efficient in terms of data management and maintenance since all data is located in one place.
3. Access Control: Access to the data is controlled by the central authority, which can grant or restrict permissions to users and regulate who can view, modify, or access the data.
4. Scalability: Scaling a centralized system can become complex and costly, especially as the volume of data or the number of users grows.
5. Risk of Failure: Centralized systems are vulnerable to single points of failure. If the central database or server experiences a technical issue, data can become inaccessible to all users.
6. Security Concerns: A breach in a centralized system could lead to a massive loss of data, as a single attack vector could compromise a significant portion of the information.
7. Data Consistency: Since all data is stored in one location, maintaining data consistency across different locations or branches can be challenging.

Data Decentralization:

1. Distributed Control: In a decentralized system, data is distributed across multiple nodes, which can be computers, devices, or servers, often connected through a network.
2. Resilience: Decentralized systems are more resilient against failures and attacks. If one node is compromised, the rest of the network remains operational.
3. Access Control: Decentralized systems can implement finer-grained access control, allowing individuals to control who can access their data through cryptographic keys and smart contracts.(Kim,2019)
4. Scalability: Decentralized systems can be more scalable as new nodes can be added to the network to accommodate increased demand or data volume.
5. Transparency: Decentralized systems can offer greater transparency, as participants have visibility into the entire network's activity and transactions.
6. Security Benefits: Decentralization can enhance security since compromising a single node has limited impact. Additionally, cryptographic techniques and consensus mechanisms are often used to secure data and transactions.
7. Data Consistency: In a decentralized system, maintaining data consistency can be more challenging, especially when data needs to be synchronized across multiple nodes.
8. Blockchain Implementation: Decentralized ledgers like blockchain use consensus mechanisms to validate and record transactions, ensuring data integrity and preventing unauthorized changes.
9. Use Cases: Decentralization is well-suited for applications where transparency, accountability, and security are paramount, such as cryptocurrencies, supply chain management, voting systems, and secure data sharing.

Data Integrity and Immutability

Conventional: In centralized systems, data integrity depends on the trustworthiness of the central authority. Records can be altered, deleted, or manipulated, leading to inaccurate information and potential legal issues.

Blockchain: Blockchain ensures data integrity through cryptographic hashing and consensus mechanisms. Each block in the chain contains a unique hash of the previous block, creating a secure link between them. Once data is added to the blockchain, it becomes nearly impossible to alter, ensuring a trustworthy and tamper-proof record. Capece, G., & Lorenzi, F. (2020).

Data Integrity:

1. **Definition:** Data integrity refers to the accuracy, reliability, and correctness of data throughout its lifecycle. It ensures that data remains unaltered, consistent, and trustworthy from creation to storage and transmission.
2. **Importance:** Data integrity is crucial to maintaining the quality and reliability of information. It ensures that data accurately represents the real-world entities it describes, and that it hasn't been tampered with or corrupted.
3. **Methods:** Data integrity can be maintained through various methods, such as encryption, checksums, hashing, digital signatures, access controls, and validation checks. These techniques help detect and prevent unauthorized modifications, errors, or data corruption.
4. **Verification:** Data integrity can be verified through regular audits, data validation processes, and comparison with trusted sources. If discrepancies or inconsistencies are found, appropriate actions can be taken to correct the data.
5. **Examples:** Ensuring that financial transaction records accurately reflect the amounts and parties involved, and that medical test results match the actual measurements, are examples of maintaining data integrity.

Immutability:

1. **Definition:** Immutability refers to the property of data that prevents it from being changed or modified once it has been created or recorded. Immutability ensures that data remains unchanged and retains its original state over time.
2. **Importance:** Immutability is essential for creating reliable and tamper-proof records. It guarantees that once data is added or recorded, it cannot be altered, deleted, or tampered with, enhancing trust and transparency.
3. **Methods:** Immutability is often achieved through cryptographic hashing and technologies like blockchain. Cryptographic hashing generates a unique fixed-size output (hash) based on the data, and any change in the data results in a completely different hash.
4. **Verification:** Immutability can be verified by comparing the current hash of the data with its original hash. If the hashes match, it confirms that the data remains unchanged.
5. **Examples:** In the context of blockchain, once a transaction is added to a block and the block is added to the chain, the transaction becomes immutable. This property is crucial for ensuring the integrity of financial transactions, land ownership records, and supply chain data.

Access Control and Privacy

Conventional: Traditional systems often rely on usernames and passwords for access control. If these credentials are compromised, unauthorized individuals can gain access to sensitive patient data.

Blockchain: Blockchain can implement stronger access control mechanisms using cryptographic keys. Patients have control over who can access their data, and permission can be granted using encryption, ensuring patient privacy and reducing the risk of unauthorized access.(Hussain, 2020)

Access Control in Conventional Systems:

1. **Centralized Control:** Conventional systems often rely on a centralized authority to manage access control. A central entity determines user roles, permissions, and levels of access.
2. **User Authentication:** Usernames and passwords are commonly used for authentication in conventional systems. Multi-factor authentication (MFA) may also be implemented for added security. Capece, G., & Lorenzi, F. (2020).
3. **Role-Based Access Control (RBAC):** RBAC is a common access control model in conventional systems. Users are assigned specific roles, and access is granted based on predefined roles and permissions.
4. **Access Control Lists (ACLs):** ACLs specify which users or groups have permissions to access specific resources, files, or data.
5. **Challenges:** Conventional access control systems can face challenges such as the risk of centralized breaches, difficulty in managing complex permission hierarchies, and potential lack of transparency in access activities.

Access Control in Blockchain:

1. **Decentralized Control:** In blockchain networks, access control can be more decentralized. Participants have control over their own cryptographic keys, which are used to sign and verify transactions.
2. **Cryptography and Keys:** Blockchain uses cryptographic keys for user authentication and access control. Private keys are kept secret by users, and public keys are used to verify their identity.
3. **Smart Contracts:** Blockchain can implement self-executing smart contracts that automate access control based on predefined conditions. These contracts enable automated and programmable access rights.
4. **Permissioned Blockchains:** In permissioned blockchains, access control can be managed by a consortium of trusted entities that collectively decide who can participate in the network and what level of access they have.

5. **Challenges:** While blockchain enhances security through cryptography and decentralization, challenges include the potential risk of key management and the need to strike a balance between transparency and privacy in public blockchains.

Privacy in Conventional Systems:

1. **Data Collection:** In conventional systems, data collection may be less transparent, and users might have limited control over how their data is collected, used, and shared.
2. **Data Sharing:** Conventional systems may involve sharing of sensitive data with third parties, often without clear user consent or visibility into the data flow.
3. **Data Protection Laws:** Privacy regulations like GDPR and CCPA have led to increased scrutiny over how conventional systems handle personal data and enforce user privacy rights.(Hussain, 2020)

Privacy in Blockchain:

1. **Data Minimization:** Blockchain can enable data minimization by allowing users to share only necessary information with specific parties through cryptographic techniques like zero- knowledge proofs.
2. **User Consent:** Blockchain-based systems can use smart contracts to enforce user consent for data sharing and establish transparent data usage policies. Capece, G., & Lorenzi, F. (2020).
3. **Anonymization:** Some blockchain implementations use techniques to anonymize or pseudonymize user data, providing a level of privacy while maintaining transparency.
4. **Data Sovereignty:** Blockchain allows users to maintain greater control over their data, decide who has access, and potentially even monetize their own data.
5. **Challenges:** While blockchain enhances privacy through transparency and user control, it can still face challenges related to data protection compliance, potential data leakage through on- chain analysis, and managing the balance between privacy and transparency.(Hussain, 2020)

Auditing and Transparency

Conventional: Auditing and tracking changes in centralized systems can be complex. It may be challenging to determine who accessed, modified, or deleted specific records.

Blockchain: Transactions on the blockchain are transparent and traceable. Each transaction is recorded and linked in a chronological order, creating an immutable audit trail. This transparency enhances accountability and makes it easy to track changes over time.

Auditing in Conventional Systems

1. **Manual Process:** In conventional systems, auditing often involves manual processes where auditors review logs, records, and transactions to verify compliance, detect anomalies, and ensure data accuracy.
2. **Limited Visibility:** Auditing in conventional systems may be limited to specific records or transactions, and the process may not provide a comprehensive view of all activities within the system.
3. **Risk of Tampering:** Audit trails in conventional systems can be susceptible to tampering, as centralized control over data and records makes it easier to modify or delete information without leaving a trace.
4. **Verification:** The verification of audit logs may require trust in the central authority managing the system and may be subject to disputes if parties disagree on the accuracy of the records.

Auditing in Blockchain:

1. **Automated and Immutable:** Blockchain provides automated and immutable audit trails. Each transaction is recorded in a transparent and tamper-proof manner, ensuring a reliable history of activities.
2. **Transparency:** The decentralized and transparent nature of blockchain ensures that audit logs are visible to all participants, creating a shared source of truth that can be independently verified.
3. **Real-time Auditing:** Blockchain's real-time updates and cryptographic hashing enable auditors to verify data integrity and transactions as they occur, reducing the need for manual, retrospective audits.
4. **Cryptographic Proof:** Blockchain's cryptographic mechanisms, such as hashes and digital signatures, provide cryptographic proof of the authenticity and integrity of each transaction, enhancing trust.(Hussain, 2020)

Transparency in Conventional Systems:

1. **Selective Transparency:** Conventional systems may offer limited transparency, with certain information visible to authorized parties. Transparency is often controlled by the central authority or organization.
2. **Lack of Trust:** The lack of transparency in some conventional systems can lead to mistrust among users and stakeholders, as they have to rely on the central authority's word regarding data accuracy. Capece, G., & Lorenzi, F. (2020).
3. **Data Sharing Challenges:** Sharing data with external parties in conventional systems can be complex, as it requires establishing trust and sharing data through intermediaries.

Transparency in Blockchain:

1. **Decentralized and Public:** Public blockchains, in particular, offer radical transparency, where all transactions and data are visible to all participants. Anyone can verify the authenticity and history of transactions.
2. **Immutable History:** Blockchain's immutability ensures that once data is recorded, it cannot be altered or deleted. This creates a permanent and trustworthy historical record.
3. **Trusted Source:** The transparent nature of blockchain removes the need for intermediaries, as parties can directly verify transactions and data without relying on a central authority.
4. **Auditable Ecosystem:** Blockchain fosters an auditable ecosystem where stakeholders can independently verify the accuracy of data, enhancing trust among participants.

Interoperability and Data Sharing

Conventional: Data sharing between different healthcare providers can be hindered by incompatible systems and data formats. This can lead to delays in patient care and coordination.

Blockchain: Blockchain can facilitate secure and standardized data sharing between different entities. Smart contracts can automate data sharing agreements, ensuring that relevant parties have access to accurate and up-to-date patient information, leading to improved care coordination.(Hussain, 2020)

Interoperability in Conventional Systems:

1. **Challenges:** Achieving interoperability in conventional systems can be challenging due to the use of different proprietary technologies, data formats, and protocols by different organizations and vendors.
2. **Custom Integration:** Organizations often need to invest significant resources in custom integration efforts to enable data exchange between disparate systems. This can lead to high costs and complexity.
3. **Third-Party Middleware:** Interoperability may require the use of third-party middleware or integration tools to facilitate communication and data exchange between different systems.
4. **Data Mapping:** Converting data from one format to another, known as data mapping, can be time-consuming and error-prone, particularly when dealing with complex data structures.
5. **Maintenance:** Ensuring continued interoperability can be challenging as systems evolve and change over time. Updates to one system might inadvertently disrupt interoperability with others.

Interoperability in Blockchain:

1. **Standards and Protocols:** Blockchain technology fosters standardized protocols and data formats, making it inherently more conducive to interoperability between different blockchain networks and applications.
2. **Smart Contracts:** Interoperability can be facilitated through the use of smart contracts that enable automated interactions between different blockchains, allowing data and value to flow seamlessly.
3. **Cross-Chain Solutions:** Various projects and technologies are emerging to address cross-chain interoperability, allowing data and assets to be transferred between different blockchain platforms.
4. **Decentralized Identity:** Blockchain can enable interoperable and self-sovereign digital identities, allowing users to control their personal information across various systems and services.

Data Sharing in Conventional Systems:

1. **Centralized Control:** Data sharing in conventional systems often involves centralized control by the data owner or the organization. Data may be shared on a case-by-case basis with specific parties.
2. **Access Challenges:** Sharing data with external parties can be complex, requiring agreements, security measures, and potentially involving intermediaries to facilitate the exchange.

3. **Data Silos:** Data sharing in conventional systems can lead to data silos, where each organization maintains its own data repository, making it difficult to achieve a comprehensive view of information.(Hussain, 2020)

Data Sharing in Blockchain:

1. **Decentralized Data Sharing:** Blockchain's decentralized nature facilitates direct data sharing between participants without relying on a central intermediary. Parties can interact with shared data in real time.
2. **Smart Contracts:** Smart contracts on blockchain can automate and enforce data sharing agreements, ensuring that data is shared according to predefined rules and conditions.
3. **Permissioned Blockchains:** In permissioned blockchains, data sharing can be controlled among authorized participants, ensuring that sensitive information is only accessible to those who have permission.
4. **Selective Data Sharing:** Some blockchain implementations allow for selective data sharing, where users can share specific data elements with specific parties while keeping the rest of the data private.
5. **Data Provenance:** Blockchain's transparent and tamper-proof ledger provides a clear record of data ownership, changes, and transactions, enhancing trust and accountability in data sharing.

Smart Contracts for Automation

Conventional: Traditional systems often lack automated processes for executing agreements and protocols. This can lead to manual errors and delays.

Blockchain: Smart contracts enable automated execution of predefined actions when specific conditions are met. For example, insurance claims could be automatically processed, reducing administrative overhead and ensuring efficient operations.

Smart Contracts in Conventional Systems:

1. **Code Integration:** In conventional systems, automation often involves integrating custom code or scripts into existing software applications. This code is typically developed and managed separately from the main application.
2. **Centralized Execution:** Automation in conventional systems relies on a centralized server or infrastructure to execute the automated processes. The control and execution of the code reside within the organization's IT infrastructure.

3. **Limited Trust:** The execution of automation scripts in conventional systems relies on trust in the central authority managing the infrastructure and code. Users may have limited visibility into the execution process.
4. **Custom Development:** Developing, testing, and maintaining automation scripts in conventional systems can be resource-intensive and may require specialized programming skills.
5. **Scope:** Automation in conventional systems is often limited to specific processes within the organization and may not be easily extensible to interactions beyond the organization's boundaries.

Smart Contracts in Blockchain:

1. **Native Automation:** Smart contracts in blockchain are built-in, self-executing code that automates processes and agreements on the blockchain itself. They are an integral part of the blockchain platform.
2. **Decentralized Execution:** Smart contracts in blockchain are executed in a decentralized manner across the entire network of nodes. The outcome of a smart contract's execution is determined by consensus among participants.
3. **Trust Through Consensus:** Smart contracts rely on consensus mechanisms, cryptographic principles, and the transparency of the blockchain to ensure trust and integrity in the execution process.
4. **Immutable Execution:** Once a smart contract is deployed to the blockchain, its code and logic become immutable. This ensures that the terms and conditions encoded in the smart contract cannot be altered.
5. **Ease of Development:** Smart contract development tools and languages are tailored to blockchain platforms, making it easier to write, test, and deploy smart contracts without extensive programming knowledge.
6. **Scope:** Smart contracts on blockchain can automate a wide range of processes beyond an individual organization, including cross-border transactions, supply chain coordination, and more.

Figure 2. Blockchain

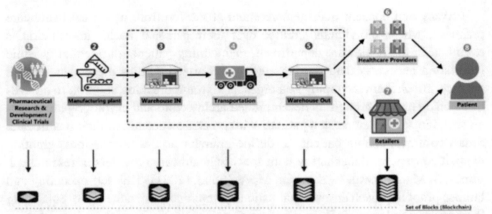

Source:- https://www.mdpi.com/applsci/applsci-09-01736/article_deploy/html/images/applsci-09-01736-g003-550.jpg

NEED OF BLOCKCHAIN IN CURRENT SECURITY PERSPECTIVE

Data Security and Integrity

Data security and integrity are paramount in the healthcare department, where the accuracy, confidentiality, and reliability of patient information play a critical role in delivering effective care. Traditional data systems often fall short in ensuring comprehensive protection against unauthorized access and tampering, leaving patient records vulnerable to breaches and fraudulent activities. In this context, blockchain technology emerges as a transformative solution. By leveraging cryptographic techniques and its immutable ledger, blockchain safeguards patient data from unauthorized alterations or deletions. Every interaction with the data is securely recorded and time-stamped, creating an unbroken chain of trust. This fortified foundation of data security ensures that patient records remain trustworthy and unassailable, establishing a new standard of integrity that bolsters patient privacy and empowers healthcare providers to deliver accurate diagnoses, well-informed treatments, and coordinated care.

Privacy and Consent Management

Privacy and consent management stand at the forefront of ethical healthcare practices, where individuals' control over their personal health information is essential. In the healthcare department, maintaining patient confidentiality while facilitating necessary data sharing among authorized entities presents a delicate balance. Blockchain technology emerges as a groundbreaking solution to address these challenges. Through its decentralized architecture and cryptographic mechanisms, blockchain empowers patients with greater ownership of their health data. Smart contracts enable patients to define granular access permissions, granting explicit consent for data sharing with specific healthcare providers or researchers. Idrees, S. M., Agarwal, P., & Alam, M. A. (Eds.). (2021). This self-executing and tamper-proof approach ensures that patients' preferences are adhered to, enhancing their privacy and control. By putting individuals at the center of their data management, blockchain revolutionizes the way healthcare institutions navigate the intricate landscape of privacy and consent, fostering a trusted environment where patients' rights are preserved and medical advancements are fostered through secure and accountable data exchanges.

Secure Sharing and Interoperability

Secure sharing and interoperability represent pivotal challenges within the healthcare sector, where seamless exchange of patient information among different healthcare providers is crucial for delivering comprehensive and coordinated care. Conventional systems often struggle to achieve this due to disparate data formats, complex integration processes, and concerns over data security. The emergence of blockchain technology offers a transformative solution. By leveraging its decentralized and standardized approach, blockchain facilitates secure data sharing and interoperability. Authorized healthcare professionals can access relevant patient data in real time, ensuring accurate diagnoses and informed decisions. Idrees, S. M., Agarwal, P., & Alam, M. A. (Eds.). (2021). Blockchain's tamper-proof and transparent ledger ensures the integrity of shared information, while smart contracts automate consent and data access, ensuring compliance with privacy regulations. This revolutionary approach not only streamlines data exchange but also enhances patient outcomes by enabling a more holistic and collaborative approach to healthcare. Blockchain's ability to bridge the gap between healthcare silos ushers in a new era of efficiency, accountability, and patient-centered care.

Clinical Trials and Research Data

Clinical trials and research data play a pivotal role in advancing medical knowledge and improving patient care within the healthcare department. However, ensuring the integrity, transparency, and security of these critical datasets remains a challenge. Traditional methods of data recording and management often lack the robustness needed to prevent tampering, data manipulation, and unauthorized access. Here, blockchain technology emerges as a game-changer. By providing an immutable and transparent ledger, blockchain ensures that each step of a clinical trial or research project is securely recorded and verifiable. Researchers can rely on an unbroken chain of data, from data collection to analysis, creating an auditable and tamper-proof record. This not only enhances the credibility and reliability of research outcomes but also fosters collaboration and trust among researchers, medical practitioners, and regulatory bodies. As blockchain transforms the landscape of clinical trials and research data, it paves the way for accelerated discoveries, innovative treatments, and a safer, more effective healthcare ecosystem.

Medical Supply Chain Security

Medical supply chain security is a critical concern within the healthcare department, as the integrity and authenticity of pharmaceuticals, medical devices, and supplies directly impact patient safety and care quality. Conventional supply chain systems often struggle to effectively track and verify the origin, handling, and distribution of medical products, leading to challenges such as counterfeit medications and compromised patient well-being. Idrees, S. M., Agarwal, P., & Alam, M. A. (Eds.). (2021) Blockchain technology emerges as a powerful solution to address these issues. By establishing an unalterable and transparent record of each step in the supply chain, blockchain ensures that products are genuine and have been handled according to established standards. This tamper-proof and traceable ledger provides a comprehensive view of the entire supply chain, making it possible to identify and eliminate any potential risks or unauthorized interventions. As blockchain bolsters medical supply chain security, it instills confidence in patients, healthcare providers, and regulatory agencies, fostering a safer and more reliable healthcare ecosystem where patient welfare remains the utmost priority.

Fraud Prevention

Fraud prevention is a critical imperative in the healthcare department, where financial and ethical concerns intersect. Traditional healthcare systems often grapple with instances of insurance fraud, billing discrepancies, and misuse of patient data, leading to compromised patient trust and significant financial losses. The introduction of blockchain technology offers a potent antidote to these challenges. By virtue of its transparent, immutable, and auditable nature, blockchain creates an environment where all transactions and activities are securely recorded and cannot be altered or deleted. This ensures a trustworthy and tamper-proof audit trail that serves as a powerful deterrent to fraudulent practices. Medical services, billing procedures, and patient interactions are all logged on the blockchain, allowing auditors and regulatory bodies to easily verify the accuracy of data and swiftly detect any anomalies or suspicious activities. As blockchain fortifies the healthcare sector against fraud, it ushers in a new era of accountability, transparency, and ethical integrity, promoting a healthcare ecosystem where patient interests are safeguarded, and resources are allocated for genuine care rather than deceptive practices.

Emergency Data Access

Emergency data access holds a critical role within the healthcare department, as swift and accurate access to patient information can be a matter of life and death. In urgent medical situations, such as accidents or sudden illnesses, healthcare providers require immediate access to a patient's medical history, allergies, medications, and other vital data. Conventional methods of accessing patient records may face delays or encounter challenges due to disparate systems and limited availability. However, with the advent of blockchain technology, emergency data access is revolutionized. Blockchain ensures that authorized healthcare professionals can securely retrieve essential patient information in real-time, regardless of geographical barriers or the availability of the primary healthcare provider. This instantaneous and comprehensive access to critical medical data empowers emergency responders and healthcare teams to make informed decisions swiftly, resulting in timely interventions and improved patient outcomes. By seamlessly bridging gaps in information sharing during urgent scenarios, blockchain transforms emergency data access into a lifesaving tool that elevates the quality of care and enhances the efficiency of the healthcare system as a whole. Idrees, S. M., Agarwal, P., & Alam, M. A. (Eds.). (2021)

Decentralization and Resilience

Decentralization and resilience are vital attributes that can reshape the healthcare landscape, ensuring a more robust and adaptable system capable of withstanding challenges and disruptions. In the healthcare department, where patient care and data security are paramount, traditional centralized systems can be vulnerable to single points of failure, cyberattacks, and technical glitches. The introduction of blockchain technology introduces a paradigm shift by distributing control and data across a network of nodes. Capece, G., & Lorenzi, F. (2020). This decentralization not only enhances security by reducing vulnerabilities but also bolsters the overall resilience of the healthcare ecosystem. In the event of system failures or external threats, decentralized networks can continue to function, ensuring uninterrupted access to patient records, critical medical data, and operational functionalities. By embracing decentralized technologies, the healthcare sector embraces a future where patient care remains uninterrupted, data remains secure, and the system is better equipped to navigate unforeseen challenges, ultimately fostering a more reliable, adaptable, and patient-centric healthcare environment.

Regulatory Compliance

Regulatory compliance serves as a cornerstone in maintaining the ethical and legal integrity of the healthcare department. The healthcare industry is governed by a complex web of regulations, standards, and guidelines aimed at safeguarding patient rights, data privacy, and quality of care. Compliance with regulations such as HIPAA (Health Insurance Portability and Accountability Act) is not only a legal obligation but also an ethical responsibility that ensures patient confidentiality and trust. However, traditional compliance processes can be intricate, time-consuming, and prone to errors, potentially compromising patient data security and leading to costly penalties. In this context, blockchain technology emerges as a transformative tool. By providing an immutable and transparent ledger, blockchain offers a real-time, auditable record of data transactions and interactions. This not only streamlines the process of demonstrating compliance but also ensures that patient data is accurately managed, shared, and protected according to regulatory standards. As blockchain automates compliance procedures and strengthens data governance, the healthcare sector can navigate the regulatory landscape with greater efficiency, minimize risks of non-compliance, and, most importantly, uphold the principles of patient-centered care while adhering to the highest ethical and legal standards. Idrees, S. M., Agarwal, P., & Alam, M. A. (Eds.). (2021)

Auditability and Accountability

Auditability and accountability constitute essential pillars in ensuring the transparency, reliability, and ethical conduct within the healthcare department. In an environment where patient care, data security, and regulatory adherence are of paramount importance, traditional methods of tracking and verifying activities may fall short in providing a comprehensive and tamper-proof record. Here, blockchain technology emerges as a transformative solution. By virtue of its immutable and transparent ledger, blockchain enables a real-time and auditable trail of every transaction, data access, and interaction within the healthcare ecosystem. Capece, G., & Lorenzi, F. (2020). This robust record-keeping mechanism not only enhances the accuracy and integrity of patient records but also facilitates swift and accurate audits by regulatory bodies and internal compliance teams. In addition, blockchain's decentralized

architecture and cryptographic mechanisms contribute to fostering account-ability by ensuring that each participant's actions are cryptographically linked to their identity, leaving no room for anonymity or evasion of responsibility. As the healthcare sector embraces blockchain for auditability and accountability, it ushers in a new era where trust is fortified, transparency is paramount, and all stakeholders are held answerable for their actions, ultimately leading to improved patient care, data security, and operational excellence.

Figure 3. Blockchain in healthcare

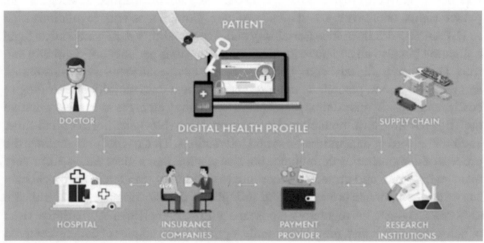

Source:- https://www.dataart.com/media/efulhi4l/picture1.png

In summary, while blockchain offers substantial benefits in healthcare, including enhanced data security, interoperability, and transparency, it also presents challenges related to scalability, integration, energy consumption, and regulatory compliance. Capece, G., & Lorenzi, F. (2020). The successful implementation of blockchain in the healthcare department requires a thorough assessment of these advantages and disadvantages, tailored to specific use cases and regulatory environments.

CHALLENGES AND RISKS INVOLVED IN IMPLEMENTATION OF BLOCKCHAIN

Implementing blockchain technology in the healthcare department brings forth various challenges and risks that need careful consideration. While blockchain offers significant benefits, addressing these challenges is essential to ensure successful adoption and integration. Here are some of the key challenges and risks, along with examples: Elangovan, D., Long, C. S., Bakrin, F. S., Tan, C. S., Goh, K. W., Hussain, Z., ... & Ming, L. C. (2020)

1. **Interoperability:** Integrating blockchain with existing healthcare systems can be complex due to the need for seamless data exchange. Different institutions may use varying data formats and standards, leading to difficulties in achieving interoperability. For instance, if a hospital adopts a blockchain-based patient records system, ensuring compatibility with other clinics' systems can be challenging.

2. **Scalability:** As the volume of data increases, blockchain networks might face scalability issues, leading to slower transaction processing times and higher costs. This can hinder real-time applications and impact the overall performance of the healthcare system, especially in scenarios like telemedicine consultations where immediate data access is crucial.

3. **Regulatory Compliance:** Blockchain's decentralized nature can conflict with existing data protection regulations, such as HIPAA and GDPR. Striking a balance between data privacy and blockchain's transparency can be complex. For example, a blockchain-based patient data sharing platform needs to ensure that patient consent and data access comply with privacy regulations.

4. **Energy Consumption:** Certain blockchain consensus mechanisms, like Proof-of-Work, can consume significant energy, leading to environmental concerns and higher operational costs. Capece, G., & Lorenzi, F. (2020).This is particularly relevant in the healthcare sector, which is increasingly focused on sustainability.

5. **Data Privacy and Security:** While blockchain enhances data security through encryption, it's not immune to cyber threats. Malicious actors could target vulnerabilities in the system, compromise private keys, or exploit smart contract flaws. Any breach of sensitive patient data stored on the blockchain could have severe consequences for patient privacy and trust.

6. **Integration Complexity:** Integrating blockchain into healthcare workflows requires significant technical expertise and investment. Ensuring smooth integration, data migration, and user adoption can be challenging, particularly for larger healthcare institutions with complex legacy systems.

7. **Adoption and Training:** Healthcare professionals may require training to effectively use blockchain- based platforms and understand the implications of this technology on their practices. Overcoming resistance to change and ensuring widespread adoption is crucial for the success of blockchain initiatives.

8. **Legal and Liability Issues:** Determining legal responsibilities and liabilities in case of errors or discrepancies in blockchain-based systems can be complex. Healthcare providers and institutions need clear legal frameworks to address disputes or errors in data stored on the blockchain.

9. **Lost Keys and Data Recovery:** If a user loses their private key, access to their data stored on the blockchain may become irrecoverable. Ensuring adequate measures for key management and data recovery is essential, especially in emergency situations.

Addressing these challenges requires a comprehensive approach involving collaboration among healthcare professionals, technologists, legal experts, and regulators. By understanding and mitigating these risks, the healthcare department can harness the transformative potential of blockchain while safeguarding patient data, regulatory compliance, and overall system integrity.

APPLICATIONS OF BLOCKCHAIN IN VARIOUS DOMAINS

Figure 4. Features of blockchain for healthcare domain

Source:- https://www.sciencedirect.com/science/article/pii/S266660302100021X?via%3Dihub#section-cited-

1. **Electronic Health Records (EHRs):** Electronic Health Records (EHRs) are a pivotal component of modern healthcare, streamlining the way patient information is stored, managed, and shared. In the healthcare department, EHRs replace traditional paper-based records with digital repositories that offer numerous benefits. One real-world example of the transformative impact of EHRs is the adoption by the Cleveland Clinic, a renowned healthcare provider in the United States. By implementing an advanced EHR system, the Cleveland Clinic improved patient care through enhanced data accessibility and interoperability. Physicians gained immediate access to comprehensive patient histories, test results, and treatment plans, allowing for more informed diagnoses and tailored treatment decisions. Moreover, EHRs enabled seamless communication among different departments and specialists, leading to coordinated and efficient care delivery. This real-world case illustrates how EHRs can elevate patient care, reduce administrative burdens, and foster collaboration among healthcare professionals. The digitalization of health records through EHRs not only enhances the quality and continuity of care but also marks a significant step forward in modernizing healthcare operations.

2. **Medical Billing and Claims Processing:** Medical billing and claims processing constitute vital functions within the healthcare department, ensuring the financial viability of healthcare services and facilitating reimbursement for patient care. Traditionally, these processes have been mired in complexity, with paper-based systems and manual interactions leading to errors, delays, and inefficiencies. However, the integration of blockchain technology presents a promising solution to these challenges. By leveraging blockchain's transparent and tamper-proof ledger, medical billing and claims processing can be transformed into streamlined and accountable procedures. For instance, blockchain's smart contracts can automate the entire billing lifecycle, from claims submission to reimbursement. These self-executing contracts can enforce predefined rules and conditions, reducing administrative overhead and minimizing errors in the billing process. Additionally, blockchain's secure and auditable nature ensures that all billing transactions are recorded in a transparent and verifiable manner, creating an accurate and immutable record of financial interactions. The benefits extend beyond accuracy and automation. With blockchain, fraudulent claims can be mitigated through the establishment of an indisputable audit trail. The shared and decentralized nature of blockchain ensures that all stakeholders have access to the same information, fostering trust and collaboration among healthcare providers, insurers, and regulatory bodies. Engelhardt, M. A. (2017).

3. **Clinical Trials and Research:** Clinical trials and research constitute the bedrock of medical advancements, shaping the landscape of healthcare by unraveling new treatments, therapies, and insights. However, the traditional process of

conducting and managing clinical trials often encounters hurdles related to transparency, data integrity, and trust. In response, blockchain's immutable and transparent ledger, clinical trials can achieve unprecedented levels of data integrity and accountability. Every step of the research process, from patient recruitment and data collection to analysis and publication, can be securely recorded on the blockchain. This tamper-proof record ensures that research findings are trustworthy and verifiable, bolstering the credibility of scientific discoveries and preventing data manipulation or selective reporting.

Moreover, blockchain introduces a new level of transparency and collaboration among stakeholders, including researchers, pharmaceutical companies, regulatory bodies, and patients. Access to research data can be securely shared in real time, enabling real-time audits and ensuring that all parties are aligned with the study's progress and outcomes.

4. **Drug Traceability and Supply Chain:** The pharmaceutical supply chain plays a crucial role in ensuring the safety and authenticity of medications and medical products that reach patients. However, traditional supply chain systems often face challenges such as counterfeit drugs and lack of transparency. Blockchain technology presents an innovative solution that can revolutionize drug trace-ability and supply chain management in the healthcare department. By utilizing blockchain's immutable and transparent ledger, every step of a drug's journey can be securely recorded and tracked. From the manufacturer to the distributor to the pharmacy, each transaction is verified and recorded, creating an unbroken chain of custody. An example is the partnership between Walmart and IBM in using blockchain to trace the origin of mangoes. Engelhardt, M. A. (2017).

5. **Telemedicine and Remote Patient Monitoring:** Telemedicine leverages digital communication platforms to enable virtual consultations between patients and healthcare professionals. Patients can seek medical advice, discuss symptoms, and receive prescriptions without the need for in-person visits. This approach not only improves access to care, particularly for individuals in remote areas or with mobility constraints, but also reduces the burden on healthcare facilities and minimizes exposure to contagious illnesses. Remote patient monitoring, on the other hand, involves the use of wearable devices and sensors to contin-uously collect and transmit patient data to healthcare providers. This real-time monitoring allows for early detection of health issues, timely interventions, and personalized treatment plans. Blockchain technology can enhance the security and privacy of data collected during remote monitoring. Elangovan, D., Long, C. S., Bakrin, F. S., Tan, C. S., Goh, K. W., Hussain, Z., ... & Ming, L. C. (2020)

An example of these technologies in action is the growth of telemedicine platforms during the COVID- 19 pandemic. Healthcare providers worldwide turned to tele-medicine to ensure continuous care while minimizing the risk of virus transmission. Patients could consult with doctors from the safety of their homes, demonstrating the value and convenience of telemedicine.

6. **Consent Management and Data Privacy:** Consent management and data privacy stand as pillars of ethical and patient-centered healthcare, ensuring individuals have control over their personal health information while fostering trust between patients and healthcare providers. In the healthcare department, where sensitive medical data is exchanged and stored, traditional consent processes and data handling may lack transparency and robustness. Blockchain's decentralized and tamper-proof ledger provides a secure and transparent platform for managing patient consent. Through blockchain-enabled smart contracts, patients can grant and revoke consent for data sharing, treatment options, and research participation. These self-executing contracts ensure that consent preferences are automatically enforced, reducing the risk of unauthorized access or usage of patient data. Moreover, blockchain enhances data privacy by allowing patients to maintain ownership and control over their health information. Patients can grant access to specific portions of their data to authorized healthcare providers, researchers, or third parties, while keeping the rest of their information secure. This empowers patients to participate in medical research and treatment decisions with confidence, knowing that their privacy rights are respected. Engelhardt, M. A. (2017).

A real-world example of blockchain's potential in this domain is the partnership between MIT Media Lab and Beth Israel Deaconess Medical Center. They developed a system called "MedRec" that uses blockchain to improve patient data access, consent management, and privacy in electronic health records.

7. **Interoperability and Health Information Exchange:** Interoperability and health information exchange represent the cornerstone of a modern and efficient healthcare system, enabling seamless communication and data sharing among different healthcare providers, facilities, and systems. In the healthcare department, where patient care often involves collaboration across various specialties and organizations, achieving interoperability has been a longstanding challenge. The integration of blockchain technology can transform the way health information is exchanged and shared. Blockchain's decentralized and standardized approach provides a secure and transparent platform for interoperability. By creating a unified and tamper-proof ledger of patient records, medical histories,

test results, and treatment plans, blockchain ensures that authorized healthcare professionals can access accurate and up-to-date information in real time. Elangovan, D., Long, C. S., Bakrin, F. S., Tan, C. S., Goh, K. W., Hussain, Z., ... & Ming, L. C. (2020)

A notable real-world example of blockchain's potential in this domain is the Synaptic Health Alliance, a consortium of healthcare organizations, including Humana, Optum, and Quest Diagnostics. They utilize blockchain to enhance data sharing and interoperability among members, streamlining administrative processes and improving patient care coordination.

8. **Personalized Medicine and Genomics:** Personalized medicine and genomics represent a paradigm shift in the healthcare department, offering a transformative approach that tailors medical treatments and interventions to an individual's unique genetic makeup. Traditional healthcare practices often follow a one-size-fits-all approach, but advancements in genomics and the integration of blockchain technology have unlocked the potential for highly personalized and precise care. **Genomics**, the study of an individual's genes and their interactions, holds the key to understanding the genetic basis of diseases and their responses to treatments. With the advent of advanced sequencing technologies, healthcare providers can analyze a patient's genetic information to identify genetic variations that may influence disease susceptibility, drug metabolism, and treatment outcomes. This information enables the development of targeted therapies and interventions that are more likely to be effective and have fewer adverse effects.

Blockchain's role in **personalized medicine** lies in securely managing and sharing genetic data. Patients can own and control access to their genomic information, granting permissions to researchers or clinicians for specific purposes. This ensures that their sensitive genetic data remains private and is used in accordance with their preferences.

A real-world example of blockchain's application in this domain is the project initiated by Nebula Genomics, which aims to give individuals ownership of their genomic data and enable them to share it with researchers through blockchain-based smart contracts. This approach revolutionizes data sharing while preserving patient privacy and control.

9. **Medical Credentialing and Licensing:** Medical credentialing and licensing are integral components of ensuring the competence and qualifications of healthcare professionals, thereby safeguarding patient safety and quality of care. In

the healthcare department, the traditional processes of verifying and maintaining credentials often involve laborious paperwork, delays, and administrative complexities. Blockchain technology presents a transformative solution that can streamline and enhance the efficiency of medical credentialing and licensing. It's transparent and tamper-proof ledger provides a secure and auditable platform for managing medical credentials and licenses. Healthcare professionals can have a digital record of their education, training, certifications, and professional achievements, all securely stored on the blockchain. This digital identity can be easily accessed and verified by authorized entities, reducing the administrative burden and potential errors associated with manual verification processes.

An real-world example is the project initiated by the Vermont Secretary of State's Office, which explored using blockchain technology for medical licensing. By utilizing blockchain, medical licenses could be securely verified and shared, enhancing mobility for healthcare professionals while maintaining stringent verification standards.

10. **Public Health Surveillance and Disease Outbreak Tracking:** Public health surveillance and disease outbreak tracking play a pivotal role in safeguarding community health and preventing the spread of infectious diseases. Traditional methods of monitoring and responding to outbreaks can be hindered by delays, data fragmentation, and limited coordination. The integration of blockchain technology can enhance the efficiency and effectiveness of public health surveillance. Blockchain's decentralized and transparent ledger provides a secure and real-time platform for recording and sharing disease-related data. Health authorities, healthcare providers, and researchers can input and access information on outbreaks, cases, and trends, ensuring that all stakeholders have access to the most up-to-date and accurate data. This real- time data sharing enables quicker detection of disease patterns and facilitates prompt responses to potential outbreaks.

An real-world example is the partnership between IBM and the Centers for Disease Control and Prevention (CDC) in the United States. They explored the use of blockchain technology to enhance disease surveillance and response, allowing for more efficient and secure data sharing among health organizations and agencies.

State of Art Architectures for Blockchain

Figure 5. Reviewing healthcare sphere with blockchain aspects

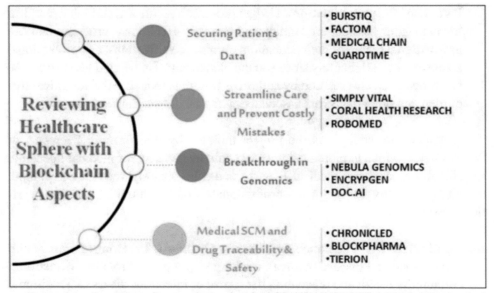

Source:- https://www.sciencedirect.com/science/article/pii/S266660302100021X?via%3Dihub#section-cited-

There are several state-of-the-art architectures and frameworks for implementing blockchain in the healthcare department using AI. These architectures aim to address the unique challenges of data security, interoperability, scalability, and regulatory compliance that arise when combining blockchain and AI in healthcare. Please note that developments may have occurred since then, and it's essential to research the latest advancements. Here are a couple of examples:

1. **Healthcare Consortium Blockchain:** This architecture involves the collaboration of multiple healthcare organizations, research institutions, and technology providers to form a consortium blockchain. Consortium blockchains are permissioned networks where participants are known and trusted, ensuring data privacy and controlled access. In the healthcare context, this architecture can facilitate secure data sharing for clinical research, patient records, and treatment insights while adhering to regulatory requirements. Huang, G., & Al Foysal, A. (2021).

Example: Synaptic Health Alliance, a consortium of leading healthcare companies including Humana, MultiPlan, and UnitedHealth Group, utilizes a blockchain-based solution to improve provider data accuracy and reduce administrative costs. By sharing provider data on a permissioned blockchain network, the consortium aims to enhance data quality and streamline administrative processes.

2. **Decentralized Data Exchange Platforms:** Decentralized platforms leverage blockchain to enable patients to own and control their health data. These platforms allow patients to share their data securely with healthcare providers, researchers, and AI algorithms while maintaining granular control over access and usage. Huang, G., & Al Foysal, A. (2021).

Example: Shivom is a blockchain-powered platform that empowers individuals to securely manage their genomic data. Patients can grant researchers access to their data for medical research, allowing AI algorithms to analyze genetic information for personalized treatment recommendations. The blockchain ensures data privacy and consent management.

3. **Blockchain-AI Hybrid Architectures:** These architectures combine the strengths of blockchain and AI to create synergistic solutions. Blockchain provides secure and transparent data sharing, while AI enhances data analysis and decision-making. AI models can be trained on blockchain-stored data to develop predictive models, diagnostic tools, and treatment recommendations.

Example: BurstIQ combines blockchain with AI and machine learning to create a health data exchange platform. Patients control their data sharing preferences on the blockchain, and AI algorithms analyze the data to provide insights for precision medicine and healthcare management.

4. **Federated Learning on Blockchain:** Federated learning enables AI models to be trained across decentralized devices while keeping data localized. When applied to healthcare, federated learning can train AI models on patient data stored on different nodes of a blockchain network, enhancing privacy while still enabling collaborative research. Huang, G., & Al Foysal, A. (2021).

Example: Doc.ai utilizes federated learning on a blockchain network to create personalized AI- powered health insights. Users contribute their health data, which remains on their devices while contributing to a collective AI model that provides insights into health conditions and treatment options.

These state-of-the-art architectures demonstrate the innovative ways in which blockchain and AI can be combined to revolutionize healthcare processes. Each architecture focuses on specific challenges and priorities, such as data privacy, data sharing, patient consent, and research collaboration, while leveraging the strengths of both technologies for improved patient outcomes and healthcare advancements.

FUTURE PERSPECTIVE OF BLOCKCHAIN IN HEALTHCARE

Figure 6. Healthcare blockchain in the cloud

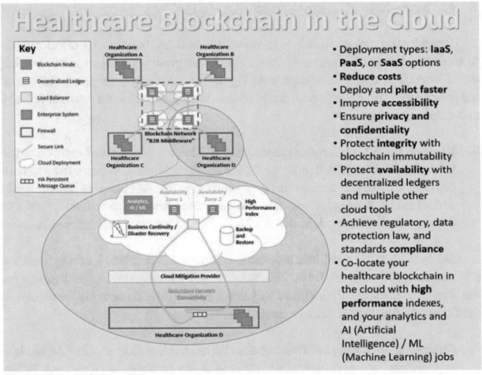

Source:- https://www.linkedin.com/pulse/healthcare-blockchain-cloud-david-houlding-cissp-cipp/

REFERENCES

Capece, G., & Lorenzi, F. (2020). Blockchain and Healthcare: Opportunities and Prospects for the EHR. *Sustainability (Basel)*, 12(22), 9693. 10.3390/su12229693

Elangovan, D., Long, C. S., Bakrin, F. S., Tan, C. S., Goh, K. W., Hussain, Z., & Ming, L. C. (2020). Application of blockchain technology in hospital information system. *Mathematical modeling and soft computing in epidemiology*, 231-246.

Engelhardt, M. A. (2017). Hitching healthcare to the chain: An introduction to blockchain technology in the healthcare sector. *Technology Innovation Management Review*, 7(10), 22–34. 10.22215/timreview/1111

Fusco, A., Dicuonzo, G., Dell'Atti, V., & Tatullo, M. (2020). Blockchain in healthcare: Insights on COVID-19. *International Journal of Environmental Research and Public Health*, 17(19), 7167. 10.3390/ijerph1719716733007951

Habib, G., Sharma, S., Ibrahim, S., Ahmad, I., Qureshi, S., & Ishfaq, M. (2022). Blockchain Technology: Benefits, Challenges, Applications, and Integration of Blockchain Technology with Cloud Computing. *Future Internet*, 14(11), 341. 10.3390/fi14110341

Huang, G., & Al Foysal, A. (2021). *Blockchain in healthcare*. Research Gate.

Idrees, S. M., Agarwal, P., & Alam, M. A. (Eds.). (2021). *Blockchain for healthcare systems: challenges, privacy, and securing of data*. CRC Press. 10.1201/9781003141471

Namasudra, S., & Deka, G. C. (Eds.). (2021). *Applications of blockchain in healthcare* (Vol. 83). Springer. 10.1007/978-981-15-9547-9

Onik, M. M. H., Aich, S., Yang, J., Kim, C. S., & Kim, H. C. (2019). Blockchain in healthcare: Challenges and solutions. In *Big data analytics for intelligent healthcare management* (pp. 197–226). Academic Press.

Shi, S., He, D., Li, L., Kumar, N., Khan, M. K., & Choo, K. R. (2020, October). Applications of blockchain in ensuring the security and privacy of electronic health record systems: A survey. *Computers & Security*, 97, 101966. 10.1016/j.cose.2020.10196632834254

Chapter 14
Challenges With the Blockchain–Powered Healthcare Secure System

P. Sumitra

Vivekanandha College of Arts and Sciences for Women(Autonomous), India

G. Sathya

Vivekanandha College of Arts and Sciences for Women (Autonomous), India

M. Sathiya

Vivekanandha College of Arts and Sciences for Women (Autonomous), India

S. Sabitha

Vivekanandha College of Arts and Sciences for Women (Autonomous), India

A. Gayathiri

Vivekanandha College of Arts and Sciences for Women (Autonomous), India

George Ghinea

Brunel University, Brunei

ABSTRACT

The expansion of the internet and the growing use of technology in the healthcare system have helped doctors monitor their patients remotely through the use of real-time smart health devices. In spite of this sophisticated system, there are many concerns regarding the sensitive data of the patients being exposed to the world by hackers. Thus, the shortcomings of the healthcare framework can be resolved by leveraging blockchain tools. The mechanism of the blockchain health system works in such a way that an id is assigned to a patient health record, and they can give access to view their health records to the specific health provider of their choice. Eventually, by using this mechanism, the patient's health record is secured from the hackers. Thus, this chapter deals with data privacy of the patient's health, research

DOI: 10.4018/979-8-3693-2268-0.ch014

Copyright © 2024, IGI Global. Copying or distributing in print or electronic forms without written permission of IGI Global is prohibited.

objectives, issues, and challenges that can be easily understandable and helpful for beginners in their research progress.

INTRODUCTION

The medical field is the main industry where the blockchain is being used to develop creative solutions in many different industries. In the healthcare field, this kind of technology is used to protect and retain patient information between testing conveniences, physicians, hospitals, clinics, prescription drugs, etc. (Tiwari et al., 2021; Yue et al., 2016). Medical administration requires an architecture that has security features for data manipulation and storage (Wang et al., 2021). The complexity and specialization of medical data has led to an increase in the importance of privacy data and refuge. Included in the package are the hospitalization, diagnosis, and registration (Schulz, 2019). The Figure 1 depicts the exchange of medical data as shown below

Figure 1. Exchange of medical data

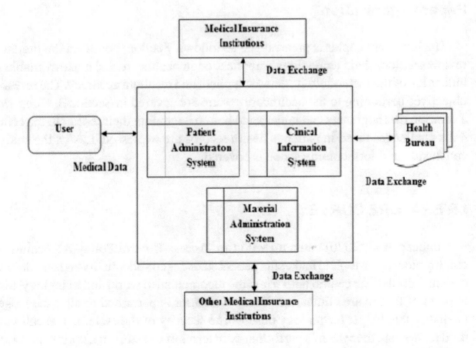

As long as healthcare institutions meet the fundamental conditions for the construction of healthcare information, data sharing amongst them will become more common place. Maximize the value of medical health data and give patients more reasonable and humanized services (Zhang & Wang, 2021). The medical field has utilized emerging Internet technology extensively, which has resulted in a diversification of methods and pathways for transmitting medical data. The transmission has gradually changed from being internal to being transmitted connecting medical institutions, between insurance and medical establishment, and between patients and medical institutions. Patient data protection has become much more difficult due to this reason (Han et al., 2022). In recent years, novel approaches to the protected storage of health data have been made possible by the use of blockchain tools.

The fundamental nature of blockchain is a database that is distributed and has the qualities of transparency, security and decentralization. The management of medical data can be improved through the use of blockchain, a distributed database that offers solution for issues in inadequate security, low efficiency, and poor sharing. On the real-time shared blockchain network, data can be captured and timestamp added to ensure immutability. Medical information is secure due to the blockchain's ability to resist tampering. To obtain data information, blockchain participants have the option to access operations on the licensed blockchain.

Paper Organization

The left over chapter is prearranged as follows. Section 2 outlines the literature review on blockchain technology's application in healthcare and make available an indication of the methodology, dataset applied, and resultant accuracy. The research objectives pertaining to the healthcare system are covered in Section 3, along with a solution that beginners can understand before beginning their research. In section 4 the challenges faced in patient's health records are expressed. Lastly, the study's conclusion and forthcoming scope is covered.

LITERATURE SURVEY

Sundeep et al (2020) came up with the "Access Control Policy Algorithm" to employ blockchain tools to make sure patient statistics confidentiality and maintaining patient records. The central authoring, the recommended work, and a single systemic point of failure are eliminated. Because no user is permitted to alter the ledger, unchangeable ledger technology ensures the security of the system. The caliper is used to evaluate the system's performance in terms of its size, time, optimization and policy. To enhance the evaluation metrics employed to calculate throughput, security and latency. Blockchain technology fundamentals, working strategies, applicable mechanism, challenges, and trends were discussed by Deepak et al. (2018). The paper also covered a brief overview of the characteristics and operation of blockchain, further explained the algorithm used in the different blockchain applications and came to a conclusion regarding the security issues.

The goal of the Abir et al. (2022) paper is to use blockchain tool and smart contracts that use information masking techniques to improve in healthcare supply chain communication networks etc. The outcomes of an intended level of security and hyperledger are both feasible. To establish a private, secure cluster of trustworthy healthcare providers, blockchain is utilized in communication, and smart contracts are employed to generate an OTH for encryption. To hide information, a segment is applied that conceals the original message within auxiliary messages. Auxiliary message is discarded by recipient and protected by a variety of encryption methods chosen by the dispatcher, while the original communication is protected by OTH. Proposed method promises a shorter execution time and greater security than traditional techniques.

In order to enable businesses to exchange information and verify data integrity through blockchain development, Francisco et al. (2019) created a software connector that resembles an Ethereum blockchain. In response to the evaluation, a simulation model is developed in order to solve issues and improve performance.

Xia et al. (2019) explained about the research studies which show various attention to the pros and cons of the system. Some of them focused on the real-time data conditions similar to the applications of blockchains in the healthcare industry. However, the authors focused in order to emphasize the importance of medical records management.

Zang et al. (2018) urges the system to become more reliable, and careful consideration should be given to models for significant system upgrades. The focus of this paper is on the elements of blockchains that are capable of handling medical data.

Innovative healthcare services for seniors that were centered on their real desire and issues were suggested by Khan et al. (2021). Researchers used machine learning techniques to better address the basic healthcare needs of senior citizens.

Chang et al. (2021) provide a solution called blockchain-based federated learning for smart healthcare that makes use of the global medical information. The edges on both sides of the nodes can easily manage the blockchain to avoid data loss, while the MIoT devices perform federated learning.

A scientific and comprehensive investigation of blockchain was proposed by the author Shuai et al. (2019). The author's groundbreaking six layer architecture served as the foundation for smart contracts. The authors have described the basic platforms and mechanisms of blockchain-enabled smart contracts. Several typical application scenarios were supplied by the authors. Main objective is to provide useful guidance and resources for future research projects.

Tsung-Kuo et al. (2018) were the first to show how blockchain tools may be used to boost the safety measures and solitude of medical data. They developed a novel algorithm and adapted blockchain technology to construct a model chain that protects privacy using machine learning.

RESEARCH METHOD

Gaining more knowledge about blockchain technology and its uses in healthcare systems is the main goal. To reach a purposeful conclusion, the following Research Question (RQ) is put forth.

RQ1: What kind of methodology may be used in the system of medical research in blockchain system?

RQ2: What uses for blockchain technology can guarantee security and privacy in the medical field?

RQ3: What are the application scenarios of blockchain in health care sector?

RQ4: What are the impacts on blockchain in healthcare sector?

RQ5: Where can I find the links to the healthcare dataset?

RQ1: What kind of methodology may be used in the system of medical research in blockchain system?

Based on the selection criteria, various articles were gathered from different libraries for selection process. It is tabulated as shown below.

Table 1. Selection criteria

Ref.No	Year	Technique Applied	Dataset applied	Framework	Proposed Methodology	Results obtained
(Omkumar et al., 2023)	2023	Blockchain	COVID-19 CT	Truffle & Ganache	BLOCKFED	Precision 0.80, Sensitivity 0.84 and Specificity 0.0040
(Xiaoguang et al., 2016)	2016	Blockchain	Medical Records	PBC and Open SSL Libraries	Light weight medical data sharing scheme	Low in computational and communication cost
(Zhijie et al., 2022)	2022	Blockchain	Medical Records	Hyperledger fabric and attribute based access control	IPFS	Safeguard and secure

continued on following page

Table 1. Continued

Ref.No	Year	Technique Applied	Dataset applied	Framework	Proposed Methodology	Results obtained
(Ashraf et al., 2023)	2023	Blockchain	Random Records	No	Federated Blockchain System	Scalability and Production Environment increased
(Sang, 2019)	2019	Blockchain	FHIR	Model View Controller	No	Support Clinical Decision making more
(Sonali et al., 2022)	2022	Blockchain, AI & IoT	Medical Records	Integration of Artificial Intelligence and Blockchain based approach	Cutting-edge blockchain based approach	Understand the technology in healthcare ecosystems and food chain
(Dris et al., 2021)	2021	IoT & Blockchain	Medical Records	SmartMedChain	1.Membership management 2. Data generating 3.EHR Generating 4.Data Sharing	Satisfies many security requirements
(Uma Maheswaran et al., 2022)	2022	Blockchain & AI	Approximate 154 individuals data from healthcare and food sector at U.K	No	Structural Equation Model (SEM)	Increase in recovery rate and service quality
(Pratima et al., 2021)	2021	Blockchain with fuzzy set	Medical Record from China	Fuzzy DEMATEL	Interpretive Structure Modeling	Effective in developing the system
(Pratima et al., 2021)	2021	Blockchain and IoT	Medical Records	Blockchain based IoT Architecture	Identity Based Encryption Algorithm	Efficiency is good compared to existing algorithm

RQ2: What uses for blockchain technology can guarantee privacy and security in the medical field?

Health Care Security

The healthcare security data can be guaranteed in a number of ways. Healthcare data is sensitive and private, so it's important to highlight a few essential security precautions and best practices. When utilizing blockchain technology in the healthcare sector, security must come first. Blockchain tools plea to the medical industry as it make available in decentralized, secure mode to exchange and accumulate data. Because it safeguards sensitive patient data like medical history etc data safety measures is essential to the healthcare production (Hamed, 2023).

The potential for blockchain technology to convey and keep sensitive patient data securely could revolutionize the healthcare sector. Data encryption and digital signatures are made possible by cryptographic procedures, which are also necessary for preserving the confidentiality and integrity of data. To protect patient data from unauthorized users, security protocols are used to restrict access. Operational controls may be used within a covered entity to accomplish this.

Privacy in Healthcare

Due to its advantages, blockchain technology is a good choice for enhancing healthcare privacy. Enhancing patient privacy and data security is one of the healthcare issues for which it has been identified as a potential solution. Although patient privacy may be enhanced by blockchain technology, certain issues still to be determined. The fact that different blockchain platforms are incompatible with one another poses a serious problem because healthcare providers can be using disparate, incompatible systems.

Blockchain tools incorporate numerous privacy-enhancing expertises to make sensitive patient data stronger. Because sensitive information in medical records must be private and privacy is especially important. Unauthorized access to this kind of information may harm patients and expose medical staff to legal risks. Encrypted ad pseudonymized data can be stored on a blockchain to safeguard confidential information while permitting authorized parties to retrieve the required data. Health information can be securely transferred and kept, with access limited to those who are authorized and have the necessary decryption keys

Blockchain uses cryptographic addresses to identify transactions, which provides an additional layer of anonymity. When the blockchain is combined with other privacy-enhancing technologies, it not only increases anonymity but also identifies transactions using cryptographic addresses rather than real-world identities.

RQ3: What are the application scenarios of blockchain in health care sector?

While blockchain-based healthcare startups are adopting some guidelines, some large organizations are experimenting with them to secure their business. The Figure 2 shows the application scenarios in healthcare sector.

Figure 2. Application scenarios of blockchain

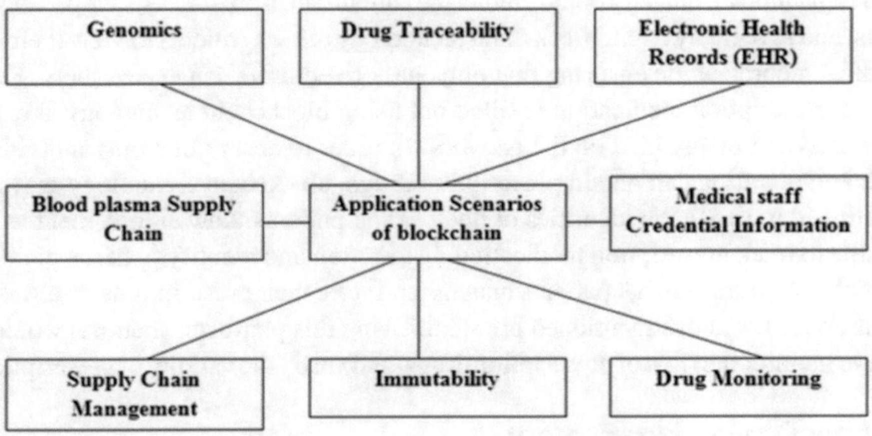

Genomics

Nebula Genomics is one of the first companies to use blockchain technology to create a decentralized platform for sharing genome data. Even after sharing their genetic data with researchers, patients are still in charge of who can access it. Many patients are reluctant to submit their genomic data due to privacy concerns. Patients can choose who have access to their genetic information and get paid for it using the organization's platform, which enables them to provide genetic information to researchers in exchange for cash.

Drug Traceability

Most drug traceability systems in use today are based on a centralized database that can be hacked or manipulated. It is the ability to track a pharmaceutical product from manufacturers to consumers along the supply chain. Blockchain tools have the prospective to completely transform drug monitoring by producing an immutable record of drug product movements. When combined with artificial intelligence and the internet of things, blockchain tools may track pharmaceutical products in real time. A blockchain-based system would track every movement of drug products in an unhackable, decentralized manner. Authorities would be able to quickly identify and get rid of counterfeit goods thanks to this. Additionally, this would enable more effective and efficient responses to medication shortages or recalls.

Electronic Health Records (EHR)

The healthcare industry could predict the patient care from illness, save production costs, and save many lives. Blockchain technology allows patients to view their own medical records while ensuring that only authorized users can access them. Every time a prescription medication is filled out using blockchain technology, a record is created and maintained on the network. In order to ensure that only individuals with authorization can obtain prescription drugs, blockchain technology may also be utilized to verify the identities of doctors and patients. Law enforcement would be able to track prescription medication distribution and identify patterns of abuse. BlockMedx, a startup that patients manage and store their prescriptions safely, is the solution for the above mentioned problem. Using this platform, chemists would be able to monitor the flow of prescription drugs, and verify the validity of prescriptions.

Supply Chain Management

A growing number of consumers are inquiring about the sources of information regarding the products they buy. Operational efficiency is increased when enterprise supply chains are mapped and visualized using traceability. Businesses can interact with customers and gain a deeper understanding of their supply chain by utilizing blockchain, which offers real, verifiable and unchangeable data. The data can be updated validated in real time.

Transparency promotes public trust by compiling crucial data, such as certifications and claims, and making it available to the general public. Once it has been registered on the Ethereum blockchain, third parties can verify its legitimacy. Fractional ownership can be used to represent tokens that represent a shareholder's interest in a specific item, in the same way that stock exchanges help make trading of company shares easier.

Immutability

Cryptographic hashes are what give blockchain its immutability. Secure hash algorithm (SHA) 256 is one among the hash functions. In hashing, input is fed through a cryptographic algorithm to produce an output. Each block in the blockchain is linked together through hashing and bound cryptography. This algorithm is a subset of the parameters that link every network block, which allows for immutability. These blocks are secured sequentially, and tampering is prohibited. The current block will disconnect from all previous blocks if someone tries to alter the data or input on the block.

Example 1: It is obvious when the toothpaste is reassembled inside the tube.

Example 2: Because an email cannot be revoked once it is sent to the recipient, they are incredibly inflexible. Convincing the recipient to remove the email is the only way to solve the issue.

Drug Monitoring

The revolutionize drug monitoring in blockchain is depicted in Figure 3 as shown below

Figure 3. Drug monitoring

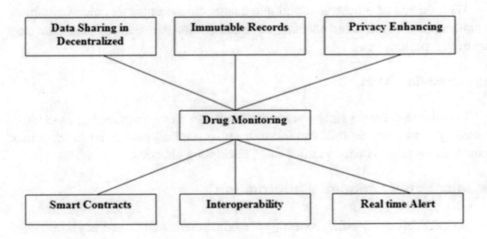

Immutable Records

Each medication and interaction between patients is stored on the blockchain as an immutable transaction. This minimizes the fraudulent activities by making sure the integrity of prescription data.

Data Sharing in Decentralized

Authorized patients medication details are secured and can be able to access with the help of blockchain.

Privacy Enhancing

The confidential information of patients can be given as the highest priority in blockchain development. To improve this, only licensed healthcare providers are agreed to access their data.

Smart Contracts

The use of smart contracts can automate patient prescription history in order to reduce workload and enhance accuracy level for healthcare providers.

Interoperability

With the aid of blockchain, multiple healthcare systems can quickly establish connections with the states, encouraging collaboration in management and keeping an eye on prescriptions.

Real time Alert

In order to promote early intervention and avoid over prescribing blockchain based systems have the ability to instantly notify medical professionals when they come across patients with questionable prescription histories.

Medical Staff Credential Information

Blockchain expedites the processing of medical credentials. Accuracy is improved and fewer exchanges and interactions are required to minimize erroneous information. Document verification, license and certificate verification, and document verification all benefit greatly from primary source verification. Peer-to-Peer networks improve data accessibility and transparency while enabling quicker verification times.

Blockchain allows a doctor or other healthcare professionals to upload credentials and background information. This may contain their prior academic records, licenses, references, certificates etc. It can also help create a secure time chain that makes it easier to view an applicant's background information and medical records quickly.

Blood Plasma Supply Chain

The technology found by EY teams in blockchain could make data about blood product usage more accessible and comprehensible by offering a platform that ensured the visibility, security, and dependability of records from donation to transfusion. The perfect technology to increase security and visibility in the blood supply network is blockchain which encodes data in a completely transparent and safe manner.

RQ4: What Are the Impacts on Blockchain in Healthcare Sector?

Blockchain tools has a number of advantages for the healthcare sector, including securing and monitoring the data. The answer to this research question may lead to benefits and the possible use of this technology to develop the industry as shown in Figure 4.

Figure 4. Impacts on blockchain in healthcare sector

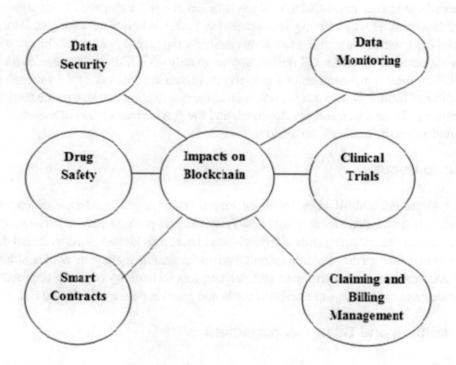

Drug Safety

Numerous procedures in the healthcare production could be streamlined with blockchain-based smart contracts. One of the major problems is drug processes in the healthcare industry. The annual cost of treating adverse drug reactions is estimated to be in the billions. Moreover, database can track the provenance of drugs throughout the supply chain. It has the ability to change the healthcare sector in medication safety. Moreover, smart contracts could be used to manage patient data and records, make certain authorized parties to access the confidential information. Furthermore, blockchain is used to track patient outcomes, making it possible to detect adverse reactions early on.

Clinical Trials

Using blockchain technology, every step of the clinical trial process would be recorded, simplifying data tracking and error detection. Blockchain technology can also be used to authenticate doctors and patients and make sure only those with permission can access clinical trial information. It has the potential to the solutions of these problems by offering a transparent and safe method of managing and storing trial information. According to a status analysis, the global market for clinical trials is expected to be worth US dollars approximately 40 billion in the year 2020. By 2027, almost compound annual growth rate grown approximately 8% to reach US dollar 54 billion. Numerous factors, such as the rise in clinical trials, the necessity of outsourcing research and development, and the commercialization of medications, are driving the market's expansion.

Drug Security

All patient health data, including doctor prescriptions and blood pressure readings, needs to be located and accessible 24/7. Blockchain protects patient privacy while facilitating data sharing among different healthcare providers. It is a distributed database that enables the safe, transparent, and unchangeable management of healthcare data. Because of its distributed architecture, this technology can help improve the management of electronic health records and provide data availability 24/7.

Claiming and Billing Management

Blockchain technology makes the process of eradicating these kinds of situations easier by recording medical data and storing it in an open digital ledger where any changes are immediately visible to all participants. Claims and billing management is the portion of the procedure that deals with submitting and handling medical claims related to a patient's diagnosis, prescription medications, and treatments.

RQ5: Where can I find the links to the healthcare dataset?

https://data.world/datasets/healthcare (World Data, n.d.)

There are nearly 250 healthcare dataset available on this website

https://catalog.data.gov/dataset (United States Government, n.d.)

There are nearly 85 healthcare dataset available on this website

https://www.kaggle.com/datasets

In this particular website U.S healthcare data set are available where mainly focused on health, drugs, nutrition and health plan strategy and disease.

https://github.com/topics/healthcare-datasets (Github, n.d.)

In this website nearly 51 healthcare dataset are available

https://data.humdata.org/organization/world-health-organization (Hum Data, n.d.)

There are nearly 207 healthcare dataset are available.

https://www.kaggle.com/search?q=healthcare+dataset (Kaggle, n.d.-b)

This is the most popular website nearly having 6900 healthcare dataset where the beginners do their research work.

CHALLENGES FACED IN BLOCKCHAIN IN HEALTHCARE SECTOR

Blockchain is a relatively new technology whose full potential has not yet been demonstrated. Blockchain presents numerous issues for the healthcare industry as shown in Figure 5.

Figure 5. Challenges in blockchain

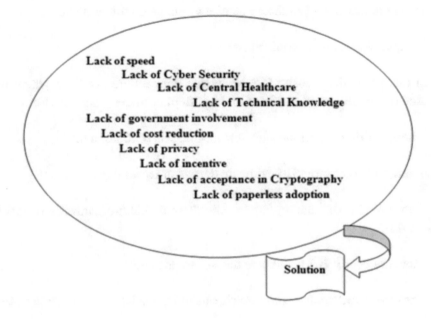

Lack of speed

When speed is considered, the pace of blockchain technology is extremely slow. In this instance, the confirmation process for sharing information automatically slows down.

Solution

There should be perfect proportions among the Blockchains. It should be up to the higher authority to define blockchain sizes. For technicians, ensuring that appropriate testing is done and that no extraneous traffic occurs is crucial. Overlapping blocks should be closely observed.

Lack of Cyber Security

There are several attacks despite the fact that blockchain technology is extremely safe and independent of outside parties. Many hackers target user's wallets in an attempt to steal money. To maximize their incentives, many hackers mine unnecessary blocks and boost network traffic.

Solution

Hospitals must employ distinct authentication for each user with unique IDs to ensure security. Private blockchain should be used by the network administrator to verify each user.

Lack of Central Healthcare

Many hospitals have more than one location. There are numerous, widely scattered healthcare systems. To maintain all medical records in one location using blockchain technology, a more efficient method is needed.

Solution

Dispersed networks are essential, and every hospital ought to have a sizable blockchain to store information and facilitate on-demand access to patient records. Certain uses of blockchain technology can assist hospitals in recognizing problems and taking the necessary action to resolve them.

Lack of Technical Knowledge

Additionally, a lot of consumers don't know about the newest technologies. It is not anticipated that all users will own high-end hardware and software.

Solution

Businesses ought to make an effort to reduce the cost of the technology. Users need to be up-to-date on the newest technologies. The media ought to actively promote this newest technology.

Lack of government involvement

The majority of hospitals are government owned. One role of the government is to enforce regulations. A few countries are unwavering in their resolve to implement the newest technologies. Blockchain is not suitable for government-owned hospitals because of its distributed, highly decentralized ledger. Without the involvement of a central authority or outside parties, decisions are made. Usually, the blockchain is in charge of making the choices.

Solution

For the government to use data for research and other purposes, it must be preserved. The government ought to give blockchain implementation in hospitals top priority as well. Blockchain offers a novel approach to combining distribution with security.

Lack of cost reduction

Hardware and software for mining are costly when using blockchain technology. When mining, electricity is necessary in blocks. The miners did not receive enough money.

Solution

Blockchain businesses ought to concentrate on cutting costs because technology is developing daily. In order to encourage more miners to participate in the blockchain, the co-operations should also raise the reward.

Lack of privacy

The information is stored in a copy of the blockchain database that is owned by each user. When there is network failure, the data is safe and can potentially be updated later.

Solution

To use a private blockchain, the network administrator must give permission. Use of small private blockchains is recommended. So, the network can only be joined by patients who are insecure.

Lack of incentive

Although blockchain offers financial independence, the rewards are insufficient. Miners receive rewards when a block is successfully verified. In comparison to the hardware and software utilized, very few incentives are generated. To raise the quantity, users attempt to mine more.

Solution

Despite the fact that blockchain offers fewer incentives, businesses are currently creating innovative strategies to optimize the benefits.

Lack of acceptance in Cryptography

The majority of physicians do not take crypto currencies as payment. The acceptance of blockchain technology before the full establishment of online payment. There is still a cash flow. As a result, it is important to execute online payments properly. Then, use of blockchain technology is necessary.

Lack of paperless adoption

Paper records are preferred by many clinicians and consumers to have a file system for medical records. Some pharmacies prefer paperless transactions. Pharmacies usually employ prescriptions to keep inventory under control. It is a challenging task for a blockchain network to do a total paperless work.

Solution

Small blockchains are a good way for doctors to become accustomed to the newest technology. They can utilize paper for X-ray plates and other surgical records. The health sector should use blockchains to store prescriptions and other file records since they are convenient to store

CONCLUSION AND FUTURE SCOPE

Many healthcare occupations could undergo a change because of blockchain technology. It improves the monetization of health information, fortifies the security of patients electronic medical data, fosters more interoperability between healthcare companies, and supports the effort to combat fake drugs. Blockchains potential in the healthcare sector is largely dependent on how well received cutting-edge technology is in the ecosystem. The improvement of patient history management, namely in the domains of insurance mediation and tracking, would expedite clinical operations while upholding the highest standards of data quality.

The way physicians and patients manage and use clinical records will eventually be revolutionized by this technology which would also significantly improve healthcare services. Healthcare data maintenance has received increase attention in recent years since it can lead to more accurate, cost-effective and efficient patient care. If blockchain technology is successfully implemented in healthcare settings, it might potentially create new opportunities for the progress of medical research. The medical sector, which employs a sizable number of professionals, including specialists in research and development, is responsible for the effective sharing of medical data and the distribution of a large amount of information.

Future Scope

Further research must be carried out and examined by shaping the framework to address numerous challenges in the public and private healthcare domains. A multi-noded computer system called blockchain can benefit doctors and patients worldwide. It functions as a database and distributed ledger. Blockchain technology can help healthcare organizations in ways beyond patient data security and confidentiality when combine with AI, IoT and Cloud Computing to automate operations.

ACKNOWLEDGMENT

The author would like to express gratitude to the management for providing the opportunity to use our college's facilities for this chapter.

REFERENCES

Abir, E. L. (2022). Blockchain-Based Distributed Information Hiding Framework for Data Privacy Preserving in Medical Supply Chain Systems. *Sensors (Basel)*, 22(4).

Ashraf, M. E., Eman, H., Khaled, W., & Fatma, A. (2023). Omara.: Federated blockchain system(FBS) for the healthcare industry. *Scientific Reports*, 2569.

Chang, Y., Fang, C., & Sun, W. (2021). *A blockchain-based Federated Learning Method for Smart Healthcare Computational Intelligence and Neuroscience*, 1-12. Wiley.

Chirag. (2024). *Breaking Barriers: Blockchain's Role in Reshaping Healthcare.* AppInventive. https://appinventiv.com/blog/blockchain-technology-in-healthcare -industry/

Dris, E. I., Hanan, E. I., & Souad, S. (2021). A Blockchain-Based Privacy-Preserving Smart Healthcare Framework. *Journal of Healthcare Engineering*.34777733

Geeks for Geeks. (n.d.). *Challenges of Blockchain in Healthcare.* Geeks for Geeks. https://www.geeksforgeeks.org/challenges-of-blockchain-in-healthcare/

Github. (n.d.). *Healthcare Datasets* [Dataset]. GitHub. https://github.com/topics/ healthcare-datasets

Hamed, T. (2023). Privacy and Security of Blockchain in Healthcare: Applications, Challenges, and Future Perspectives. *SCI, 5*(4).

Han, D., Pan, N., & Li, K. C. (2022). A traceable and revocable cipher text-policy attribute-based encryption scheme based on privacy protection. *IEEE Transactions on Dependable and Secure Computing*, 19(1), 316–327. 10.1109/TDSC.2020.2977646

Hum Data. (n.d.). *Organizations: WHO.* Hum Data. https://data.humdata.org/ organization/world-health-organization

Kaggle. (n.d.-a). *Datasets* [Dataset]. Kaggle. https://www.kaggle.com/datasets

Kaggle. (n.d.-b). *Healthcare Datasets* [Dataset]. Kaggle. https://www.kaggle.com/ search?q=healthcare+dataset

Khan, M. F., Ghazal, T. M., Said, R. A., Fatima, A., Abbas, S., Khan, M. A., Issa, G. F., Ahmad, M., & Khan, M. A. (2021). An iomt-enabled smart healthcare model to monitor elderly people using machine learning technique. *Computational Intelligence and Neuroscience*, 2021, 1–10. 10.1155/2021/248775934868288

Kuo, T.T. & Ohno-Machado, L. (2018). *Modelchain: Decentralized privacy-preserving healthcare predictive modeling framework on private blockchain networks.*

Letizia, N. (2019). Blockchain-enabled supply chain: An experimental study. *Science Direct,136*, 57-69.

Omkumar, C. U., Sudhakaran, G., Balaji, V., Nhaveen, A., & Balakrishnan, S. (2023). Securing healthcare data through blockchain enabled collaborative machine learning. *Solftcomputing*, 27, 9941–9954.

Pratima, S., Rao, M., Namasudra, S., Vimal, S., & Ching-Hsien, H. (2021). *Blockchain-based IoT architecture to secure healthcare system using identity-based encryption*. Wiley.

Puthal, D., Malik, N., Mohanty, S. P., Kougianos, E., & Das, G. (2018). Everything you wanted to know about the Blockchain: Its Promise, Components, Processes, and Problems. *IEEE Consumer Electronics Magazine*, 7(4), 6–14. 10.1109/MCE.2018.2816299

Sang, Y. L. (2019). Medical Data Framework Using Blockchain Technology. *International Journal of Advanced Trends in Computer Science and Engineering*, 8(5).

Schulz, S. (2019). Standards in healthcare data. *Fundamentals of Clinical Data Science*, 19-26.

Sonali, V., Mohammad, S., Prajjawal, P., Rama Parvathy, L., & Issac, O. (2022). Integration of Artificial Intelligence and Blockchain Technology in Healthcare and Agriculture,Hindawi. *Journal of Food Quality*.

Sudeep, T., Karan, P., & Richard, E. (2020). Blockchain-based electronic healthcare record system for healthcare 4.0 applications. *Journal of Information Security and Applications, 50*.

Tiwari, A., Dhiman, V., Iesa, M. A. M., Alsarhan, H., Mehbodniya, A., & Shabaz, M. (2021). Patient behavioral analysis with smart healthcare and IoT. *Behavioural Neurology*, 2021, 1–9. 10.1155/2021/402876134900023

Uma Maheswaran, S. K., Gaganpreet, K., Pankajam, A., Firos, A., Piyush, V., Vikas, T., & Hussien, S. (2022). Empirical Analysis for Improving Food Quality Using Artificial Intelligence Technology for Enhancing Healthcare Sector. *Journal of Food Quality*, 2022, 1–13. 10.1155/2022/1447326

United States Government. (n.d.). *Data Catalog* [Dataset]. United States Government. https://catalog.data.gov/dataset

Vazirani, , A. (2019). Implementing Blockchains for Efficient Healthcare: Systematic Review. *Journal of Medical Internet Research, 2*.

Wang, J., Xia, C., Sharma, A., Gaba, G. S., & Shabaz, M. (2021). Chest CT findings and differential diagnosis of mycoplasma pneumonia and mycoplasma pneumonia combine with streptococcal pneumonia in children. *Journal of Healthcare Engineering*, 1–10.

Wang, S., Ouyang, L., Yuan, Y., Ni, X., Han, X., & Wang, F. Y. (2019). Blockchain enabled smart contracts: Architecture, applications, and future trends. *IEEE Transactions on Systems, Man, and Cybernetics. Systems*, 49(11), 2266–2277. 10.1109/TSMC.2019.2895123

World Data. (n.d.). *Healthcare*. [Dataset]. World Data. https://data.world/datasets/healthcare

Xiaoguang, L., Ziqing, W., Chunhua, J., Fagen, L., & Gaoping, Li. (2016). A Blockchain-based Medical Data Sharing and Protection Scheme. *IEEE Access : Practical Innovations, Open Solutions*, 4, 1–11.

Xiaomin, Du. (2021). Research on the Application of Blockchain in Smart Healthcare: Constructing a Hierarchical Framework. *Journal of Healthcare Engineering*.

Yue, X., Wang, H., Jin, D., Li, M., & Jiang, W. (2016). Healthcare data gateways: Found healthcare intelligence on blockchain with novel privacy risk control. *Journal of Medical Systems*, 40(10), 218–8. 10.1007/s10916-016-0574-627565509

Zhang, P. (2018). Blockchain technology use cases in healthcare. In *advances in Computers*. Elsevier.

Zhang, X., & Wang, Y. (2021). Research on intelligent medical big data system based on hadoop and blockchain. *EURASIP Journal on Wireless Communications and Networking*, 2021(1), 1–21. 10.1186/s13638-020-01858-3

Zhijie, S., Dezhi, H., Dun, Li., Xiangsheng, W., Chin-Chen, C., & Zhongdai, W. (2022). A blockchain-based secure storage scheme for medical information. *EURASIP Journal on Wireless Communications and Networking*, 40.

Chapter 15
Graph–Theoretic Approaches to Optimizing Connectivity and Security in Ubiquitous Healthcare Systems

R. Sowrirajan
https://orcid.org/0000-0001-9556-5482
Dr. N.G.P. Arts and Science College, India

S. Manimekalai
https://orcid.org/0000-0002-9777-1682
Dr. N.G.P. Arts and Science College, India

ABSTRACT

Graph theory in computer science is an innovative answer to the increasingly complicated modern infrastructure of healthcare, where security and connection are critical and it has a wide range of applications, such as drug development, epidemiological analysis, personalized medicine, and so on. Through the utilization of graph databases and analytics, healthcare practitioners can obtain significant knowledge, improve their decision-making procedures, and optimize their operations. Real-world case studies illustrate successful implementations, such as remote patient monitoring and smart healthcare environments through graph-theoretic solutions The healthcare sector stands to gain from increased patient outcomes, data-driven decision support, and increased efficiency through the incorporation of graph tech-

DOI: 10.4018/979-8-3693-2268-0.ch015

Copyright © 2024, IGI Global. Copying or distributing in print or electronic forms without written permission of IGI Global is prohibited.

nology. The study describes the field's challenges and future directions. It looks at new trends, untapped applications of graph theory in healthcare optimization, and approaches to ethical and legal issues.

INTRODUCTION

Brief Overview of Ubiquitous Healthcare Systems

Ubiquitous healthcare systems aim to transform traditional healthcare delivery by leveraging technology to create a more patient-centric, preventive, and data-driven approach to healthcare. These systems hold the potential to improve outcomes, enhance patient experiences, and increase the efficiency of healthcare services. Ubiquitous healthcare involves the use of wearable devices, such as smart watches and fitness trackers, equipped with sensors to monitor various health parameters like heart rate, activity levels, and sleep patterns (Abdul Majeed & Ibtisam Rauf, 2020). Advanced systems may include implantable sensors or body-worn devices for continuous monitoring of specific health conditions. Integration with medical devices, such as glucometers, blood pressure monitors, and ECG machines, allows real-time data transmission to healthcare providers.

Ubiquitous healthcare systems emphasize the seamless integration of electronic health records, ensuring that patient information is accessible across different healthcare settings.

Interoperability standards enable the exchange of health information among various healthcare entities, supporting coordinated and collaborative care. Ubiquitous healthcare leverages data analytics and artificial intelligence to analyse large datasets, providing insights into patient behaviour, treatment efficacy, and disease trends. By continuously collecting and analyzing health data, healthcare providers can tailor treatment plans to individual patients, optimizing outcomes. Ensuring the privacy and security of health data during transmission is critical, requiring the implementation of secure communication protocols (Abdul Majeed & ibtisam rauf, 2020).

Role of Connectivity and Security in Enhancing Healthcare Infrastructure

A secure and connected healthcare infrastructure fosters patient trust by ensuring the confidentiality and integrity of their health information. The seamless flow of information facilitated by connectivity streamlines healthcare operations, reducing administrative burden and improving resource utilization. Connectivity and security enable the integration of emerging technologies, such as artificial intelligence and machine learning, fostering innovation in diagnostics, treatment plans, and healthcare delivery. So the symbiotic relationship between connectivity and security forms the foundation of a modern and effective healthcare infrastructure, ultimately leading to improved patient care and outcomes(Angel, 2022). It's essential for healthcare organizations to invest in both areas to create a robust and resilient healthcare ecosystem.

Introduction to the Integration of Graph Theory in Computer Science for Healthcare Optimization

Graph-theoretic approaches can be valuable in optimizing connectivity and security in ubiquitous healthcare systems (Anirudh& Thiagarajan, 2019). Ubiquitous healthcare systems involve the seamless integration of various devices, sensors, and networks to monitor and manage health-related data. GT concepts were adopted by a majority of scientists in their works. Recently, graphs are extensively used in many disciplines including social networks (SNs) modelling, big data analysis, natural language processing (NLP), complex network analysis, and patter recognition applications. Here are some ways graph theory can be applied to enhance connectivity and security in such systems:

Network Topology Modeling

Graphs can represent the network topology of ubiquitous healthcare systems. Nodes in the graph can represent devices or components, and edges can represent the connections between them. Analyzing the graph structure can help optimize the layout and connectivity of devices for efficient data exchange (Chithra & Menon, 2020).

Optimizing Communication Paths

Graph algorithms, such as shortest path algorithms (e.g., Dijkstra's algorithm), can be applied to find the most efficient communication paths between healthcare devices. This optimization can improve data transfer speed and reduce latency in the system.

Vulnerability Assessment

Graph theory can be used to model potential vulnerabilities in the healthcare network. By identifying critical nodes and edges, security professionals can focus on securing those points to prevent unauthorized access and data breaches (Bilyeau, 2021).

Role-Based Access Control

Representing user roles and their relationships in a graph allows for the implementation of role-based access control. Nodes can represent users, and edges can represent the permissions or relationships between users and resources. This ensures that only authorized personnel can access specific parts of the healthcare system.

Anomaly Detection

Graph-based anomaly detection techniques can be employed to identify unusual patterns or behaviors in the network. Detecting anomalies can help in the early identification of security threats, such as malicious activities or compromised devices.

Scalability Analysis

Graph theory can assist in analyzing the scalability of the healthcare system. As the number of devices and users increases, understanding how the network's performance scales can guide decisions on infrastructure upgrades and optimizations.

Resilience Analysis

By modeling the healthcare system as a graph, it becomes possible to analyze its resilience to failures or attacks. Graph connectivity analysis can help identify weak points and design strategies to enhance the system's overall resilience.

Graph Encryption Techniques

Graph-based encryption methods can be explored to secure data transmission within the healthcare network. This involves encrypting subgraphs or specific edges to protect sensitive information as it travels between devices.

Dynamic Network Reconfiguration

Graph theory can be applied to dynamically reconfigure the network in response to changing conditions or security threats. This adaptability enhances the system's ability to withstand attacks and ensures continuous connectivity.

Interoperability Optimization

Graphs can represent the relationships and dependencies between different healthcare standards and protocols. Optimizing these interconnections can improve the overall interoperability of the system, allowing for seamless data exchange between diverse healthcare devices.

GRAPH THEORY FUNDAMENTALS

Graph Structures

Graph neural networks (GNNs) have emerged as powerful tools for directly modeling graph representations of electrical physiological data and medical images, spanning modalities such as fMRI, EEG, MRI, and CT data (Xie& Qin, 2005). Despite advancements, defining the graph connectivity structure for specific tasks remains a challenge, often requiring manual design in surveyed proposals(Gopinath et al, 2019). The absence of a standardized method for constructing graphs for GNN models has led some researchers to employ innovative techniques like bootstrapped versions of Graph Convolutional Networks (GCNs) to mitigate sensitivity to initial graph structure initialization (Dadario& Sughrue, 2022).

Models capable of inferring graph topology from data hold significant value, particularly in representing diverse medical signals with multiple nodes and edges. For example, Rakhimberdina et al. utilized a method to analyze various configurations, constructing a set of graphs and identifying the best-performing one for ASD analysis. Similarly, Jang et al. proposed a model that autonomously extracts a multi-layer graph structure and feature representation from raw EEG data for affective mental states analysis (David Ahmedt-Aristizabal et al, 2021; Hernández-Ortiz, 2021,). However, there are essential requirements to enhance the generation process:

1. Dynamic Weights and Node Connectivity: Instead of relying on predetermined connectivity, the adjacency matrix should dynamically learn during training to capture the dynamic latent graph structure (Jang et al 2019; Kazi et al, 2019; Lin et al, 2009; Lin et al, 2020). Such approaches have been suggested for MDD, ASD, and emotion recognition tasks, emphasizing the importance of learning both local and global spatial information to facilitate better information exchange between distant nodes (Hasudungan et al, 2019).

2. Edge Attributes: The exploration of edge embeddings in graphs remains relatively unexplored. While learning predominantly focuses on vertices, incorporating edge attributes as auxiliary information shows promise, particularly in edge-weighted models for ASD and BD analysis.

3. Embedding Knowledge: Leveraging domain-specific knowledge, especially from the medical field, can address specific challenges by creating networks that emulate medical professionals' data analysis methods. Graph-based mapping with label representations, like word embeddings, plays a crucial role in guiding information propagation among nodes. This approach encourages researchers to integrate task-specific prior knowledge, such as disease label embeddings, when constructing graph representations, as demonstrated in chest pathology analysis studies (Meikang Qiu et al, 2013; Onur Tanglay et al, 2023; Parisot et al, 2017;Rakhimberdina, 2020; Yao et al 2020)

The concept of building graph generation models through neural networks has grown, especially with complex topologies and properties of constrained structures. Frameworks like GraphRNN and GRANs offer scalable auto-regressive approaches within the medical domain. While progress has been made in estimating graph structures from data, further exploration is needed, especially in automated graph generation, which remains relatively unexplored in the clinical domain.

Further graphs can be classified as valued and non-valued. Valued graphs assign numerical values to edges, representing intensity, strength, quantity, or frequency between nodes. In contrast, non-valued graphs focus on the connection/relationship between nodes without numerical values. For example, in social networks, edges can represent relationships or interaction frequencies between users, illustrating the distinction between valued and non-valued graphs(Wang et al, 2020)

Types of Graphs Relevant to Healthcare Connectivity

There are five broad types of graphs that can be related to Health care industry

Social graph: A graph that connects individuals or users, commonly seen in social media platforms.

Intent graph: This graph focuses on reasoning and motivation, often observed in platforms like Twitter where user tweets are analyzed to extract intents. These intents can be categorized into areas such as food, travel, career and so on.

Consumption graph: This is widely used in the retail industry by e-commerce giants like eBay, Amazon, and Walmart to monitor customer consumption patterns. This graph aids in tasks such as credit risk analysis and chargeback management.

Interest graph: This type concentrates on user's interests and preferences through organizing web content based on interests rather than simply indexing webpages.

Mobile graph: Derived from mobile data sources, this graph incorporates browsing data from the web, digital gadgets and Internet of Things devices, providing insights into user behaviour and interactions across various digital platforms

INFRASTRUCTURE DESIGN AND OPTIMIZATION

Designing and optimizing infrastructure is a critical aspect of ensuring the efficiency, reliability, and scalability of IT systems (Quan& Guo, 2021). While planning a new infrastructure or looking to improve an existing one, we have to follow considerations like

- Clearly define the business and technical requirements. Understand current and future workloads, data storage, and processing needs.
- Design for scalability to accommodate growth in users, data, and traffic. Consider horizontal and vertical scaling based on the application and workload characteristics.
- Implement redundancy and failover mechanisms to ensure continuous operation. Use load balancing and distributed architecture to prevent single points of failure.
- Incorporate security measures at every level (network, data, application). Regularly update and patch software to address vulnerabilities. Implement access controls, encryption, and monitoring. Use cost-effective solutions without compromising performance. Leverage cloud services for flexibility in resource allocation and pay-as-you-go models.
- Regularly monitor and analyze performance metrics. Optimize code, database queries, and network configurations. Use content delivery networks (CDNs) for faster content delivery.
- Implement automation for deployment, scaling, and monitoring. Use Infrastructure as Code (IaC) tools for consistent and repeatable infrastructure deployments.
- Utilize monitoring tools for real-time insights into system performance. Set up alerts to detect and respond to issues promptly. Analyze data to identify optimization opportunities.
- Design a robust and scalable network architecture. Optimize routing, implement firewalls, and use VPNs for secure communication.
- Implement efficient data storage and retrieval mechanisms. Consider database sharding, indexing, and caching strategies. Regularly back up data and implement disaster recovery plans.

- Comply with industry regulations and standards. Regularly audit and update security and compliance measures. Maintain comprehensive documentation for the entire infrastructure. Document configurations, processes, and troubleshooting steps.

- Foster collaboration between development, operations, and security teams. Encourage communication to address issues and improvements collaboratively.

- Establish a feedback loop for continuous improvement. Collect feedback from users and stakeholders to make informed adjustments.

- Consider environmental impacts and sustainability in infrastructure design. Optimize resource usage to minimize energy consumption. By carefully addressing these considerations, we can design and optimize infrastructure that meets business needs, adapts to changes, and operates efficiently and securely.

Network Topology Modeling for Healthcare Devices

Sensor Network Deployment Strategies

Sensor network deployment involves strategically placing sensors to efficiently and effectively collect data in a given environment. The choice of deployment strategy depends on the specific goals of the sensor network, the characteristics of the environment, and the available resources. Here are some common sensor network deployment strategies:

In random deployment sensors are randomly scattered across the deployment area and simple to implement but may lead to uneven coverage or redundant sensor placement. Suitable for large-scale monitoring where uniform coverage is not critical. In Grid deployment sensors are placed at regular intervals in a grid pattern, ensures more uniform coverage but may result in redundancy. Suitable for applications where consistent data resolution is required. Cluster-based deployment have sensors organized into clusters, with each cluster covering a specific area, improves network efficiency by reducing communication overhead. Barrier coverage deployment have sensors that strategically placed to create a barrier against intrusions. Mobile Sensor Deployment have sensors that mounted on mobile platforms like robots or drones, enables dynamic adaptation to changing conditions and targeted data collection (Zhang et al, 2020).

In Hierarchical Deployment sensors are organized in a hierarchical structure with different levels of sensing capability, efficiently uses resources by having lower-level sensors process data before transmitting to higher-level nodes. Commonly used in large-scale sensor networks to reduce communication overhead. Event-Driven deployment having sensors deployed based on the expected occurrence of events. Optimizes energy usage by activating sensors only when needed. In adaptive deployment sensors adjust their positions based on changing environmental conditions or the quality of data collected, Utilizes feedback mechanisms to optimize coverage and resource usage over time.

In collaborative deployment sensors collaborate to optimize coverage and reduce redundancy. Requires communication between sensors to coordinate deployment or adjust positions based on the network's needs. In localized deployment sensors are placed in localized clusters to focus on specific regions of interest. Useful for applications where detailed data is required in specific areas. In relocation strategies sensors can be designed to relocate themselves based on changing conditions. Enables dynamic adaptation to environmental changes or resource constraints.

In energy-aware deployment consider energy efficiency when deploying sensors, especially in battery-powered systems. Optimize sensor placement to balance data collection needs with energy consumption. In fault-tolerant deployment deploy redundant sensors to ensure continued operation in case of sensor failures. Useful in critical applications where uninterrupted data collection is essential.

Scalability and Reliability Considerations in Graph-Based Networks

In graph-based networks, scalability and reliability are paramount considerations for ensuring the efficient handling of growing workloads and maintaining consistent performance. To achieve scalability, the network can leverage techniques such as graph partitioning, horizontal scaling, parallel processing, and distributed computation frameworks. Horizontal scaling allows for the addition of nodes to handle increased demand, while distributed computation and parallel processing enhance computational efficiency. Reliability is addressed through strategies like data replication for fault tolerance, consistency models tailored to application needs, and robust monitoring with proactive alerts. Additionally, fault-tolerant practices, such as redundancy, backups, and geographic dispersion of data centers, contribute to system resilience. Regular testing, simulations, and adherence to best practices in distributed systems play a crucial role in maintaining a scalable and reliable graph-based network, ensuring it can adapt to evolving demands while sustaining continuous operation even in the face of failures.

Routing Algorithms Optimization

Optimizing routing algorithms is essential for enhancing the efficiency and performance of network communication. Various strategies can be employed to improve routing in computer networks. One approach involves refining traditional algorithms, such as Dijkstra's or Bellman-Ford, by incorporating heuristics or optimizations tailored to specific network characteristics. Additionally, the implementation of adaptive routing algorithms enables dynamic adjustments based on real-time network conditions, leading to more efficient path selection. Load balancing mechanisms distribute traffic evenly across network paths, preventing congestion and optimizing resource utilization. In large-scale and complex networks, hierarchical routing structures or protocols like Open Shortest Path First (OSPF) can be employed to improve scalability. Furthermore, the integration of machine learning and artificial intelligence techniques allows routing algorithms to adapt and optimize based on historical traffic patterns and predictive analytics. Continuous monitoring, feedback loops, and the use of Quality of Service (QoS) metrics contribute to ongoing optimization efforts, ensuring that routing algorithms evolve to meet the demands of modern, dynamic network environments.

Efficient Data Transmission Using Graph Algorithms

Efficient Data Transmission using Graph Algorithms Efficient data transmission is crucial in modern networked systems, and graph algorithms play a major role in optimizing the routing and delivery of information. Graph-based approaches, such as Dijkstra's algorithm or variants like A* search, are employed to find the most optimal paths for data transmission across network nodes. By modeling the network with nodes representing devices or routers and edges denote communication links, these algorithms efficiently navigate the network topology, considering factors like bandwidth, latency, and congestion. Additionally, spanning tree algorithms like Prim's or Kruskal's are utilized to create efficient broadcast or multicast trees, minimizing redundant transmissions. Graph-based optimizations contribute to load balancing, as algorithms like Max Flow-Min Cut are applied to maximize the flow of data through the network while avoiding bottlenecks. Furthermore, advances in distributed graph processing frameworks, called as Apache Giraph or Apache Flink, enable the parallel execution of graph algorithms, enhancing the scalability and speed of data transmission. Incorporating graph algorithms into the network infrastructure ensures that data is transmitted in a manner that is not only expedient but also intelligently adapts to the dynamic conditions of modern communication environments.

Redundancy and Fault Tolerance in Healthcare Networks

Redundancy and fault tolerance are critical considerations in healthcare networks to ensure uninterrupted and reliable delivery of medical services and information. Healthcare systems rely heavily on network infrastructure for tasks ranging from electronic health records (EHR) management to real-time communication among healthcare professionals. Redundancy, achieved through duplicate hardware, network paths, and server clusters, mitigates the risk of single points of failure. This redundancy is vital in healthcare networks where the availability of critical information and communication can be a matter of life and death. Fault tolerance mechanisms, such as automatic failover and load balancing, are implemented to swiftly redirect traffic and workload in the event of hardware failures or network disruptions. Additionally, the use of geographically dispersed data centres and cloud-based solutions contributes to overall fault tolerance, ensuring that healthcare services remain accessible even during localized outages or unforeseen disasters. The integration of these redundancy and fault tolerance measures not only safeguards patient data but also supports the continuous and reliable operation of healthcare networks, promoting the delivery of high-quality and timely patient care.

PATIENT MONITORING AND DATA ANALYTICS

Graph-Based Models for Patient Interaction

Graph-based models have become increasingly significant in modeling patient interactions within healthcare systems. By representing patients and healthcare entities as nodes and their interactions as edges, these models offer a versatile framework for analyzing complex relationships. In the context of patient interactions, graphs can capture dependencies among patients, healthcare providers, and medical facilities. Algorithms such as community detection can identify groups of patients with similar health profiles, aiding in personalized treatment plans. Link prediction algorithms can anticipate potential collaborations or shared health risks among patients. Moreover, graph-based models are instrumental in understanding the flow of patient information, enhancing care coordination, and optimizing healthcare workflows. These models can be applied to electronic health records, enabling the identification of patterns and correlations that contribute enhanced decision-making by healthcare professionals. Leveraging graph-based models in patient interactions not only increase the overall efficiency of healthcare systems but also supports the step towards patient-centered and data-driven healthcare delivery.

Utilizing Graph Structures for Patient-to-Patient Interaction

Leveraging graph structures for patient-to-patient interaction introduces a powerful paradigm in healthcare that captures the intricacies of relationships and collaborations within patient communities. By representing patients as nodes and their interactions as edges, graph models provide a holistic view of shared health experiences, allowing for personalized and community-driven healthcare initiatives. These models enable the identification of patient clusters with similar medical conditions, facilitating targeted support groups and shared resources. Additionally, graph algorithms such as centrality measures can pinpoint influential patients who may serve as peer influencers or mentors within the community. The application of these models extends to enhancing patient engagement through recommendation systems, suggesting relevant health content or connecting individuals with shared health goals. Furthermore, graph-based approaches can aid healthcare professionals in understanding the social determinants of health, contributing to more comprehensive and individualized care plans. Overall, by harnessing the structure of patient interactions through graph modeling, healthcare systems can foster a sense of community, facilitate knowledge exchange, and improve overall well-being within patient networks.

Patient-to-Device Interaction Graphs in Healthcare Monitoring

In healthcare monitoring, the concept of patient-to-device interaction graphs has emerged as a valuable framework for understanding and optimizing the connections between patients and medical devices. Representing patients and devices as nodes connected by edges, these graphs offer insights into the dynamics of data exchange and communication within a healthcare ecosystem. By modeling interactions, such as sensor data collection or device-triggered alerts, these graphs enable a comprehensive view of how patients engage with various monitoring technologies. Graph-based analytics can identify patterns in patient-device interactions, helping healthcare providers tailor interventions, adjust device settings, and enhance overall patient care. Moreover, these models facilitate the identification of potential connectivity issues, allowing for proactive troubleshooting and maintenance. As the Internet of Things (IoT) continues to play a significant role in healthcare, patient-to-device interaction graphs become instrumental in optimizing the deployment and effectiveness of monitoring solutions. By leveraging the power of graph structures, healthcare systems can achieve a more nuanced understanding of patient-device relationships, leading to improved care outcomes and a more responsive and adaptive healthcare environment.Top of Form

Predictive Analytics Using Graph Theory

Early Warning Systems Based on Graph Analysis

Early Warning Systems (EWS) based on graph analysis have emerged as a sophisticated approach to proactively identify and mitigate potential risks in various domains, particularly in healthcare. By representing interconnected entities as nodes and their relationships as edges, graph-based models offer a dynamic representation of complex systems. In healthcare, these systems often include patients, medical conditions, treatments, and other relevant variables. Graph algorithms can then analyze the interconnectedness within this network, identifying patterns that may signal impending issues or deteriorating conditions. For instance, anomalies in patient vital signs or changes in medication adherence can be detected through graph-based anomaly detection algorithms. Additionally, community detection algorithms can identify clusters of patients with similar risk profiles, enabling targeted interventions. The strength of graph-based EWS lies in its ability to consider the holistic context of patient data, allowing for the integration of diverse information sources. As a result, healthcare professionals can receive early alerts and make timely, informed decisions to prevent adverse events, ultimately improving patient outcomes and reducing the burden on healthcare resources. The application of graph-based Early Warning Systems showcases the potential of data-driven approaches in enhancing the predictive capabilities of healthcare systems for more proactive and personalized patient care.

Disease Spread Modeling Through Graph-Based Approaches

Disease spread modeling through graph-based approaches has become a cornerstone in understanding and managing infectious outbreaks. By representing individuals as nodes and their interactions as edges, graph models provide a dynamic framework to simulate and analyze the transmission dynamics of diseases within populations. Nodes in the graph can represent individuals, while edges denote the potential for disease transmission through contact or proximity. Epidemiological models, such as the Susceptible-Infectious-Recovered (SIR) model, can be adapted to graph structures to simulate the progression of diseases. Graph-based algorithms, including centrality measures and community detection, offer insights into the most influential nodes and identify high-risk clusters for targeted intervention. These models can incorporate real-world complexities such as travel patterns, social networks, and demographic data to enhance the accuracy of predictions. As witnessed in recent global events, graph-based disease spread modeling plays a crucial role in informing public health strategies, optimizing resource allocation, and mitigating the impact of infectious diseases on communities. The versatility of graph-based approaches allows for the exploration of different scenarios, aiding policymakers and healthcare professionals in devising effective strategies to curb the spread of diseases.

HEALTHCARE RESOURCE MANAGEMENT

Allocation and Scheduling Optimization Through Graph-Based Approaches to Bed Management Systems

Healthcare resource management is a critical aspect of ensuring efficient and effective delivery of care. One key component is the optimization of resource allocation and scheduling, which can be significantly enhanced through graph-based approaches. In bed management systems, Graph-Based Approaches offer a dynamic framework for modeling patient flow, bed availability, and occupancy patterns. By representing beds as nodes and patient movements as edges, graph algorithms can optimize bed utilization, predict potential bottlenecks, and facilitate timely patient placements. This not only improves patient outcomes by minimizing wait times but also enhances overall resource efficiency.

Personnel Scheduling Optimization Using Graph Algorithms

Similarly, personnel scheduling optimization is paramount in healthcare settings, and graph algorithms play a pivotal role in achieving efficient staffing solutions. By representing healthcare professionals and their skills as nodes connected by edges indicating task dependencies or collaborative requirements, graph models facilitate optimized personnel scheduling. Algorithms such as Dijkstra's or A* can efficiently determine the most effective scheduling routes, ensuring appropriate staffing levels at different times and locations within the healthcare facility. This approach not only minimizes labor costs but also maximizes workforce productivity and patient care quality.

Optimal Placement of Medical Equipment via Graph-Based Techniques

Moving to facility layout planning, the optimal placement of medical equipment is crucial for streamlining workflows and minimizing operational bottlenecks. Graph-based techniques can model the spatial relationships between different departments, medical equipment, and patient areas. Algorithms like Minimum Spanning Trees or Shortest Path Algorithms can assist in determining the most efficient layouts, minimizing travel distances for both patients and healthcare providers. This approach enhances the overall functionality of the healthcare facility, improving accessibility and reducing patient transfer times.

Workflow Optimization in Healthcare Facilities Using Graph Models

Workflow optimization within healthcare facilities is another area where graph models prove invaluable. By representing various workflow stages and dependencies as nodes and edges, these models enable the identification of bottlenecks, delays, and redundant processes. Graph algorithms, such as topological sorting or cycle detection, can optimize the sequential order of tasks, ensuring a streamlined and efficient workflow. This not only enhances patient satisfaction through reduced waiting times but also contributes to improved resource utilization and overall operational efficiency.

Graph-based approaches offer versatile solutions for healthcare resource management, from optimizing bed utilization and personnel scheduling to designing optimal facility layouts and streamlining workflows. These techniques empower healthcare facilities to enhance patient care quality, improve resource efficiency, and ultimately contribute to the overall effectiveness of healthcare delivery.

SECURITY AND PRIVACY IN UBIQUITOUS HEALTHCARE: GRAPH-BASED SECURITY MODELS

Yang et al. introduced a group-based security model that considers varying service qualities within the system. In this model, the overall system security strength is determined as a weighted sum of the security strengths of the selected security algorithms. However, accurately articulating the comprehensive security strength remains a challenge and an open issue.

Access Control and Authentication in Healthcare Networks

Security and privacy are paramount in the realm of ubiquitous healthcare, where the seamless integration of technology introduces new challenges. Graph-based security models provide a robust framework for addressing these concerns within healthcare networks. Access control and authentication, critical components of healthcare cyber security, can be effectively managed using graph structures. Nodes in the graph represent entities such as users or devices, while edges signify relationships or permissions. Through graph-based access control models, healthcare systems can implement fine-grained permissions, ensuring that only authorized individuals have access to specific patient data or critical medical resources. Authentication processes can benefit from graph algorithms that verify user identities based on their relationships and interactions within the network, enhancing the overall security posture.

Anomaly Detection Using Graph Structures

Graph-based approaches also prove invaluable in anomaly detection within healthcare networks. By modeling normal behavior patterns as interconnected nodes and edges, any deviations or anomalies can be identified through graph analysis. This method provides a dynamic and contextual understanding of network activities, allowing for the prompt detection of suspicious behavior. Anomalies may include unauthorized access attempts, irregular data transfers, or abnormal usage patterns. Graph-based anomaly detection enhances the security of ubiquitous healthcare systems by providing real-time insights into potential threats, allowing for swift response and mitigation.

Privacy-Preserving Graph Algorithms: Patient Data Anonymization Through Graph-Based Techniques and Secure Communication Protocols Using Graph-Theoretic Approaches

In the realm of privacy-preserving techniques, graph algorithms offer innovative solutions to safeguard patient data. Patient data anonymization, a critical aspect of privacy protection, can be achieved through graph-based techniques. Graph structures allow for the creation of pseudonymous identifiers linked to patients while preserving the relationships and connectivity in the data. This ensures that valuable insights can still be derived without compromising individual privacy. Additionally, secure communication protocols within healthcare networks can benefit from graph-theoretic approaches. By representing communication channels and encryption keys as nodes and edges, these models enable the development of robust and scalable encryption schemes. This ensures that sensitive health information remains confidential during transmission, safeguarding patient privacy in ubiquitous healthcare environments.

Graph-based security models and privacy-preserving graph algorithms are instrumental in fortifying the security and privacy of ubiquitous healthcare systems. From access control and authentication to anomaly detection and patient data anonymization, these approaches provide a comprehensive framework to address the unique challenges posed by the integration of technology in healthcare. As the healthcare landscape continues to evolve, leveraging graph-based techniques becomes essential in ensuring the confidentiality, integrity, and availability of patient information in ubiquitous healthcare settings.

Security and privacy are paramount in the realm of ubiquitous healthcare, where the seamless integration of technology introduces new challenges. Graph-based security models provide a robust framework for addressing these concerns within healthcare networks. Access control and authentication, critical components of healthcare cybersecurity, can be effectively managed using graph structures. Nodes in the graph represent entities such as users or devices, while edges signify relationships or permissions. Through graph-based access control models, healthcare systems can implement fine-grained permissions, ensuring that only authorized individuals have access to specific patient data or critical medical resources. Authentication processes can benefit from graph algorithms that verify user identities based on their relationships and interactions within the network, enhancing the overall security posture.

Graph-based approaches also prove invaluable in anomaly detection within healthcare networks. By modeling normal behaviour patterns as interconnected nodes and edges, any deviations or anomalies can be identified through graph analysis. This method provides a dynamic and contextual understanding of network activities, allowing for the prompt detection of suspicious behaviour. Anomalies may include unauthorized access attempts, irregular data transfers, or abnormal usage patterns. Graph-based anomaly detection enhances the security of ubiquitous healthcare systems by providing real-time insights into potential threats, allowing for swift response and mitigation.

In the realm of privacy-preserving techniques, graph algorithms offer innovative solutions to safeguard patient data. Patient data anonymization, a critical aspect of privacy protection, can be achieved through graph-based techniques. Graph structures allow for the creation of pseudonymous identifiers linked to patients while preserving the relationships and connectivity in the data. This ensures that valuable insights can still be derived without compromising individual privacy. Additionally, secure communication protocols within healthcare networks can benefit from graph-theoretic approaches. By representing communication channels and encryption keys as nodes and edges, these models enable the development of robust and scalable encryption schemes. This ensures that sensitive health information remains confidential during transmission, safeguarding patient privacy in ubiquitous healthcare environments.

In summary, graph-based security models and privacy-preserving graph algorithms are instrumental in fortifying the security and privacy of ubiquitous healthcare systems. From access control and authentication to anomaly detection and patient data anonymization, these approaches provide a comprehensive framework to address the unique challenges posed by the integration of technology in healthcare. As the healthcare landscape continues to evolve, leveraging graph-based techniques becomes essential in ensuring the confidentiality, integrity, and availability of patient information in ubiquitous healthcare settings.

CASE STUDIES AND APPLICATIONS

1. Drug retargeting: During the race to discover a vaccine for Cancer is if certain existing drugs can be repurposed to fight cancer. This approach is called drug retargeting or repositioning. Drug retargeting is useful when it comes to diseases that trouble only a very small number of people(orphan disease). New drug research for these orphan diseases is not always a priority for pharma companies. Most pharmaceutical drugs act by targeting proteins research could be expedited through a drug retargeting graph, constructed with three types of nodes: disease, protein and drug nodes. A connection is created between a disease and a protein, where it is known that a problem with the protein causes the disease. Likewise, a connection is created between a drug and a protein, where the protein is a known target for the drug. By analyzing such a graph with multiple types of nodes, new target proteins for existing drugs can be identified, consequently discovering a new treatment for diseases base on clinical trials.

2. Graph theory provides a mathematical representation of brain architecture, consisting of nodes and edges. The definition of nodes and edges depends on the scale and technique used to study the brain. Broadly, graphs may model structural or functional connectivity based on a group of brain regions, known as a brain network.

3. Fraud detection: If a fraudulent claim is filed in the name of the customer by nefarious parties without the customer's knowledge, the specific treatment or test or equipment cannot be availed of by the customer when they need it. Graph technology helps health insurance companies go beyond traditional fraud detection methods that involve looking at a single claim or a single doctor. Graph methods now allow looking at the entire network of doctors to detect collusion, cartelization, kickbacks, fake referrals, etc.

4. Genomic and disease: Analyzing a graph constructed using both diseases and genes with connections between comorbid diseases, related genes and known disease gene associations could help uncover new disease-gene associations.

5. Advances in our understanding of human brain structure and function have been facilitated through improved mapping of the structural and functional neural connections throughout the human brain 'connectome'. By utilizing different statistical techniques and non-invasive imaging modalities to capture the structural and functional properties of the brain connectome, such as with diffusion or functional MRI, the brain can also be represented as a graph of individual

nodes which are connected throughout a network. Previously, the neurosurgical community has often relied on traditional maps of the human brain to identify highly functional regions, often called 'eloquent', but these regions differ between patients and do not always provide an adequate guide to reliably prevent functional deficits. Through graphically representing the brain, mathematical graph theory approaches may be able to provide additional information on important inter-individual network properties and functionally eloquent brain regions. This review attempts to outline and review the applicability of graph theory for neurosurgery.

Real-World Implementations of Graph Theory in Ubiquitous Healthcare

1. *Remote Patient Monitoring Systems with Graph-Based Connectivity:* Several healthcare providers have embraced remote patient monitoring systems that leverage graph theory to optimize connectivity. In these systems, patients, healthcare devices, and data sources are represented as nodes interconnected through edges that signify the flow of information. Graph algorithms facilitate the creation of dynamic networks where patient data, vital signs, and treatment plans are seamlessly integrated. This approach enables healthcare professionals to remotely monitor patients in real-time, ensuring timely interventions and personalized care. The connectivity established through graph-based models contributes to a more efficient and responsive healthcare ecosystem.

2. *Smart Healthcare Environments using Graph-Based Security Measures:* Graph theory has been instrumental in designing smart healthcare environments with robust security measures. By modeling the various elements of the healthcare ecosystem as nodes and their interactions as edges, graph-based security measures help protect sensitive patient data and maintain the integrity of medical systems. This approach facilitates the implementation of access control, authentication, and anomaly detection mechanisms. Smart healthcare environments benefit from secure communication protocols modeled through graph structures, ensuring the confidentiality and privacy of patient information. These implementations showcase the role of graph theory in fortifying the security and reliability of ubiquitous healthcare systems.

Success Stories and Challenges Faced

1. *Improved Healthcare Connectivity and Security Outcomes:* Real-world implementations of graph theory in healthcare have yielded significant successes, particularly in terms of enhanced connectivity and security. Remote patient monitoring systems utilizing graph-based connectivity have demonstrated improved patient outcomes through continuous monitoring and timely interventions. Additionally, smart healthcare environments fortified with graph-based security measures have safeguarded patient data, mitigated risks, and fostered a secure and interconnected healthcare infrastructure. These successes underscore the potential of graph theory to revolutionize healthcare delivery and management.

2. *Technical and Ethical Challenges Addressed through Graph-Theoretic Approaches:* While the successes are notable, the adoption of graph theory in healthcare has also faced challenges. Technical challenges include the need for robust algorithms to handle large-scale and dynamic healthcare data. Ethical concerns, such as patient privacy and data anonymization, have been addressed through innovative graph-theoretic approaches. For instance, the use of pseudonymous identifiers in patient data graphs ensures privacy while maintaining the relationships needed for effective healthcare analytics. Overcoming these challenges has required interdisciplinary collaboration between graph theorists, healthcare professionals, and ethicists to ensure the responsible and ethical use of graph-based models in ubiquitous healthcare. The real-world implementations of graph theory in ubiquitous healthcare, particularly in remote patient monitoring and smart healthcare environments, have showcased significant successes in improving connectivity, security, and patient outcomes. However, addressing technical and ethical challenges remains an ongoing effort, emphasizing the need for continued research and collaboration to maximize the potential benefits of graph-theoretic approaches in the evolving landscape of healthcare technology.

3. Challenges of data sharing using graph theory: Balancing the benefits of enhanced data access and sharing with the risks, while considering legitimate private, national, and public interests. This may require reducing unjustified barriers to cross-border data flows. Reinforcing trust and empowering users through pro-active stakeholder engagements and community building to facilitate data sharing and help maximise the value of data reuse. This may involve significant costs including for the development of data-related skills, infrastructures and standards as well as for maintaining community engagement. Encouraging the provision of data through coherent incentive mechanisms and sustainable business models while acknowledging the limitations of (data) markets. This may require addressing uncertainties about data ownership and clarification of the role of privacy, intellectual property rights (IPRs) and other ownership-like

rights, which ideally should be undertaken by appropriate expert agency and organisations.

EMERGING TRENDS IN UBIQUITOUS HEALTHCARE SYSTEMS

The future of ubiquitous healthcare systems holds promising developments driven by emerging trends. Advances in wearable technologies, Internet of Things (IoT) devices, and edge computing are poised to reshape the landscape. Graph-based models will likely play a pivotal role in integrating these diverse data sources, enabling more comprehensive patient monitoring and personalized healthcare interventions. The utilization of artificial intelligence and machine learning algorithms within graph structures is anticipated to enhance predictive analytics, supporting early disease detection and preventive care. Additionally, the growth of telemedicine and virtual care platforms will demand sophisticated graph-based connectivity solutions to ensure seamless interactions between patients, healthcare providers, and devices.

Unexplored Opportunities for Graph Theory in Healthcare Optimization

There exist unexplored opportunities for leveraging graph theory to optimize healthcare processes further. The potential integration of patient-generated health data, social determinants of health, and genetic information within a graph-based framework presents an untapped avenue for comprehensive health analysis. Exploring graph algorithms for predictive modeling of disease progression, treatment responses, and patient outcomes could revolutionize clinical decision support systems. Moreover, extending graph-based approaches to optimize supply chain management in healthcare, from pharmaceutical distribution to medical equipment procurement, remains an intriguing yet underexplored application. These opportunities underscore the need for ongoing research to unlock the full potential of graph theory in advancing healthcare optimization.

Addressing Ethical and Regulatory Concerns in Graph-Based Healthcare Solutions

As graph-based healthcare solutions continue to evolve, addressing ethical and regulatory concerns is imperative. The privacy implications of patient data representation in graph structures necessitate robust anonymization techniques to protect sensitive information while maintaining the usage of data for research and care. Ensuring transparency in the use of graph algorithms and obtaining informed consent from patients for data sharing and analysis are essential ethical practices. Regulations must be framed to accommodate the unique challenges posed by graph-based healthcare solutions, including data ownership, accountability, and the potential biases embedded in algorithmic decision-making. Collaborative efforts involving healthcare professionals, technologists, ethicists, and policymakers are crucial to establishing ethical guidelines and regulatory frameworks that foster responsible and equitable deployment of graph-based models in healthcare systems. Notice that the right balance between ethical practice and innovation is mandatory to realize the full potential of graph-based healthcare solutions in the future.

CONCLUSION

Graph-theoretic approaches present a robust framework for optimizing connectivity and security within ubiquitous healthcare systems. Through the application of graph modeling and algorithms, healthcare providers can improve network efficiency, identify and mitigate security vulnerabilities, and ensure the resilience of interconnected services. This paper advocates for the extensive utilization of graph theory in cyber security within the healthcare domain. With the majority of patient records now digitized, the effective monitoring and maintenance of hospital networks are paramount to safeguarding patient care and confidentiality. By emphasizing the application of graph theory in network monitoring, this chapter underscores the importance of maintaining the security of patient information. The chapter specifically addresses the secure domination and vertex cover problems within graph structures, particularly in blooms architecture, demonstrating the practical benefits of this research in enhancing the security of healthcare systems. Furthermore, this research contributes to alleviating challenges faced by cyber security personnel, who are often burdened with heavy workloads. By leveraging graph-theoretic methodologies, healthcare organizations can streamline their security protocols, thereby optimizing operational efficiency and ensuring the integrity of patient data.

REFERENCES

Ahmedt-Aristizabal, D., Armin, M. A., Denman, S., Fookes, C., & Petersson, L. (2021). Graph-Based Deep Learning for Medical Diagnosis and Analysis: Past, Present and Future. *Sensors (Basel)*, 21(14), 4758. 10.3390/s2114475834300498

Angel, D. (2022). *Protection of Medical Information Systems Against Cyber Attacks: A Graph Theoretical Approach.*

Anirudh, R., & Thiagarajan, J. J. (2019). Bootstrapping graph convolutional neural networks for autism spectrum disorder classification. *In Proceedings of the IEEE International Conference on Acoustics. Speech and Signal Processing.* IEEE.

Bilyeau, N. (2021). Newest Target of Cyber Attacks: America's Hospitals. *The Crime Report*. https://thecrimereport.org/2021/08/18/hospitals-cyberattacks/

Chithra, M. R., & Menon, M. K. (2020). Secure domination of honeycomb networks. [CrossRef] [Google Scholar]. *Journal of Combinatorial Optimization*, 40(1), 98–109. 10.1007/s10878-020-00570-8

Dadario, N. B., & Sughrue, M. E. (2022). Should Neurosurgeons Try to Preserve Non-Traditional Brain Networks? A Systematic Review of the Neuroscientific Evidence. *Journal of Personalized Medicine*, 12(4), 587. 10.3390/jpm1204058735455703

Gopinath, K., Desrosiers, C., & Lombaert, H. (2019 June) Adaptive graph convolution pooling for brain surface analysis. In *Proceedings of the 26th International Conference Information Processing in Medical Imaging*, Hong Kong, China.

Hasudungan, R., Pangestuty, D. M., Latifah, A. J., & Rudiman, . (2019). Solving minimum vertex cover problem using DNA computing. *Journal of Physics: Conference Series*, 1361(1), 012038. 10.1088/1742-6596/1361/1/012038

Hernández-Ortiz, R., Montejano, L. P., & Rodríguez-Velázquez, J. A. (2021). Secure domination in rooted product graphs. [CrossRef] [Google Scholar]. *Journal of Combinatorial Optimization*, 41(2), 401–413. 10.1007/s10878-020-00679-w

. Jang, S., Moon, S.E., & Lee, J.S. (2019). *Signal Classification via Learning Connectivity Structure.* arXiv:1905.11678

Kazi, A., Shekarforoush, S., Krishna, S. A., Burwinkel, H., Vivar, G., Kortüm, K., Ahmadi, S. A., Albarqouni, S., & Navab, N. (2019). Inception GCN: Receptive field aware graph convolutional network for disease prediction. *Proceedings of the 26th International Conference Information Processing in Medical Imaging*, Hong Kong, China.

Li, X., Zhou, Y., Dvornek, N. C., Zhang, M., Zhuang, J., Ventola, P., & Duncan, J. S. (2020). *Pooling regularized graph neural network for fmri biomarker analysis*. In *Proceedings of the 23rd Medical Image Computing and Computer Assisted Intervention*, Lima. Peru. 10.1007/978-3-030-59728-3_61

Lin, M., Yang, L. T., Qin, X., Zheng, N., Wu, Z., & Qiu, M. (2009). Static security optimization for real-time systems. *IEEE Transactions on Industrial Informatics*, 5(1), 22–37. 10.1109/TII.2009.2014055

Majeed, A. & Rauf, I. (2020). Graph Theory: A Comprehensive Survey about Graph Theory Applications in Computer Science and Social Networks. *Inventions 2020*. 5. 10. doi: 5010010.10.3390/inventions

Parisot, S., Ktena, S. I., Ferrante, E., Lee, M., Moreno, R. G., Glocker, B., & Rueckert, D. (2017). Spectral graph convolutions for population-based disease prediction. In *Proceedings of the Medical Image Computing and Computer Assisted Intervention*, Quebec City, QC, Canada. 10.1007/978-3-319-66179-7_21

Qiu, M., Zhang, L., Ming, Z., Chen, Z., Qin, X., & Yang, L. T. (2013). Security-aware optimization for ubiquitous computing systems with SEAT graph approach. *Journal of Computer and System Sciences*, 79(5), 518–529. 10.1016/j.jcss.2012.11.002

Quan, C., & Guo, P. (2021). A local search method based on edge age strategy for minimum vertex cover problem in massive graphs. [CrossRef] [Google Scholar]. *Expert Systems with Applications*, 182, 115185. 10.1016/j.eswa.2021.115185

Rakhimberdina, Z., Liu, X., & Murata, T. (2020). Population Graph-Based Multi-Model Ensemble Method for Diagnosing Autism Spectrum Disorder. *Sensors (Basel)*, 20(21), 6001. 10.3390/s2021600133105909

Tanglay, O., Dadario, N. B., Chong, E. H. N., Tang, S. J., Young, I. M., & Sughrue, M. E. (2023). Graph Theory Measures and Their Application to Neurosurgical Eloquence. *Cancers (Basel)*, 15(2), 556. 10.3390/cancers1502055636672504

Wang, J., Liang, S., He, D., Wang, Y., Wu, Y., & Zhang, Y. (2020). A Sequential Graph Convolutional Network with Frequency-domain Complex Network of EEG Signals for Epilepsy Detection. *Proceedings of the 2020 IEEE International Conference on Bioinformatics and Biomedicine (BIBM)*, Seoul, Korea. 10.1109/BIBM49941.2020.9313232

Xie, T., & Qin, X. (2005). A new allocation scheme for parallel applications with deadline and security constraints on cluster. *Proc. of the 7th IEEE International Conference on Cluster Computing*, (pp. 1–10). IEEE. 10.1109/CLUSTR.2005.347057

Yang, H., Li, X., Wu, Y., Li, S., Lu, S., Duncan, J. S., Gee, J. C., & Gu, S. (2019). Interpretable multimodality embedding of cerebral cortex using attention graph network for identifying bipolar disorder. In *Proceedings of the Medical Image Computing and Computer Assisted Intervention*, Shenzhen, China. 10.1007/978-3-030-32248-9_89

Yao, D., Sui, J., Yang, E., Yap, P. T., Shen, D., & Liu, M. (2020). Temporal-Adaptive Graph Convolutional Network for Automated Identification of Major Depressive Disorder Using Resting-State fMRI. In *Proceedings of the 11th International Workshop on Machine Learning in Medical Imaging*, Lima, Peru. 10.1007/978-3-030-59861-7_1

Zhang, Y., Wang, X., Xu, Z., Yu, Q., Yuille, A., & Xu, D. (2020). *When radiology report generation meets knowledge graph.* In *Proceedings of the AAAI Conference on Artificial Intelligence*, New York, NY, USA. 10.1609/aaai.v34i07.6989

Chapter 16
Navigating Complexity:
Unraveling the IVHM Requirements Puzzle in Unmanned Aerial Systems Through Innovative IVHM–RD Method

Rita Komalasari
https://orcid.org/0000-0001-9963-2363
Yarsi University, Indonesia

ABSTRACT

This chapter aims to establish an approach for IVHM requirements elucidation. A meticulous literature study served as the bedrock of this research, offering critical insights into existing methodologies and challenges in IVHM for UAS. Leveraging this knowledge, the study innovatively introduced the IVHM-RD method, a culmination of extensive data analysis. This approach not only grounded the study in established theories but also pushed the boundaries of understanding in IVHM, ushering in transformative possibilities for UAS design. This method consolidates diverse stakeholder demands through extensive data analysis, resulting in a prioritized set of IVHM requirements. The study's innovative approach, bridging the gap between theory and practice, promises transformative implications for UAS design processes.

DOI: 10.4018/979-8-3693-2268-0.ch016

Copyright © 2024, IGI Global. Copying or distributing in print or electronic forms without written permission of IGI Global is prohibited.

INTRODUCTION

In the vast expanse of a rugged mountain range, a fleet of unmanned aerial systems (UAS) embarks on a critical reconnaissance mission. Their objective: to survey inaccessible terrain for potential hazards and gather vital intelligence for disaster response teams. As the UAS navigate through unpredictable weather conditions and harsh environments, they encounter unforeseen technical glitches and mechanical failures. Without immediate intervention, these malfunctions could jeopardize the success of the mission and compromise the safety of personnel on the ground. The UAS market has experienced significant growth due to technological advancements and increasing demand in various fields, including logistics and delivery (Fan et al., 2020). The incorporation of Integrated Vehicle Health Management (IVHM) is becoming increasingly important to ensure the efficiency, safety, and dependability of UAS (Ranasinghe et al., 2022). The global IVHM market is predicted to grow at a CAGR of 7.7% from 2018 to 2023, reflecting the importance of IVHM in UAS, as it represents the growing realization of the advantages of preventive maintenance and real-time health monitoring (Ezhilarasu et al., 2019). The increasing complexity of UAS operations makes the need for advanced health management systems evident. Autonomy and automation describe the degree to which unmanned aerial systems (UAS) can make decisions without human intervention, thanks to complex computer programs (Montazeri et al., 2021). The Department of Defence sets ten levels of autonomy, including remote guidance, real-time health and diagnosis, adapting to flight conditions and failures, re-planning the group's route on the fly, distributed control, group strategic goals, group tactical objectives, and fully autonomous swarms. Regulatory bodies are placing greater emphasis on safety in the UAS sector, such as the Federal Aviation Administration (FAA), which emphasizes the importance of incorporating effective IVHM practices to meet safety standards. This research has the potential to benefit various individuals, groups, and entities involved in the UAS industry and related fields. The research results may help regulatory agencies like the FAA and other aviation authorities understand what works regarding IVHM, improve safety and regulatory compliance by informing the creation of standards and guidelines for the use of IVHM in UAS operations. UAS operators and service providers may apply the prioritised IVHM requirements to maximize the efficiency of their fleets' operations and maintenance, leading to more effective mission execution, less downtime, and better dependability. IVHM technology companies and entrepreneurs may use the study's findings to improve solutions or create new ones that meet the prioritised needs. Innovation in the sector may flourish due to new possibilities for UAS-specific health monitoring systems. This study helps advance the UAS industry and allied disciplines by outlining a systematic and evidence-based method for determining IVHM needs.

BACKGROUND

IVHM (Integrated Vehicle Health Management) emerged as a response to the growing complexity of aviation maintenance (Ezhilarasu et al., 2019). It integrates physical components for maintenance with UAS and fleet health management, serving as a product-service system (PSS). The goal is to save expenses, increase availability, and ensure safety. IVHM elements include integrated logistics, fault management, fault isolation, diagnostic analysis, and prognostic analysis (Campean et al., 2019). The European roadmap acknowledges the need for UAS health monitoring, and modular design and IVHM subsystems could work together if standardised interfaces are established. The results of this research have the potential to significantly impact the world of practice in unmanned aerial systems (UAS) and contribute to expanding the body of knowledge in applied research. UAS manufacturers and operators can directly implement the prioritised set of IVHM requirements derived from the study, leading to more reliable, efficient, and safer UAS designs and optimized operational practices. The study provides practical guidance for incorporating health management features into real-world UAS applications, leading to an empirical understanding of how IVHM integration influences UAS performance in real-world scenarios. Technology providers and innovators can use the study's insights to refine existing IVHM technologies or develop new solutions tailored specifically for UAS applications. This can result in technological advancements that address the unique challenges of health management in unmanned aerial systems. Educational institutions and training programs can incorporate the study's findings into their curricula, ensuring future professionals in the UAS industry are well-versed in effective IVHM practices. IVHM has the potential to significantly impact the UAS practice world by promoting continuous improvement and fostering a culture of continuous improvement within the industry.

Method

Integrating Vehicle Health Management (IVHM) for Unmanned Aerial Systems (UAS) is a complex field, and this research relies heavily on a literature review that sheds light on current approaches and obstacles. This method serves as a comprehensive exploration of theoretical foundations, guiding the development of the IVHM-RD methodology. Rigour data analysis further underpins the study, ensuring robust comparative analysis and validation exercises. This dual approach grounds the research in established theories and pushes the boundaries of understanding in IVHM, facilitating a transformative bridge between theory and practice in UAS design.

TECHNOLOGICAL ADVANCEMENTS

Diagnostic

The IVHM provides diagnostic analysis and other functional needs for the Unmanned Aircraft System (UAS) to monitor a vehicle's landing gear and other systems (Ciliberti et al., 2022). The IVHM's dependability is one example of a non-functional requirement that specifies standards for evaluating the performance of a system. The typical needs of an IVHM system include the following: fault isolation, deterioration detection, impact assessment, severity assessment, anomaly detection, and future performance prediction (Tang et al., 2022). In addition to reporting problems to the pilot and maintenance staff, the IVHM checks the fleet's health and transmits data to or from other systems inside or outside the vehicle. The IVHM keeps track of hard landings, other events, health statistics, and data for a specific amount of time (Fu & Avdelidis, 2023). The requirements analysis presents several challenges, such as ensuring the IVHM is trustworthy and addressing the inherent limitations of the process. The development of UAS has impacted the fast-paced industry of IVHM, or Infrastructure Vehicles for Human Use. Thanks to developments in sensors, CPUs, networking, and databases, these IVHM-like systems have come a long way. Thanks to these developments and the shrinking size and cost of components, many organisations have experimented with them, leading to better algorithms and programming for UAS diagnostics and prognostics, autonomous flight control, automation, and other similar applications. These advancements have caused new markets, such as environmental monitoring for UAS and availability-based contracting for IVHM, while disrupting existing ones, like selling replacement parts for IVHM and power line inspection for UAS. These issues are not particular to IVHM requirements; they affect all systems equally. An integral part of UAS model development, IVHM provides supplementary advantages such as flight control and autonomy, long endurance missions, and the ability to do hazardous and filthy tasks (Dasgupta, 2019). Thanks to the additional information this data provides on the UAS's autonomy, mission planning, and flight control computer, longer flights and more comprehensive maintenance procedures are accomplished. In order to assess the possible consequences on system life, IVHM may also consider the amount and timing of pollution in a polluted region. The IVHM system may also notify ground personnel of any UAS contamination so they can take the necessary precautions when the plane lands (Berkcan & Aksoy, 2022). Since UAS includes various aircraft and may be configured in various ways into a SoS, our present understanding of IVHM is restricted. Final customers, UAS operators, operations staff, flight schedulers, and maintenance personnel are just a few of the many groups whose needs must be considered throughout the creation of IVHM. Unmanned Aerial Systems (UAS) have all the necessary components to operate. The safety and efficiency of aviation systems rely on IVHM systems. However, its layout is not usually considered an integral aspect of the asset's design, and solutions are generally implemented in isolation. The context of the IVHM is important, as it depends on UAS elements such as failure rates and regulations. Designers and manufacturers of UAS need to consider IVHM early in the design process. There is a lack of operational knowledge on which components of IVHM will best assist a UAS in its operation, and customers often fail to see the value of IVHM to themselves (Holland, 2020). It is critical to create standards for IVHM, but the steps to do so are unclear. There are advantages and disadvantages to the current methods and technologies used to collect and organise requirements. To satisfy stakeholders and assist the UAS in its operation, accomplishing the IVHM objectives of boosting availability, reducing costs, and ensuring safety, the designer must thoroughly understand the complicated requirements (Vachtsevanos & Raja-mani, 2023). An analysis of how IVHM design might boost consumer happiness is included in the review. However, there is no standardised method for designers to consider the many perspectives and requirements of the IVHM's stakeholders. The UAS's IVHM designer will benefit from a firm grasp of the relative significance of needs. According to the results, the IVHM design inspired the project's goals and objectives. IVHM is a linear approach to designing a health monitoring system, focusing on gathering relevant documents and information, assessing the information, and performing new analyses (Li et al., 2020). The system continues by recording functional failure types and how they impact the UAS systems. It then evaluates the fallout from failures and uses that information to do preventative maintenance. IVHM design techniques do not always provide enough information for others to replicate the steps. While some firms provide design techniques to highlight their newest technology and demonstrate their competence, academic research on creating IVHM for UAS is scarce. These approaches may not be theoretically sound, and they might pay attention to one part of a UAS system, ignoring how crucial that part is to the vehicle's overall health.

Prognostic

Establishing and analysing IVHM requirements is costly and important. Key technologies for implementing IVHM include sensors, diagnostics and prognostics, networks and databases, and computer reasoning (Vogl et al., 2019). Connected sensors monitor the state of the system by collecting KPIs. Diagnostics use algorithms to find problems and outliers, pinpoint where the system is headed for failure, and estimate when it will happen. By spotting performance decline and estimating when the system will fail, prognostics make it possible to do maintenance before the actual failure. Thanks to databases and networks, health information may be sent to the appropriate departments, such as operations and maintenance, so that they can make well-informed choices. The operational behaviour of a fleet of vehicles may be better understood using databases that store their historical data. Hardware that runs diagnostic or prognostic algorithms is known as computer reasoning, and it is essential for monitoring various subsystems. IVHM is a broad field with several health monitoring approaches and technology sets. Engine heat monitoring (EHM), structural health monitoring, and avionics built-in testing are just a few examples of the many methods developed due to advancements in maintenance design (Enrico et al., 2019). IVHM combines these many methods to integrate individual system or subsystem health monitoring. However, subcontractors who want to provide their health monitoring service to the subsystems they supply may find IVHM controversial. For instance, instead of using the UAS manufacturer's IVHM service, an engine manufacturer may want to supply their own EHM solution. This thesis does not intend to address the inter-organisational politics that may affect the design of IVHM for a UAS. The Unmanned Aerial Systems (UAS) and fleet rely on IVHM to integrate vendor health monitoring systems (Koschlik et al., 2023). IVHM may benefit from the standards set forth by IEEE, such as AI-ESTATE and SIMICA (Ochella et al., 2021). One standard architecture is OSA-CBM or open systems architecture for condition-based maintenance. It addresses the structure and exchange of medical records. It follows the guidelines laid down in ISO 13,374. Seven layers comprise OSA-CBM: data acquisition, data manipulation, state detection, health assessment, prognosis assessment, and decision support (Mbiyana et al., 2021). The widespread implementation of IVHM open standards would lend credence to an open platform by allowing service providers to cater to a wider range of customers by providing them with compatible systems and components. Since there is not yet a standard set of features for all health monitoring systems, it is hard for designers to choose the best parts, algorithms, and systems. If IVHM and related technologies could handle a set of requirements, it would be helpful for designers. Information and Communication Systems, or IVHM, are vital to the well-being of UAS (Sabatini et al., 2020). The MIMOSA OSA-CBM standard provides a uniform framework for transferring data inside condition-based maintenance systems, letting designers anticipate the precise kind and format of data received from each subsystem or component (Mihai et al., 2022). As a result of further advancements and industry acceptance of standards, the implementation of IVHM becomes more cost-effective, resulting in greater savings in the lifespan expenses of a UAS. Nevertheless, the absence of IVHM norms and regulations may restrict the sustainability of any specific IVHM design for UAS in the long run (Scott et al., 2022). Since developing an IVHM system for a UAS is similar to developing any other system, it is feasible to utilise technologies established for other purposes. To fully use existing health monitoring tools and procedures, it is vital to understand which systems are generally harmful to UAS and need monitoring. If we want our unmanned aerial systems (UAS) to be safe, reliable, and efficient in an ever-changing industry, we must practice integrated vehicle health management (IVHM). Here are some examples of how the study has helped put IVHM into practice in UAS design and operations: The innovative Integrated Vehicle Health Management Requirements Determination (IVHM-RD) approach is introduced due to this research, demonstrating the study's dedication to practicalities (Bhatti et al., 2021). An exhaustive examination of the available data led to the development of this technique, which offers a methodical and organised framework for ascertaining the needs of UAS health management. In the IVHM-RD approach, decisions are heavily based on data. The process guarantees that the specified needs are based on facts and practical knowledge by carefully analysing the material. The prioritised list of IVHM criteria is not made up but rather based on a solid body of evidence, which makes it more useful and relevant for UAS operations and design. A rigid comparative study, including a thorough investigation of current techniques and obstacles in IVHM for UAS, yielded the prioritised list of needs. By comparing and contrasting, we can ensure that the criteria we seek are appropriate and consider all the intricacies of the UAS setting. The IVHM-RD technique provides an organised and methodical approach to requirement determination. Health management elements may be easily included in the design and operational procedures with the help of this practical guidance for UAS operators and designers. The research enables practitioners to transform theoretical ideas into concrete advances in UAS design and operations by methodically establishing needs and supporting a smooth integration of IVHM. The study has real-world consequences for UAS design and operations, as shown by the evidence given. The IVHM-RD technique offers a methodical and tangible way to determine health management needs. It was created through intensive comparative research and comprehensive data analysis. In order to improve the efficiency and dependability of unmanned aerial systems, this part lays the groundwork for the next investigation into the actual application of these criteria. Beyond abstract concepts, the study has real-world ramifications that may help those involved in making and operating unmanned aerial systems (UAS). A new age of improved efficiency, compliance, and dependability is about to dawn on UAS designers and operators thanks to the criteria determined via the Integrated Vehicle Health Management Criteria Determination (IVHM-RD) approach. Producers and designers of UASs bring their wares into line with norms and best practices in the industry by directly applying the specified IVHM criteria (Brat et al., 2023). The IVHM-RD methodology offers a systematic approach that guarantees the smooth integration of health management components, matching regulatory standards and industry expectations. A more efficient and dependable UAS may be created considering the specified needs.The prioritised list of needs is used as a guide to maximise operating efficiency, reduce the likelihood of in-flight problems, and improve UAS health monitoring capabilities. UAS operators may achieve improved mission success rates by directly incorporating the prioritised IVHM criteria into their operating practices. Operators may find and fix problems before they become worse using proactive health monitoring tools, which increases the chances of mission success and decreases the possibility of unexpected failures. Operators may now proactively control the health of their UAS, thanks to the inclusion of IVHM regulations, which reduce unplanned downtimes. The IVHM features help find problems early and fix them, leading to a more dependable operating schedule and optimising mission planning by minimising interruptions (Zhang & Li, 2023). Beyond mere compliance, improving UAS system performance results from incorporating IVHM regulations into operating procedures. Assuring that UASs run at maximum efficiency throughout their operational lifetimes is possible when operators have access to real-time health monitoring data, which allows them to make educated choices about optimising UAS performance. The study findings have real-world implications for UAS operators and manufacturers, as the reasoning given shows. The established IVHM criteria may be directly integrated into design processes and operating practices to ensure UAS performance, efficiency, and dependability that exceed industry norms. This method connects theory with practice, encouraging a change in thinking about the design, operation, and maintenance of UAS in the ever-changing field of unmanned aerial systems.

REGULATORY CONSIDERATIONS

Importantly, this study examines how Integrated Vehicle Health Management (IVHM) affects the rules and regulations that control Unmanned Aerial Systems (UAS) use (Barrado et al., 2020). According to the provided data, the study has shaped regulatory viewpoints, highlighted safety, and laid the groundwork for recommendations that address the unique issues of IVHM in UAS (Wang et al., 2021). Insights from current regulatory agencies, such as the FAA and other international aviation authorities, are included in the research. The study is based on knowledge of the safety and compliance regulations that control UAS operations, as it incorporates insights from regulatory viewpoints (Xu et al., 2020). The data supports the regulatory landscape's focus on safety and compliance, aligning with the aviation sector's objectives.The study highlights the importance of following regulations, which presents IVHM as a means to improve safety measures and guarantee adherence to rules. This study has the potential to shape regulatory frameworks by offering detailed knowledge of the connection between IVHM and UAS safety. The study shows that the views of current regulatory bodies help build a holistic strategy that incorporates IVHM and complies with aviation industry regulations. The study findings provide a solid basis for regulatory agencies to be informed about the real-world consequences of IVHM in UAS operations. These findings may be used to create regulatory frameworks that tackle the unique problems and possibilities of integrating health management systems in UAS. The data shows that we need to ensure operations are safe while encouraging innovation in UAS technology (Gheisari & Esmaeili, 2019). The study adds to the continuing discussion on how regulatory frameworks might change to include IVHM's innovations, enabling innovation while keeping safety a top priority. The impact of this study on the development of rules and regulations governing the use of unmanned aerial systems (UAS) is emphasised here. Contributing to the continuing discussion on IVHM's function in the aviation industry, the research draws on the expertise of current regulatory agencies while stressing the significance of safety and compliance. The data given lend credence to the idea that these studies might help shape regulations for UAS that consider the specific difficulties of IVHM and work together to create a seamless regulatory framework.

The IVHM-RD Approach and the Industry's Focus on Preventative Maintenance

This study's IVHM-RD technique results from thorough data analysis and fits well with the industry's overall emphasis on UAS safety management systems and proactive maintenance (Rajamani, 2020). Examining the data that backs up this alignment, this part highlights how the IVHM-RD approach handles important issues mentioned in aviation rules. Consistent with standard practice in the field, the IVHM-RD approach prioritises preventative maintenance. The technique helps with proactive maintenance practices by methodically identifying health management needs, which in turn aids in creating UAS designs that emphasise early problem identification and treatment (Subramanian, 2021). Because safety is so important in the aviation industry, the technique works well with safety management systems. The IVHM-RD technique takes into account the importance of safety in UAS operations. It ensures that the most important criteria are used to build systems that improve overall safety by continuously monitoring health. Since conformity with aviation rules is essential, the IVHM-RD technique makes regulatory compliance a key component (Shukla et al., 2020). This technique guarantees that unmanned aerial system (UAS) designs with IVHM characteristics are ground-breaking and conform with aviation rules by tackling important issues mentioned in those documents. An important step in keeping UAS designs and operating practices compliant with regulations and safety standards is to match the IVHM-RD approach with industry priorities on safety management systems and proactive maintenance (Maindze et al., 2019). This alignment allows for the smooth incorporation of IVHM while simultaneously addressing the goals and concerns stated in aviation regulations, connecting theoretical frameworks with real industry demands. By providing guidelines for creating UAS that can identify and resolve any problems before their escalation, the IVHM-RD approach aids in proactive maintenance. There will be fewer in-flight breakdowns and interruptions because of proactive maintenance made possible by the IVHM features, which increase the durability and dependability of UAS components. The IVHM-RD approach allows for continuous monitoring, which strengthens safety management systems. Including safety concerns in the prioritised criteria makes it possible for UAS operators to see how their systems are doing in real-time and make choices that improve safety for everyone.This section emphasises how the IVHM-RD approach aligns with the industry's focus on safety management systems and proactive maintenance. This technique guarantees that the integration of IVHM in UAS is both innovative and by industry best practices by addressing significant issues specified in aviation laws (Walthall, 2020). The data given highlights this. In the ever-changing world of UAS, this harmony helps achieve aviation's broad objectives by encouraging a safety-first mindset, preventative maintenance, and regulatory conformity. This study's conclusions will greatly affect the rules and regulations governing UAS. In this part, the author makes a strong case for how regulatory agencies may use the study's results to shape the creation of actionable standards that reflect business interests. The UAS industry's safety, dependability, and compliance are greatly improved by its alignment with regulatory imperatives. Regulatory agencies may greatly benefit from the study's findings, based on an exhaustive investigation of IVHM in UAS. The research's practical recommendations provide a methodical way to incorporate IVHM into current and future regulatory frameworks, which might be useful for regulatory authorities. Key problems and difficulties related to the integration of IVHM in UAS operations are identified and addressed in the study. Guidelines must be developed to handle the particular intricacies of health management in unmanned aerial systems, and this research helps by alerting regulatory agencies to regulatory gaps and difficulties. Because they are manufactured in blocks with somewhat varied systems, IVHM systems are vital for the well-being and security of UAS systems. Confusion and increased logistical costs result from a lack of planning for UAS assistance and an inadequate understanding of how the new capacity may be properly used and redesigned. In order to prevent logistical issues later on, it is clear that the supportability of a UAS must be seriously studied from its inception. The reasons why unmanned aerial systems (UAS) fail or crash are not well documented, and the little data that is available may vary greatly from one UAS to another. It would be wiser to treat each UAS as a distinct case or group depending on size, purpose, and operational state rather than implementing IVHM systems for all UAS sizes and kinds. IVHM is critical in designing health monitoring systems for un-crewed aerial vehicles (UAS) (Bisanti et al., 2023). However, new UAS designers may struggle to understand the system failure patterns, especially for less conven-tional UASs. Designing health monitoring systems for UAS is the subject of two articles from General Atomics, PHM Technology, and Agent-Oriented Software (AOS) (Grübel et al., 2022). Equally important is the use of Failure Modes, Effects, and Criticality Analysis (FMECA) to determine the consequences of functional UAS failures. The study's alignment with regulatory priorities ensures that the guidelines developed are theoretically sound and practically applicable to the UAS industry. By addressing safety, reliability, and compliance concerns, the research contributes to developing guidelines that resonate with the core priorities of regu-latory bodies. A focus on safety within regulatory frameworks is emphasised as a key contribution of the research. Health management is essential to regulatory concerns, and the recommendations promote a safety culture in the UAS sector by including IVHM best practices (Verhagen et al., 2023). The study can improve industry practices by providing practical recommendations that producers and op-erators of unmanned aerial systems (UAS) may use to manage health better. The practical effects include more stringent adherence to regulations, enhanced depend-ability, and better safety precautions. The argument highlights how the study may impact regulatory authorities and how recommendations for integrating IVHM in UAS operations are developed. The research helps to set up a regulatory framework that improves UAS safety, dependability, and compliance by lining up regulatory goals and handling important problems. In the ever-changing realm of unmanned aerial systems, the real-world influence is substantial, shaping industrial practices and encouraging a culture of accountable and efficient health management. This study's findings contribute to current theoretical frameworks and have significant implications for developing unmanned aerial systems (UAS) technology. In this part, we outline how the study's prioritised criteria for Integrated Vehicle Health Management (IVHM) provide technology vendors with a clear path forward. Rec-ognising that UAS technology is ever-evolving further highlights the need for creative and adaptable IVHM solutions. Providers of UAS technology may greatly benefit from the research's prioritisation of IVHM needs. From this data, it is clear that the study's findings provide a clear direction for technology businesses to satisfy the specific health management needs of the UAS industry. The research recognises the need for creative and adaptable solutions by openly addressing the ever-changing nature of UAS technology.The study highlights the significance of IVHM systems that can adapt to shifting operating settings and technical improvements by address-ing the dynamic nature of UAS technology. This section argues that the study's findings affect technical advancement and innovation in the UAS sector. According to the prioritised IVHM criteria, technology providers must offer solutions that cater to industry expectations and can adjust to the always-evolving UAS technology. Technology providers may use the priority IVHM demands as a roadmap to develop solutions that tackle the unique challenges of UAS health management. Thus, technological advancements may affect the study's practical requirements rather than the reverse. This argument demonstrates how the study considers the dynamic character of operational settings and UAS technology. Therefore, the IVHM solutions proposed in the research are designed to be naturally flexible in order to address the constantly evolving technological and operational challenges faced by UAS vendors.

IVHM-RD Methodology and Rigorous Data Analysis

Implications for the long-term health of the UAS market are borne out of the study's focus on novel and adaptable IVHM solutions (Ochella et al., 2022). The study's findings demonstrate that technology suppliers can contribute to innovation in the industry by developing solutions that address current and future needs. This part delves into how the research has aided advancements and innovations in UAS technology. The assertion that technology providers may design flexible solutions that keep up with the dynamic UAS sector by referring to the prioritised IVHM criteria is supported by evidence. This study has a significant effect on the state of unmanned aerial systems technology. The findings of this study will hopefully lead to new developments in UAS technology. This section argues that technology vendors may tackle the unique challenges faced by UAS with creative IVHM solutions based on the study's findings. The study adds to theoretical discussions and provides useful data that business innovators can use to enhance UAS health management. According to the study's conclusions, IT businesses have a once-in-a-lifetime opportunity to construct revolutionary IVHM solutions on top of current research. The results imply that technology providers may use the priority criteria based on research to address the complicated problems associated with UAS health management. In this line of reasoning, the particular issues brought on by UAS are emphasised rather than the study's findings applying to a broader context. Technology suppliers may provide successful solutions that respond to unmanned aerial systems' operational complexity and environmental variables (UAS) by adapting to their particular needs. The research stands out by providing insights beyond theoretical considerations and offering practical guidance for industry innovators. Technology providers can translate the theoretical constructs into tangible advancements, resulting in IVHM technologies that have a meaningful impact on the operational efficiency and reliability of UAS. The argument establishes that the research contributes to technological advancements within the UAS sector. By offering practical insights, the study empowers industry innovators to meet current technological demands and pioneer advancements that push the boundaries of UAS health management capabilities. Technology providers equipped with the study's insights have the power to shape the future of UAS health management by creating innovative and advanced technologies. This section asserts that the study's findings empower technology providers to lead the charge in developing state-of-the-art IVHM technologies for UAS, which goes beyond the theoretical realm and contributes to operational excellence in UAS. The argument proves that the study helps with theory and practice, improving unmanned aerial systems' operational capabilities via real-world technology. These developments have far-reaching consequences beyond the lab, influencing how UAS health management will evolve to be more agile, responsive, and technologically advanced.

OPERATIONAL CHALLENGES

This section focuses on how the study has affected UAS-related challenges. The study's prospective incorporation into educational programmes is shown by its focus on a methodical technique and data analysis. In addition, one must recognise that to shape the educational environment in UAS health management, it is essential to provide future professionals with skills that align with what the business wants (Li, 2022). A systematic method with applications in research and education, the IVHM-RD technique, is presented in the study. This evidence supports the claim that the study systematically plans how to teach IVHM at UAS while integrating it with preexisting curricula. The course devotes much time to teaching students how to analyse data, which is crucial for UAS health management (Richardson et al., 2021). This section argues that educational programmes may benefit from including practical data analysis tasks in their curricula, given that the study's results highlight practical abilities and provide a systematic approach. In general, courses may benefit from the study, which recognises the significance of practical skills. This research provides valuable information for educational courses looking to train future professionals in IVHM in UAS by including these factors. The basic technique of the study provides the groundwork for learning IVHM. Despite the difficulty of health management in UAS, this structured method should help students grasp the subject well. The study's focus on data analysis aligns with the pragmatic aspects of UAS health management. Students may acquire skills directly relevant to the UAS business by participating in educational programmes that provide data analysis activities. The argument stresses the significance of training the workforce of the future with competencies that are in demand by various sectors. By incorporating the study's results into their curricula, educational programmes may better educate students to meet the growing demands of the unmanned aerial system (UAS) business and its health management concerns. This part explains how the study has affected UAS-related training and education initiatives. Offering a systematic approach and emphasising abilities that directly align with industry objectives, the given data and reasoning highlight the practical application of the study's conclusions. These results may impact the training of future UAS professionals by highlighting the need to understand IVHM in UAS and providing them with the hands-on experience they need to solve real-world challenges (Thibault, 2020). In this part, the argument is made that schools and programmes may use the research's results to improve their courses of study so that students can be prepared for the changing UAS sector with theoretical knowledge and practical abilities. A workforce prepared to tackle the ever-changing difficulties of UAS health management is greatly enhanced by including the subject in educational programmes (Goulart et al., 2022). Institutions of higher learning may include this information in their course offerings to guarantee that students leave with a solid grounding in IVHM theory and practice. Data analysis and the systematic IVHM-RD approach are two areas where the research highlights the significance of practical skills in UAS health management. By incorporating these hands-on components into their curricula, educational programmes may better equip students to meet the expectations of the unmanned aerial system (UAS) sector. The argument is that the study's incorporation into the curriculum enables students to put theoretical principles into practice. Graduates can connect the dots between academic requirements and those of businesses because they have a firm grasp of theoretical frameworks and the practical skills to put them into practice. Educational institutions can help prepare students for unmanned aerial systems (UAS) careers by using the study's findings in their curricula (Lercel & Hupy, 2020). Graduates will have the theoretical background and hands-on experience to be valuable assets to the industry, and they will be able to make a difference in UAS health management practices immediately. Recognising the ever-changing nature of the UAS industry, the research results align with its changing demands. By incorporating these findings into educational programmes, students are guaranteed to be prepared to adapt to new circumstances and make valuable contributions to the ongoing improvement of UAS health management activities. This section highlights how the study results profoundly affect UAS-related training programmes and educational institutions. The claim here is that students will be better equipped to handle the ever-changing demands of the UAS sector if this research is woven into the school curriculum. Training programmes help produce professionals with the theoretical background and hands-on experience necessary to handle the complex issues that arise in the actual world of unmanned aerial system (UAS) health management.

IVHM-RD Research and Continuous UAS-Related Improvement

Here the author look at how the research has helped spread a mindset of constant refinement and cyclical study in unmanned aerial systems (UAS) (Mesas et al., 2019). The study's findings highlight the importance of the structured Integrated Vehicle Health Management (IVHM)-RD approach in fostering an improvement cycle. To remain ahead of the curve, conducting continuous assessments and modifications is crucial since the UAS market is always evolving. The IVHM-RD technique introduces the study as a systematic way to identify the needs for UAS health management (Bolick et al., 2022). This data lends credence to the claim that the research encourages constant development by outlining a process that can be tested and improved upon in light of user input. Since both technology and operational requirements in the UAS business are subject to change, the research considers this. The research argues that the outcomes have a transformative impact on instilling a mindset of continuous improvement and iterative research within the UAS community (McGee & Campbell, 2019). IVHM practices should be evaluated and adjusted continuously to ensure their relevance and effectiveness. The data strongly suggests that the IVHM-RD approach offers a solid framework for iterative applications. This, in turn, promotes an environment where feedback and real-life experiences are valued and used to improve UAS health management practices continuously. The IVHM-RD approach provides an iterative application and refining vehicle (Menkhoff et al., 2022). Organisations may use this technique to keep up with the changing demands of the industry by providing a systematic approach to UAS health management practices that can be evaluated and improved based on real-world input. The argument stresses that the study recognises the ever-changing UAS market. This acknowledgement highlights the significance of ongoing development to adjust to technological progress, enabling UAS health management practices to maintain a leading edge in innovation. Given the ever-changing nature of the UAS sector, the study emphasises the requirement of continuous assessments and modifications. Organisations and researchers may use this advice to remain relevant by consistently evaluating and adjusting their methods for UAS health management in line with developments in the industry. Here, the author highlight how the research has revolutionised the UAS sector by encouraging a mindset of constant refinement and incremental study. In order to provide a formal basis for continual improvements in UAS health management practices, the offered evidence and reasoning highlight the significance of the IVHM-RD approach. Organisations can stay ahead of the curve in UAS health management by adopting a growth mindset and recognising that the industry is always changing (Antonenko, 2022). The research findings should motivate those working in the Unmanned Aerial Systems (UAS) field to improve their processes constantly. This part aims to provide the study as a foundation for practitioners to build upon, adjusting IVHM practices according to real-world experiences and the changing needs of the UAS industry. With each iteration, our understanding of IVHM in UAS is informed and refined, and the applied research knowledge continues to grow. This is because these practice advancements are iterative. This study's findings could benefit health management practices using unmanned aerial systems (UAS). As a foundation, the structured IVHM-RD methodology gives practitioners a systematic approach that may be modified and tailored to the demands and difficulties of their operating settings. The argument stresses that practitioners who want to enhance their IVHM practices continuously may use the study as a reference. The IVHM-RD technique provides practitioners with a framework for organised evaluations, modifications, and improvements that may be applied continuously. Practitioners can modify IVHM practices by incorporating feedback and real-life experiences. Applying the IVHM-RD technique iteratively helps practitioners learn from real-world implementations, pinpointing where they can improve and how to tackle the specific issues of UAS operations better. The study takes into account the ever-changing demands of the UAS market (Bhuyan et al., 2020). In order to keep up with the industry's ever-changing demands and make the most of new technologies and operational changes, practitioners may use the study as a roadmap to adjust their IVHM practices. According to the idea, the knowledge base of applied research continues to grow because of the iterative nature of practice improvements. The more iterations of applying the IVHM-RD approach there are, the more we learn about IVHM in UAS, and the more our knowledge reflects the complexities and reality of health management in UAS (Janke et al., 2022). The findings encourage a mindset of constant improvement and new ideas among professionals in the field. By learning more about IVHM with each iteration of the improvement process, practitioners may encourage a spirit of creativity and add to the body of knowledge in UAS health management applied research (Félix et al., 2022). Presented below are some of the most important takeaways for those working in unmanned aerial systems (UAS). The argument emphasises how the study may serve as a foundation for ongoing progress by letting practitioners adjust IVHM practices according to industry needs and real-life experiences. By continuously improving UAS health management, these enhancements not only make the system more successful but also add to the growing body of knowledge from practical research, making the field of unmanned aerial system IVHM more dynamic and informed. In the long run, the long-term efficacy of the IVHM-RD approach in various UAS operating circumstances should be the subject of future studies examining its real-world deployment.

SOLUTIONS AND RECOMMENDATIONS

Encourage a safety-conscious and innovative culture by incorporating the study's findings into industry norms. IVHM (Integrated Vehicle Health Management) is a crucial aspect of UAS health management, requiring continuous improvement and iterative research. To achieve this, a collaborative platform should be established for practitioners to share best practices and lessons learned from IVHM-RD methodology. This can be achieved through industry conferences, workshops, and online forums, fostering a culture of knowledge-sharing among stakeholders.Educational and training programs should be developed in collaboration with industry experts to integrate IVHM-RD methodology into UAS-related programs. Partnerships between educational institutions and industry leaders should be formed to ensure curricula stay aligned with the latest advancements and industry needs. Internship programs and practical training opportunities should be established to expose students to real-world applications of IVHM in UAS. Regulatory frameworks should be engaged in a collaborative effort to develop guidelines and standards based on IVHM-RD methodology. Regular workshops and webinars should be conducted to educate regulatory authorities on the benefits and practical implications of integrating IVHM into UAS operations.Technology and innovation advancements should be fostered through research and development grants, industry-academic partnerships, and open-source initiatives. By implementing these solutions, the UAS industry can foster a collaborative, innovative, and well-informed ecosystem that maximizes the benefits of IVHM.

FUTURE RESEARCH DIRECTIONS

The efficiency of the IVHM-RD technique in various UAS operating settings should be evaluated in future research that focuses on real-world application. IVHM is a crucial technology for unmanned aerial systems (UAS), enhancing the performance, safety, and sustainability of these systems. Future research should focus on integrating human factors, cybersecurity, AI and machine learning, interoperability standards, environmental impact assessment, dynamic risk assessment, human-machine teaming, adaptive maintenance strategies, edge computing for real-time analysis, and human-centric training programs. These suggestions aim to expand the scope of IVHM in UAS, address emerging challenges, and explore new frontiers to optimize the performance, safety, and sustainability of unmanned aerial systems. IVHM systems can be enhanced by incorporating user-centric design principles, enhancing cybersecurity, and utilizing advanced AI and machine learning techniques. Interoperability standards should be developed to ensure seamless integration across different UAS platforms and manufacturers, fostering a more cohesive and interconnected UAS health management ecosystem. Additionally, the integration of human-machine teaming concepts within IVHM frameworks can optimize decision-making processes and ensure effective human oversight in critical situations.

CONCLUSION

In conclusion, this chapter underscores the multidimensional impact of Integrated Vehicle Health Management (IVHM) on unmanned aerial systems (UAS), reinforcing its significance in shaping future research, regulatory frameworks, and operational practices. As we look ahead, several areas emerge as focal points for future investigation and technological advancement. Firstly, the efficiency of the IVHM-RD technique in various UAS operating settings should be rigorously evaluated in future research, focusing on real-world application scenarios to validate its effectiveness and scalability. This empirical approach will provide valuable insights into the practical implementation and performance optimization of IVHM systems in diverse operational environments. Moreover, future research endeavors should prioritize the integration of key technological innovations such as human factors, cybersecurity, AI and machine learning, interoperability standards, environmental impact assessment, dynamic risk assessment, human-machine teaming, adaptive maintenance strategies, edge computing for real-time analysis, and human-centric training programs. By embracing these interdisciplinary perspectives, we can expand the scope of IVHM in UAS, address emerging challenges, and explore new frontiers to optimize the performance, safety, and sustainability of unmanned aerial systems. Furthermore, IVHM systems can be enhanced by incorporating user-centric design principles, enhancing cybersecurity measures, and leveraging advanced AI and machine learning techniques to improve predictive analytics and decision-making capabilities. Developing interoperability standards will also be crucial to ensure seamless integration across different UAS platforms and manufacturers, fostering a more cohesive and interconnected UAS health management ecosystem. Lastly, the integration of human-machine teaming concepts within IVHM frameworks holds immense potential to optimize decision-making processes and ensure effective human oversight in critical situations. By harnessing the complementary strengths of humans and machines, we can enhance operational efficiency, situational awareness, and mission effectiveness in UAS operations. This conclusion reiterates the relevance and impact of IVHM in addressing real-world challenges faced by unmanned aerial systems, echoing the narrative introduced in the introduction. It emphasizes the need for continued research, technological innovation, and collaboration to realize the full potential of IVHM and unlock new opportunities for UAS advancement.

REFERENCES

Antonenko, I. M. P. (2022). Unmanned aerial vehicles as educational technology systems in construction engineering education. *Journal of information technology in construction*, 27. 10.36680/j.itcon.2022.014

Barrado, C., Boyero, M., Brucculeri, L., Ferrara, G., Hately, A., Hullah, P., Martin-Marrero, D., Pastor, E., Rushton, A. P., & Volkert, A. (2020). U-space concept of operations: A key enabler for opening airspace to emerging low-altitude operations. *Aerospace (Basel, Switzerland)*, 7(3), 24. 10.3390/aerospace7030024

Berkcan, O., & Aksoy, T. (2022). Assessing the effect of proactive maintenance scheduling on maintenance costs and airline profitability: The case of Turkish Airlines Technic. *International Journal of Research in Business and Social Science*. 10.20525/ijrbs.v11i4.1780

Bhatti, G., Mohan, H., & Singh, R. R. (2021). Towards the future of smart electric vehicles: Digital twin technology. *Renewable & Sustainable Energy Reviews*, 141, 110801. 10.1016/j.rser.2021.110801

Bhuyan, J., Wu, F., Thomas, C., Koong, K., Hur, J. W., & Wang, C. H. (2020). Aerial drone: An effective tool to teach information technology and cybersecurity through project based learning to minority high school students in the US. *TechTrends*, 64(6), 899–910. 10.1007/s11528-020-00502-734396368

Bisanti, G. M., Mainetti, L., Montanaro, T., Patrono, L., & Sergi, I. (2023). Digital twins for aircraft maintenance and operation: A systematic literature review and an IoT-enabled modular architecture. *Internet of Things : Engineering Cyber Physical Human Systems*, 100991, 100991. 10.1016/j.iot.2023.100991

Bolick, M. M., Mikhailova, E. A., & Post, C. J. (2022). Teaching innovation in STEM education using an unmanned aerial vehicle (UAV). *Education Sciences*, 12(3), 224. 10.3390/educsci12030224

Brat, G. P., Yu, H., Atkins, E., Sharma, P., Cofer, D., Durling, M., & Bakirtzis, G. (2023). *Autonomy Verification & Validation Roadmap and Vision2045* (No. NASA/TM-20230003734).

Campean, F., Neagu, D., Doikin, A., Soleimani, M., Byrne, T., & Sherratt, A. (2019, July). Automotive IVHM: towards intelligent personalised systems healthcare. In *Proceedings of the design society: international conference on engineering design* (*Vol. 1*, No. 1, pp. 857-866). Cambridge University Press. https://doi.org/10.1017/dsi.2019.90

Ciliberti, D., Della Vecchia, P., Memmolo, V., Nicolosi, F., Wortmann, G., & Ricci, F. (2022). The Enabling Technologies for a Quasi-Zero Emissions Commuter Aircraft. *Aerospace (Basel, Switzerland)*, 2022(9), 319. 10.3390/aerospace9060319

Dasgupta, S. (2019). Emerging frontiers for Development of Military UAVs: An Indian Perspective. *Journal of Aerospace Sciences and Technologies*, 126–134.

Enrico, Z., Mengfei, F., Zhiguo, Z., & Rui, K. (2019). Application of reliability technologies in civil aviation: Lessons learnt and perspectives. *Chinese Journal of Aeronautics*, 32(1), 143–158. 10.1016/j.cja.2018.05.014

Ezhilarasu, C. M., Skaf, Z., & Jennions, I. K. (2019). The application of reasoning to aerospace Integrated Vehicle Health Management (IVHM): Challenges and opportunities. *Progress in Aerospace Sciences*, 105, 60–73. 10.1016/j.paerosci.2019.01.001

Ezhilarasu, C. M., Skaf, Z., & Jennions, I. K. (2019, October). Understanding the role of a digital twin in integrated vehicle health management (IVHM). In *2019 IEEE International Conference on Systems, Man and Cybernetics* (SMC) (pp. 1484-1491). IEEE. https://doi.org/10.1109/SMC.2019.8914244

Fan, B., Li, Y., Zhang, R., & Fu, Q. (2020). Review on the technological development and application of UAV systems. *Chinese Journal of Electronics*, 29(2), 199–207. 10.1049/cje.2019.12.006

Félix-Herrán, L. C., Izaguirre-Espinosa, C., Parra-Vega, V., Sánchez-Orta, A., Benitez, V. H., & Lozoya-Santos, J. D. J. (2022). A Challenge-Based Learning Intensive Course for Competency Development in Undergraduate Engineering Students: Case Study on UAVs. *Electronics (Basel)*, 11(9), 1349. 10.3390/electronics11091349

Fu, S., & Avdelidis, N. P. (2023). Prognostic and Health Management of Critical Aircraft Systems and Components: An Overview. *Sensors (Basel)*, 23(19), 8124. 10.3390/s2319812437836954

Gheisari, M., & Esmaeili, B. (2019). Applications and requirements of unmanned aerial systems (UASs) for construction safety. *Safety Science*, 118, 230–240. 10.1016/j.ssci.2019.05.015

Goulart, V. G., Liboni, L. B., & Cezarino, L. O. (2022). Balancing skills in the digital transformation era: The future of jobs and the role of higher education. *Industry and Higher Education*, 36(2), 118–127. 10.1177/09504222211029796

Grübel, J., Thrash, T., Aguilar, L., Gath-Morad, M., Chatain, J., Sumner, R. W., Hölscher, C., & Schinazi, V. R. (2022). The hitchhiker's guide to fused twins: A review of access to digital twins in situ in smart cities. *Remote Sensing (Basel)*, 14(13), 3095. 10.3390/rs14133095

Holland, S. (2020). *Unsettled Technology Opportunities for Vehicle Health Management and the Role for Health-Ready Components* (No. EPR2020003). SAE Technical Paper. 10.4271/epr2020003

Janke, C., Luthi, K., Kleinke, S., & Lin, Y. (2022). Using Small UAS for STEM Education: Introducing Robotics and Mechatronics with Drones. In *Florida Conference for Recent Advances in Robotics 2022* (p. 1). Embry-Riddle Aeronautical University. https://doi.org/10.5038/QQGN3785

Koschlik, A. K., Meyer, H., Arts, E., Conen, P., Jacob, G., Soria-Gomez, M., & Wende, G. (2023, June). Towards an Integrated Vehicle Health Management for Maintenance of Unmanned Air Systems. In *2023 International Conference on Unmanned Aircraft Systems* (ICUAS) (pp. 463-470). IEEE. 10.1109/ICUAS57906.2023.10155995

Lercel, D. J., & Hupy, J. P. (2020). Developing a competency learning model for students of unmanned aerial systems. *The Collegiate Aviation Review International*, 38(2). 10.22488/okstate.20.100212

Li, L. (2022). Reskilling and upskilling the future-ready workforce for industry 4.0 and beyond. *Information Systems Frontiers*, 1–16. 10.1007/s10796-022-10308-y35855776

Li, R., Verhagen, W. J., & Curran, R. (2020). Toward a methodology of requirements definition for prognostics and health management system to support aircraft predictive maintenance. *Aerospace Science and Technology*, 102, 105877. 10.1016/j.ast.2020.105877

Maindze, A., Skaf, Z., & Jennions, I. (2019, September). Towards an Enhanced Data-and Knowledge Management Capability: A Data Life Cycle Model Proposition for Integrated Vehicle Health Management. In *Annual Conference of the PHMS*, Scottsdale, AZ, USA. 10.36001/phmconf.2019.v11i1.842

Mbiyana, K., Kans, M., & Campos, J. (2021, December). A data-driven approach for gravel road maintenance. In *2021 International Conference on Maintenance and Intelligent Asset Management* (ICMIAM) (pp. 1-6). IEEE. 10.1109/ICMIAM54662.2021.9715196

McGee, J. A., & Campbell, J. B. (2019). The sUAS Educational Frontier: Mapping an Educational Pathway for the Future Workforce. In *Applications of Small Unmanned Aircraft Systems* (pp. 57–79). CRC Press. 10.1201/9780429244117-4

Menkhoff, T., Kan, S. N., Tan, E. K., & Foong, S. (2022). Future-proofing students in higher education with unmanned aerial vehicles technology: A knowledge management case study. *Knowledge Management & E-Learning: An International Journal*, 14(2), 223–244. 10.34105/j.kmel.2022.14.013

Mesas-Carrascosa, F. J., Pérez Porras, F., Triviño-Tarradas, P., Meroño de Larriva, J. E., & García-Ferrer, A. (2019). Project-based learning applied to unmanned aerial systems and remote sensing. *Remote Sensing (Basel)*, 11(20), 2413. 10.3390/rs11202413

Mihai, S., Yaqoob, M., Hung, D. V., Davis, W., Towakel, P., Raza, M., Karamanoglu, M., Barn, B., Shetve, D., Prasad, R. V., Venkataraman, H., Trestian, R., & Nguyen, H. X. (2022). Digital twins: A survey on enabling technologies, challenges, trends and future prospects. *IEEE Communications Surveys and Tutorials*, 24(4), 2255–2291. 10.1109/COMST.2022.3208773

Montazeri, A., Can, A., & Imran, I. H. (2021). Unmanned aerial systems: autonomy, cognition, and control. In *Unmanned aerial systems* (pp. 47–80). Academic Press. 10.1016/B978-0-12-820276-0.00010-8

Ochella, S., Shafiee, M., & Dinmohammadi, F. (2022). Artificial intelligence in prognostics and health management of engineering systems. *Engineering Applications of Artificial Intelligence*, 108, 104552. 10.1016/j.engappai.2021.104552

Ochella, S., Shafiee, M., & Sansom, C. (2021, September). Requirements for Standards and Regulations in AI-Enabled Prognostics and Health Management. In *2021 26th International Conference on Automation and Computing* (ICAC) (pp. 1-6). IEEE. https://doi.org/10.23919/ICAC50006.2021.9594069

Rajamani, R. (2020). *Unsettled Issues Concerning Integrated Vehicle Health Management Systems and Maintenance Credits* (No. EPR2020006). SAE Technical Paper. https://doi.org/10.4271/epr2020006

Ranasinghe, K., Sabatini, R., Gardi, A., Bijjahalli, S., Kapoor, R., Fahey, T., & Thangavel, K. (2022). Advances in Integrated System Health Management for mission-essential and safety-critical aerospace applications. *Progress in Aerospace Sciences*, 128, 100758. 10.1016/j.paerosci.2021.100758

Richardson, D., Kinnear, B., Hauer, K. E., Turner, T. L., Warm, E. J., Hall, A. K., Ross, S., Thoma, B., & Van Melle, E.ICBME Collaborators. (2021). Growth mindset in competency-based medical education. *Medical Teacher*, 43(7), 751–757. 10.1080/0142159X.2021.192803634410891

Sabatini, R., Roy, A., Blasch, E., Kramer, K. A., Fasano, G., Majid, I., & Major, R. O. (2020). Avionics systems panel research and innovation perspectives. *IEEE Aerospace and Electronic Systems Magazine*, 35(12), 58–72. 10.1109/MAES.2020.3033475

Scott, M. J., Verhagen, W. J., Bieber, M. T., & Marzocca, P. (2022). A Systematic Literature Review of Predictive Maintenance for Defence Fixed-Wing Aircraft Sustainment and Operations. *Sensors (Basel)*, 22(18), 7070. 10.3390/s2218707036146419

Shukla, B., Fan, I. S., & Jennions, I. (2020, July). Opportunities for explainable artificial intelligence in aerospace predictive maintenance. In *PHM Society European Conference* (Vol. 5, No. 1, pp. 11-11). IEEE. 10.36001/phme.2020.v5i1.1231

Subramanian, C. (2021, February). An appraisal on intelligent and smart systems. In *AIP Conference Proceedings (Vol. 2316*, No. 1). AIP Publishing. 10.1063/5.0037534

Tang, X., Yung, K. L., & Hu, B. (2022). Reliability and health management of spacecraft. In *IoT and Spacecraft Informatics* (pp. 307–335). Elsevier. 10.1016/B978-0-12-821051-2.00012-X

Thibault, G. E. (2020). The future of health professions education: Emerging trends in the United States. *FASEB bioAdvances*, 2(12), 685–694. 10.1096/fba.2020-0006133336156

Vachtsevanos, G., & Rajamani, R. (2023). Criticality of Prognostics in the Operations of Autonomous Aircraft. *SAE International Journal of Aerospace*, *16*. 10.4271/01-16-03-0022

Verhagen, W. J., Santos, B. F., Freeman, F., van Kessel, P., Zarouchas, D., Loutas, T., Yeun, R. C. K., & Heiets, I. (2023). Condition-Based Maintenance in Aviation: Challenges and Opportunities. *Aerospace (Basel, Switzerland)*, 10(9), 762. 10.3390/aerospace10090762

Vogl, G. W., Weiss, B. A., & Helu, M. (2019). A review of diagnostic and prognostic capabilities and best practices for manufacturing. *Journal of Intelligent Manufacturing*, 30(1), 79–95. 10.1007/s10845-016-1228-830820072

Walthall, R. (2020). *Unsettled Topics on the Use of IVHM in the Active Control Loop* (No. EPR2020011). SAE Technical Paper. 10.4271/epr2020011

Wang, J., Liu, Y., & Song, H. (2021). Counter-unmanned aircraft system (s)(C-UAS): State of the art, challenges, and future trends. *IEEE Aerospace and Electronic Systems Magazine*, 36(3), 4–29. 10.1109/MAES.2020.3015537

Xu, C., Liao, X., Tan, J., Ye, H., & Lu, H. (2020). Recent research progress of unmanned aerial vehicle regulation policies and technologies in urban low altitude. *IEEE Access : Practical Innovations, Open Solutions*, 8, 74175–74194. 10.1109/ACCESS.2020.2987622

Zhang, J., & Li, J. (2023). *High-Reliability Autonomous Management Systems for Spacecraft*. Elsevier.

ADDITIONAL READINGS

Azizan, A., Zahra, S., & Sophia, S. (2024). Navigating the Maritime: Technology for the Defense of the Indonesian National Capital City (IKN) in the Makassar Strait. *Jurnal Pertahanan: Media Informasi tentang Kajian dan Strategi Pertahanan yang Mengedepankan Identity, Nasionalism dan Integrity*, *10*(1), 155-168.

Komalasari, R. (2022). A Social Ecological Model (SEM) to Manage Methadone Programmes in Prisons. In *Handbook of Research on Mathematical Modeling for Smart Healthcare Systems* (pp. 374-382). IGI Global. 10.4018/978-1-6684-4580-8.ch020

Komalasari, R. (2023). The Relationship Between Cybersecurity and Public Health. In *Handbook of Research on Current Trends in Cybersecurity and Educational Technology* (pp. 78–91). IGI Global. 10.4018/978-1-6684-6092-4.ch005

Komalasari, R. (2023). Postnatal Mental Distress: Exploring the Experiences of Mothers Navigating the Healthcare System. In *Perspectives and Considerations on Navigating the Mental Healthcare System* (pp. 159-181). IGI Global. 10.4018/978-1-6684-5049-9.ch007

Komalasari, R. (2023). Designing Health Systems for Better, Faster, and Less Expensive Treatment. In *Exploring the Convergence of Computer and Medical Science Through Cloud Healthcare* (pp. 1–13). IGI Global. 10.4018/978-1-6684-5260-8.ch001

Komalasari, R. (2023). The Ethical Consideration of Using Artificial Intelligence (AI) in Medicine. In *Advanced Bioinspiration Methods for Healthcare Standards, Policies, and Reform* (pp. 1-16). IGI Global. 10.4018/978-1-6684-5656-9.ch001

Komalasari, R. (2023). Healthcare for the Elderly With Digital Twins. In *Digital Twins and Healthcare: Trends, Techniques, and Challenges* (pp. 145-156). IGI Global. 10.4018/978-1-6684-5925-6.ch010

Komalasari, R. (2023). Cloud Computing's Usage in Healthcare. In *Recent Advancements in Smart Remote Patient Monitoring, Wearable Devices, and Diagnostics Systems* (pp. 183-194). IGI Global. 10.4018/978-1-6684-6434-2.ch009

Komalasari, R. (2023). History and Legislative Changes Governing Medical Cannabis in Indonesia. In *Medical Cannabis and the Effects of Cannabinoids on Fighting Cancer, Multiple Sclerosis, Epilepsy, Parkinson's, and Other Neurodegenerative Diseases* (pp. 274-284). IGI Global. 10.4018/978-1-6684-5652-1.ch012

Komalasari, R. (2023). Ambient Assisted Living (AAL) Systems to Help Older People. In *Exploring Future Opportunities of Brain-Inspired Artificial Intelligence* (pp. 84-99). IGI Global. 10.4018/978-1-6684-6980-4.ch006

Komalasari, R. (2023). Telemedicine in Pandemic Times in Indonesia: Healthcare Professional's Perspective. In *Health Informatics and Patient Safety in Times of Crisis* (pp. 138-153). IGI Global. 10.4018/978-1-6684-5499-2.ch008

Komalasari, R. (2023). Cloud Computing's Usage in Healthcare. In *Recent Advancements in Smart Remote Patient Monitoring, Wearable Devices, and Diagnostics Systems* (pp. 183-194). IGI Global. 10.4018/978-1-6684-6434-2.ch009

Komalasari, R. (2023). The Relationship Between Cybersecurity and Public Health. In *Handbook of Research on Current Trends in Cybersecurity and Educational Technology* (pp. 78–91). IGI Global. 10.4018/978-1-6684-6092-4.ch005

Komalasari, R. (2023). Treatment of Menstrual Discomfort in Young Women and a Cognitive Behavior Therapy (CBT) Program. In *Perspectives on Coping Strategies for Menstrual and Premenstrual Distress* (pp. 194-211). IGI Global. 10.4018/978-1-6684-5088-8.ch011

Komalasari, R. (2023). Healthcare for the Elderly With Digital Twins. In *Digital Twins and Healthcare: Trends, Techniques, and Challenges* (pp. 145-156). IGI Global. 10.4018/978-1-6684-5925-6.ch010

Komalasari, R. (2023). Telemedicine in Pandemic Times in Indonesia: Healthcare Professional's Perspective. In *Health Informatics and Patient Safety in Times of Crisis* (pp. 138-153). IGI Global. 10.4018/978-1-6684-5499-2.ch008

Komalasari, R. (2023). Regulatory Shift Healthcare Applications in Industry 5.0. In *Advanced Research and Real-World Applications of Industry 5.0* (pp. 149-165). IGI Global. 10.4018/978-1-7998-8805-5.ch008

Komalasari, R. (2023). Exploring Pedagogies Of Affect In Secondary School Physical Education For Enhanced Emotional Well-Being. *Pedagogik: Jurnal Pendidikan Guru Sekolah Dasar*, 11(2), 117–127. 10.33558/pedagogik.v11i2.7374

Komalasari, R. (2023). Integrating Sport education model and the athletics challenges approach for transformative physical education in Indonesian Middle Schools. *Motion: Jurnal Riset Physical Education*, 13(2), 118–135. 10.33558/motion.v13i2.7372

Komalasari, R. (2023). Rancangan Program Bagi Keberhasilan Gerakan Mencuci Tangan Yang Sehat Bagi Para Ibu Dan Anak. *Sulolipu: Media Komunikasi Sivitas Akademika dan Masyarakat, 23*(1), 55-60. 10.32382/sulolipu.v23i1.3103

Komalasari, R. (2023). Culture as A Catalyst: Unveiling the Nexus Between Health Services Performance Management and National Identity. *Journal of Business and Political Economy: Biannual Review of The Indonesian Economy,* 5(1).

Komalasari, R. (2023). Exploring Pedagogies Of Affect In Secondary School Physical Education For Enhanced Emotional Well-Being. *Pedagogik: Jurnal Pendidikan Guru Sekolah Dasar,* 11(2), 117–127. 10.33558/pedagogik.v11i2.7374

Komalasari, R. (2023). Integrating sport education model and the athletics challenges approach for transformative physical education in Indonesian Middle Schools. *Motion: Jurnal Riset Physical Education,* 13(2), 118–135. 10.33558/motion.v13i2.7372

Komalasari, R. (2023). Efek Ganja Medis pada Pasien Parkinson: A Literature Review of Clinical Evidence. *Journal of Islamic Pharmacy,* 8(1), 44–48. 10.18860/jip.v8i1.17832

Komalasari, R. (2023). Rancangan Program Bagi Keberhasilan Gerakan Mencuci Tangan Yang Sehat Bagi Para Ibu Dan Anak. *Sulolipu: Media Komunikasi Sivitas Akademika dan Masyarakat, 23*(1), 55-60. 10.32382/sulolipu.v23i1.3103

Komalasari, R. (2023). Culture As A Catalyst: Unveiling The Nexus Between Health Services Performance Management and National Identity. *Journal of Business and Political Economy,* 5(1), 25–47. 10.46851/138

Komalasari, R. (2024). Decoding the Genomic and Proteomic Landscape: Dissemination and Mechanisms of Antibiotic Resistance in Environmental Staphylococci. In Grewal, A., Dhingra, A., Nepali, K., Deswal, G., & Srivastav, A. (Eds.), *Frontiers in Combating Antibacterial Resistance: Current Perspectives and Future Horizons* (pp. 163–195). IGI Global. 10.4018/979-8-3693-4139-1.ch008

Komalasari, R. (2024). Unravelling the Veil: Exploring the Nexus of Insecure Attachment and Functional Somatic Disorders in Adults. In Burrell, D. (Ed.), *Change Dynamics in Healthcare, Technological Innovations, and Complex Scenarios* (pp. 1–27). IGI Global. 10.4018/979-8-3693-3555-0.ch001

Komalasari, R. (2024). Advancing Healthcare: Economic Implications of Immediate MRI in Suspected Scaphoid Fractures - A Comprehensive Exploration. In Sharma, A., Chanderwal, N., Tyagi, S., & Upadhyay, P. (Eds.), *Future of AI in Medical Imaging* (pp. 224–246). IGI Global. 10.4018/979-8-3693-2359-5.ch014

Komalasari, R. (2024). Women's perceptions of midlife mothering during perimenopause: the impact on health and well-being through life's transitions. In *Utilizing AI Techniques for the Perimenopause to Menopause Transition*. IGI Global.

Komalasari, R. (2024). Machine Learning in Health Information Security: Unraveling Patterns, Concealing Secrets, and Mitigating Vulnerabilities. In *Enhancing Steganography Through Deep Learning Approaches*. IGI Global.

Komalasari, R. (2024). Exploring the Potential of Augmented Reality in Schools for the Health and Safety of Teenagers. In *Modern Technology in Healthcare and Medical Education: Blockchain, IoT, AR, and VR* (pp. 159-185). IGI Global. 10.4018/979-8-3693-5493-3.ch010

Komalasari, R. (2024). Optimizing Prostate Cancer Radiotherapy: Advanced Machine Learning in Virtual Patient-Specific Plan Verification. *Indonesian Journal of Cancer*.

Komalasari, R. (2024). Navigating Complexity: Unraveling the IVHM Requirements Puzzle in Unmanned Aerial Systems Through Innovative IVHM-RD Methodology and Rigorous Data Analysis. In *Ubiquitous Computing and Technological Innovation for Universal Healthcare*. IGI Global.

Komalasari, R. (2024). Trust Dynamics in Remote Patient-Expert Communication: Unraveling the Role of ICT in Indonesia's Private Healthcare Sector. In Geada, N. (Ed.), *Improving Security, Privacy, and Connectivity Among Telemedicine Platforms* (pp. 198–219). IGI Global. 10.4018/979-8-3693-2141-6.ch010

Komalasari, R. (2024). Cyberbullying in the Healthcare Workplace: How to Find Your Way Through the Digital Maze. In Aslam, M., Kim, Y., & Linchao, Q. (Eds.), *Workplace Cyberbullying and Behavior in Health Professions* (pp. 84–112). IGI Global. 10.4018/979-8-3693-1139-4.ch004

Komalasari, R. (2024). Harmonizing Minds and Machines: A Transformative AI-Based Mental Health Care Framework in Medical Tourism. In *Impact of AI and Robotics on the Medical Tourism Industry*. IGI Global. 10.4018/979-8-3693-2248-2.ch002

Komalasari, R. (2024). Navigating the Future of Healthcare: A User-Centric Approach to Designing Lucrative Business Models for the IoMT. In *Lightweight Digital Trust Architectures in the Internet of Medical Things (IoMT)*. IGI Global. 10.4018/979-8-3693-2109-6.ch020

Komalasari, R. (2024). Biospheric Reverie: Unraveling Indoor Air Quality Through Bio-Inspired Textiles, Awareness, and Decision-Making. In Jaganathan, R., Mehta, S., & Krishan, R. (Eds.), *Intelligent Decision Making Through Bio-Inspired Optimization* (pp. 227–244). IGI Global. 10.4018/979-8-3693-2073-0.ch013

Komalasari, R. (2024). Transformative Insights: Harnessing Artificial Intelligence for Enhanced Ovarian Cancer Prediction and Prognosis. In *Biomedical Research Developments for Improved Healthcare* (pp. 184-207). IGI Global.

Komalasari, R. (2024). Bridging the Gap: Theory of Change-Guided Digital Health Implementation in Indonesian Primary Care. In *Analyzing Current Digital Healthcare Trends Using Social Networks* (pp. 12-25). IGI Global.

Komalasari, R. (2024). Navigating the Digital Frontier: A Socio-Technical Review of Indonesia's NHS E-Health Strategy and the Path to Seamless Healthcare Transformation. In *Inclusivity and Accessibility in Digital Health* (pp. 174–194). IGI Global. 10.4018/979-8-3693-1463-0.ch012

Komalasari, R. (2024). Trust Dynamics in Remote Patient-Expert Communication: Unraveling the Role of ICT in Indonesia's Private Healthcare Sector. In *Improving Security, Privacy, and Connectivity Among Telemedicine Platforms* (pp. 198-219). IGI Global.

Komalasari, R. (2024). Harmonizing Midlife Motherhood: Navigating the Intersection of First-Time Maternity and Perimenopause. In *Utilizing AI Techniques for the Perimenopause to Menopause Transition*. IGI Global.

Komalasari, R. (2024). In Pursuit of Excellence: A Comprehensive Framework for Ensuring Quality in Digital Health Apps. In Chatterjee, L., & Gani, N. (Eds.), *Multi-Sector Analysis of the Digital Healthcare Industry* (pp. 133–163). IGI Global. 10.4018/979-8-3693-0928-5.ch005

Komalasari, R. (2024). Fostering Transparency in AI for Disease Detection: Exploring Meaningful Explanations and Interactive Modalities in Healthcare. In *Federated Learning and Privacy-Preserving in Healthcare AI*. IGI Global.

Komalasari, R. (2024). Predictive Pioneers: Bridging the Mental Health Gap in Older Adults through Advanced Digital Technologies. In *Using Machine Learning to Detect Emotions and Predict Human Psychology*. IGI Global. 10.4018/979-8-3693-1910-9.ch005

Komalasari, R. (2024). Unravelling the Veil: Exploring the Nexus of Insecure Attachment and Functional Somatic Disorders in Adults. In Burrell, D. (Ed.), *Change Dynamics in Healthcare, Technological Innovations, and Complex Scenarios* (pp. 1–27). IGI Global. 10.4018/979-8-3693-3555-0.ch001

Komalasari, R. (2024). Cyberbullying in the Health Care Workplace: How to Find Your Way Through the Digital Maze. In *Workplace Cyberbullying and Behavior in Health Professions*. IGI Global. 10.4018/979-8-3693-1139-4.ch004

Komalasari, R. (2024). Navigating Mental Health Crises: Understanding Pivotal Phases, Health Campaigns, and Community Resilience for Recovery and Reform. In *The Role of Health Literacy in Major Healthcare Crises*. IGI Global.

Komalasari, R. (2024). Decoding the Genomic and Proteomic Landscape: Dissemination and Mechanisms of Antibiotic Resistance in Environmental Staphylococci. In *Frontiers in Combating Antibacterial Resistance: Current Perspectives and Future Horizons* (pp. 163-195). IGI Global.

Komalasari, R. (2024). Unveiling the Future: Blockchain-Powered Digital Twins for Personalized Privacy Preservation in Metaverse Healthcare Data. In Burrell, D. (Ed.), *Innovations, Securities, and Case Studies Across Healthcare, Business, and Technology* (pp. 321–342). IGI Global. 10.4018/979-8-3693-1906-2.ch017

Komalasari, R. (2024). Predictive Pioneers: Bridging the Mental Health Gap in Older Adults through Advanced Digital Technologies. In *Using Machine Learning to Detect Emotions and Predict Human Psychology*. IGI Global. 10.4018/979-8-3693-1910-9.ch005

Komalasari, R. (2024). Unravelling the Veil: Exploring the Nexus of Insecure Attachment and Functional Somatic Disorders in Adults. In *Discourses, Inquiries, and Case Studies in Healthcare, Social Sciences, and Technology*. IGI Global. 10.4018/979-8-3693-3555-0.ch001

Komalasari, R. (2024). Cyberbullying in the Health Care Workplace: How to Find Your Way Through the Digital Maze. In *Workplace Cyberbullying and Behavior in Health Professions*. IGI Global. 10.4018/979-8-3693-1139-4.ch004

Komalasari, R. (2024). Navigating Mental Health Crises: Understanding Pivotal Phases, Health Campaigns, and Community Resilience for Recovery and Reform. In *The Role of Health Literacy in Major Healthcare Crises*. IGI Global. 10.4018/978-1-7998-9652-4.ch008

Komalasari, R. (2024). Safeguarding the Future: Cutting-Edge Time-Stamping Services and Blockchain Technologies for Maintaining EHR Data Integrity Over the Long Term. In *Blockchain and IoT Approaches for Secure Electronic Health Records (EHR)*. IGI Global. 10.4018/979-8-3693-1662-7.ch003

Komalasari, R. (2024). Empowering Informed Healthcare Choices in Rural Areas: SIKDA - A Novel Model for Enhancing Patient Access to Reliable Consumer Health Information in Indonesia. In *Emerging Technologies for Health Literacy and Medical Practice*. IGI Global.

Komalasari, R. (2024). Advancing Trauma Care: Contemporary Cranio-Maxillo-Facial Surgery in Indonesia and Beyond. In *Contemporary Cranio-Maxillo-Facial Surgery: From Trauma to Reconstruction*. IGI Global.

Komalasari, R. (2024). Innovations in Neurodegenerative Disease Diagnosis: Unraveling the Transformative Potential of Deep Learning and MRI Integration. In *Deep Learning Approaches for Early Diagnosis of Neurodegenerative Diseases*. IGI Global.

Komalasari, R. (2024). Secure and privacy-preserving federated learning with explainable artificial intelligence for smart healthcare systems. In *Federated Learning and AI for Healthcare 5.0*. IGI Global.

Komalasari, R. (2024) Optimizing Prostate Cancer Radiotherapy: Advanced Machine Learning in Virtual Patient-Specific Plan Verification. *Indonesian Journal of Cancer*.

Komalasari, R. (2024). Unveiling the Future: Blockchain-Powered Digital Twins for Personalized Privacy Preservation in Metaverse Healthcare Data. In Burrell, D. (Ed.), *Innovations, Securities, and Case Studies Across Healthcare, Business, and Technology* (pp. 321–342). IGI Global. 10.4018/979-8-3693-1906-2.ch017

Komalasari, R. (2024). Predictive Pioneers: Bridging the Mental Health Gap in Older Adults Through Advanced Digital Technologies. In Rai, M., & Pandey, J. (Eds.), *Using Machine Learning to Detect Emotions and Predict Human Psychology* (pp. 99–129). IGI Global. 10.4018/979-8-3693-1910-9.ch005

Komalasari, R. (2024). Unravelling the Veil: Exploring the Nexus of Insecure Attachment and Functional Somatic Disorders in Adults. In Burrell, D. (Ed.), *Change Dynamics in Healthcare, Technological Innovations, and Complex Scenarios* (pp. 1–27). IGI Global. 10.4018/979-8-3693-3555-0.ch001

Komalasari, R. (2024). Cyberbullying in the Healthcare Workplace: How to Find Your Way Through the Digital Maze. In Aslam, M., Kim, Y., & Linchao, Q. (Eds.), *Workplace Cyberbullying and Behavior in Health Professions* (pp. 84–112). IGI Global. 10.4018/979-8-3693-1139-4.ch004

Komalasari, R. (2024). Navigating Mental Health Crises: Understanding Pivotal Phases, Health Campaigns, and Community Resilience for Recovery and Reform. In Papalois, V., & Papalois, K. (Eds.), *The Role of Health Literacy in Major Healthcare Crises* (pp. 144–174). IGI Global. 10.4018/978-1-7998-9652-4.ch008

Komalasari, R. (2024). Bridging Uncertainties: Exploring the Lived Experiences of Pediatric Long-COVID-19 Through ME/CFS Caregiver Narratives. In Rao, G., & Dhamdhere-Rao, S. (Eds.), *Clinical Practice and Post-Infection Care for COVID-19 Patients* (pp. 207–227). IGI Global. 10.4018/978-1-6684-6855-5.ch009

Komalasari, R., & Khang, A. (2024). An Integrated Approach to Next-Generation Telemedicine and Health Advice Systems Through AI Applications in Disease Diagnosis. In Khang, A. (Ed.), *Driving Smart Medical Diagnosis Through AI-Powered Technologies and Applications* (pp. 258–274). IGI Global. 10.4018/979-8-3693-3679-3.ch016

Komalasari, R., & Khang, A. (2024). An Integrated Approach to Next-Generation Telemedicine and Health Advice Systems Through AI Applications in Disease Diagnosis. In Khang, A. (Ed.), *Driving Smart Medical Diagnosis Through AI-Powered Technologies and Applications* (pp. 258–274). IGI Global. 10.4018/979-8-3693-3679-3.ch016

Komalasari, R., & Mustafa, C. (2023). A Healthy Game-Theoretic Evaluation of NATO and Indonesia's Policies in the Context of International Law. Jurnal Pertahanan: Media Informasi tentang Kajian & Strategi Pertahanan yang Mengedepankan Identity. *Nasionalism & Integrity*, 9(2), 333–349. 10.33172/jp.v9i2.16794

Komalasari, R., & Mustafa, C. (2023) Combating International Cyber Conflict: A Healthy Just War and International Law Analysis of NATO and Indonesian Policies. *Jurnal Pertahanan: Media Informasi tentang Kajian & Strategi Pertahanan yang Mengedepankan Identity, Nasionalism & Integrity, 9*(3).

Komalasari, R., & Mustafa, C. (2023). Combating International Cyber Conflict: A Healthy Just War and International Law Analysis of NATO and Indonesian Policies. *Jurnal Pertahanan: Media Informasi tentang Kajian & Strategi Pertahanan yang Mengedepankan IdentityNasionalism & Integrity*, 9(3), 559–570. 10.33172/jp.v9i2.16794

Komalasari, R., & Mustafa, C. (2023). Analysis Of The Propulsion And Maneuvering Characteristics Of Autonomous Underwater Vehicles And Their Strategic Defense. *Propeller Jurnal Permesinan, 1*(2).

Komalasari, R., & Mustafa, C. (2023). Amphibious Forces in the Total War Age: Exploring Indonesia's Multifaceted Contributions to Statecraft in the Asia-Pacific Region. *Jurnal Strategi Pertahanan Laut*, 9(2), 62–77. 10.33172/spl.v9i2.12606

Komalasari, R., & Mustafa, C. (2023). The Evolution and Institutionalization of the Naval Partnership between Indonesia and ASEAN. *Jurnal Strategi Pertahanan Laut*, 9(2), 1–18. 10.33172/spl.v9i2.12576

Komalasari, R., & Mustafa, C. (2023). A Healthy Game-Theoretic Evaluation of NATO and Indonesia's Policies in the Context of International Law. *Jurnal Pertahanan: Media Informasi tentang Kajian & Strategi Pertahanan yang Mengedepankan Identity. Nasionalism & Integrity*, 9(2), 333–349. 10.33172/jp.v9i2.16794

Komalasari, R., & Mustafa, C. (2024). Rehabilitasi Pengguna Narkoba: Tantangan dan Peluang. *Arena Hukum*, *14*(4).

Komalasari, R., & Mustafa, C. (2024). *Healthy Competition Policy Dynamics: the Influence of Domestic-Specific Factors in a Globalized Landscape*. Jurnal Persaingan Usaha.

Komalasari, R., & Mustafa, C. (2024). *Comparative Analysis of Healthy Electoral Fraud Legislation in Established Democracies*. Jurnal Adhyasta Pemilu.

Komalasari, R., & Mustafa, C. (2024). Navigating governance for equitable health systems: Ethical dimensions, ideological impacts, and evidence-based improvements. *Governance: An International Journal of Policy, Administration and Institutions*, 12(1), 49–62.

Komalasari, R., & Mustafa, C. (2024). Strengthening National Security Through Integrated Farming Systems: A Comprehensive Assessment and Strategic Outlook. *Jurnal Pertanian Terpadu*, 1(1), 19–33.

Komalasari, R., & Mustafa, C. (2024). Dimensi Sosial-Ekologi Pengelolaan Danau Tropis Berkelanjutan: Pelajaran Dari Danau Toba, Indonesia. *Jurnal Perikanan dan Kelautan Nusantara*, *1*(1), 8-17.

Komalasari, R., & Mustafa, C. (2024). Navigating governance for equitable health systems: Ethical dimensions, ideological impacts, and evidence-based improvements. *Governance: An International Journal of Policy, Administration and Institutions*, 12(1), 49–62.

Komalasari, R., & Mustafa, C. (2024). Strengthening National Security Through Integrated Farming Systems: A Comprehensive Assessment and Strategic Outlook. *Jurnal Pertanian Terpadu*, 1(1), 19–33.

Komalasari, R., & Mustafa, C. (2024). Dimensi Sosial-Ekologi Pengelolaan Danau Tropis Berkelanjutan: Pelajaran Dari Danau Toba, Indonesia. *Wrasse Jurnal Perikanan dan Kelautan Nusantara*, *1*(1).

Komalasari, R., Nurhayati, N., & Mustafa, C. (2022). Enhancing the Online Learning Environment for Medical Education: Lessons From COVID-19. In *Policies and procedures for the implementation of safe and healthy eaducational environments: Post-COVID-19 perspectives* (pp. 138-154). IGI Global. 10.4018/978-1-7998-9297-7. ch009

Komalasari, R., Nurhayati, N., & Mustafa, C. (2022). Insider/outsider issues: Reflections on qualitative research. *The Qualitative Report*, 27(3), 744–751. 10.46743/2160-3715/2022.5259

Komalasari, R., Nurhayati, N., & Mustafa, C. (2022). Professional Education and Training in Indonesia. In *Public Affairs Education and Training in the 21st Century* (pp. 125–138). IGI Global. 10.4018/978-1-7998-8243-5.ch008

Komalasari, R., & Puspitasari, M. (2024). Medical Educators (ME) and Their Continuous Professional Development (CPD). In *The Lifelong Learning Journey of Health Professionals: Continuing Education and Professional Development* (pp. 54-76). IGI Global. 10.4018/978-1-6684-6756-5.ch003

Komalasari, R., Wilson, S., & Haw, S. (2021). A systematic review of qualitative evidence on barriers to and facilitators of the implementation of opioid agonist treatment (OAT) programmes in prisons. *The International Journal on Drug Policy*, 87, 102978. 10.1016/j.drugpo.2020.10297833129135

Komalasari, R., Wilson, S., & Haw, S. (2021). A social ecological model (SEM) to exploring barriers of and facilitators to the implementation of opioid agonist treatment (OAT) programmes in prisons. *International Journal of Prisoner Health*, 17(4), 477–496. 10.1108/IJPH-04-2020-002038902897

Komalasari, R., Wilson, S., Nasir, S., & Haw, S. (2020). Multiple burdens of stigma for prisoners participating in Opioid Antagonist Treatment (OAT) programmes in Indonesian prisons: A qualitative study. *International Journal of Prisoner Health*, 17(2), 156–170. 10.1108/IJPH-03-2020-0018

Mustafa, C. (2020). The influence of sunni islamic values on rehabilitation as judicial decision for minor drug users in Indonesian court. *Ijtihad: Jurnal Wacana Hukum Islam dan Kemanusiaan*, 20(1), 79-96. 10.18326/ijtihad.v20i1.79-96

Mustafa, C. (2020). The perceptions of Indonesian judges in sentencing minor drug offenders: challenges and opportunities. *Jurnal Hukum dan Peradilan, 9*(1), 1-26. 10.25216/jhp.9.1.2020.1-26

Mustafa, C. (2021). Qualitative Method Used in Researching the Judiciary: Quality Assurance Steps to Enhance the Validity and Reliability of the Findings. *The Qualitative Report*, 26(1), 176–185. 10.46743/2160-3715/2021.4319

Mustafa, C. (2021). Key Finding: Result of a Qualitative Study of Judicial Perspectives on the Sentencing of Minor Drug Offenders in Indonesia: Structural Inequality. *The Qualitative Report*, 26(5), 1678–1692. 10.46743/2160-3715/2021.4436

Mustafa, C. (2021). The view of judicial activism and public legitimacy. *Crime, Law, and Social Change*, 76(1), 23–34. 10.1007/s10611-021-09955-0

Mustafa, C. (2021). The News Media Representation of Acts of Mass Violence in Indonesia. In *Mitigating Mass Violence and Managing Threats in Contemporary Society* (pp. 127–140). IGI Global. 10.4018/978-1-7998-4957-5.ch008

Mustafa, C. (2021). The Challenges to Improving Public Services and Judicial Operations: A unique balance between pursuing justice and public service in Indonesia. In *Handbook of research on global challenges for improving public services and government operations* (pp. 117-132). IGI Global. 10.4018/978-1-7998-4978-0.ch007

Mustafa, C. (2023) Electronic Evidence In The Healthy Justice System: Reimagined. *Jurnal Hukum dan Peradilan, 12*(3), 547-580. 10.25216/jhp.13.1.2025.547-580

Mustafa, C. (2024). Integritas Chain Of Custody Pada Pemeriksaan Bukti Digital. *Judex Laguens*, 2(1), 75–96.

Mustafa, C., & Komalasari, R. (2024). Gender Equality in the Criminal Justice System in Dubai: Between Sharia and Human Rights. *Shar-E: Jurnal Kajian Ekonomi Hukum Syariah*, 10(1), 52–62. 10.37567/shar-e.v10i1.2726

Mustafa, C., & Komalasari, R. (2024). Harmony Unveiled: Sharia Law and Human Rights in Dubai's Justice. *Jurnal Alwatzikhoebillah: Kajian Islam, Pendidikan, Ekonomi. Humaniora*, 10(2), 272–284.

Mustafa, C., & Komalasari, R. (2024). Gender Equality in the Criminal Justice System in Dubai: Between Sharia and Human Rights. *Shar-E: Jurnal Kajian Ekonomi Hukum Syariah*, 10(1), 52–62. 10.37567/shar-e.v10i1.2726

Mustafa, C., & Komalasari, R. (2024). Gender Equality in the Criminal Justice System in Dubai: Between Sharia and Human Rights. *Shar-E: Jurnal Kajian Ekonomi Hukum Syariah*, 10(1), 52–62. 10.37567/shar-e.v10i1.2726

Mustafa, C., Malloch, M., & Hamilton Smith, N. (2020). Judicial perspectives on the sentencing of minor drug offenders in Indonesia: Discretionary practice and compassionate approaches. *Crime, Law, and Social Change*, 74(3), 297–313. 10.1007/s10611-020-09896-0

Suhariyanto, B., Mustafa, C., & Santoso, T. (2021). Liability incorporate between transnational corruption cases Indonesia and the United States of America. *J. Legal Ethical & Regul. Isses*, 24, 1.

KEY TERMS AND DEFINITIONS

Continuous Improvement: This refers to a programme that systematically seeks to improve a service, product, or process over time by identifying areas of inefficiency and making small but significant adjustments to fix them.

Data Analysis: In order to find relevant patterns, draw conclusions, and aid in decision-making, data must first be inspected, cleaned, transformed, and modelled. Data visualisation, machine learning, and statistical analysis are a few methods used.

Integrated Vehicle Health Management: IVHM is an all-encompassing method for tracking how well vehicles (like planes or drones) are doing. IVHM optimises maintenance and enhances operational dependability using real-time data, diagnostics, and prognostics.

Technology Innovation: Technical innovation entails introducing new or improved technological processes, equipment, commodities, or services to accomplish a certain objective. It is part of research and development, developing new ideas and using them to solve problems or satisfy changing demands. Topics Covered: Innovation in Technology, Unmanned Aerial Systems (UAS), Data Analysis, and Integrated Vehicle Health Management (IVHM)

Unmanned Aerial Systems: This describes planes that fly without a pilot. Drones are another name for this kind of aircraft. They serve several purposes, such as data collection, reconnaissance, and remote control, and they may even function independently.

Chapter 17
A Bright Future for AR and VR on Mobile:
Current Status, Obstacles, and Perceptions

G. Sathya
Vivekanandha College of Arts and Sciences for Women(Autonomous), India

M. Sathiya
Vivekanandha College of Arts and Sciences for Women (Autonomous), India

A. Gayathiri
Vivekanandha College of Arts and Sciences for Women (Autonomous), India

S. Sabitha
Vivekanandha College of Arts and Sciences for Women (Autonomous), India

P. Sumitra
Vivekanandha College of Arts and Sciences for Women (Autonomous), India

George Ghinea
Brunel University, Brunei

ABSTRACT

This chapter is conceptual in character and concentrates on two more recent technology innovations the fashion industry is making use of both virtual reality (VR) and augmented reality (AR).Using examples from contemporary fashion, the technology acceptance model (TAM) will be used to further assess the perceived utility and usability of AR and VR from a consumer perspective. The chapter ends with a discussion of potential future study areas. Academics and business alike are paying an increasing amount of attention to mobile augmented reality, or mobile AR. Application-based and hardware-based are the two leading platforms for mobile augmented reality applications. Even with the deployment through apps requiring

DOI: 10.4018/979-8-3693-2268-0.ch017

Copyright © 2024, IGI Global. Copying or distributing in print or electronic forms without written permission of IGI Global is prohibited.

additional downloading and installation beforehand making it painstaking for many platforms distribution, mobile augmented reality implementation through hardware is known to be costly and lacking in flexibility. This chapter looks at the newest technological advancements, active mobile augmented reality deployments, auxiliary technologies, and issues that come up with AR.

INTRODUCTION

A collection of technologies known collectively as augmented reality (AR) allow computer-generated evidence to be combined in real time with live image display. AR is built on methods found in virtual reality (Villari et al., 2016) and engages with both the actual world and a virtual one to some extent. Hugues11 asserts that "augmenting" reality has no intrinsic value. But as soon as we put the human person and his view of the world back in the forefront, this word starts to make sense. Although reality cannot be increased, perceptions of it may. Even if we define augmented reality as a "heightened perception of reality," we will nonetheless refer to it by that word.

In Ronald Azuma and his colleagues conducted insightful and thorough studies in the realm of augmented reality. But the past ten years have seen a particularly high level of advancement in this expanding field of study, opening up prospects for the use of augmented reality across a range of application disciplines. To the best of our knowledge, no current study have comprehensively covered AR technologies (Agrawal, 2018) in the literature with regard to the many application sectors, the influence of mobile technology, and the connection between AR and VR. This study offers an overview of current technology, prospective applications, constraints, and future developments of AR systems for anybody interested in learning more about the topic. The document's outstanding sections are organized as follows: Within Section 2 the technologies that provide an augmented reality experience are presented. The differences between AR and VR are elucidated, and the role played by mobile technology in AR is highlighted. The applications of augmented reality that have been identified are categorized into 12 different areas in Section 3, which includes well-known industries including robotics, entertainment, manufacturing, healthcare, and visualization. Along with these beginning disciplines, it also covers tourism, urban planning, civil engineering, education, marketing, GIS, navigation, and path planning. Section 4 delineates and deliberates upon the prevalent technical obstacles and constraints concerning technology and human issues.

AUGMENTED REALITY

Definition

Computer science interface research is where augmented reality technology developed (Ahmed, 2014; Alam & Hadgraft, 2014). At least since the 1984 film The Terminator and the 1987 film RoboCop, many of the fundamental ideas of augmented reality have been included into science fiction and motion pictures. In these films, cyborg the main characters see the outside world through the lens of a continuous stream of annotations and graphical overlays created by their vision systems. Tom Caudell, a researcher at Boeing, initially suggested the phrase "augmented reality" in 1990 when he was requested to enhance the pricey marking devices and diagrams that were utilized by workers on the production the ground (Krüger et al., 2019). He suggested swapping out the big plywood boards with the individual wiring instructions for every plane for a head-mounted device which transfers the aircraft's unique designs onto reusable, multipurpose boards before displaying them onto high-tech spectacles. The conceptualization of augmented reality (AR) that many writers agree upon requires the usage of head-mounted displays (HMDs) (Al Ansi & Al-Ansi, 2020). But instead of restricting AR to particular technology, we suggest characterizing AR as technologies that possess the following traits: blends the actual and virtual;2) allows for real-time communication; and3) is 3-dimensionally captured. This definition seeks to permit more technologies, including mobile technology, in addition to HMDs while keeping the fundamental elements of AR intact (Al-Ansi, 2022). Interactive rates are possible for 2-D virtual overlays over live video, but in 3-D the overlays are not integrated with the real world (Belimpasakis et al., 2010). This definition, however, excludes mobile devices, see-through headgear, monocular systems, and monitor-based interfaces.

Elements

Augmented reality systems, according to Bimber and Raskar (Sun et al., 2012), are composed of three main building blocks: real-time rendering, display technology, and tracking and registration. To begin with, augmented reality technology must to be three-dimensional and real-time interactive. Accurate tracking and registration are crucial when attempting to create a credible augmented picture. This is because the actual camera should be mapped to the virtual one in a way that ensures the viewpoints of the two worlds match perfectly in order to present the user with a convincing image (Sun et al., 2012). The computer-generated item should appear to be fixed, therefore the system must continuously determine the user's location within the environment around the virtual object, especially if the user is moving (Sun et al., 2012).

Virtual and Augmented Reality

The mainstream media frequently refers to imagined worlds that exist just in our imaginations and on computers as virtual realities. Let's define the phrase more accurately first, though. Virtual is defined as existing in essence or effect but not in reality, per Schmalstieg et al. (2007). As opposed to anything that is just apparent, reality is defined as something that is real or actual and exists regardless of concepts that form it. Fortunately, more recent research has defined virtual reality as an artificial environment where actions taken by users affect the environment's results and is perceived through sensory inputs (such sounds and pictures) provided by a computer. A virtual reality, as defined by Cheok et al. (2003), is an artificially created space that can be interacted with practically exactly the same as a real one.

Figure 1. VR and AR

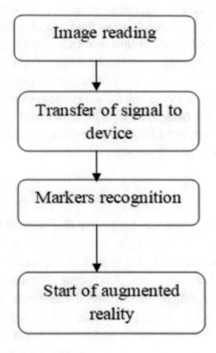

AR and VR technology have the ability to completely change how we use mobile applications.

There are certainly many benefits to creating a fully immersive experience for consumers using AR and VR, namely improved user experience, greater involvement, and a competitive advantage..

AR's Potential for Mobile App Development

The future of AR in mobile app development looks bright. The following are some of the opportunities AR presents for developing mobile apps:

Improved User Experience

Augmented Reality (AR) has the possible to enhance user experience by superimposing digital data onto the physical world. For instance, when a user points their phone's camera at a product, an augmented reality mobile app can show information about it in real-time. This can be especially helpful for e-commerce applications that let users preview products in-person before buying them.

Enhanced Effectiveness

AR has the potential to improve mobile app efficiency as well. For instance, an augmented reality-enabled mobile app can eliminate the need for written or spoken instructions by offering step-by-step guidance for a specific task or procedure.

Enhanced Security

By giving consumers information that can help them avoid dangers, augmented reality (AR) can also increase safety in mobile apps. For instance, a construction worker can identify possible risks in their workplace and take the appropriate safety measures by utilizing a mobile app with augmented reality capabilities.

VR's Potential for Mobile App Development

VR has a promising future in the creation of mobile apps as well. The following are some of the VR-related opportunities for mobile app development:

Better Experience With Games

Users of mobile apps may enjoy a more engaging and dynamic gaming experience with VR. Users can have a more engaging experience with VR because it gives them an appearance that they are really in the game.

Better Instruction and Guidance

Virtual reality (VR) can also be used through mobile apps for training and education. An application for smart phones for medical students, for instance, can simulate surgical procedures using virtual reality, giving students practice in an atmosphere of safety.

Online Tours

Virtual reality (VR) can also be utilized for virtual tours of locations like historical sites or museums. Users can have an immersive and instructive experience by using virtual reality (VR) to experience these locations as if they were really there.

Obstacles

Despite AR and VR have a bright future in mobile app development, these technologies also present certain difficulties. Among the difficulties are the following:

Technical Difficulties of VR and AR in Mobile Applications

Since AR and VR are still relatively new, integrating them into mobile apps can be challenging from a technical standpoint. Smaller businesses may find this prohibitive because it can take a lot of resources and experience.

The Price of AR and VR in a Mobile App

It can be costly to integrate AR and VR technologies into mobile applications. For organizations with tight budgets and resources, this could be a barrier.

Usage of AR and VR in Mobile Applications

Since AR and VR technologies are still relatively new, users might not be familiar with them. This may result in a lack of enthusiasm or uptake for mobile applications utilizing AR and VR technologies.

REVIEW OF LITERATURE AND DEVELOPMENT OF HYPOTHESES

Qualities With Current Studies

In the quickly evolving field of technological devices, virtual reality (VR) and augmented reality (AR), two sides of the same coin, have certain characteristics in common as well as some unique aspects. The market for VR and AR integration in education is expected to reach 19.6 trillion by 2023, rising at a 16.2% annual pace, as reported on Maunders' (2018) homepage.

The main elements of the augmented reality system are conceptuality the simultaneous combination of the virtual and real worlds interactivity simultaneously, and spatiality in the 3D world. The primary characteristics of virtual reality are represented in imaginary space, immersion in virtual space, sensory feedback, and interactivity. These qualities allowed for the possibility of using virtual and augmented reality for education.

Virtual and augmented worlds are growing popularity as a result of a recent quantum come in the development of VR and AR technology. However, some recent research in the realm of education utilizing AR, VR, and XR examined quality changes in learning environments during COVID-19.

H1. Research on AR and VR in education has grown significantly in the last ten years.

H2. Since the start of the Covid-19 epidemic, there has been a dramatic enhance in the use of VR and AR in the classroom.

Possibilities and Difficulties

The real-world application of virtual reality and augmented reality in education is proved by enhancing the interaction, motivation, and communication between teachers and students, despite the innumerable advantages and opportunities these technologies offer. AR and VR have a positive effect on learning effectiveness. Two of the most innovative technical advancements are virtual and augmented reality, which have the potential to significantly improve the educational system. Teachers can offer engaging, interactive classes with AR and VR that students can access from anywhere, including with virtual field trips. AR and VR can be used to provide immersive learning experiences for students. They can perform activities in a virtual environment and receive feedback on their work. Moreover, utilizing AR and VR in the classroom could reduce costs associated with learning resources.

The application of augmented reality (AR) and virtual reality (VR) in education is growing because they offer a distinctive and engaging learning experience. However, a number of problems must be fixed before these innovations may be effectively utilized. Education is one of the main expense associated with AR and VR.Due to the high expense of modern technologies, schools may possibly not have the resources to purchase the necessary gear and software. Furthermore, since the software that creates the immersive experiences needs to be updated frequently, there can be additional everyday expenditure.

Even though AR and VR have a lot to offer the educational sector, there are still obstacles that need to be removed before they can be used effectively. However, when used properly, AR and VR in learning are capable of be a very effective implement for teaching and attracting learners. This corpus of study led us to formulate the third assumption.

H3. In online instruction, VR and AR have improved interaction and engagement between students and teachers.

Platforms and Application for Mobile

Mobile applications have gained popularity in the education sector in recent years. Due to the widespread use of smart phones and tablets, a vast array of educational applications, including games and language learning programs, have been developed (Huang et al., 2019).

Numerous advantages come with mobile apps for education: instantaneous access to knowledge possessions, motivation and appointment among students, and the opportunity used for self-paced learning.

H4. The usage of VR and AR in education has significantly increased during the COVID-19 pandemic..

Current Advancements in AR and VR

Virtual reality (VR) and augmented reality (AR) technological developments are drastically altering the nature of educational. Immersion educational experiences enabled by AR and VR, according to academics, can raise students' understanding and level of involvement with the subject matter. Building virtual simulations of a variety of scenarios using augmented reality and virtual reality applications can be beneficial for teaching kids about science, the economy, and histories.

For instance, physics students may utilize an AR or VR simulator to explore the properties of a black hole, or Educational platforms and apps provide many benefits, such as enhanced student motivation and engagement, anytime, anywhere access to course content, and the ability of enabling students to learn at their own speed. Two further characteristics of mobile apps that benefit teachers in better understanding their pupils and adjusting their teaching methods are real-time feedback and progress monitoring. In view of these data, we propose the fourth hypothesis.

H5: The VR and AR education landscape is being dominated by mobile applications and platform.

During and After the COVID-19 Pandemic, AR, and VR

The Covid-19 epidemic has significantly changed how people live, work, and attend school. Social distance and other safety measures have forced businesses and educational institutions to quickly adapt and come up with new strategies to maintain operations. These days, virtual reality (VR) and augmented reality (AR) technologies are crucial resources for continuing studying and being in touch..

One application of AR and VR during the pandemic has been to facilitate remote learning. Students no longer need to be present in the actual classroom to investigate and engage among their surroundings in a more immersive way thanks to VR and AR.

Current Advancements in AR and VR

nnovations in technology like virtual reality (VR) and augmented reality (AR) are fundamentally changing the way that learning is delivered. Experiential possibilities for learning provided by AR and VR have the ability to improve students' comprehension and engagement with the material, as evidenced by When teaching science, economics, and history to pupils, researchers who are creating virtual replicas of various scenarios utilizing augmented reality and virtual reality applications may find their work useful. Teachers study geography or physics, for instance, can tour reconstructed historical sites or use an AR or VR simulator to learn about the characteristics of a black hole.

Furthermore, individuals can engage and play with 3D objects in ways that don't belong to feasible in the real world by using AR and VR to build interactive learning environments. Utilizing augmented reality and virtual reality, students can explore interactive environments or examine an object from multiple perspectives in a 3D depiction. Experiences that offer children with unique requirements a secure and stimulating educational setting have also been created using AR and VR technologies.

H6. Virtual reality and augmented reality in education are being researched in relation to forthcoming business patterns and the job market.

APPROACH AND OUTCOMES

Research Environments

VR and AR for learning can access 5122 documents from all time, without any limitations, by using the Scopus database. The ensuing arrangement was implemented to glance for pertinent works published among 2011 and 2022 (excluding the current year, 2023).

Analysis of Documents

Articles from various Scopus-based journals incorporated both AR and VR in learning. In order to increase the accuracy and feasibility of the analysis, 84 documents were chosen based on a single criterion: the document had to be limited to articles and include both AR and VR in communal discipline learning.

Figure 2. Different between AR, VR, and XR

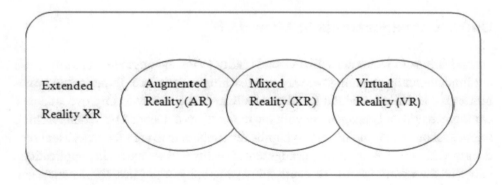

DIFFERENT WEB AR IMPLEMENTATION APPROACHES

Researchers and businesses are at present look for additional efficient approaches to implementation to connection the gap linking the user knowledge of mobile AR applications in addition to the constrained mobile devices that enable to fully capitalize on the promise of AR applications. The Web browser's efficiency. A subset of mobile augmented reality called web augmented reality has been attracting a lot of attention lately because of its cross-platform compatibility and portability. Depending on the various computer paradigms, there are actually two categories of Web AR implementation approaches: (1) The standalone method (also known as the offline strategy) uses the mobile device to carry out all functions locally.

The benefit of this approach is that it is less reliant on mobile networks, so that extra communication latency won't impair real-time tracking performance. However, the mobile device's wasteful computational power turns into its fatal flaw: these tasks are still too difficult for current mobile devices to perform adequately, especially for the Web. (2) Outsourcing of Computation Method makes use of the cloud servers' processing and storage power, and it typically offers a more satisfying user experience than the previously mentioned self-contained one. However, because of this method's heavy reliance on mobile networks, network conditions can quickly impact the workings of Web AR applications.

Individualized Approach

The self-contained method can be implemented using one of two primary methods. One is to create plug-ins or libraries that are solely based on JavaScript in order to supply Mobile AR services on the Web. The other is to improve the performance of Web AR applications by extending the browser kernel. We will now go over these two strategies in more depth. 1) Direct JavaScript Plug-in or Library: As previously indicated, fiducially tracking-based mobile augmented reality implementation techniques can consistently offer accurate and trustworthy identifying and tracking efficiency as a result of their little processing complexity. To support AR services on the Web, numerous specialized JavaScript libraries and plug-ins are already available. These include JSARToolkit which is based on the original ARToolKit, JSARArUco, which is a port of the ArUco to JavaScript, JSARToolKit5, which is an emscripten port of ARToolKit, and many more. The most advanced Web AR solution is AR.js, which was just suggested in 2017 and is based on Three.js and JSARToolKit5. It can operate on any platform and in any browser that supports WebRTC and WebGL, and it can even attain 60 frames per second (FPS), which is stable on the Nexus 6P. Unfortunately, because it only requires basic matrix operations, AR.js can only handle fiducial markers at this time. AR.js still has difficulties when it comes to supporting natural feature objects.

MOBILE AR PRINCIPLES AND COMMON APPLICATIONS MECHANISMS

In 1997, Azuma characterized augmented reality as a technology that allows interaction and seamlessly merges virtual objects with the 3D real environment in real time. In this In this section, we provide an overview of the fundamentals of mobile augmented reality (AR) and list the three common ways it can be implemented. We next discuss the difficulties that arise when using AR in practical situations. In conclusion, we go over a few enabling Web technologies that are either essential or suggested for the use of Web AR.

Mobile AR Principles

AR is a image technology between Virtual Reality (VR) and Real Reality (RR). By superimposing computer-generated virtual comfortable over the real world, AR can without difficulty help users to better appreciate their ambient atmosphere.

Figure 3 is an illustration of a typical AR procedure. Information about the user's surroundings is continuously gathered via the camera and other kinds of sensors. In order to recognize and perceive objects in the real world, the environment perception examines the recorded data (such as image/video, position, and orientation). Meanwhile, the sensors record information about the user's interactions, which is subsequently processed to monitor things. The outcomes of the interaction and perception of the surroundings are both utilized to create a smooth transition between virtual and physical content; this is accomplished by rendering, which presents the user with a "augmented" reality.

Figure 3. Android augment reality process

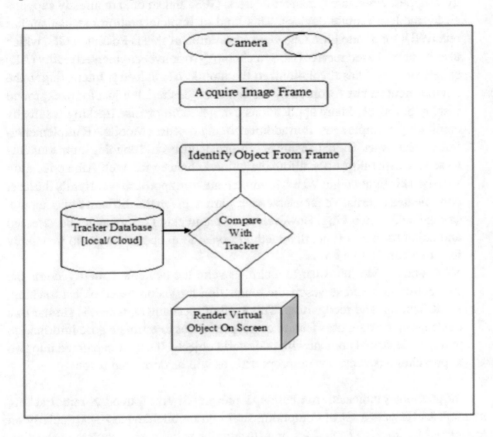

Typical Implementation Mechanisms

Additionally, there are now numerous possibilities for implementing augmented reality applications because to advancements in mobile devices, including computing and display platforms. Following the tracking technologies, we present the conventional Mobile AR implementation in depth. Mechanisms, involving sensor-based, vision-based, and hybrid tracking techniques, are examined from three different angles. Naturally, different implementation strategies have varying levels of computational, networking, and storage complexity. The sensor-based technique is a comparative light-weight Mobile AR implementation strategy, whereas the vision-based approach places a heavy demand on the runtime platform's compute, storage, and network capabilities.

A Bright Future for AR and VR on Mobile

1) Sensor-based Mechanisms: A wide range of sensors, including accelerometers, gyroscopes, compasses, magnetometers, GPS, and so on, are already supported by modern mobile devices. This kind of implementation mechanism has received a lot of attention One clear illustration of this is Pokémon GO, which uses location-based service (LBS) technology to deliver augmented reality (AR) experiences and has revolutionized the mobile AR industry. Interestingly, the environment can be recorded by the camera if desired, but just for background display purposes. Many applications can get more precise tracking results by combining multiple sensors in addition to single-sensor Mobile AR implementation mechanisms. The expansion of sensor categories and ongoing improvements to sensor capability offer a foundation and chances for Web AR application variety. This lightweight Web AR implementation approach is currently the least complicated alternative for users to get started, given the difficulty of compute, storage, and networking. However, since the tracking error cannot be assessed and adjusted in real time, this method's open loop operation would inevitably lead to a cumulative error.

2) Vision-based Mechanisms: In a similar vein, the device's camera records the world around it and serves as the foundation for vision-based object tracking, identification, and recognition. This kind of mechanism, which is similar to a closed loop system, uses feature correspondences to estimate pose information to align the virtual content with real-world objects. It can be separated into two approaches based on several properties, as will be described below.

The previously indicated error buildup is prevented by the frame-by-frame tracking method. But it puts a lot of computing strain on mobile devices—particularly on techniques for tracking natural features. In addition to increasing device capabilities, network advancements (such as the impending 5G networks) will offer compute outsourcing as a solution to the issue of inefficient Web AR application performance. The marker-based method, which includes two methods—natural feature tracking and fiducially feature tracking—uses a predetermined marker to satisfy the tracking requirement. (1) The shape, size, color, and features of the fiducially technique are predetermined. (2) Because it circumvents the challenges of the previously mentioned fiducial tracking method, the natural feature tracking method provides a wider range of applications.

A subset of mobile augmented reality called web augmented reality has gained a lot of attention lately because of its cross-platform compatibility and portability. We can divide Web AR implementation strategies into two categories based on the various computer paradigms: (1) Independent All tasks are carried out locally on the mobile device (i.e., offline approach). Because of this method's reduced reliance on mobile networks, real-time tracking performance won't be negatively impacted by extra communication delays. (2) Outsourcing of Computation Method makes use of the cloud servers' processing and storage power, and it typically offers a more satisfying user experience than the previously mentioned self-contained one. However, because of this method's heavy reliance on mobile networks, network circumstances can quickly alter how well Web AR applications run.

Compatibility

The goal of Web AR is to promote AR apps widely by providing a cross-platform, lightweight implementation of mobile augmented reality. But one of the biggest issues right now is the compatibility issue as well. 1) Enabling Technology Compatibility: There are significant differences in the way that different browsers support and work with different Web AR enabling technologies, like Web Assembly, Web GL, Web RTC, and others. These browsers include native ones like Chrome, Firefox, and Safari, as well as built-in ones where the application is designed hybrid like Face book, Twitter, and We Chat. This complicates program creation in addition to impeding the widespread promotion of Web AR applications.

2) Web AR Browser Compatibility: Another compatibility problem stems from the non-standardization of Web AR browsers. As of right now, every specialized Web AR browser is segregated from the others; an AR application built on one Web browser can't be used on another. The W3C group has lately made some attempts, and given users' increasing enthusiasm for Web AR, standardization also has to be addressed. This calls for collaboration between academia and industry.
3) 3D model Format Compatibility:

Three.js and Web 3D models created with various tools (such as 3DMax, MAYA, and Blender) do not work well together, which degrades the animation effects of Web AR applications. Standardization of a Web 3D model format is additionally anticipated in order for it to be cross-platform.

CONCLUSION

Technologies like AR and VR have the power to completely change how we use mobile apps. There is no denying that AR and VR have a lot of potential, and their use in mobile app development is growing. Numerous industries, including healthcare, education, gaming, retail, and tourism, are already utilizing these technologies. Without a doubt, AR and VR will continue to be important in the development of mobile apps, given the growing popularity of smart phones and other mobile devices. Developers must therefore stay up to date on the most recent developments in these technologies and incorporate them into their projects. Technology like the use of augmented reality (AR) and the virtual world (VR) have the potential to completely transform education while giving students a captivating, interactive learning experience. Instructors can spark students' interest in the subject matter by immersing them in a variety of unusual sights, audio signals, and experimentation through the use of various techniques. Additionally, these developments can be leveraged to construct more engaging virtual worlds, which could make for an engaging and stimulating atmosphere for education. The Web XR Editor draft was released in March 2018 and is an outcome of the W3C group's recent concerted attention to the Web-based AR implementation technique. Additionally, network slicing can improve the effectiveness of data transfer for Web AR, and Device-to-Device (D2D) technology enables an efficient method for devices to cooperate in communication.

FUTURE OF VR AND AR

There are several AR/VR devices accessible on the market, including headsets, tablets, smart phones, wearable's, and consoles, as we already mentioned. While each AR/VR gadget offers an experience that is distinctive across the reality spectrum, they are all bound to certain limitations. The content of many virtual reality headsets can be viewed on smart phones. Even though these gadgets serve as a good starting point for VR, they don't have the visual fidelity essential to make available an immersive experience. Furthermore, headsets are typically heavy, making long-term usage unlikely.

What does the future hold for our gadgets? How are they going to change in light of virtual and augmented reality? Think about being able to look past the screens that surround us on a daily basis. In the future, tethered systems and standalone units will be the two forms that virtual and augmented reality technology takes. Tethered systems will consist of a head-worn device or wearable with a wire connecting it to a processing unit. All systems, from processing to display, will be housed within standalone units, which will also be offered as wearable. Manufacturers are selecting a combination of standalone and tethered units, so we're already seeing early indications of these trends.

These devices are more complicated and challenging to install, even though some standalone units are already on the market. With regard to augmented and virtual reality devices, we are in a compromise state these days. Users cannot get a fully immersive, limitless, or comprehensive experience from any of the current systems. The majority of the systems don't have a wide, natural field of view (FOV), low brightness, a short battery life, a restricted display resolution, or 3D sensing capabilities. It will take an additional three to five years to witness genuine, unrestricted AR/VR applications. Despite being less developed than virtual reality due to its limitations, lack of standards, and higher cost, augmented reality technology is already being used in a number of sectors, including logistics, manufacturing, and healthcare. There are early indications that augmented authenticity, which is primarily experienced through headsets like Meta, ODG, Vuzix, and HoloLens, is going to revolutionize the commercial and manufacturing markets. Before these technologies become broadly use, though, there is still work to be done.

ACKNOWLEDGMENT

The author would like to express gratitude to the management for providing the opportunity to use our college facilities for this chapter.

REFERENCES

Agrawal, A. K. (2018). *The role of ICT in higher education for the 21st century: ICT as a change agent for education.Multidisciplinary Higher Education, Research, Dynamics & Concepts: Opportunities & Challenges for Sustainable Development, 1*(1), 76–83.

Ahmed, T. B. (2014). Between school factors and teacher factors: what inhibits Malaysian science teachers from using ICT? *Malaysian Online Journal of Educational Technology, 2*(1).

Al-Ansi, A. (2022). Investigating characteristics of learning environments during the COVID-19 pandemic: A systematic review. *Canadian Journal of Learning and Technology, 48*(1).

Al Ansi, A. M., & Al-Ansi, A. (2020). Future of education post covid-19 pandemic: Reviewing changes in learning environments and latest trends. *Solid State Technology*, 63(6), 201584–201600.

Alam, F., & Hadgraft, R. A. (2014). eLearning – Challenges and Opportunities. *Using Technology Tools to Innovate Assessment, Reporting, and Teaching Practices in Engineering Education*. IGI Global.

Belimpasakis, P., Selonen, P., & You, Y. (2010). Bringing user-generated content from internet services to mobile augmented reality clients. *Proceedings of the IEEE Cloud–Mobile Convergence for Virtual Reality Workshop (CMCVR),* (pp. 14–17). IEEE. 10.1109/CMCVR.2010.5560611

Cheok, A. D., Fong, S. W., Goh, K. H., Yang, X., Liu, W., Farzbiz, F., & Li, Y. (2003). Human pacman: A mobile entertainment system with ubiquitous computing and tangible interaction over a wide outdoor area. *International Conference on Mobile Human–Computer Interaction*. Springer. 10.1007/978-3-540-45233-1_16

Krüger, J. M., Buchholz, A., & Bodemer, D. (2019). Augmented reality in education: Three unique characteristics from a user's perspective. In *Proc. 27th Int. Conf. on Comput. in Educ*, 412–422.

Schmalstieg, D., Schall, G., Wagner, D., Barakonyi, I., Reitmayr, G., Newman, J., & Ledermann, F. (2007). Managing complex augmented reality models. *IEEE Computer Graphics and Applications*, 27(4), 48–57. 10.1109/MCG.2007.8517713234

Sun, Z., Purohit, A., Pan, S., Mokaya, F., Bose, R., & Zhang, P. (2012). Polaris: Getting accurate indoor orientations for mobile devices using ubiquitous visual patterns on ceilings. *Proceedings of the Twelfth Workshop on Mobile Computing Systems & Applications*. ACM. 10.1145/2162081.2162101

Villari, M., Fazio, M., Dustdar, S., Rana, O., & Ranjan, R. (2016). Osmoticcomputing: A new paradigm for edge/cloud integration. *IEEE Cloud Computing*, 3(6), 76–83. 10.1109/MCC.2016.124

Compilation of References

Aazam, M., Zeadally, S., & Flushing, E. F. (2021). Task offloading in edge computing for machine learning-based smart healthcare. *Computer Networks*, 191, 108019. 10.1016/j.comnet.2021.108019

Abdulrab, H., Babkin, E., & Kozyrev, O. (2011). *Semantically Enriched Integration Framework for Ubiquitous Computing Environment*. Ubiquitous Computing. https://doi.org/10.5772/15262

Abir, E. L. (2022). Blockchain-Based Distributed Information Hiding Framework for Data Privacy Preserving in Medical Supply Chain Systems. *Sensors (Basel)*, 22(4).

Agarwal, J., Christa, S., Pai, A., Kumar, M. A., & Prasad, G. (2023, January). Machine Learning Application for News Text Classification. In *2023 13th International Conference on Cloud Computing, Data Science & Engineering (Confluence)* (pp. 463-466). IEEE. 10.1109/Confluence56041.2023.10048856

Agrawal, A. K. (2018). *The role of ICT in higher education for the 21st century: ICT as a change agent for education.Multidisciplinary Higher Education, Research, Dynamics & Concepts: Opportunities & Challenges for Sustainable Development, 1*(1), 76–83.

Ahmad, S. A., & Mohamad, D. (2017). A comparative analysis between fuzzy topsis and simplified fuzzy topsis. *AIP Conference Proceedings*, 040072. 10.1063/1.4995904

Ahmed, T. B. (2014). Between school factors and teacher factors: what inhibits Malaysian science teachers from using ICT? *Malaysian Online Journal of Educational Technology, 2*(1).

Ahmedt-Aristizabal, D., Armin, M. A., Denman, S., Fookes, C., & Petersson, L. (2021). Graph-Based Deep Learning for Medical Diagnosis and Analysis: Past, Present and Future. *Sensors (Basel)*, 21(14), 4758. 10.3390/s2114475834300498

Ahsan, M. N., & Kamal, M. M. (2021). A survey on encryption techniques for secure healthcare data transmission. *Health Information Science and Systems*, 9(1), 1–12.33235709

Akram, M., Shumaiza, , & Arshad, M. (2019). Bipolar fuzzy TOPSIS and bipolar fuzzy ELECTRE-I methods to diagnosis. *Computational & Applied Mathematics*, 39(1), 7. 10.1007/s40314-019-0980-8

Al Ansi, A. M., & Al-Ansi, A. (2020). Future of education post covid-19 pandemic: Reviewing changes in learning environments and latest trends. *Solid State Technology*, 63(6), 201584–201600.

Al Mohamed, A. A., Al Mohamed, S., & Zino, M. (2023). Application of fuzzy multicriteria decision-making model in selecting pandemic hospital site. *Future Business Journal*, 9(1), 14. 10.1186/s43093-023-00185-5

Alam, F., & Hadgraft, R. A. (2014). eLearning – Challenges and Opportunities. *Using Technology Tools to Innovate Assessment, Reporting, and Teaching Practices in Engineering Education.* IGI Global.

Al-Ansi, A. (2022). Investigating characteristics of learning environments during the COVID-19 pandemic: A systematic review. *Canadian Journal of Learning and Technology, 48*(1).

Ali, M., Naeem, F., Kaddoum, G., & Hossain, E. (2023). Metaverse communications, networking, security, and applications: Research issues, state-of-the-art, and future directions. *IEEE Communications Surveys and Tutorials.*

All India Council for Technical Education. (2022). *Invitation of Proposals.* All India Council for Technical Education. https://www.aicte-india.org/sites/default/files/40-35_AICTE_SWAYAM _EOI_2017.pdf

Al-lQubaydhi, N., Alenezi, A., Alanazi, T., Senyor, A., Alanezi, N., Alotaibi, B., Alotaibi, M., Razaque, A., & Hariri, S. (2024). Deep learning for unmanned aerial vehicles detection: A review. *Computer Science Review*, 51, 100614. 10.1016/j.cosrev.2023.100614

Alowais, S. A., Alghamdi, S. S., Alsuhebany, N., Alqahtani, T., Alshaya, A. I., Almohareb, S. N., Aldairem, A., Alrashed, M., Bin Saleh, K., Badreldin, H. A., Al Yami, M. S., Al Harbi, S., & Albekairy, A. M. (2023). Revolutionizing healthcare: The role of artificial intelligence in clinical practice. *BMC Medical Education*, 23(1), 689. 10.1186/s12909-023-04698-z37740191

Amer, A., & Peralez, P. (2014, October). Affordable altered perspectives: Making augmented and virtual reality technology accessible. In *IEEE global humanitarian technology conference (GHTC 2014)* (pp. 603-608). IEEE.

Angel, D. (2022). *Protection of Medical Information Systems Against Cyber Attacks: A Graph Theoretical Approach.*

Angelica, C., Purnama, H., & Purnomo, F. (2021, October). Impact of computer vision with deep learning approach in medical imaging diagnosis. In *2021 1st International Conference on Computer Science and Artificial Intelligence (ICCSAI)* (Vol. 1, pp. 37-41). IEEE.

Anirudh, R., & Thiagarajan, J. J. (2019). Bootstrapping graph convolutional neural networks for autism spectrum disorder classification. *In Proceedings of the IEEE International Conference on Acoustics. Speech and Signal Processing.* IEEE.

Antonenko, I. M. P. (2022). Unmanned aerial vehicles as educational technology systems in construction engineering education. *Journal of information technology in construction, 27.* 10.36680/j.itcon.2022.014

Compilation of References

Ashraf, M. E., Eman, H., Khaled, W., & Fatma, A. (2023). Omara.: Federated blockchain system(FBS) for the healthcare industry. *Scientific Reports*, 2569.

Athar, A., Ali, S. M., Mozumder, M. I., Ali, S., & Kim, H. C. (2023b). *Applications and Possible Challenges of Healthcare Metaverse*. IEEE Xplore. 10.23919/ICACT56868.2023.10079314

Avinash, S., Naveen Kumar, H. N., Guru Prasad, M. S., Mohan Naik, R., & Parveen, G. (2023). Early Detection of Malignant Tumor in Lungs Using Feed-Forward Neural Network and K-Nearest Neighbor Classifier. *SN Computer Science*, 4(2), 195. 10.1007/s42979-022-01606-y

Aziz, K., Tarapiah, S., Ismail, S. H., & Atalla, S. (2016). Smart real-time healthcare monitoring and tracking system using GSM/GPS technologies. *2016 3rd MEC International Conference on Big Data and Smart City (ICBDSC)*. IEEE._10.1109/ICBDSC.2016.7460394

Bacon, J. (2002). Toward pervasive computing. *IEEE Pervasive Computing*, 1(2), 84. https://doi.org/10.1109/mprv.2002.1012341

Balasingam, M. (2017). Drones in medicine—The rise of the machines. *International Journal of Clinical Practice*, 71(9), e12989. 10.1111/ijcp.1298928851081

Bálint, L. (1995). HCI methods and tools in computer-supported interpersonal communication: Towards error-free information exchange in human-to-human interaction. Symbiosis of Human and Artifact - Future Computing and Design for Human-Computer Interaction, Proceedings of the Sixth International Conference on Human-Computer Interaction, (HCI International '95), 819–824. https://doi.org/10.1016/s0921-2647(06)80129-2

Ball, M. (2022). *The Metaverse: And How It Will Revolutionize Everything*. Liveright. 10.15358/9783800669400

Bansal, G., Rajgopal, K., Chamola, V., Xiong, Z., & Niyato, D. (2022). Healthcare in metaverse: A survey on current metaverse applications in healthcare. *IEEE Access : Practical Innovations, Open Solutions*, 10, 119914–119946. 10.1109/ACCESS.2022.3219845

Barrado, C., Boyero, M., Brucculeri, L., Ferrara, G., Hately, A., Hullah, P., Martin-Marrero, D., Pastor, E., Rushton, A. P., & Volkert, A. (2020). U-space concept of operations: A key enabler for opening airspace to emerging low-altitude operations. *Aerospace (Basel, Switzerland)*, 7(3), 24. 10.3390/aerospace7030024

Bashshur, R. L., Shannon, G. W., Krupinski, E. A., & Grigsby, J. (2011). The empirical foundations of telemedicine interventions for chronic disease management. *Telemedicine Journal and e-Health*, 17(6), 484–516. 10.1089/tmj.2011.010321718114

Bauer, J., Moormann, D., Strametz, R., & Groneberg, D. A. (2021). Development of unmanned aerial vehicle (UAV) networks delivering early defibrillation for out-of-hospital cardiac arrests (OHCA) in areas lacking timely access to emergency medical services (EMS) in Germany: A comparative economic study. *BMJ Open*, 11(1), e043791. 10.1136/bmjopen-2020-04379133483448

Bayoudh, K., Knani, R., Hamdaoui, F., & Mtibaa, A. (2022). A survey on deep multimodal learning for computer vision: Advances, trends, applications, and datasets. *The Visual Computer*, 38(8), 2939–2970. 10.1007/s00371-021-02166-734131356

Belchior, R., Vasconcelos, A., Guerreiro, S., & Correia, M. (2021). A survey on blockchain interoperability: Past, present, and future trends. *ACM Computing Surveys*, 54(8), 1–41. 10.1145/3471140

Belimpasakis, P., Selonen, P., & You, Y. (2010). Bringing user-generated content from internet services to mobile augmented reality clients. *Proceedings of the IEEE Cloud–Mobile Convergence for Virtual Reality Workshop (CMCVR)*, (pp. 14–17). IEEE. 10.1109/CMCVR.2010.5560611

Bellato, E., Marini, E., Castoldi, F., Barbasetti, N., Mattei, L., Bonasia, D. E., & Blonna, D. (2012). Fibromyalgia syndrome: Etiology, pathogenesis, diagnosis, and treatment. *Pain Research and Treatment*, 426130, 1–17. 10.1155/2012/42613023213512

Bennett, R. M., Jones, J., Turk, D. C., Russell, I. J., & Matallana, L. (2007). An internet survey of 2,596 people with Fibromyalgia. *BMC Musculoskeletal Disorders*, 8(1), 27. 10.1186/1471-2474-8-2717349056

Berkcan, O., & Aksoy, T. (2022). Assessing the effect of proactive maintenance scheduling on maintenance costs and airline profitability: The case of Turkish Airlines Technic. *International Journal of Research in Business and Social Science*. 10.20525/ijrbs.v11i4.1780

Bhaskar, A. S., Khan, A., & Patre, S. R. (2020). Application potential of fuzzy embedded TOPSIS approach to solve MCDM based problems. *Intelligent Manufacturing*, 99-121. .10.1007/978-3-030-50312-3_5

Bhattacharya, P., Obaidat, M. S., Savaliya, D., Sanghavi, S., Tanwar, S., & Sadaun, B. (2022). Metaverse assisted Telesurgery in Healthcare 5.0: An interplay of Blockchain and Explainable AI. *IEEE Xplore -2022 International Conference on Computer, Information and Telecommunication Systems (CITS)*. IEEE. 10.1109/CITS55221.2022.9832978

Bhatti, G., Mohan, H., & Singh, R. R. (2021). Towards the future of smart electric vehicles: Digital twin technology. *Renewable & Sustainable Energy Reviews*, 141, 110801. 10.1016/j.rser.2021.110801

Bhutta, M. N. M., Khwaja, A. A., Nadeem, A., Ahmad, H. F., Khan, M. K., Hanif, M. A., Song, H., Alshamari, M., & Cao, Y. (2021). A survey on blockchain technology: Evolution, architecture and security. *IEEE Access : Practical Innovations, Open Solutions*, 9, 61048–61073. 10.1109/ACCESS.2021.3072849

Bhuyan, J., Wu, F., Thomas, C., Koong, K., Hur, J. W., & Wang, C. H. (2020). Aerial drone: An effective tool to teach information technology and cybersecurity through project based learning to minority high school students in the US. *TechTrends*, 64(6), 899–910. 10.1007/s11528-020-00502-734396368

Compilation of References

Bibri, S. E., & Jagatheesaperumal, S. K. (2023). Harnessing the potential of the metaverse and artificial intelligence for the internet of city things: Cost-effective XReality and synergistic AIoT technologies. *Smart Cities*, 6(5), 2397–2429. 10.3390/smartcities6050109

Bilyeau, N. (2021). Newest Target of Cyber Attacks: America's Hospitals. *The Crime Report*. https://thecrimereport.org/2021/08/18/hospitals-cyberattacks/

Binns, R., & Gillett, G. (2021). Ethical frameworks for virtual health technologies: Addressing issues of equity and access. *Health Care Analysis*, 29(4), 463–475.

Bisanti, G. M., Mainetti, L., Montanaro, T., Patrono, L., & Sergi, I. (2023). Digital twins for aircraft maintenance and operation: A systematic literature review and an IoT-enabled modular architecture. *Internet of Things : Engineering Cyber Physical Human Systems*, 100991, 100991. 10.1016/j.iot.2023.100991

Bolick, M. M., Mikhailova, E. A., & Post, C. J. (2022). Teaching innovation in STEM education using an unmanned aerial vehicle (UAV). *Education Sciences*, 12(3), 224. 10.3390/educsci12030224

Bozorgzadeh, E. (2017). *Embedded Systems for Pervasive Computing*. Springer. https://www.springeropen.com/collections/espc

Brat, G. P., Yu, H., Atkins, E., Sharma, P., Cofer, D., Durling, M., & Bakirtzis, G. (2023). *Autonomy Verification & Validation Roadmap and Vision2045* (No. NASA/TM-20230003734).

Budiyono, A., & Higashino, S. I. (2023). A Review of the Latest Innovations in UAV Technology. Journal of Instrumentation. *Automation and Systems*, 10(1), 7–16.

Büyüközkan, G., & Mukul, E. (2020). Evaluation of smart health technologies with hesitant fuzzy linguistic MCDM methods. *Journal of Intelligent & Fuzzy Systems*, 39(5), 6363–6375. 10.3233/JIFS-189103

Campean, F., Neagu, D., Doikin, A., Soleimani, M., Byrne, T., & Sherratt, A. (2019, July). Automotive IVHM: towards intelligent personalised systems healthcare. In *Proceedings of the design society: international conference on engineering design* (Vol. 1, No. 1, pp. 857-866). Cambridge University Press. https://doi.org/10.1017/dsi.2019.90

Capece, G., & Lorenzi, F. (2020). Blockchain and Healthcare: Opportunities and Prospects for the EHR. *Sustainability (Basel)*, 12(22), 9693. 10.3390/su12229693

Cawthorne, D., & Robbins-van Wynsberghe, A. (2020). An ethical framework for the design, development, implementation, and assessment of drones used in public healthcare. *Science and Engineering Ethics*, 26(5), 2867–2891. 10.1007/s11948-020-00233-132578062

Chandrappa, S., Dharmanna, L., & Neetha, K. I. R. (2019, July). Automatic elimination of noises and enhancement of medical eye images through image processing techniques for better glaucoma diagnosis. In *2019 1st International Conference on Advances in Information Technology (ICAIT)* (pp. 551-557). IEEE. 10.1109/ICAIT47043.2019.8987312

Chandrappa, S., Dharmanna, L., & Basavaraj, A. (2022). A novel approach for early detection of neovascular glaucoma using fractal geometry. *Int J Image Graph Signal Process*, 14(1), 26–39. 10.5815/ijigsp.2022.01.03

Chandrappa, S., Guruprasad, M. S., Kumar, H. N., Raju, K., & Kumar, D. S. (2023). An IOT-Based Automotive and Intelligent Toll Gate Using RFID. *SN Computer Science*, 4(2), 154. 10.1007/s42979-022-01569-0

Chang, Y., Fang, C., & Sun, W. (2021). *A blockchain-based Federated Learning Method for Smart Healthcare Computational Intelligence and Neuroscience*, 1-12. Wiley.

Chen, D., & Zhang, R. (2022). Exploring research trends of emerging technologies in health metaverse: A bibliometric analysis. SSRN *Electron.* J. 10.2139/ssrn.3998068

Chengoden, R., Victor, N., Huynh-The, T., Yenduri, G., Jhaveri, R. H., Alazab, M., Bhattacharya, S., Hegde, P., Maddikunta, P. K. R., & Gadekallu, T. R. (2022). *Metaverse for healthcare: A survey on potential applications, challenges and future directions.* arXiv preprint arXiv:2209.04160.

Chengoden, R., Victor, N., Huynh-The, T., Yenduri, G., Jhaveri, R. H., Alazab, M., Bhattacharya, S., Hegde, P., Maddikunta, P. K. R., & Gadekallu, T. R. (2023b). Metaverse for Healthcare: A survey on potential applications, challenges and future directions. *IEEE Access : Practical Innovations, Open Solutions*, 11, 12765–12795. 10.1109/ACCESS.2023.3241628

Chen, Z., Yeh, S., Chamberland, J. F., & Huff, G. H. (2019). A Sensor-Driven Analysis of Distributed Direction Finding Systems Based on UAV Swarms. *Sensors (Basel)*, 19(12), 2659. 10.3390/s1912265931212836

Cheok, A. D., Fong, S. W., Goh, K. H., Yang, X., Liu, W., Farzbiz, F., & Li, Y. (2003). Human pacman: A mobile entertainment system with ubiquitous computing and tangible interaction over a wide outdoor area. *International Conference on Mobile Human–Computer Interaction*. Springer. 10.1007/978-3-540-45233-1_16

Chirag. (2024). *Breaking Barriers: Blockchain's Role in Reshaping Healthcare.* AppInventive. https://appinventiv.com/blog/blockchain-technology-in-healthcare-industry/

Chithra, M. R., & Menon, M. K. (2020). Secure domination of honeycomb networks. [Cross-Ref] [Google Scholar]. *Journal of Combinatorial Optimization*, 40(1), 98–109. 10.1007/s10878-020-00570-8

Chui, K., Alhalabi, W., Pang, S., Pablos, P., Liu, R., & Zhao, M. (2017). Disease diagnosis in smart healthcare: Innovation, technologies and applications. *Sustainability (Basel)*, 9(12), 2309. 10.3390/su9122309

Ciliberti, D., Della Vecchia, P., Memmolo, V., Nicolosi, F., Wortmann, G., & Ricci, F. (2022). The Enabling Technologies for a Quasi-Zero Emissions Commuter Aircraft. *Aerospace (Basel, Switzerland)*, 2022(9), 319. 10.3390/aerospace9060319

Cohen, I. G., & Mello, M. M. (2018). Ethical and legal issues in virtual health care. *The Journal of Law, Medicine & Ethics*, 46(2), 245–259.

Compilation of References

Coles, T. R., Meglan, D., & John, N. W. (2010). The role of haptics in medical training simulators: A survey of the state of the art. *IEEE Transactions on Haptics*, 4(1), 51–66. 10.1109/TOH.2010.1926962955

Condoluci, M., Araniti, G., Mahmoodi, T., & Dohler, M. (2016). Enabling the iot machine age with 5g: Machine-type multicast services for innovative real-time applications. *IEEE Access, 4*.

Cordeiro, T. F. K., Ishihara, J. Y., & Ferreira, H. C. (2020). A Decentralized Low-Chattering Sliding Mode Formation Flight Controller for a Swarm of UAVs. *Sensors (Basel)*, 20(11), 3094. 10.3390/s2011309432486183

Cottenier, T. (2020). *Adaptive Embedded Services for Pervasive Computing*. Illinois Institute of Technology.

Dadario, N. B., & Sughrue, M. E. (2022). Should Neurosurgeons Try to Preserve Non-Traditional Brain Networks? A Systematic Review of the Neuroscientific Evidence. *Journal of Personalized Medicine*, 12(4), 587. 10.3390/jpm1204058735455703

Damar, M. (2022). What the literature on medicine, nursing, public health, midwifery, and dentistry reveals: An overview of the rapidly approaching metaverse. *Journal of Metaverse*, 2(2), 62–70. 10.57019/jmv.1132962

Dara, S., Dhamercherla, S., Jadav, S. S., Babu, C. M., & Ahsan, M. J. (2022). Machine learning in drug discovery: A review. *Artificial Intelligence Review*, 55(3), 1947–1999. 10.1007/s10462-021-10058-434393317

Dasgupta, S. (2019). Emerging frontiers for Development of Military UAVs: An Indian Perspective. *Journal of Aerospace Sciences and Technologies*, 126–134.

Davies, N., Langheinrich, M., Clinch, S., Elhart, I., Friday, A., Kubitza, T., & Surajbali, B. (2014). *Proceedings of the 32nd annual ACM conference on Human factors in computing systems - CHI '14 - Personalisation and privacy in future pervasive display networks*. ACM. 10.1145/2556288.2557287

Davies, N. (2013). Ethics in Pervasive Computing Research. *IEEE Pervasive Computing*, 12(3), 2–4. https://doi.org/10.1109/mprv.2013.48

Davis, A., Murphy, J., Owens, D., Khazanchi, D., & Zigurs, I. (2009). Avatars, people, and virtual worlds: Foundations for research in metaverses. *Journal of the Association for Information Systems*, 10(2), 1. 10.17705/1jais.00183

Deepa, N., Pham, Q.-V., Nguyen, D. C., Bhattacharya, S., Prabadevi, B., Gadekallu, T. R., Maddikunta, P. K. R., Fang, F., & Pathirana, P. N. (2022). A survey on blockchain for big data: Approaches, opportunities, and future directions. *Future Generation Computer Systems*, 131, 209–226. 10.1016/j.future.2022.01.017

Devadas, R. M., Hiremani, V., Bidwe, R. V., Zope, B., Jadhav, V., & Jadhav, R. (2023). Identifying factors in congenital heart disease transition using fuzzy DEMATEL. *International Journal of Advanced Computer Science and Applications*, 14(12). 10.14569/IJACSA.2023.0141218

Devadas, R., & Srinivasan, G. N. (2019). Review Of Different Fuzzy Logic Approaches for Prioritizing Software Requirements. *International Journal of Scientific & Technology Research.*, 8(09), 296–298.

Dincelli, E., & Yayla, A. (2022b). Immersive virtual reality in the age of the Metaverse: A hybrid-narrative review based on the technology affordance perspective. *The Journal of Strategic Information Systems*, 31(2), 101717. 10.1016/j.jsis.2022.101717

Dionisio, J. D. N., Burns, W. G.III, & Gilbert, R. (2013). 3D Virtual Worlds and the Metaverse: Current Status and Future Possibilities. *ACM Computing Surveys*, 45(3), 1–38. 10.1145/2480741.2480751

Dris, E. I., Hanan, E. I., & Souad, S. (2021). A Blockchain-Based Privacy-Preserving Smart Healthcare Framework. *Journal of Healthcare Engineering*.34777733

Duan, H., Li, J., Fan, S., Lin, Z., Wu, X., & Cai, W. (2021). Metaverse for social good: A university campus prototype. *Proceedings of the 29th ACM International Conference on Multimedia*, (pp. 153–161). ACM. 10.1145/3474085.3479238

Duquenoy, P., & Burmeister, O. K. (2009). *Ethical Issues and Pervasive Computing*. Risk Assessment and Management in Pervasive Computing., https://doi.org/10.4018/9781605662206.ch014

Dwivedi, Y. K., Hughes, L., Baabdullah, A. M., Ribeiro-Navarrete, S., Giannakis, M., Al-Debei, M. M., Dennehy, D., Metri, B. A., Buhalis, D., Cheung, C. M. K., Conboy, K., Doyle, R., Dubey, R., Dutot, V., Felix, R., Goyal, D., Gustafsson, A., Hinsch, C., Jebabli, I., & Wamba, S. F. (2022). Metaverse beyond the hype: Multidisciplinary perspectives on emerging challenges, opportunities, and agenda for research, practice and policy. *International Journal of Information Management*, 66, 102542. 10.1016/j.ijinfomgt.2022.102542

Elangovan, D., Long, C. S., Bakrin, F. S., Tan, C. S., Goh, K. W., Hussain, Z., & Ming, L. C. (2020). Application of blockchain technology in hospital information system. *Mathematical modeling and soft computing in epidemiology*, 231-246.

ElHeneidi, S., & Li, S. (2020). Blockchain-based healthcare data security and privacy: A review. *Journal of Healthcare Engineering*, 2020, 1–13.

Engelhardt, M. A. (2017). Hitching healthcare to the chain: An introduction to blockchain technology in the healthcare sector. *Technology Innovation Management Review*, 7(10), 22–34. 10.22215/timreview/1111

Enrico, Z., Mengfei, F., Zhiguo, Z., & Rui, K. (2019). Application of reliability technologies in civil aviation: Lessons learnt and perspectives. *Chinese Journal of Aeronautics*, 32(1), 143–158. 10.1016/j.cja.2018.05.014

Ezhilarasu, C. M., Skaf, Z., & Jennions, I. K. (2019). The application of reasoning to aerospace Integrated Vehicle Health Management (IVHM): Challenges and opportunities. *Progress in Aerospace Sciences*, 105, 60–73. 10.1016/j.paerosci.2019.01.001

Compilation of References

Ezhilarasu, C. M., Skaf, Z., & Jennions, I. K. (2019, October). Understanding the role of a digital twin in integrated vehicle health management (IVHM). In *2019 IEEE International Conference on Systems, Man and Cybernetics* (SMC) (pp. 1484-1491). IEEE. https://doi.org/10.1109/SMC .2019.8914244

Fan, B., Li, Y., Zhang, R., & Fu, Q. (2020). Review on the technological development and application of UAV systems. *Chinese Journal of Electronics*, 29(2), 199–207. 10.1049/cje.2019.12.006

Farahat, M. A., Darwish, A., & Hassanien, A. E. (2023). The implication of metaverse in the traditional medical environment and healthcare sector: Applications and challenges. In *Studies in big data* (pp. 105–133). Springer. 10.1007/978-3-031-29132-6_7

Félix-Herrán, L. C., Izaguirre-Espinosa, C., Parra-Vega, V., Sánchez-Orta, A., Benitez, V. H., & Lozoya-Santos, J. D. J. (2022). A Challenge-Based Learning Intensive Course for Competency Development in Undergraduate Engineering Students: Case Study on UAVs. *Electronics (Basel)*, 11(9), 1349. 10.3390/electronics11091349

Fotouhi, A., Ding, M., & Hassan, M. (2017). Understanding autonomous drone maneuverability for internet of things applications. *A World of Wireless, Mobile and Multimedia Networks (WoWMoM), IEEE 18th International Symposium*. IEEE.

French, S. (1996). Multicriteria Methodology for Decision Aiding. *The Journal of the Operational Research Society*, 48, 1257–1258.

Friedewald, M. (2011). *Ubiquitous computing: An overview of technology impacts Author links open overlay panel*. Science Direct.

Fu, S., & Avdelidis, N. P. (2023). Prognostic and Health Management of Critical Aircraft Systems and Components: An Overview. *Sensors (Basel)*, 23(19), 8124. 10.3390/s2319812437836954

Fusco, A., Dicuonzo, G., Dell'Atti, V., & Tatullo, M. (2020). Blockchain in healthcare: Insights on COVID-19. *International Journal of Environmental Research and Public Health*, 17(19), 7167. 10.3390/ijerph1719716733007951

Gad, G., Farrag, A., Aboulfotouh, A., Bedda, K., Fadlullah, Z. M., & Fouda, M. M. (2024). Joint Self-Organizing Maps and Knowledge Distillation-Based Communication-Efficient Federated Learning for Resource-Constrained UAV-IoT Systems. *IEEE Internet of Things Journal*, 11(9), 15504–15522. 10.1109/JIOT.2023.3349295

Gajjar, M. (2010). *Ubiquitous Computing Smart Things*. Science Direct. https://www.sciencedirect .com/topics/computer-science/ubiquitous-computing

Galvez-Sánchez, C. M., & Reyes Del Paso, G. A. (2020). Diagnostic Criteria for Fibromyalgia: Critical Review and Future Perspectives. *Journal of Clinical Medicine*, 9(4), 1219. 10.3390/ jcm904121932340369

Gao, J., Wang, H., & Shen, H. (2020). Machine learning based workload prediction in cloud computing. In *2020 29th international conference on computer communications and networks (ICCCN)* (pp. 1-9). IEEE. 10.1109/ICCCN49398.2020.9209730

Gao, J., Xu, X., Qi, L., Dou, W., Xia, X., & Zhou, X. (2024). Distributed Computation Offloading and Power Control for UAV-Enabled Internet of Medical Things. *ACM Transactions on Internet Technology*, 3652513. 10.1145/3652513

Gao, J., Yang, Y., Lin, P., & Park, D. S. (2018). Computer vision in healthcare applications. *Journal of Healthcare Engineering*, 2018.29686826

Geeks for Geeks. (2020). *Introduction to Pervasive Computing*. Geeks for Geeks.https://www.geeksforgeeks.org/introduction-to-pervasive-computing/

Geeks for Geeks. (n.d.). *Challenges of Blockchain in Healthcare.* Geeks for Geeks. https://www.geeksforgeeks.org/challenges-of-blockchain-in-healthcare/

Gerdle, B., Björk, J., Cöster, L., Henriksson, K., Henriksson, C., & Bengtsson, A. (2008). Prevalence of widespread pain and associations with work status: A population study. *BMC Musculoskeletal Disorders*, 9(1), 102. 10.1186/1471-2474-9-10218627605

Gettinger, D. (2017). *Drones at Home: Public Safety Drones*. Center for the Study of the Drone at Bard College.

Gheisari, M., & Esmaeili, B. (2019). Applications and requirements of unmanned aerial systems (UASs) for construction safety. *Safety Science*, 118, 230–240. 10.1016/j.ssci.2019.05.015

Github. (n.d.). *Healthcare Datasets* [Dataset]. GitHub. https://github.com/topics/healthcare-datasets

Gopinath, K., Desrosiers, C., & Lombaert, H. (2019 June) Adaptive graph convolution pooling for brain surface analysis. In *Proceedings of the 26th International Conference Information Processing in Medical Imaging*, Hong Kong, China.

Gordon, N. P., & O'Connor, P. J. (2020). The impact of the Internet on telehealth: Data transmission and service delivery. *Journal of Telemedicine and Telecare*, 26(5), 267–273.

Gordon, S. S., & Spetz, J. (2019). Regulatory issues and compliance for virtual health care: A review. *Journal of Telemedicine and Telecare*, 25(6), 335–341.

Goulart, V. G., Liboni, L. B., & Cezarino, L. O. (2022). Balancing skills in the digital transformation era: The future of jobs and the role of higher education. *Industry and Higher Education*, 36(2), 118–127. 10.1177/09504222211029796

Grübel, J., Thrash, T., Aguilar, L., Gath-Morad, M., Chatain, J., Sumner, R. W., Hölscher, C., & Schinazi, V. R. (2022). The hitchhiker's guide to fused twins: A review of access to digital twins in situ in smart cities. *Remote Sensing (Basel)*, 14(13), 3095. 10.3390/rs14133095

Gujjar, J. P., Kumar, H. P., & Prasad, M. G. (2023, March). Advanced NLP Framework for Text Processing. In *2023 6th International Conference on Information Systems and Computer Networks (ISCON)* (pp. 1-3). IEEE.

Compilation of References

Gupta, L., Jain, R., & Vaszkun, G. (2016). Survey of important issues in UAV communication networks. *IEEE Communications Surveys and Tutorials*, 18(2), 1123–1152. 10.1109/COMST.2015.2495297

Guru Prasad, M. S., Naveen Kumar, H. N., Raju, K., Santhosh Kumar, D. K., & Chandrappa, S. (2023). Glaucoma detection using clustering and segmentation of the optic disc region from retinal fundus images. *SN Computer Science*, 4(2), 192. 10.1007/s42979-022-01592-1

Guru, P. M., Praveen, G. J., Dodmane, R., Sardar, T. H., Ashwitha, A., & Yeole, A. N. (2023, March). Brain Tumor Identification and Classification using a Novel Extraction Method based on Adapted Alexnet Architecture. In *2023 6th International Conference on Information Systems and Computer Networks (ISCON)* (pp. 1-5). IEEE. 10.1109/ISCON57294.2023.10112075

Habib, G., Sharma, S., Ibrahim, S., Ahmad, I., Qureshi, S., & Ishfaq, M. (2022). Blockchain Technology: Benefits, Challenges, Applications, and Integration of Blockchain Technology with Cloud Computing. *Future Internet*, 14(11), 341. 10.3390/fi14110341

Hamed, T. (2023). Privacy and Security of Blockchain in Healthcare: Applications, Challenges, and Future Perspectives. *SCI, 5*(4).

Hamilton, S. (2022). Deep Learning Computer Vision Algorithms, Customer Engagement Tools, and Virtual Marketplace Dynamics Data in the Metaverse Economy. *Journal of Self-Governance and Management Economics*, 10(2), 37–51.

Han, D., Pan, N., & Li, K. C. (2022). A traceable and revocable cipher text-policy attribute-based encryption scheme based on privacy protection. *IEEE Transactions on Dependable and Secure Computing*, 19(1), 316–327. 10.1109/TDSC.2020.2977646

Harrington, A., & Cahill, V. (2011). Model-driven engineering of planning and optimization algorithms for pervasive computing environments. *Pervasive and Mobile Computing*, 7(6), 705–726. https://doi.org/10.1016/j.pmcj.2011.09.005

Hasudungan, R., Pangestuty, D. M., Latifah, A. J., & Rudiman, . (2019). Solving minimum vertex cover problem using DNA computing. *Journal of Physics: Conference Series*, 1361(1), 012038. 10.1088/1742-6596/1361/1/012038

Hemachandran, K., & Rodriguez, R. V. (Eds.). (2023). *The Business of the Metaverse: How to Maintain the Human Element Within this New Business Reality*. CRC Press.

Hernández-Ortiz, R., Montejano, L. P., & Rodríguez-Velázquez, J. A. (2021). Secure domination in rooted product graphs. [CrossRef] [Google Scholar]. *Journal of Combinatorial Optimization*, 41(2), 401–413. 10.1007/s10878-020-00679-w

Holland, S. (2020). *Unsettled Technology Opportunities for Vehicle Health Management and the Role for Health-Ready Components* (No. EPR2020003). SAE Technical Paper. 10.4271/epr2020003

Hong, J. (2017). The Privacy Landscape of Pervasive Computing. *IEEE Pervasive Computing*, 16(3), 40–48. https://doi.org/10.1109/mprv.2017.2940957

Huang, G., & Al Foysal, A. (2021). *Blockchain in healthcare*. Research Gate.

Huang, Y., & Wu, K. (2020). Vibration-based pervasive computing and intelligent sensing. *CCF Transactions on Pervasive Computing and Interaction*, 2(4), 219–239. https://doi.org/10.1007/s42486-020-00049-9

Hum Data. (n.d.). *Organizations: WHO*. Hum Data. https://data.humdata.org/organization/world-health-organization

Huo, R., Zeng, S., Wang, Z., Shang, J., Chen, W., Huang, S., Wang, T., Yu, F., & Liu, Y. (2022). A comprehensive survey on blockchain in industrial internet of things: Motivations, research progresses, and future challenges. *IEEE Commun. Surv. Tutor*. IEEE.

Hwang, C., & Yoon, K. (1981). Methods for multiple attribute decision making. *Multiple Attribute Decision Making*, 58-191. Springer. .10.1007/978-3-642-48318-9_3

Hwang, C., & Yoon, K. (2012). *Multiple attribute decision making: Methods and applications a state-of-the-Art survey*. Springer Science & Business Media.

ICT-317669 METIS Project. Scenarios, Requirements and KPIs for 5G Mobile and WirelessSystem.Availableonline:https://cordis.europa.eu/docs/projects/cnect/9/317669/080/deliverables/001-ETISD11v1pdf.pdf

Idrees, S. M., Agarwal, P., & Alam, M. A. (Eds.). (2021). *Blockchain for healthcare systems: challenges, privacy, and securing of data*. CRC Press. 10.1201/9781003141471

Jabbar, R., Fetais, N., Krichen, M., & Barkaoui, K. (2020). Blockchain technology for healthcare: Enhancing shared electronic health record interoperability and integrity. *IEEE International Conference on Informatics, IoT, and Enabling Technologies (ICIoT), (pp. 310–317)*. IEEE.

Janke, C., Luthi, K., Kleinke, S., & Lin, Y. (2022). Using Small UAS for STEM Education: Introducing Robotics and Mechatronics with Drones. In *Florida Conference for Recent Advances in Robotics 2022* (p. 1). Embry-Riddle Aeronautical University. https://doi.org/10.5038/QQGN3785

Jaziri, A., Nasri, R., & Chahed, T. (2016). *Congestion mitigation in 5G networks using drone relays*. In *Proceedings of the 2016 International Wireless Communications and Mobile Computing Conference (IWCMC)*, Paphos, Cyprus. 10.1109/IWCMC.2016.7577063

Jeon, H.-j., Youn, H.-c., Ko, S.-m., & Kim, T.-h. (2022). Blockchain and AI meet in the metaverse. In *Advances in the Convergence of Blockchain and Artificial Intelligence* (p. 73). BoD–Books on Demand. 10.5772/intechopen.99114

Jing, Q., Vasilakos, A. V., Wan, J., Lu, J., & Qiu, D. (2014). Security of the internet of things: Perspectives and challenges. *Wireless Networks*, 20(8), 2481–2501. 10.1007/s11276-014-0761-7

Kaggle. (n.d.-a). *Datasets* [Dataset]. Kaggle. https://www.kaggle.com/datasets

Kaggle. (n.d.-b). *Healthcare Datasets* [Dataset]. Kaggle. https://www.kaggle.com/search?q=healthcare+dataset

Compilation of References

Kazi, A., Shekarforoush, S., Krishna, S. A., Burwinkel, H., Vivar, G., Kortüm, K., Ahmadi, S. A., Albarqouni, S., & Navab, N. (2019). Inception GCN: Receptive field aware graph convolutional network for disease prediction. *Proceedings of the 26th International Conference Information Processing in Medical Imaging*, Hong Kong, China.

Keeney, R. L., & Raiffa, H. (1976). *Decisions with multiple objectives: Preferences and value tradeoffs*. Cambridge University Press.

Keesara, S., Jonas, A., & Schulman, K. (2020). COVID-19 and health care's digital revolution. *The New England Journal of Medicine*, 382(23), e82. 10.1056/NEJMp200583532240581

Khaer, A., Sarker, M. S. H., Progga, P. H., Lamim, S. M., & Islam, M. M. (2023). UAVs in Green Health Care for Energy Efficiency and Real-Time Data Transmission. In *International Conference on Intelligent Sustainable Systems* (pp. 773-788). Singapore: Springer Nature Singapore. 10.1007/978-981-99-1726-6_60

Khan, M. F., Ghazal, T. M., Said, R. A., Fatima, A., Abbas, S., Khan, M. A., Issa, G. F., Ahmad, M., & Khan, M. A. (2021). An iomt-enabled smart healthcare model to monitor elderly people using machine learning technique. *Computational Intelligence and Neuroscience*, 2021, 1–10. 10.1155/2021/248775934868288

Khan, R., & McDaniel, P. (2019). Sensor-based healthcare monitoring system: A review of recent advances. *Sensors (Basel)*, 19(10), 2290.31108994

Khoo, B. (2011). RFID as an Enabler of the Internet of Things: Issues of Security and Privacy. *Internet of Things (iThings/CPSCom), International Conference on and 4th International Conference on Cyber, Physical and Social Computing*. IEEE. 10.1109/iThings/CPSCom.2011.83

Kim, M. J., Maher, M. L., & Gu, N. (2012). *Mobile and Pervasive Computing: The Future for Design Collaboration. Mobile and Pervasive Computing in Construction*. Portico. https://doi.org/10.1002/9781118422281.ch9

Kirubasri, G., Sankar, S., Guru Prasad, M. S., Naga Chandrika, G., & Ramasubbareddy, S. (2023). LQETA-RP: Link quality based energy and trust aware routing protocol for wireless multimedia sensor networks. *International Journal of System Assurance Engineering and Management*, ●●●, 1–13.

Kirubasri, G., Sankar, S., Guru Prasad, M. S., Naga Chandrika, G., & Ramasubbareddy, S. (2023). LQETA-RP: Link quality-based energy and trust aware routing protocol for wireless multimedia sensor networks. *International Journal of System Assurance Engineering and Management*, 1–13.

Kolpashchikov, D., Gerget, O., & Meshcheryakov, R. (2022). *Robotics in healthcare. Handbook of Artificial Intelligence in Healthcare* (Vol. 2). Practicalities and Prospects.

Kong, X., Cao, J., Wu, H., & Hsu, C.-H. (Robert). (2020). Mobile Crowdsourcing and Pervasive Computing for Smart Cities. *Pervasive and Mobile Computing*, 61, 101114. https://doi.org/10.1016/j.pmcj.2020.101114

Koohang, A., Nord, J. H., Ooi, K., Tan, G. W., Al-Emran, M., Aw, E. C., Baabdullah, A. M., Buhalis, D., Cham, T., Dennis, C., Dutot, V., Dwivedi, Y. K., Hughes, L., Mogaji, E., Pandey, N., Phau, I., Raman, R., Sharma, A., Σιγάλα, M., & Wong, L. (2023c). Shaping the Metaverse into Reality: A Holistic Multidisciplinary Understanding of Opportunities, Challenges, and Avenues for Future Investigation. *Journal of Computer Information Systems*, 63(3), 735–765. 10.1080/08874417.2023.2165197

Koschlik, A. K., Meyer, H., Arts, E., Conen, P., Jacob, G., Soria-Gomez, M., & Wende, G. (2023, June). Towards an Integrated Vehicle Health Management for Maintenance of Unmanned Air Systems. In *2023 International Conference on Unmanned Aircraft Systems* (ICUAS) (pp. 463-470). IEEE. 10.1109/ICUAS57906.2023.10155995

Kotiyal, A., Kumar, D. S., Prasad, M. G., Manjunath, S. R., Chandrappa, S., & Prabhu, B. A. (2023, June). Real-Time Drowsiness Detection System Using Machine Learning. In *International Conference on Advanced Communication and Intelligent Systems* (pp. 49-58). Cham: Springer Nature Switzerland. 10.1007/978-3-031-45121-8_5

Krüger, J. M., Buchholz, A., & Bodemer, D. (2019). Augmented reality in education: Three unique characteristics from a user's perspective. In *Proc. 27th Int. Conf. on Comput. in Educ*, 412–422.

Kruk, M. E., Gage, A. D., Joseph, N. T., Danaei, G., García-Saisó, S., & Salomon, J. A. (2018). Mortality due to low-quality health systems in the universal health coverage era: A systematic analysis of amenable deaths in 137 countries. *Lancet*, 392(10160), 2203–2212. 10.1016/S0140-6736(18)31668-430195398

Kukreti, A., Prasad, G., Ram, M., & Naik, P. K. (2023, October). Detection and Classification of Brain Tumour Using EfficientNet and Transfer Learning Techniques. In *2023 International Conference on Computer Science and Emerging Technologies (CSET)* (pp. 1-5). IEEE. 10.1109/CSET58993.2023.10346858

Kumar, M. A., Pai, A. H., Agarwal, J., Christa, S., Prasad, G. M., & Saifi, S. (2023, January). Deep Learning Model to Defend against Covert Channel Attacks in the SDN Networks. In *2023 Advanced Computing and Communication Technologies for High Performance Applications (ACCTHPA)* (pp. 1-5). IEEE. 10.1109/ACCTHPA57160.2023.10083336

Kumar, H. N. N., Kumar, A. S., Prasad, M. S. G., & Shah, M. A. (2023). Automatic facial expression recognition combining texture and shape features from prominent facial regions. *IET Image Processing*, 17(4), 1111–1125. 10.1049/ipr2.12700

Kumar, M. A., Abirami, N., Prasad, M. G., & Mohankumar, M. (2022, May). Stroke Disease Prediction based on ECG Signals using Deep Learning Techniques. In *2022 International Conference on Computational Intelligence and Sustainable Engineering Solutions (CISES)* (pp. 453-458). IEEE.

Kumar, M., & Zambonelli, F. (2007). Middleware for pervasive computing. *Pervasive and Mobile Computing*, 3(4), 329–331. https://doi.org/10.1016/j.pmcj.2007.04.005

Compilation of References

Kumar, P., Kumar, R., Srivastava, G., Gupta, G. P., Tripathi, R., Gadekallu, T. R., & Xiong, N. N. (2021). PPSF: A privacy-preserving and secure framework using blockchain-based machine-learning for IoT-driven smart cities. *IEEE Transactions on Network Science and Engineering*, 8(3), 2326–2341. 10.1109/TNSE.2021.3089435

Kun, A. L. (2019). Reader and Teacher: Fourteen Books That Can Inspire Teaching in Pervasive Computing (and beyond). *IEEE Pervasive Computing*, 18(2), 85–90. https://doi.org/10.1109/mprv.2019.2912257

Kuo, T.T. & Ohno-Machado, L. (2018). *Modelchain: Decentralized privacy-preserving healthcare predictive modeling framework on private blockchain networks.*

Kutlu Gündoğdu, F., & Kahraman, C. (2019). Spherical fuzzy sets and spherical fuzzy TOPSIS method. *Journal of Intelligent & Fuzzy Systems*, 36(1), 337–352. 10.3233/JIFS-181401

Lee, L., Braud, T., Zhou, P., Wang, L., Xu, D., Lin, Z., & Hui, P. (2021). All One Needs to Know about Metaverse: A Complete Survey on Technological Singularity, Virtual Ecosystem, and Research Agenda. *arXiv preprint arXiv:2110.05352.*

Lee, C. W. (2022b). Application of Metaverse Service to Healthcare Industry: A Strategic perspective. *International Journal of Environmental Research and Public Health*, 19(20), 13038. 10.3390/ijerph19201303836293609

Lercel, D. J., & Hupy, J. P. (2020). Developing a competency learning model for students of unmanned aerial systems. *The Collegiate Aviation Review International*, 38(2). 10.22488/okstate.20.100212

Letizia, N. (2019). Blockchain-enabled supply chain: An experimental study. *Science Direct,136*, 57-69.

Lien, S. Y., Chen, K. C., & Lin, Y. (2011). Toward ubiquitous massive accesses in 3GPP machine-to-machine communications. *IEEE Communications Magazine*, 49(4), 66–74. 10.1109/MCOM.2011.5741148

Li, K., Cui, Y., Li, W., Lv, T., Yuan, X., Li, S., Ni, W., Simsek, M., & Dressler, F. (2022). When internet of things meets metaverse: Convergence of physical and cyber worlds. *IEEE Internet of Things Journal*, 10(5), 4148–4173. 10.1109/JIOT.2022.3232845

Li, L. (2022). Reskilling and upskilling the future-ready workforce for industry 4.0 and beyond. *Information Systems Frontiers*, 1–16. 10.1007/s10796-022-10308-y35855776

Lin, M., Yang, L. T., Qin, X., Zheng, N., Wu, Z., & Qiu, M. (2009). Static security optimization for real-time systems. *IEEE Transactions on Industrial Informatics*, 5(1), 22–37. 10.1109/TII.2009.2014055

Lin, Q., & Shi, X. (2006). A Message Filtering System in Pervasive Computing. *2006 First International Symposium on Pervasive Computing and Applications*. IEEE. 10.1109/SPCA.2006.297446

Li, R., Verhagen, W. J., & Curran, R. (2020). Toward a methodology of requirements definition for prognostics and health management system to support aircraft predictive maintenance. *Aerospace Science and Technology*, 102, 105877. 10.1016/j.ast.2020.105877

Li, X., Zhou, Y., Dvornek, N. C., Zhang, M., Zhuang, J., Ventola, P., & Duncan, J. S. (2020). *Pooling regularized graph neural network for fmri biomarker analysis*. In *Proceedings of the 23rd Medical Image Computing and Computer Assisted Intervention*, Lima. Peru. 10.1007/978-3-030-59728-3_61

Lucke, U., & Steinmetz, R. (2014). Special issue on "Pervasive Education.". *Pervasive and Mobile Computing*, 14, 1–2. https://doi.org/10.1016/j.pmcj.2014.08.001

Luo, J. (2022). Advances in Atherosclerotic Disease Screening Using Pervasive Healthcare. *IEEE Rev Biomed*. doi:10.1109/RBME.2021.3081180.Epub

MacCallum, K., & Parsons, D. (2019, September). Teacher perspectives on mobile augmented reality: The potential of metaverse for learning. In *World Conference on Mobile and Contextual Learning* (pp. 21-28). IEEE.

Madhavanunni, A. N., Kumar, V. A., & Panicker, M. R. (2023). A Portable Ultrasound Imaging Pipeline Implementation with GPU Acceleration on Nvidia CLARA AGX. *arXiv preprint arXiv:2311.00482*.

Maindze, A., Skaf, Z., & Jennions, I. (2019, September). Towards an Enhanced Data-and Knowledge Management Capability: A Data Life Cycle Model Proposition for Integrated Vehicle Health Management. In *Annual Conference of the PHMS*, Scottsdale, AZ, USA. 10.36001/phmconf.2019.v11i1.842

Maizes, V., Rakel, D., & Niemiec, C. (2009). Integrative medicine and patient-centered care. *Explore (New York, N.Y.)*, 5(5), 277–289. 10.1016/j.explore.2009.06.00819733814

Majeed, A. & Rauf, I. (2020). Graph Theory: A Comprehensive Survey about Graph Theory Applications in Computer Science and Social Networks. *Inventions 2020*. 5. 10. doi: 5010010.10.3390/inventions

Malasinghe, L. P., Ramzan, N., & Dahal, K. (2019). Remote patient monitoring: A comprehensive study. *Journal of Ambient Intelligence and Humanized Computing*, 10(1), 57–76. 10.1007/s12652-017-0598-x

Mangaraj, B. K., & Aparajita, U. (2010). Cultural Dimension in the Future of Pervasive Computing. Ubiquitous and Pervasive Computing, 974–992. https://doi.org/10.4018/978-1-60566-960-1.ch060

Mascagni, P., Alapatt, D., Sestini, L., Altieri, M. S., Madani, A., Watanabe, Y., & Hashimoto, D. A. (2022). Computer vision in surgery: From potential to clinical value. *npj. Digital Medicine*, 5(1), 163.36307544

Mason, D. J., & Jones, D. A. (2021). Bridging the digital divide: Strategies for improving access to healthcare technology. *Journal of Nursing Scholarship*, 53(2), 129–138.

Compilation of References

Mathew, M., Chakrabortty, R. K., & Ryan, M. J. (2020). A novel approach integrating AHP and TOPSIS under spherical fuzzy sets for advanced manufacturing system selection. *Engineering Applications of Artificial Intelligence*, 96, 103988. 10.1016/j.engappai.2020.103988

Mathur, K. (2015). Review and Future Prospects of Ubiquitous Computing. *Indian journal of Research, Palak Chauhan, 4.*

Ma, X., Liu, T., Liu, S., Kacimi, R., & Dhaou, R. (2020). Priority-Based Data Collection for UAV-Aided Mobile Sensor Network. *Sensors (Basel)*, 20(11), 3034. 10.3390/s2011303432471092

Mbiyana, K., Kans, M., & Campos, J. (2021, December). A data-driven approach for gravel road maintenance. In *2021 International Conference on Maintenance and Intelligent Asset Management* (ICMIAM) (pp. 1-6). IEEE. 10.1109/ICMIAM54662.2021.9715196

McCormick, J. B., & Greenberg, J. (2019). Ethical considerations in the use of telehealth technologies. *Telemedicine Journal and e-Health*, 25(10), 939–944.

McGee, J. A., & Campbell, J. B. (2019). The sUAS Educational Frontier: Mapping an Educational Pathway for the Future Workforce. In *Applications of Small Unmanned Aircraft Systems* (pp. 57–79). CRC Press. 10.1201/9780429244117-4

Mejia, J. M. R., & Rawat, D. B. (2022b). Recent advances in a medical domain metaverse: status, challenges, and perspective. *2022 Thirteenth International Conference on Ubiquitous and Future Networks (ICUFN)*. IEEE. 10.1109/ICUFN55119.2022.9829645

Menkhoff, T., Kan, S. N., Tan, E. K., & Foong, S. (2022). Future-proofing students in higher education with unmanned aerial vehicles technology: A knowledge management case study. *Knowledge Management & E-Learning: An International Journal*, 14(2), 223–244. 10.34105/j.kmel.2022.14.013

Merei, A., Mcheick, H., & Ghaddar, A. (2023). Survey on Path Planning for UAVs in Healthcare Missions. *Journal of Medical Systems*, 47(1), 79. 10.1007/s10916-023-01972-x37498478

Mesas-Carrascosa, F. J., Pérez Porras, F., Triviño-Tarradas, P., Meroño de Larriva, J. E., & García-Ferrer, A. (2019). Project-based learning applied to unmanned aerial systems and remote sensing. *Remote Sensing (Basel)*, 11(20), 2413. 10.3390/rs11202413

Meshram, V. (2016). *A Survey On Ubiquitous Computing*. Department of Computer Engineering, Vishwakarma Institute of Information Technology, India.10.21917/ijsc.2016.0157

Mihai, S., Yaqoob, M., Hung, D. V., Davis, W., Towakel, P., Raza, M., Karamanoglu, M., Barn, B., Shetve, D., Prasad, R. V., Venkataraman, H., Trestian, R., & Nguyen, H. X. (2022). Digital twins: A survey on enabling technologies, challenges, trends and future prospects. *IEEE Communications Surveys and Tutorials*, 24(4), 2255–2291. 10.1109/COMST.2022.3208773

Mir, M. H., Jamwal, S., Islam, S., & Khan, Q. R. (2021). Machine learning techniques and computing technologies for IoT based smart healthcare (COVID-19 case study). In *2021 3rd International Conference on Advances in Computing, Communication Control and Networking (ICAC3N)* (pp. 2089-2095). IEEE.

Montazeri, A., Can, A., & Imran, I. H. (2021). Unmanned aerial systems: autonomy, cognition, and control. In *Unmanned aerial systems* (pp. 47–80). Academic Press. 10.1016/B978-0-12-820276-0.00010-8

Morley, J., Machado, C. C., & Silva, C. A. (2020). The ethics of artificial intelligence in healthcare: A review. *Health and Technology*, 10(6), 1029–1038.

Motlagh, N., Taleb, T., & Arouk, O. (2016). Low-altitude unmanned aerial vehicles-based internet of things services: Comprehensive survey and future perspectives. *IEEE Internet of Things Journal, 3*(6).

Motlagh, N. H., Bagaa, M., & Taleb, T. (2017). UAV-based IoT platform: A crowd surveillance use case. *IEEE Communications Magazine*, 55(2), 128–134. 10.1109/MCOM.2017.1600587CM

Motlagh, N. H., Bagaa, M., Taleb, T., & Song, J. (2017). Connection steering mechanism between mobile networks for reliable UAV's IoT platform. In *Proceedings of the 2017 IEEE International Conference on Communications (ICC)*, Paris, France. 10.1109/ICC.2017.7996718

Motlagh, N. H., Taleb, T., & Arouk, O. (2016). Low-Altitude Unmanned Aerial Vehicles-Based Internet of Things Services: Comprehensive Survey and Future Perspectives. *IEEE Internet of Things Journal*, 3(6), 899–922. 10.1109/JIOT.2016.2612119

Mozaffari, M., Saad, W., Bennis, M., & Debbah, M. (2016). Unmanned Aerial Vehicle With Underlaid Device-to-Device Communications: Performance and Tradeoffs. *IEEE Transactions on Wireless Communications*, 15(6), 3949–3963. 10.1109/TWC.2016.2531652

Mozumder, M. I., Armand, T. P. T., Uddin, S. M. I., Athar, A., Sumon, R. I., Hussain, A., & Kim, H. C. (2023). Metaverse for Digital Anti-Aging Healthcare: An overview of potential use cases based on artificial intelligence, blockchain, IoT technologies, its challenges, and future directions. *Applied Sciences (Basel, Switzerland)*, 13(8), 5127. 10.3390/app13085127

Munawar, H. S., Inam, H., Ullah, F., Qayyum, S., Kouzani, A. Z., & Mahmud, M. P. (2021). Towards smart healthcare: Uav-based optimized path planning for delivering COVID-19 self-testing kits using cutting edge technologies. *Sustainability (Basel)*, 13(18), 10426. 10.3390/su131810426

Murala, D. K., Panda, S. K., & Dash, S. P. (2023). MedMetaverse: Medical Care of Chronic Disease Patients and Managing Data Using Artificial Intelligence, Blockchain, and Wearable Devices State-of-the-Art Methodology. *IEEE Access : Practical Innovations, Open Solutions*, 11, 138954–138985. 10.1109/ACCESS.2023.3340791

Musamih, A., Yaqoob, I., Salah, K., Jayaraman, R., Al-Hammadi, Y., Omar, M., & Ellahham, S. (2023b). Metaverse in healthcare: Applications, challenges, and future directions. *IEEE Consumer Electronics Magazine*, 12(4), 33–46. 10.1109/MCE.2022.3223522

Mystakidis, S. (2022). Metaverse. *Encyclopedia*, 2(1), 486–497. 10.3390/encyclopedia2010031

Naeem, K., Riaz, M., & Karaaslan, F. (2021). A mathematical approach to medical diagnosis via pythagorean fuzzy soft TOPSIS, VIKOR and generalized aggregation operators. *Complex & Intelligent Systems*, 7(5), 2783–2795. 10.1007/s40747-021-00458-y

Compilation of References

Nagesh, H. R., Prasad, G., Shivaraj, B. G., Jain, D., Puneeth, B. R., & Anadkumar, M. (2022, December). E-Voting System Using Blockchain Technology. In *2022 4th International Conference on Advances in Computing, Communication Control and Networking (ICAC3N)* (pp. 2106-2111). IEEE.

Nagesh, H. R., & Prabhu, S. (2017). High performance computation of big data: Performance optimization approach towards a parallel frequent item set mining algorithm for transaction data based on hadoop MapReduce framework. *International Journal of Intelligent Systems and Applications*, 9(1), 75–84. 10.5815/ijisa.2017.01.08

Nair, S., & Choi, K. S. (2021). Frameworks for compliance in emerging virtual health care environments. *Health Law Journal*, 28(4), 304–317.

Namasudra, S., & Deka, G. C. (Eds.). (2021). *Applications of blockchain in healthcare* (Vol. 83). Springer. 10.1007/978-981-15-9547-9

Narang, M., Liu, W., Gutierrez, J., & Chiaraviglio, L. (2017). A cyber physical buses-and-drones mobile edge infrastructure for large scale disaster emergency communications. *2017 IEEE 37th International Conference on Distributed Computing Systems Workshops (ICDCSW)*. IEEE.

Nawaz, H., Ali, H. M., & Laghari, A. A. (2021). UAV communication networks issues: A review. *Archives of Computational Methods in Engineering*, 28(3), 1349–1369. 10.1007/s11831-020-09418-0

Ning, H., Wang, H., Lin, Y., Wang, W., Dhelim, S., Farha, F., Ding, J., & Daneshmand, M. (2021). A survey on metaverse: the state-of-the-art, technologies, applications, and challenges, , arXiv preprint arXiv:2111.09673.

O'Neill, E., Conlan, O., & Lewis, D. (2013). Situation-based testing for pervasive computing environments. *Pervasive and Mobile Computing*, 9(1), 76–97. https://doi.org/10.1016/j.pmcj.2011.12.002

Ochella, S., Shafiee, M., & Sansom, C. (2021, September). Requirements for Standards and Regulations in AI-Enabled Prognostics and Health Management. In *2021 26th International Conference on Automation and Computing* (ICAC) (pp. 1-6). IEEE. https://doi.org/10.23919/ICAC50006.2021.9594069

Ochella, S., Shafiee, M., & Dinmohammadi, F. (2022). Artificial intelligence in prognostics and health management of engineering systems. *Engineering Applications of Artificial Intelligence*, 108, 104552. 10.1016/j.engappai.2021.104552

Omkumar, C. U., Sudhakaran, G., Balaji, V., Nhaveen, A., & Balakrishnan, S. (2023). Securing healthcare data through blockchain enabled collaborative machine learning. *Solftcomputing*, 27, 9941–9954.

Onik, M. M. H., Aich, S., Yang, J., Kim, C. S., & Kim, H. C. (2019). Blockchain in healthcare: Challenges and solutions. In *Big data analytics for intelligent healthcare management* (pp. 197–226). Academic Press.

Ouahouah, S., Taleb, T., Song, J., & Benzaid, C. (2017). *Efficient offloading mechanism for UAVs-based value added services*. In *Proceedings of the 2017 IEEE International Conference on Communications (ICC)*, Paris, France. 10.1109/ICC.2017.7997362

Ozturkcan, S. (2023). Technology and disaster relief: The Türkiye-Syria earthquake case study. In L. Aldieri (Ed.), *Innovation-Research and development for human, economic and institutional growth*.

Pai, A., Anandkumar, M., Prasad, G., Agarwal, J., & Christa, S. (2023, January). Designing a Secure Audio/Text Based Captcha Using Neural Network. In *2023 13th International Conference on Cloud Computing, Data Science & Engineering (Confluence)* (pp. 510-514). IEEE.

Pal, M., Arora, H. D., Kumar, V., & Kumar, D. S. (2019). Application of TOPSIS in the Diagnosis of Vector Borne Diseases. *International Journal of Engineering and Advanced Technology*, 8(6), 5217–5223. 10.35940/ijeat.F8585.088619

Pandey, A., Chirputkar, A., & Ashok, P. (2023b). Metaverse: An Innovative Model for Healthcare Domain. *IEEE-2023 International Conference on Innovative Data Communication Technologies and Application (ICIDCA)*. IEEE. 10.1109/ICIDCA56705.2023.10099764

Parisi, T. (2015). *Learning virtual reality: Developing immersive experiences and applications for desktop, web, and mobile*. O'Reilly Media, Inc.

Parisot, S., Ktena, S. I., Ferrante, E., Lee, M., Moreno, R. G., Glocker, B., & Rueckert, D. (2017). Spectral graph convolutions for population-based disease prediction. In *Proceedings of the Medical Image Computing and Computer Assisted Intervention*, Quebec City, QC, Canada. 10.1007/978-3-319-66179-7_21

Park, Y. C. (2014). Pervasive Computing and Communication Technologies for U-learning. *Journal of International Education Research (JIER), 10*(4), 265–270. https://www.aicte-india.org/sites/default/files/40-35_AICTE_SWAYAM_EOI_2017.pdf10.19030/jier.v10i4.8836

Patil, A. V., Somasundaram, K. V., & Goyal, R. C. (2002). Current health scenario in rural India. *The Australian Journal of Rural Health*, 10(2), 129–135. 10.1111/j.1440-1584.2002.tb00022.x12047509

Paucar, C., Morales, L., Pinto, K., Sánchez, M., Rodríguez, R., Gutierrez, M., & Palacios, L. (2018). Use of drones for surveillance and reconnaissance of military areas. In *Developments and Advances in Defense and Security:Proceedings of the Multidisciplinary International Conference of Research Applied to Defense and Security (MICRADS 2018)* (pp. 119-132). Springer International Publishing. 10.1007/978-3-319-78605-6_10

Pereira, A. (2016). *Pervasive Business Intelligence: A New Trend in Critical Healthcare*. EU-SPN/ICTH.

Poljak, M., & Šterbenc, A. J. C. M. (2020). Use of drones in clinical microbiology and infectious diseases: Current status, challenges and barriers. *Clinical Microbiology and Infection*, 26(4), 425–430. 10.1016/j.cmi.2019.09.01431574337

Compilation of References

Prabhu, S., Rodrigues, A. P., Prasad, G., & Nagesh, H. R. (2015, March). Performance enhancement of Hadoop MapReduce framework for analyzing BigData. In *2015 IEEE International Conference on Electrical, Computer and Communication Technologies (ICECCT)* (pp. 1-8). IEEE. 10.1109/ICECCT.2015.7226049

Prasad, G., Gujjar, P., Kumar, H. N., Kumar, M. A., & Chandrappa, S. (2023). Advances of Cyber Security in the Healthcare Domain for Analyzing Data. In *Cyber Trafficking, Threat Behavior, and Malicious Activity Monitoring for Healthcare Organizations* (pp. 1-14). IGI Global.

Prasad, M. G., Kumar, D. S., Pratap, M. S., Kiran, J., Chandrappa, S., & Kotiyal, A. (2023, June). Enhanced Prediction of Heart Disease Using Machine Learning and Deep Learning. In *International Conference on Advanced Communication and Intelligent Systems* (pp. 1-12). Cham: Springer Nature Switzerland. 10.1007/978-3-031-45121-8_1

Prasad, G., Jain, A. K., Jain, P., & Nagesh, H. R.Nagesh H. R. (2019). A Novel Approach to Optimize the Performance of Hadoop Frameworks for Sentiment Analysis. [IJOSSP]. *International Journal of Open Source Software and Processes*, 10(4), 44–59. 10.4018/IJOSSP.2019100103

Prasad, G., Kumar, A. S., Srivastava, S., Srivastava, A., & Srivastava, A. (2023). An iomt and machine learning model aimed at the development of a personalized lifestyle recommendation system facilitating improved health. In *Dynamics of Swarm Intelligence Health Analysis for the Next Generation* (pp. 162–185). IGI Global. 10.4018/978-1-6684-6894-4.ch009

Prasad, M. G., Agarwal, J., Christa, S., Pai, H. A., Kumar, M. A., & Kukreti, A. (2023, January). An Improved Water Body Segmentation from Satellite Images using MSAA-Net. In *2023 International Conference on Machine Intelligence for GeoAnalytics and Remote Sensing (MIGARS)* (Vol. 1, pp. 1-4). IEEE. 10.1109/MIGARS57353.2023.10064508

Prasad, M. G., Pratap, M. S., Jain, P., Gujjar, J. P., Kumar, M. A., & Kukreti, A. (2022, December). RDI-SD: An Efficient Rice Disease Identification based on Apache Spark and Deep Learning Technique. In *2022 International Conference on Artificial Intelligence and Data Engineering (AIDE)* (pp. 277-282). IEEE. 10.1109/AIDE57180.2022.10060157

Pratima, S., Rao, M., Namasudra, S., Vimal, S., & Ching-Hsien, H. (2021). *Blockchain-based IoT architecture to secure healthcare system using identity-based encryption.* Wiley.

Prawiyogi, A. G., Purnama, S., & Meria, L. (2022). Smart Cities Using Machine Learning and Intelligent Applications. *International Transactions on Artificial Intelligence*, 1(1), 102–116. 10.33050/italic.v1i1.204

Priyadarshini, S. B. B., Bagjadab, A. B., & Mishra, B. K. (2020). A brief overview of natural language processing and artificial intelligence. *Natural Language Processing in Artificial Intelligence*, 211-224.

Puthal, D., Malik, N., Mohanty, S. P., Kougianos, E., & Das, G. (2018). Everything you wanted to know about the Blockchain: Its Promise, Components, Processes, and Problems. *IEEE Consumer Electronics Magazine*, 7(4), 6–14. 10.1109/MCE.2018.2816299

Qin, Z., Dong, C., Wang, W., & Xu, Z. (2019). Trajectory Planning for Data Collection of Energy-Constrained Heterogeneous UAVs. *Sensors (Basel)*, 19(22), 4884. 10.3390/s1922488431717421

Qin, Z., Li, A., Dong, C., Dai, H., & Xu, Z. (2019). Completion Time Minimization for Multi-UAV InformationCollection via Trajectory Planning. *Sensors (Basel)*, 19(18), 4032. 10.3390/s1918403231540537

Qiu, M., Zhang, L., Ming, Z., Chen, Z., Qin, X., & Yang, L. T. (2013). Security-aware optimization for ubiquitous computing systems with SEAT graph approach. *Journal of Computer and System Sciences*, 79(5), 518–529. 10.1016/j.jcss.2012.11.002

Qu, Q., Hatami, M., Xu, R., Nagothu, D., Chen, Y., Li, X.E., Blasch, E., Ardiles-Cruz, E. & Chen, G. (2024). *Microverse: A Task-Oriented Edge-Scale Metaverse.*

Quan, C., & Guo, P. (2021). A local search method based on edge age strategy for minimum vertex cover problem in massive graphs. [CrossRef] [Google Scholar]. *Expert Systems with Applications*, 182, 115185. 10.1016/j.eswa.2021.115185

Radha, S., & Babu, C. (2018). An Enhancement of Cloud Based Sentiment Analysis and BDAAs Using SVM Based Lexicon Dictionary and Adaptive Resource Scheduling. *Journal of Computational and Theoretical Nanoscience*, 15(2), 437–445. 10.1166/jctn.2018.7107

Rajamani, R. (2020). *Unsettled Issues Concerning Integrated Vehicle Health Management Systems and Maintenance Credits* (No. EPR2020006). SAE Technical Paper. https://doi.org/10.4271/epr2020006

Rakhimberdina, Z., Liu, X., & Murata, T. (2020). Population Graph-Based Multi-Model Ensemble Method for Diagnosing Autism Spectrum Disorder. *Sensors (Basel)*, 20(21), 6001. 10.3390/s2021600133105909

Ranasinghe, K., Sabatini, R., Gardi, A., Bijjahalli, S., Kapoor, R., Fahey, T., & Thangavel, K. (2022). Advances in Integrated System Health Management for mission-essential and safety-critical aerospace applications. *Progress in Aerospace Sciences*, 128, 100758. 10.1016/j.paerosci.2021.100758

Richardson, D., Kinnear, B., Hauer, K. E., Turner, T. L., Warm, E. J., Hall, A. K., Ross, S., Thoma, B., & Van Melle, E.ICBME Collaborators. (2021). Growth mindset in competency-based medical education. *Medical Teacher*, 43(7), 751–757. 10.1080/0142159X.2021.192803634410891

Román, A., Heredia, S., Windle, A. E., Tovar-Sánchez, A., & Navarro, G. (2024). Enhancing Georeferencing and Mosaicking Techniques over Water Surfaces with High-Resolution Unmanned Aerial Vehicle (UAV) Imagery. *Remote Sensing (Basel)*, 16(2), 290. 10.3390/rs16020290

Rong, G., Mendez, A., Bou Assi, E., Zhao, B., & Sawan, M. (2020). Arnaldo Mendez, Elie Bou Assi, Bo Zhao, Mohamad Sawan: Artificial Intelligence in Healthcare: Review and Prediction Case Studies, Elsevier. *Engineering (Beijing)*, 6(3), 291–301. 10.1016/j.eng.2019.08.015

Roth, M. (2019). *Computer vision in healthcare–current applications.*

Compilation of References

Saaty, T. L. (1988). The analytic hierarchy process, (2nd ed). New York: McGraw-Hill.

Sabatini, R., Roy, A., Blasch, E., Kramer, K. A., Fasano, G., Majid, I., & Major, R. O. (2020). Avionics systems panel research and innovation perspectives. *IEEE Aerospace and Electronic Systems Magazine*, 35(12), 58–72. 10.1109/MAES.2020.3033475

Saha, D. (2005). *Pervasive computing: A vision to Realize.* Elsevier. .10.1016/S0065-2458(04)64005-8

Samarati, P., & de Vimercati, S. C. (2000). Access control: Policies, models, and mechanisms. In *International school on foundations of security analysis and design* (pp. 137–196). Springer Berlin Heidelberg.

Sanchez-Aguero, V., Valera, F., Vidal, I., Tipantuna, C., & Hesselbach, X. (2020). Energy-Aware Management in Multi-UAV Deployments: Modelling and Strategies. *Sensors (Basel)*, 20(10), 2791. 10.3390/s2010279132422970

Sang, Y. L. (2019). Medical Data Framework Using Blockchain Technology. *International Journal of Advanced Trends in Computer Science and Engineering*, 8(5).

Saunders, J., Saeedi, S., & Li, W. (2024). Autonomous aerial robotics for package delivery: A technical review. *Journal of Field Robotics*, 41(1), 3–49. 10.1002/rob.22231

Schmalstieg, D., Schall, G., Wagner, D., Barakonyi, I., Reitmayr, G., Newman, J., & Ledermann, F. (2007). Managing complex augmented reality models. *IEEE Computer Graphics and Applications*, 27(4), 48–57. 10.1109/MCG.2007.8517713234

Schulz, S. (2019). Standards in healthcare data. *Fundamentals of Clinical Data Science*, 19-26.

Scott, M. J., Verhagen, W. J., Bieber, M. T., & Marzocca, P. (2022). A Systematic Literature Review of Predictive Maintenance for Defence Fixed-Wing Aircraft Sustainment and Operations. *Sensors (Basel)*, 22(18), 7070. 10.3390/s2218707036146419

Shaikh, Z., Baidya, S., & Levorato, M. (2018). Robust Multi-Path Communications for UAVs in the Urban IoT. In *Proceedings of the 2018 IEEE International Conference on Sensing, Communication and Networking (SECON Workshops)*, (pp. 1–5). IEEE. 10.1109/SECONW.2018.8396356

Shankar, N., Nallakaruppan, M. K., Ravindranath, V., Senthilkumar, M., & Bhagavath, B. P. (2022). Smart IoMT Framework for Supporting UAV Systems with AI. *Electronics (Basel)*, 12(1), 86. 10.3390/electronics12010086

Sharma, S. (2013). *Embedded Systems -- A Security Paradigm for Pervasive Computing, Surendra Sharma*. Semantic Scholar.

Sherlaw-Johnson, C., Gallivan, S., Treasure, T., & Nashef, S. A. M. (2004). Computer tools to assist the monitoring of outcomes in surgery. *European Journal of Cardio-Thoracic Surgery*, 26(5), 1032–1036. 10.1016/j.ejcts.2004.07.02615519199

Shi, S., He, D., Li, L., Kumar, N., Khan, M. K., & Choo, K. R. (2020, October). Applications of blockchain in ensuring the security and privacy of electronic health record systems: A survey. *Computers & Security*, 97, 101966. 10.1016/j.cose.2020.10196632834254

Shukla, B., Fan, I. S., & Jennions, I. (2020, July). Opportunities for explainable artificial intelligence in aerospace predictive maintenance. In *PHM Society European Conference* (Vol. 5, No. 1, pp. 11-11). IEEE. 10.36001/phme.2020.v5i1.1231

Singh, P., Tripathi, V., Singh, K. D., Guru Prasad, M. S., & Aditya Pai, H. (2023, April). A Task Scheduling Algorithm for Optimizing Quality of Service in Smart Healthcare System. In *International Conference on IoT, Intelligent Computing and Security: Select Proceedings of IICS 2021* (pp. 43-50). Singapore: Springer Nature Singapore. 10.1007/978-981-19-8136-4_4

Skalidis, I., Muller, O., & Fournier, S. (2023). CardioVerse: The cardiovascular medicine in the era of Metaverse. *Trends in Cardiovascular Medicine*, 33(8), 471–476. 10.1016/j.tcm.2022.05.00435568263

Slater, M., Gonzalez-Liencres, C., Haggard, P., Vinkers, C., Gregory-Clarke, R., Jelley, S., Watson, Z., Breen, G., Schwarz, R., Steptoe, W., Szostak, D., Halan, S., Fox, D., & Silver, J. (2020). The Ethics of Realism in Virtual and Augmented Reality. *Frontiers in Virtual Reality*, 1, 1. 10.3389/frvir.2020.00001

Smith, A. C., Thomas, E., Snoswell, J. A., Haydon, H., & Caffery, L. J. (2020). Telehealth for patients with chronic disease: A review of the evidence. *Journal of Telemedicine and Telecare*, 26(5), 283–293.32196391

Sonali, V., Mohammad, S., Prajjawal, P., Rama Parvathy, L., & Issac, O. (2022). Integration of Artificial Intelligence and Blockchain Technology in Healthcare and Agriculture,Hindawi. *Journal of Food Quality*.

Song, Y., & Qin, J. (2022b). Metaverse and personal healthcare. *Procedia Computer Science*, 210, 189–197. 10.1016/j.procs.2022.10.136

Srivastav, A., & Sharma, A. (2022). *Healthcare Platform for Online Consultation*.

Stalling, D., Westerhoff, M., & Hege, H. C. (2005). Amira: A highly interactive system for visual data analysis. *The visualization handbook, 38*, 749-67.

Stanberry, B. (2000). Telemedicine: Barriers and opportunities in the 21st century. *Journal of Internal Medicine*, 247(6), 615–628. 10.1046/j.1365-2796.2000.00699.x10886483

Stephenson, N. (1992). *Snow Crash*. Bantam Books.

Subramanian, C. (2021, February). An appraisal on intelligent and smart systems. In *AIP Conference Proceedings (Vol. 2316*, No. 1). AIP Publishing. 10.1063/5.0037534

Sudeep, T., Karan, P., & Richard, E. (2020). Blockchain-based electronic healthcare record system for healthcare 4.0 applications. *Journal of Information Security and Applications, 50*.

Compilation of References

Sun, H., Duo, B., Wang, Z., Lin, X., & Gao, C. (2019). Aerial Cooperative Jamming for Cellular-Enabled UAV Secure Communication Network: Joint Trajectory and Power Control Design. *Sensors (Basel)*, 19(20), 4440. 10.3390/s1920444031614986

Sun, Z., Purohit, A., Pan, S., Mokaya, F., Bose, R., & Zhang, P. (2012). Polaris: Getting accurate indoor orientations for mobile devices using ubiquitous visual patterns on ceilings. *Proceedings of the Twelfth Workshop on Mobile Computing Systems & Applications*. ACM. 10.1145/2162081.2162101

Suzuki, S. N., Kanematsu, H., Barry, D. M., Ogawa, N., Yajima, K., Nakahira, K. T., Shirai, T., Kawaguchi, M., Kobayashi, T., & Yoshitake, M. (2020). Virtual Experiments in Metaverse and their Applications to Collaborative Projects: The framework and its significance. *Procedia Computer Science*, 176, 2125–2132. 10.1016/j.procs.2020.09.249

Szeliski, R. (2022). *Computer vision: algorithms and applications*. Springer Nature. Chen, X., & Konukoglu, E. (2022). Unsupervised abnormality detection in medical images with deep generative methods. In *Biomedical Image Synthesis and Simulation* (pp. 303–324). Academic Press.

Tailor, J. H. (2012). Green it: Sustainability Plan of Green Computing. *Global Journal for Research Analysis*, 3(4), 38–39. https://doi.org/10.15373/22778160/apr2014/13

Tan, T. F., Li, Y., Lim, J., Gunasekeran, D. V., Teo, Z. L., Ng, W. Y., & Ting, D. S. (2022). Metaverse and Virtual Health Care in Ophthalmology: Opportunities and Challenges. *Asia-Pacific Journal of Ophthalmology, 11*(3), 237–246. .10.1097/APO.0000000000000537

Tanglay, O., Dadario, N. B., Chong, E. H. N., Tang, S. J., Young, I. M., & Sughrue, M. E. (2023). Graph Theory Measures and Their Application to Neurosurgical Eloquence. *Cancers (Basel)*, 15(2), 556. 10.3390/cancers1502055636672504

Tang, X., Yung, K. L., & Hu, B. (2022). Reliability and health management of spacecraft. In *IoT and Spacecraft Informatics* (pp. 307–335). Elsevier. 10.1016/B978-0-12-821051-2.00012-X

Tao, F., Zhang, M., Liu, Y., & Nee, A. Y. C. (2019). Digital twin-driven smart manufacturing: Connotation, reference model, applications and research issues. *Robotics and Computer-integrated Manufacturing*, 61, 101–112.

Taylor, A. (2009). Ethnography in Ubiquitous Computing. Ubiquitous Computing Fundamentals, 203–236. https://doi.org/10.1201/9781420093612.ch5

Tedeschi, P., Al Nuaimi, F. A., Awad, A. I., & Natalizio, E. (2023). Privacy-Aware Remote Identification for Unmanned Aerial Vehicles: Current Solutions, Potential Threats, and Future Directions. *IEEE Transactions on Industrial Informatics*.

Thibault, G. E. (2020). The future of health professions education: Emerging trends in the United States. *FASEB bioAdvances*, 2(12), 685–694. 10.1096/fba.2020-0006133336156

Tiwari, A., Dhiman, V., Iesa, M. A. M., Alsarhan, H., Mehbodniya, A., & Shabaz, M. (2021). Patient behavioral analysis with smart healthcare and IoT. *Behavioural Neurology*, 2021, 1–9. 10.1155/2021/402876134900023

Tomita, R. M., Russ, S. L., Sridhar, R., & Naughton, M. B. J. (2010). Smart home with healthcare technologies for community-dwelling older adults. *Smart Home Systems.*, 1, 139–158. 10.5772/8411

Tripathi, G., Abdul Ahad, M., & Paiva, S. (2020). SMS: A Secure Healthcare Model for Smart Cities. *Electronics (Basel)*, 9(7), 1135. 10.3390/electronics9071135

Turab, M., & Jamil, S. (2023). A comprehensive survey of digital twins in healthcare in the era of Metaverse. *BioMedInformatics*, 3(3), 563–584. 10.3390/biomedinformatics3030039

Ullah, H., Manickam, S., Obaidat, M., Laghari, S. A., & Uddin, M. (2023). Exploring the potential of metaverse technology in healthcare: Applications, challenges, and future directions. *IEEE Access : Practical Innovations, Open Solutions*, 11, 69686–69707. 10.1109/ACCESS.2023.3286696

Ullah, S., Kim, K. I., Kim, K. H., Imran, M., Khan, P., Tovar, E., & Ali, F. (2019). UAV-enabled healthcare architecture: Issues and challenges. *Future Generation Computer Systems*, 97, 425–432. 10.1016/j.future.2019.01.028

Uma Maheswaran, S. K., Gaganpreet, K., Pankajam, A., Firos, A., Piyush, V., Vikas, T., & Hussien, S. (2022). Empirical Analysis for Improving Food Quality Using Artificial Intelligence Technology for Enhancing Healthcare Sector. *Journal of Food Quality*, 2022, 1–13. 10.1155/2022/1447326

United States Government. (n.d.). *Data Catalog* [Dataset]. United States Government. https://catalog.data.gov/dataset

Vachtsevanos, G., & Rajamani, R. (2023). Criticality of Prognostics in the Operations of Autonomous Aircraft. *SAE International Journal of Aerospace*, 16. 10.4271/01-16-03-0022

Vazirani, , A. (2019). Implementing Blockchains for Efficient Healthcare: Systematic Review. *Journal of Medical Internet Research*, 2.

Verghese, A., & Shah, N. H. (2017). Virtual care and the future of medicine: A review of telemedicine. *Health Affairs*, 36(12), 2182–2188.

Verhagen, W. J., Santos, B. F., Freeman, F., van Kessel, P., Zarouchas, D., Loutas, T., Yeun, R. C. K., & Heiets, I. (2023). Condition-Based Maintenance in Aviation: Challenges and Opportunities. *Aerospace (Basel, Switzerland)*, 10(9), 762. 10.3390/aerospace10090762

Vijitha Ananthi, J., & Subha Hency Jose, P. (2023). Optimal design of artificial bee colony based UAV routing (ABCUR) algorithm for healthcare applications. *International Journal of Intelligent Unmanned Systems*, 11(2), 285–295. 10.1108/IJIUS-08-2021-0099

Villari, M., Fazio, M., Dustdar, S., Rana, O., & Ranjan, R. (2016). Osmoticcomputing: A new paradigm for edge/cloud integration. *IEEE Cloud Computing*, 3(6), 76–83. 10.1109/MCC.2016.124

Vogl, G. W., Weiss, B. A., & Helu, M. (2019). A review of diagnostic and prognostic capabilities and best practices for manufacturing. *Journal of Intelligent Manufacturing*, 30(1), 79–95. 10.1007/s10845-016-1228-830820072

Compilation of References

Walthall, R. (2020). *Unsettled Topics on the Use of IVHM in the Active Control Loop* (No. EPR2020011). SAE Technical Paper. 10.4271/epr2020011

Wang, N., Christen, M. & Hunt, M. (2021). *Ethical Considerations Associated with "Humanitarian Drones": A Scoping.* Springer.

Wang, D., Bai, L., Zhang, X., Guan, W., & Chen, C. (2012). Collaborative relay beamforming strategies for multiple destinations with guaranteed QoS in wireless machine-to-machine networks. *International Journal of Distributed Sensor Networks*, 8(8), 525640. 10.1155/2012/525640

Wang, J., Liang, S., He, D., Wang, Y., Wu, Y., & Zhang, Y. (2020). A Sequential Graph Convolutional Network with Frequency-domain Complex Network of EEG Signals for Epilepsy Detection. *Proceedings of the 2020 IEEE International Conference on Bioinformatics and Biomedicine (BIBM)*, Seoul, Korea. 10.1109/BIBM49941.2020.9313232

Wang, J., Liu, Y., & Song, H. (2021). Counter-unmanned aircraft system (s)(C-UAS): State of the art, challenges, and future trends. *IEEE Aerospace and Electronic Systems Magazine*, 36(3), 4–29. 10.1109/MAES.2020.3015537

Wang, J., Xia, C., Sharma, A., Gaba, G. S., & Shabaz, M. (2021). Chest CT findings and differential diagnosis of mycoplasma pneumonia and mycoplasma pneumonia combine with streptococcal pneumonia in children. *Journal of Healthcare Engineering*, 1–10.

Wang, N. (2021). "As it is Africa, it is ok"? Ethical considerations of development use of drones for delivery in Malawi. *IEEE Transactions on Technology and Society*, 2(1), 20–30. 10.1109/TTS.2021.3058669

Wang, S., Ouyang, L., Yuan, Y., Ni, X., Han, X., & Wang, F. Y. (2019). Blockchain enabled smart contracts: Architecture, applications, and future trends. *IEEE Transactions on Systems, Man, and Cybernetics. Systems*, 49(11), 2266–2277. 10.1109/TSMC.2019.2895123

Want, R. (2009). An Introduction to Ubiquitous Computing. Ubiquitous Computing Fundamentals, 1–35. https://doi.org/10.1201/9781420093612.ch1

Wolfe, F., Ross, K., Anderson, J., Russell, I. J., & Hebert, L. (1995). The prevalence and characteristics of Fibromyalgia in the general population. *Arthritis and Rheumatism*, 38(1), 19–28. 10.1002/art.17803801047818567

World Data. (n.d.). *Healthcare.* [Dataset]. World Data. https://data.world/datasets/healthcare

World Health Organization. (2019). *World health statistics overview 2019: monitoring health for the SDGs, sustainable development goals (No. WHO/DAD/2019.1).* World Health Organization.

World Health Organization. (2022). *Health workforce in India: where to invest, how much and why?* WHO.

Wu, T., & Ho, C. B. (2023b). A scoping review of metaverse in emergency medicine. *Australasian Emergency Care (Online)*, 26(1), 75–83. 10.1016/j.auec.2022.08.00235953392

Xiaoguang, L., Ziqing, W., Chunhua, J., Fagen, L., & Gaoping, Li. (2016). A Blockchain-based Medical Data Sharing and Protection Scheme. *IEEE Access : Practical Innovations, Open Solutions*, 4, 1–11.

Xiaomin, Du. (2021). Research on the Application of Blockchain in Smart Healthcare: Constructing a Hierarchical Framework. *Journal of Healthcare Engineering*.

Xie, L., Su, Z., Xu, Q., Chen, N., Fan, Y., & Benslimane, A. (2024). A Secure UAV Cooperative Communication Framework: Prospect Theory Based Approach. *IEEE Transactions on Mobile Computing*, 1–16. 10.1109/TMC.2024.3367124

Xie, T., & Qin, X. (2005). A new allocation scheme for parallel applications with deadline and security constraints on cluster. *Proc. of the 7th IEEE International Conference on Cluster Computing*, (pp. 1–10). IEEE. 10.1109/CLUSTR.2005.347057

Xie, Y., Xu, X., & Wang, X. (2021). A survey on data privacy and security issues in virtual healthcare environments. *Journal of Medical Systems*, 45(8), 1–12.

Xi, N., Chen, J., Gama, F., Riar, M., & Hamari, J. (2022). The challenges of entering the metaverse: An experiment on the effect of extended reality on workload. *Information Systems Frontiers*, 1–22. 10.1007/s10796-022-10244-x35194390

Xu, C., Liao, X., Tan, J., Ye, H., & Lu, H. (2020). Recent research progress of unmanned aerial vehicle regulation policies and technologies in urban low altitude. *IEEE Access : Practical Innovations, Open Solutions*, 8, 74175–74194. 10.1109/ACCESS.2020.2987622

Yang, C., Tampubolon, H., Setyoko, A., Hua, K., Tanveer M., & Wei, W. (2023). Secure and Privacy-Preserving Human Interaction Recognition of Pervasive Healthcare Monitoring. *IEEE Transactions on Network Science and Engineering, 10*(5), 2439-2454. .10.1109/TNSE.2022.3223281

Yang, D. (2022). *Expert consensus on the metaverse in medicine*. Clinical eHealth.

Yang, H., Li, X., Wu, Y., Li, S., Lu, S., Duncan, J. S., Gee, J. C., & Gu, S. (2019). Interpretable multimodality embedding of cerebral cortex using attention graph network for identifying bipolar disorder. In *Proceedings of the Medical Image Computing and Computer Assisted Intervention*, Shenzhen, China. 10.1007/978-3-030-32248-9_89

Yang, P., Cao, X., Yin, C., Xiao, Z., Xi, X., & Wu, D. (2017). Proactive Drone-Cell Deployment: Overload Relief for a Cellular Network Under Flash Crowd Traffic. *IEEE Transactions on Intelligent Transportation Systems*, 18(10), 2877–2892. 10.1109/TITS.2017.2700432

Yanmaz, E. (2022). Positioning aerial relays to maintain connectivity during drone team missions. *Ad Hoc Networks*, 128, 102800. 10.1016/j.adhoc.2022.102800

Yao, D., Sui, J., Yang, E., Yap, P. T., Shen, D., & Liu, M. (2020).Temporal-Adaptive Graph Convolutional Network for Automated Identification of Major Depressive Disorder Using Resting-State fMRI. In *Proceedings of the 11th International Workshop on Machine Learning in Medical Imaging*, Lima, Peru. 10.1007/978-3-030-59861-7_1

Compilation of References

Ye, J., Dobson, S., & McKeever, S. (2012). Situation identification techniques in pervasive computing: A review. *Pervasive and Mobile Computing*, 8(1), 36–66. https://doi.org/10.1016/j .pmcj.2011.01.004

Yue, X., Wang, H., Jin, D., Li, M., & Jiang, W. (2016). Healthcare data gateways: Found healthcare intelligence on blockchain with novel privacy risk control. *Journal of Medical Systems*, 40(10), 218–8. 10.1007/s10916-016-0574-627565509

Zadeh, L. A. (1965). Fuzzy Sets. *Information and Control*, 8(3), 338–353. 10.1016/ S0019-9958(65)90241-X

Zarefsky, J., & Kogan, S. (2022). Privacy and security concerns in the metaverse healthcare: A systematic review. *Healthcare Informatics Research*, 28(1), 54–63.

Zègre-Hemsey, J. K., Bogle, B., Cunningham, C. J., Snyder, K., & Rosamond, W. (2018). Delivery of automated external defibrillators (AED) by drones: Implications for emergency cardiac care. *Current Cardiovascular Risk Reports*, 12(11), 25. 10.1007/s12170-018-0589-230443281

Zeng, Y., & Zhang, R. (2017). Energy-Efficient UAV Communication With Trajectory Optimization. *IEEE Transactions on Wireless Communications*, 16(6), 3747–3760. 10.1109/ TWC.2017.2688328

Zeng, Y., Zhang, R., & Lim, T. J. (2016). Throughput Maximization for UAV-Enabled Mobile Relaying Systems. *IEEE Transactions on Communications*, 64(12), 4983–4996. 10.1109/ TCOMM.2016.2611512

Zeng, Y., Zhang, R., & Lim, T. J. (2016). Wireless communications with unmanned aerial vehicles: Opportunities and challenges. *IEEE Communications Magazine*, 54(5), 36–42. 10.1109/ MCOM.2016.7470933

Zhang, P. (2018). Blockchain technology use cases in healthcare. In *advances in Computers*. Elsevier.

Zhang, Z.-K., Cho, M. C. Y., Wang, C.-W., Hsu, C.-W., Chen, C.-K., & Shieh, S. (2014). IoT security: ongoing challenges and research opportunities. *2014 IEEE 7th International Conference on Service-Oriented Computing and Applications*. IEEE. 10.1109/SOCA.2014.58

Zhang, J., & Li, J. (2023). *High-Reliability Autonomous Management Systems for Spacecraft*. Elsevier.

Zhang, J., Zeng, Y., & Zhang, R. (2017). Spectrum and energy efficiency maximization in UAV-enabled mobile relaying. In *Proceedings of the 2017 IEEE International Conference on Communications (ICC)*, Paris, France. 10.1109/ICC.2017.7997208

Zhang, L., Li, F., Wang, P., Su, R., & Chi, Z. (2021). A blockchain-assisted massive IoT data collection intelligent framework. *IEEE Internet of Things Journal*.

Zhang, L., Zhang, Z., Wang, W., Jin, Z., Su, Y., & Chen, H. (2021). Research on a covert communication model realized by using smart contracts in blockchain environment. *IEEE Systems Journal*.

Zhang, X., & Wang, Y. (2021). Research on intelligent medical big data system based on hadoop and blockchain. *EURASIP Journal on Wireless Communications and Networking*, 2021(1), 1–21. 10.1186/s13638-020-01858-3

Zhang, X., Zhang, H., Sun, K., Long, K., & Li, Y. (2024). Human-Centric Irregular RIS-Assisted Multi-UAV Networks with Resource Allocation and Reflecting Design for Metaverse. *IEEE Journal on Selected Areas in Communications*, 42(3), 603–615. 10.1109/JSAC.2023.3345426

Zhang, Y., Wang, X., Xu, Z., Yu, Q., Yuille, A., & Xu, D. (2020). *When radiology report generation meets knowledge graph*. In *Proceedings of the AAAI Conference on Artificial Intelligence*, New York, NY, USA. 10.1609/aaai.v34i07.6989

Zhang, Y., Xu, X., & Liu, Y. (2019). Cloud computing for digital twins in healthcare: A review and future research directions. *Future Generation Computer Systems*, 98, 220–237.

Zhao, R., Zhang, Y., Zhu, Y., Lan, R., & Hua, Z. (2022). Metaverse: Security and Privacy Concerns. arXiv, arXiv:2203.03854.

Zhao, G., Xu, X., Li, B., & Liu, W. (2020). Blockchain technology for digital twins: A review and future directions. *Journal of Cleaner Production*, 275.

Zhao, H., Wu, S., Wen, Y., Liu, W., & Wu, X. (2019). Modeling and Flight Experiments for Swarms of High Dynamic UAVs: A Stochastic Configuration Control System with Multiplicative Noises. *Sensors (Basel)*, 19(15), 3278. 10.3390/s1915327831349676

Zhi,-yong, Q. (2011). Pervasive Computing Environment for Embedded System. *Computer Science, 38*(3), 179-181.

Zhijie, S., Dezhi, H., Dun, Li., Xiangsheng, W., Chin-Chen, C., & Zhongdai, W. (2022). A blockchain-based secure storage scheme for medical information. *EURASIP Journal on Wireless Communications and Networking*, 40.

Zhou, H., Gao, J., & Chen, Y. (2022). The paradigm and future value of the metaverse for the intervention of cognitive decline. *Frontiers in Public Health*, 10, 1016680. 10.3389/fpubh.2022.101668036339131

Zhu, F., Carpenter, S., & Kulkarni, A. (2012). Understanding identity exposure in pervasive computing environments. *Pervasive and Mobile Computing*, 8(5), 777–794. https://doi.org/10.1016/j.pmcj.2011.06.007

About the Contributors

Suresh Kumar Arumugam Graduated in Computer Science and Engineering (B.E) from Periyar University, India in 2003. Master's (M.E) in Computer Science and Engineering from Anna University, India in 2010. He was awarded a Ph.D in Computer Science and Engineering from Anna University, Chennai in 2017. He has 18+ Teaching and Research experience in various institutions, and presently working as a Professor in the School of Computer Science and Engineering at Jain (Deemed to be University), Bengaluru. He has published 20 SCI articles and more than 30 Scopus articles in peer-reviewed journals. He has published 7 Indian patents and received 1 Innovation Grand patent from Germany Patent. He has actively participated as a reviewer in some of the international journals and senior member of IEEE, IAENG, and CSI societies. His main research interest is in the area of Wireless Sensor Networks, Internet of Things, Artificial Intelligence, and Machine Learning

Geetha G. holds a Ph.D. in Computer Science, with an impressive background in teaching, research, administration, and software development. She is a certified Microsoft Programmer and Solution Developer. With over 26 years of teaching experience, research, and administration, she is a seasoned professional in academia. She has 7 years of experience in software development and project scheduling. With a strong focus on research excellence, she has been granted four patents, including one from the United States and has published 70+ research papers in Scopus-indexed journals. Besides, she has guided 9 Ph.D. scholars. Dr. Geetha G., has established specialized labs, including the CISCO Net Academy, Medhavi Automotive Research Center, and Center for Space Research in collaboration with the Ecquadorian Space Agency. She has also secured funding from the European Union to create the Central Instrumentation Facility, Erasmus Resource Center, and Green Lab.

Ramesh Sekaran is a Professor and Program Head in the School of Computer Science and Engineering (Data Science) at JAIN (Deemed-to-be University). He obtained his Ph.D. from Anna University, Chennai, in 2015, along with a Master's Degree in Information Technology from Anna University, Coimbatore, and a Bachelor's Degree in Information Technology from Anna University, Chennai. With expertise in IoT Networking, Wireless Networks, Network Security, and Optimization Techniques, Dr. Sekaran's research interests span various domains of computer science. He has published over 100 refereed publications in renowned journals and conferences and authored 10 textbooks, emphasizing his dedication to knowledge dissemination. Dr. Ramesh Sekaran's contributions extend beyond research, as he serves as a reviewer for esteemed journals and holds numerous Indian and Australian patents. His outstanding work in IoT Networking earned him recognition as an Innovative Researcher by the World Research Council and the American Medical Council in 2020.

Krishnan Batri possesses an extensive background in teaching, research, administration, and management spanning over 17+ years, and brings a wealth of knowledge and expertise to the field. Dr. Batri's educational journey includes BE, ME, and a Ph.D. in Computer Science and Engineering, from the National Institute of Technology, Tiruchirappalli. Areas of interest that captivate Dr. Krishnan Batri's expertise encompass Information Retrieval, Genetic Algorithm, Tabu Search, Artificial Intelligence, Microprocessor and Microcontrollers, and Embedded Systems. Dr. Batri has published several research papers in renowned journals. Additionally, he holds the distinction of being a Wipro Certified Faculty. Dr. Krishnan Batri has played a pivotal role in guiding Ph.D. scholars, with 13 successfully awarded degrees under his guidance.

N.V. Kousik is a Associate Prof., and currently work as a Lecturer in Computing and ICT dept. at Stanmore College, United Kingdom. Further on as an Editor work for Innovative science and technology publications. His current project is 'Energy Efficient Analysis for Routing in Datacenter MANET'.

***

A. Gayathiri currently working as Assistant Professor in Vivekanandha College of Arts and Sciences for Women (Autonomous), Tiruchengode, Namakkal District in South Tamilnadu State, India. I have more than 17+ of experience in the teaching field. Done my B.Sc Computer Science, M.Sc Computer Science, M.Phil Computer Science, MCA and Pursuing Ph.D in Computer Science. Interest to learn new innovatives is my hobby.

Praveen Gujjar is an academician with 13 years of teaching experience. He has served in engineering and management institute. His research article is published in science direct.

Vani Hiremani is currently working as an Assistant Professor in the Department of Computer Science and Engineering at Symbiosis Institute of Technology, Deemed University, Pune. She completed her Master of Technology in Computer Science and Engineering from BEC Bagalkot, Autonomous College under Visveswaraya Technological University Karnataka and PhD in Computer Science and Engineering from Birla Institute of Technology, MESRA. She has more than 12 years of teaching and research experience. She has published more than 30 peer reviewed papers on various national and international journals of repute. She has delivered invited talk at various national and international seminars, conference, symposium, and workshop. She is member of many national and international societies. She is also member in various program committees of many International conference and chaired the session. She is also editor of many International and National Journal of high repute. She has also conducted many workshops in her organization on various topic.

Rita Komalasari is a lecturer at YARSI University. Her current work is focused on Navigating Complexity: Unraveling the IVHM Requirements Puzzle in Unmanned Aerial Systems Through Innovative IVHM-RD Methodology and Rigorous Data Analysis.

M. Vasim Babu received his B.E. degree in the discipline of Electronics and Communication Engineering from Sethu Institute of Technology (Affiliated to Anna University), India, M.E Degree in the discipline of Communication Systems from K.L.N College of Engineering (Affiliated to Anna University), India, Ph.D. degree in the discipline of Information and Communication Engineering from Anna University, India. His area of interest is in Localization in Wireless Sensor Networks, Mobile Adhoc network, ANFIS and Signal processing. He is an active member of International Association of Engineers, Seventh sense research group, International Association of Computer Science and Information Technology, Universal Association of Computer and Electronics Engineers, American Association for science and technology and the Institute of Engineers. Currently, he is working as an Associate Professor, Department of ECE in KKR & KSR Institute of Technology & Sciences, Guntur, AP, India.

About the Contributors

Nandini Mahanag is a highly motivated and ambitious student of computer science, currently pursuing her Bachelor of Technology in Computer Science from Vellore University of Technology, Andhra Pradesh. She has a thorough understanding of programming languages such as Java, and is an excellent software developer and problem solver. Her enthusiasm for exploring innovative technologies in her personal projects, which demonstrate her dedication to innovation and personal and professional development. She ensures that new and different technology should be used to make a real difference in the world, making her an ideal candidate for a leadership role in computer science.

Sabyasachi Pramanik is a professional IEEE member. He obtained a PhD in Computer Science and Engineering from Sri Satya Sai University of Technology and Medical Sciences, Bhopal, India. Presently, he is an Associate Professor, Department of Computer Science and Engineering, Haldia Institute of Technology, India. He has many publications in various reputed international conferences, journals, and book chapters (Indexed by SCIE, Scopus, ESCI, etc). He is doing research in the fields of Artificial Intelligence, Data Privacy, Cybersecurity, Network Security, and Machine Learning. He also serves on the editorial boards of several international journals. He is a reviewer of journal articles from IEEE, Springer, Elsevier, Inderscience, IET and IGI Global. He has reviewed many conference papers, has been a keynote speaker, session chair, and technical program committee member at many international conferences. He has authored a book on Wireless Sensor Network. He has edited 8 books from IGI Global, CRC Press, Springer and Wiley Publications.

R. Sowrirajan is wording as a head of the department of Mathematics in Dr.N.G.P. Arts and Science College, Coimbatore for the past 8 years. With a total of 15 years of teaching and research experience, his research interests are partial differential equations, Mathematical Finance and Inverse problems. He has organised many national and international conferences, workshops funded by various agencies like DST, SERB and CSIR.

Manikandan Ramachandran obtained his Ph.D. in VLSI Physical design from SASTRA Deemed University, India in 2014. He received his Bachelor of Engineering in Computer Science from Bharathidasan University in 1996 and Master of Technology in VLSI Design from SASTRA Deemed University in 2002. He possesses three decades of academic and 15 years of research experience in the field of Computer Science and Engineering. He has more than 200 research contributions to his credit, which are published in referred and indexed journals, book chapters and conferences. He is presently working as Senior Assistant Professor at SASTRA Deemed University for the last 17 years. He has delivered many lectures and has attended and presented in International Conferences in India and Abroad. He has edited more than 200 research articles to his credit, which includes his editorial experience across refereed and indexed journals, conferences and book chapters at national and international levels. His contemporary research interests include Big Data, Data Analytics, VLSI Design, IoT and Health Care Applications.

Akshay Bhuvaneswari Ramakrishnan is currently pursuing a B.Tech. in Computer Science and Engineering at SASTRA University, Thanjavur. With a strong passion for machine learning and AI, Akshay possesses extensive experience and expertise in these cutting-edge technologies.As an Intel ambassador, Akshay has demonstrated his prowess by emerging victorious in numerous hackathons and serving as a mentor for startups. His commitment to knowledge sharing is evident through his role as a speaker, having conducted over 50 sessions on Data Science and successfully trained more than 5000 students across India.Akshay's dedication to staying at the forefront of the field is underscored by his certification as an Intel Certified MLOps Professional. Furthermore, his research contributions are noteworthy, with 2 international conference papers, 1 sci paper, 3 Scopus papers, and 4 book chapters to his credit.Currently serving as a Management Trainee Intern at Hitachi Energy, Akshay continues to expand his horizons in the industry. His multifaceted involvement and achievements underscore his commitment to the ever-evolving landscape of technology.

S. Magesh is a notable academician and a passionate entrepreneur. He commenced his academic career as Lecturer in the year 1999 and thereafter elevated to the level of Assistant Professor, Associate Professor, and Head in the Department of Computer Science and Engineering with his distinguished career spanning in engineering institutions over a period of 15 years and 9 years of Corporate Experience. He has published 12 refereed international journal and a book with ISBN. He received the Distinguished Innovator & Edupreneur Award in the year 2017 and Lifetime Achievement Award in the year 2019. Presently he serves as the Chairman & Director of Magestic Technology Solutions (P) Ltd, CEO of Maruthi Technocrat E-Services and Director, Jupiter Publications Consortium, Chennai, Tamil Nadu, India.

Manimekalai S has 15 years of teaching experience. She has compiled a book "Business Mathematics and Statistics" by Mc-Graw Hill and One Book chapter Published by Book Publishers international. She has published nearly 20 research papers in national and international journals and MOOC courses. Reviewer for various journals - Journal of Pharmaceutical Research International, Arabian Journal of Chemistry, Asian Research Journal of Mathematics, Asian Journal of Mathematics and Computer Research. Organized more than 10 seminars/workshops/Conferences. More than 25 numbers of conference presentations and more than 100 attended seminars/workshops/FDPs. Received Best work paper in the year of 2020 by Sri Nalla goundar Awards. Received Best researcher in International Research Awards on Science Health and Engineering SHEN research Awards at 2020. Received PAVAIASIRIAR VIRUTHU by Yavarum Kelir.

Srijanani S is a student who is pursuing B.E Computer Science and Engineering in Velammal Engineering College .Srijanani is an accomplished web developer with a strong passion for creating dynamic and user-friendly websites. Her academic background provided a solid foundation in programming, web development, and software engineering. Her journey is marked by valuable experiences, diverse internships, and notable participation in hackathons. Srijanani' s idea of blood warmer system for blood transfusion using Hardware and IOT secured best place in Hackathon organised in Velammal Engineering College. Her significant contribution in designing of Health Monitoring System for detecting sudden abnormalities using IOT has been shortlisted for the Smart India Hackathon. Srijanani has enriched her professional portfolio with internships at four different companies, each offering unique challenges and learning opportunities. Srijanani' technical skill set includes proficiency in HTML, CSS, JavaScript, various JavaScript frameworks such as React and Angular. She is also well-versed in back-end technologies like Node.js and Express, as well as database management systems like MongoDB and SQL.

S. Annamalai is an Associate Professor in the School of Computer Science and Engineering - Data Science at Jain (Deemed-to-be University), Bangalore, India with a Master's Degree in Computer Science and Engineering from Anna University Chennai and a Ph.D. Degree from Anna University Chennai, Dr.S.Annamalai brings a strong academic foundation to his role by combining several years of industry experience with a teaching career that began in 2005, Dr.S.Annamalai possesses a comprehensive perspective in computer science. His research interests span Cloud Computing, Internet of Things (IoT), Big Data, and Data Science, driving him to explore innovative approaches and contribute to existing knowledge. As an accomplished researcher, Dr.S.Annamalai has authored numerous research papers in international journals and conference proceedings.

Daksh Srivastava is an energetic and committed student of computer science. Currently pursuing his Btech in computer science from Vellore institute of technology in Andhra Pradesh, he has a good command over programming languages such as Java, python and is an expert in software development. He has a keen interest in emerging technologies, especially in the fields of AI, blockchain, and is actively participating in coding competitions & hackathons. He has a great work ethic and is a team player. Apart from technical skills, he is passionate about mentorship, organising coding workshops and contributing to OS projects, which reflects his drive to motivate and innovate in the ever-changing world of computer science.

About the Contributors

S. Radha obtained her Bachelor's degree in Computer Science & Engineering from Periyar University in 2004.Then she obtained her Master's degree in Computer Science & Engineering from Mahendra Engineering College in 2010. and Currently, she is an Associate Professor at the Department of Information Technology, Vivekanandha College of Engineering for Women, Namakkal. Her specializations include Data mining, Networking and Networking. Her current research interests are spatial data mining, co located pattern recognition and pattern mining.

Index

Publishing Tomorrow's Research Today

Uncover Current Insights and Future Trends in
Scientific, Technical, & Medical (STM)
with IGI Global's Cutting-Edge Recommended Books

Print Only, E-Book Only, or Print + E-Book.
Order direct through IGI Global's Online Bookstore at **www.igi-global.com** or through your preferred provider.

ISBN: 9798369303689
© 2024; 299 pp.
List Price: US$ 300

ISBN: 9798369314791
© 2024; 287 pp.
List Price: US$ 330

ISBN: 9798369300442
© 2023; 542 pp.
List Price: US$ 270

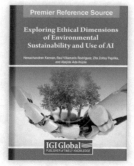

ISBN: 9798369308929
© 2024; 426 pp.
List Price: US$ 265

ISBN: 9781668489383
© 2023; 299 pp.
List Price: US$ 325

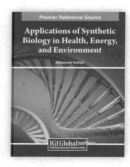

ISBN: 9781668465776
© 2023; 454 pp.
List Price: US$ 325

Do you want to stay current on the latest research trends, product announcements, news, and special offers?
Join IGI Global's mailing list to receive customized recommendations, exclusive discounts, and more.
Sign up at: www.igi-global.com/newsletters.

Scan the QR Code here to view more related titles in STM.

www.igi-global.com   Sign up at www.igi-global.com/newsletters   facebook.com/igiglobal   twitter.com/igiglobal   linkedin.com/igiglobal

Ensure Quality Research is Introduced to the Academic Community

Become a Reviewer for IGI Global Authored Book Projects

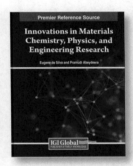

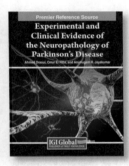

The overall success of an authored book project is dependent on quality and timely manuscript evaluations.

Applications and Inquiries may be sent to:
development@igi-global.com

Applicants must have a doctorate (or equivalent degree) as well as publishing, research, and reviewing experience. Authored Book Evaluators are appointed for one-year terms and are expected to complete at least three evaluations per term. Upon successful completion of this term, evaluators can be considered for an additional term.

If you have a colleague that may be interested in this opportunity, we encourage you to share this information with them.

www.igi-global.com

Publishing Tomorrow's Research Today

IGI Global's Open Access Journal Program

Including Nearly 200 Peer-Reviewed, Gold (Full) Open Access Journals across IGI Global's Three Academic Subject Areas:
Business & Management; Scientific, Technical, and Medical (STM); and Education

**Consider Submitting Your Manuscript to One of These Nearly 200
Open Access Journals for to Increase Their Discoverability & Citation Impact**

Web of Science Impact Factor	**6.5**	Web of Science Impact Factor	**4.7**	Web of Science Impact Factor	**3.2**	Web of Science Impact Factor	**2.6**

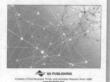

JOURNAL OF
**Organizational and
End User Computing**

JOURNAL OF
**Global Information
Management**

INTERNATIONAL JOURNAL ON
**Semantic Web and
Information Systems**

JOURNAL OF
**Database
Management**

Choosing IGI Global's Open Access Journal Program
Can Greatly Increase the Reach of Your Research

Higher Usage
Open access papers are 2-3 times
more likely to be read than
non-open access papers.

Higher Download Rates
Open access papers benefit from
89% higher download rates than
non-open access papers.

Higher Citation Rates
Open access papers are 47% more
likely to be cited than non-open
access papers.

Submitting an article to a journal offers an invaluable opportunity for you to share your work with the
broader academic community, fostering knowledge dissemination and constructive feedback.

Submit an Article and Browse the IGI
Global Call for Papers Pages

We can work with you to find the journal most well-suited for your next research manuscript.
For open access publishing support, contact: journaleditor@igi-global.com

Publishing Tomorrow's Research Today

IGI Global
e-Book Collection

Including Essential Reference Books Within Three Fundamental Academic Areas

Business & Management
Scientific, Technical, & Medical (STM)
Education

- Acquisition options include Perpetual, Subscription, and Read & Publish
- No Additional Charge for Multi-User Licensing
- No Maintenance, Hosting, or Archiving Fees
- Continually Enhanced Accessibility Compliance Features (WCAG)

| Over 150,000+ Chapters | Contributions From 200,000+ Scholars Worldwide | More Than 1,000,000+ Citations | Majority of e-Books Indexed in Web of Science & Scopus | Consists of Tomorrow's Research Available Today! |

Recommended Titles from our e-Book Collection

Innovation Capabilities and Entrepreneurial Opportunities of Smart Working
ISBN: 9781799887973

Advanced Applications of Generative AI and Natural Language Processing Models
ISBN: 9798369305027

Using Influencer Marketing as a Digital Business Strategy
ISBN: 9798369305515

Human-Centered Approaches in Industry 5.0
ISBN: 9798369326473

Modeling and Monitoring Extreme Hydrometeorological Events
ISBN: 9781668487716

Data-Driven Intelligent Business Sustainability
ISBN: 9798369300497

Information Logistics for Organizational Empowerment and Effective Supply Chain Management
ISBN: 9798369301593

Data Envelopment Analysis (DEA) Methods for Maximizing Efficiency
ISBN: 9798369302552

Request More Information, or Recommend the IGI Global e-Book Collection to Your Institution's Librarian

For More Information or to Request a Free Trial, Contact IGI Global's e-Collections Team: eresources@igi-global.com | 1-866-342-6657 ext. 100 | 717-533-8845 ext. 100

Printed in the United States
by Baker & Taylor Publisher Services